1995 UPDATE
appears on page 275,
following Index

WILDERNESS PRESS • BERKELEY

Yosemite National Park

A Natural-History Guide to Yosemite and Its Trails

Jeffrey P. Schaffer

First edition 1978
Second printing March 1982
Second edition 1983
Second printing January 1985
Third printing July 1986
Fourth printing April 1987
Fifth printing January 1988
Revised sixth printing September 1989
Seventh printing March 1991
THIRD EDITION June 1992
Second printing November 1993
Third printing July 1995

Drawings, maps and design by the author
Cover design by Larry Van Dyke
Topographic map in pocket revised and updated by author,
    based on U.S. Geological Survey overlays
Library of Congress Card Catalog Number 89-22444
International Standard Book Number 0-89997-107-5

Manufactured in the United States of America
Published by Wilderness Press
                2440 Bancroft Way
                Berkeley, CA   94704
                (510) 843-8080
                Write for free catalog

Photo Credits

All the photos were taken by the author except the following:
Ben Schifrin: pages 28, 30, 32, 34, 35, 48, 57, 58 and 108 bottom
Ken Ng: 97 top
National Park Service: 8, 9, 10, 12, 68, 102, and 210
U.S. Geological Survey: 246

Cover: **Vernal Fall and Liberty Cap**
Title page: **Liberty Cap and Nevada Fall, seen along Hike 78**

Library of Congress Cataloging-in-Publication Data

Schaffer, Jeffrey P.
    Yosemite National Park : a natural-history guide to Yosemite and
its trails / Jeffrey P. Schaffer. — 3rd ed.
        p. cm.
    Includes bibliographical references.
    ISBN 0-89997-107-5
    1. Hiking—California—Yosemite National Park—Guidebooks.
    2. Trails—California—Yosemite National Park—Guidebooks.
    3. Natural history—California—Yosemite National Park—Guidebooks.
    4. Yosemite National Park (Calif.)—Guidebooks.   I. Title.
GV199.42.C22Y677 1992
917.94'47045—dc20
                                                        89-22444
                                                          CIP

Contents

Acknowledgments

"I'm going to map all the trails of Yosemite and the adjacent area in one summer," I told a park ranger when I was beginning field work on the first edition. I had to eat those words. Even if I hadn't had a three-month-long knee ailment, I would have been hard pressed to complete the field mapping in *two* summers. Fortunately, during the second summer I had Ben Schifrin, a first-rate mapper and observant naturalist, helping me. Ben, now a medical doctor living in the Sierra's foothills, wrote all the prose for Hikes 3–5, 9–10 and 12–14 and most of the prose for Hikes 2, 6, 8 and 11. He made helpful comments for other parts of the original edition and provided photographs for his section and other sections. For the 1992 edition I've revised Ben's sections based on prose in his 1990 *Emigrant Wilderness and Northwestern Yosemite,* also by Wilderness Press.

Supplying additional prose was Thomas Winnett, a veteran backpacker and the publisher of Wilderness Press. I've borrowed his trail descriptions for about one half of the trails in the Tuolumne Meadows quadrangle, and also for a few sections in the Mono Craters quadrangle.

In order to try to understand what really had occurred in the Sierra Nevada, geologically speaking, I put an enormous amount of energy into producing Chapter 4 (Geology). For the original chapter in 1978, several books and more than 100 technical articles had to be digested and resynthesized. For the first part of the 1992-vintage chapter, a few hundred additional technical articles were read between 1988 and '92. For the second part, I greatly condensed my Ph.D. dissertation, which was nearing completion as this book was going to press in June 1992. Giving constructive criticism of the initial, short-version draft of my dissertation were two Cal Berkeley professors, Ted Oberlander (Geography) and Bill Dietrich (Geology).

Over the years I have also benefited from discussions with Howard Schorn (Paleontology) and Clyde Wahrhaftig (Geology, now retired).

I've also benefited from criticisms on my former Sierran ideas by N. King Huber of the U.S. Geological Survey. Some of his comments ultimately forced me to totally abandon the longstanding interpretation of how Yosemite Valley had been formed. Once freed from its many erroneous assumptions, I was then able to produce a new interpretation based on one simple assumption: fractured rocks erode faster than unfractured ones.

For comments and criticisms on Chapter 5 (Biology), I am indebted in part to Dave Graber, a grad student at Cal during the 1970s while at the same time being Yosemite's bear expert. Also, Dr. Carl Sharsmith of the Yosemite Association gave me a solid introduction to alpine wildflowers, and he reviewed an early form of this chapter. Thanks also go to Dr. Thomas Harvey of San Jose State University, who reviewed Hike 93, which deals with giant-sequoia ecology. That hike's description is based largely on work done by Harvey, Hartesveldt and others. Finally, Len McKenzie, Yosemite's Chief Park Interpreter, read much of the manuscript's natural-history sections.

Giving me encouragement at every step of the way was Ron Mackie, Jr., the Chief Back-country Ranger, who not only shared Park philosophy and management problems with me, but also gave me a *carte blanche* that enabled me to do unrestricted field work in the Park. Ron also read all 100 hikes of the manuscript and made numerous valuable comments, particularly with regard to safety. Lending moral support to the project were Ken Ng, who accompanied me on several hiking excursions, and Steve Medley. Back in the '70s Steve was the Park's librarian and photo curator. Now he is president of the Yosemite Association and author of *The Complete Guidebook to Yosemite National Park*. Lastly, I would like to thank Les Arnberger, a former Park Superintendent, who contributed the Foreword to the original edition.

Jeffrey P. Schaffer
June 1992

Foreword/Dedication

The trails of Yosemite are timeless, having been traveled by Indians, frontiersmen, shepherds, the cavalry, backpackers and generations of hikers. Each trail offers a distinct experience—perhaps new vistas, a special sunset, insight to oneself or a shared experience with family or friends. Yosemite's trails open up the Yosemite experience. In so doing they provide a legacy. They offer a source of enjoyment to be handed down from generation to generation.

The Schiller family from the San Francisco Bay Area has shared these experiences through three generations. Leon Schiller with his wife, Beulah, has hiked Yosemite's trails through four decades. At the age of 72, Leon hiked to the top of Clouds Rest. The Schillers honeymooned at the Ahwahnee, and their son, Keith, believes that he was conceived at Yosemite.

Keith took the Yosemite experience a few steps farther. After having read the first (1978) edition of this guidebook, Keith decided to hike all the trails in the Park. By early 1992, as the third edition was going to press, he had completed 94 of the book's 100 routes. In this course of time he had brought dozens of friends and fellow Yosemite lovers to the Park. After becoming alarmed at deteriorating conditions in the backcountry, Keith resolved to help preserve Yosemite. He founded the East Bay Chapter of the Yosemite Fund. His friends became the initial nucleus for this all-volunteer organization, which by 1992 had raised approximately $200,000 for the restoration of the Happy Isles area in Yosemite Valley.

The experiencing and sharing of Yosemite's grandeur is vital to its preservation. It is for our children and future generations that we owe it to enable them to marvel at nature's greatest masterpiece. Jordan Dean Schiller (see photograph) is the youngest beneficiary of the Yosemite experience in the Schiller family.

At the age of four, Jordan hiked down from Columbia Point to the Valley floor without help. At the age of five, he hiked to Vernal and Nevada falls, encouraging others by saying, "It's a piece of cake." At the age of eight, he hiked to the top of Mt. Hoffmann. He knows that Yosemite is more than the few crowded trails most people take. There are great opportunities for families, kids, everyone to enjoy Yosemite's trails. He especially likes Pothole Dome, Sentinel Dome, the Fissures at Taft Point, the lakes of the Tuolumne Meadows area and just tossing rocks in the Merced River. He also likes to help raise money for Yosemite.

Therefore, this book is dedicated to Jordan Dean Schiller. To that purpose we honor a vision that the trails of Yosemite can be enjoyed by future generations and preserved for renewal of the Yosemite experience.

Chapter 1

Introduction

Yosemite National Park certainly is one of the world's finest parks. Although most of Yosemite's visitors are Californians, people here come from all 50 states. And, if you talk to people you meet in the Park, you also discover that the Park's attraction is truly international. However, most out-of-state visitors view Yosemite as one scenic attraction among many on their list, and consequently spend little time in the Park. They may visit only Yosemite Valley and Glacier Point, or, if their schedule permits, they may drive scenic Highway 120 up to Tuolumne Meadows and Tioga Pass.

This Yosemite guide is primarily a *hiking* guide, but if you plan to visit the Park for only one day, you'll hardly have time to get out of your car. Given only one day, you can best sample Yosemite's greatness by driving across it. Starting in Oakhurst or Fish Camp, drive up Highway 41 to the entrance station, then drive up to the Mariposa Grove for a tram ride among the giant sequoias. Next, continue on Highway 41 (the Wawona Road) to Chinquapin, drive up the Glacier Point Road, and stop at Washburn and Glacier points. Backtrack to Chinquapin, then descend to Yosemite Valley. Park at the Bridalveil Fall lot and walk up the short path toward that fall (start of Hike 62). Then drive through the Valley and walk to the base of Lower Yosemite Fall (end of Hike 64). Leave the Valley, drive up to Crane Flat, then up Highway 120 past Tenaya Lake, through Tuolumne Meadows, over Tioga Pass, and spend a very exhausting evening recuperating in Lee Vining. Of course, you can make this trip in reverse.

One hopes you'll have more than one day to spend in Yosemite. With two or more days, you'll have time to hit the trail, stretch your muscles, get away from the highway noise, breathe the fresh mountain air, and experience Yosemite more intimately. If you have only two days, you can spend one full day hiking, and Hike 78—to Vernal and Nevada falls—is probably your best bet. Given three days, you might spend your second hiking day up in the High Sierra and make one of several very rewarding hikes: Lembert Dome and/or Dog Lake (Hike 45), Glen Aulin (Hike 39), or, if you can handle its thin air, the top of Mt. Dana (Hike 61).

All pertinent day-hiking and backpacking information is presented on the back side of this book's topographic map. If you plan to day hike or backpack, read this information first. In particular, backpackers should be aware that they'll probably need a wilderness permit and that certain camping restrictions apply. All hikers should be aware of disease-producing micro-organisms, *Giardia lamblia*—see "Drinking Water" in column 4 on the back side of the book's topographic map.

Left: **Half Dome and Yosemite Valley, viewed from Eagle Peak, Hike 69**

1

Purpose of This Book

Many people return to Yosemite time and time again to experience the appeal of its multifaceted landscape. For these hikers in particular, this book was written. The author hopes all hikers will benefit from this book in at least three ways. First, this book describes every single trail in Yosemite that is worth taking, and it also describes many trails just outside the Park. With this information, arranged in 100 hikes, you can leisurely *plan* your hike. Table 1 will aid you in planning your hike, for with it you can see at a glance the basic characteristics of each hike. When you see a hike that matches your desires—say, a 2-day hike that is 10-15 miles long—turn to that hike and read its description. Often, photos included in the hike will help you decide if it has the kind of scenery you want to visit.

Second, this book is a *guide*. Yosemite's trails are as well-signed as any in the nation, but if you are caught in a blizzard or are hiking a largely snow-covered trail, then directions are important. In addition, there are a few places where a trail may not be obvious, and the text identifies these. This book also gives you advice you won't find on signs, such as avalanche dangers, bear problems, difficult fords, and trails on the edges of cliffs.

Third, by stressing natural history, this book aims at *increasing your awareness and understanding* of the landscape you traverse. Many veteran hikers come to the High Sierra year after year and never extend their natural-history knowledge past the identification of a few prominent tree species. The fact is, the more you know about the environment, the more you will appreciate, protect and defend it. And you will develop a better feeling for man's role in it. For these reasons, natural history is stressed in this book's 100 hikes. In addition to trailside nature notes, this book goes into considerable detail about geology (Chapter 4) and biology (Chapter 5). The remainder of this chapter offers information you'll need to make your Yosemite visit safer and more enjoyable.

Accommodations

Many visitors who stay overnight in the Yosemite area would like to do so in camp-grounds, which are shown on the topographic map included with this book. Reservations are required for campsites in Yosemite Valley's campgrounds (except for its two walk-in camp-grounds), for Hodgdon Meadow and Crane Flat campgrounds, and for one half of the sites in Tuolumne Meadows Campground. Reservations can be made 8 weeks in advance for family sites, 12 weeks in advance for group sites. Make reservations by phoning MISTIX at (800) 365-2267 Monday-Friday, 7 A.M.–6 P.M. or Saturday–Sunday 7 A.M.–4 P.M. Pacific time. You can also write MISTIX at P.O. Box 85705, San Diego, CA 92138-5705. Be aware that especially for summer, the campgrounds fill up very early.

Other visitors to Yosemite National Park would like to stay at a hotel, lodge or camp operated by the Yosemite Park and Curry Company. As with the Park's campgrounds, rooms quickly fill up, and you will have better luck at reserving a room if you do so out-of-season, preferably for week days as opposed to a weekend. The prime season is summer, but holidays and school vacations are also very popular, and weekends are likely to be busy year-round. To make reservations—up to 366 days in advance—phone the company at (209) 252-4848, Monday-Friday, 8 A.M.–5 P.M. You can also write to the company at Yosemite Reservations, 5410 East Home Avenue, Fresno, CA 93727. The company's summer-only High Sierra Camps operate on a different schedule. The company accepts written requests starting on the first Monday in December of the previous year, and accepts phone requests starting on the first Monday in January of the given year.

In Yosemite Valley the Yosemite Park and Curry Company operates three complexes: the Ahwahnee Hotel, Yosemite Lodge and Curry Village. The Ahwahnee Hotel, a "world class" hotel, charges world-class prices. Yosemite Lodge is comfortable and moderately priced, having hotel rooms plus cabins. Some of the cabins lack private baths. Curry Village, the least expensive of the Valley's accommoda-tions, has hotel rooms, cabins, tent cabins and a house-keeping campground. Most of its accom-modations lack private baths. The Yosemite Park and Curry Company also operates the Wawona Hotel, near the Park's south border. This historic complex, which is closed from after Christmas until early spring, is a cut above Yosemite Lodge in both ambience and price. During the summer the company operates five High Sierra camps (mentioned above) and two lodges. White Wolf Lodge is about a mile off the Tioga Road, and is halfway between Tuolumne Meadows and Yosemite Valley. Tuolumne

Lodge is near the east end of the meadows. Both are popular, so as with all the other establishments, make a reservation well in advance.

In addition to accommodations provided by the Yosemite Park and Curry Company, you can also lodge at four other establishments. Two are on a private tract of land in North Wawona, near the Park's south boundary: the Redwoods (P.O. Box 2085, Wawona, CA 95389; 209-375-6666) and the Chilnualna Cabins (P.O. Box 2095, Wawona, CA 95389; 209-375-6295). The units range from one-bedroom cabins up to five-bedroom homes. Most have fireplaces, and all have kitchens, though you have the option of eating out at the nearby Wawona Hotel. The other two establishments are in Yosemite West, which is just beyond the Park's west boundary. However, to reach Yosemite West, you'll have to enter the Park and drive along the Wawona Road. The spur road to it is just under ½ mile south of the Glacier Point Road junction. Yosemite West Condominiums are moderately priced (reservations: 5410 East Home Avenue, Fresno, CA 93727; 209-454-2033), whereas Yosemite West Cottages have a low-to-high price range, since the units range in size from studio apartments to ample homes (P.O. Box 36, Yosemite, CA 95389; 209-642-2211). The advantage of these two establishments is that from them you can reach each of three popular destinations in under ½ hour: Yosemite Valley, Glacier Point and Wawona.

Outside the Park there are dozens of motels, lodges and bed-and-breakfasts—far too many to mention here. Especially if you are traveling from out of state, you likely will not find accommodations within the Park but instead will have to settle for a room in one of the Park's satellite towns—such as Sonora, Groveland, Mariposa, El Portal, Oakhurst, Fish Camp, Bass Lake, Lee Vining or Bridgeport—or for a room in one of a number of establishments along Highways 41, 120, 140 and 395. Mammoth Lakes, just southeast of the Yosemite area, is a vacationland unto itself—a bustling Lake Tahoe *sans* the lake and casinos. You can usually find all kinds of accommodations in and about this small city, plus lots of lakes, scenery and trails nearby.

Yosemite Activities Other Than Hiking

Horseback Rides: Just because this book is mainly a guide to Yosemite's trails doesn't mean that you have to hike to enjoy them; you can also ride horses along most of them. In summer, saddle and pack animals can be rented at stables

Fishing at Lukens Lake, Hikes 23 and 24

in Yosemite Valley, Tuolumne Meadows, Wawona and White Wolf. These stables are operated by the Yosemite Park and Curry Company (see the previous section for address and phone numbers). Other pack stations are found outside the Park at Cherry Reservoir, Kennedy Meadows, Leavitt Meadow and Clover Meadow, near Fish Camp, and along the Park's east border.

Fishing: Originally, trout were native only to the Merced and Tuolumne rivers below their mid-elevation cascades. The vast majority of Yosemite's streams and virtually all its lakes were barren. As recently as 1972, about 160 of the Park's lakes were regularly stocked with rainbow and brook trout, and, to a lesser extent, with brown, golden and cut-throat trout. The Park Service in the late 1970s greatly reduced the number of lakes to be stocked, then in 1991 completely stopped stocking them. Hence some of the once-stocked lakes may go barren. Certainly there will be fewer trout to catch.

As one might expect, lakes close to Highway 120 and lakes along popular trails attract the most fishermen, so you might do better to select a more remote lake or stream to fish in. However, avoid lakes at the higher elevations, for they tend to be barren or to have only undersized trout. In the past, information was dispensed on fishing pressure at the Park's lakes. The result was that many fishermen flocked to sites that were said to have light pressure (and therefore presumably excellent fishing). This flocking radically changed the fishing pressure at these lakes and played havoc with planning the fish-planting schedule. This book mentions the kind of trout found at lakes in the past, but the fish situation can change, especially after stocking is ended. If you do fish, be sure you have a California fishing license, which can be bought in Yosemite Valley or in Tuolumne Meadows as well as in your own town.

Cooling off in Tenaya Creek

Swimming and Rafting: Many hikers swim in Yosemite's lakes, the warmer of which get up into the high 60s by midsummer. You can also swim in the Merced River through Yosemite Valley. Although the water temperature is cool, the often hot afternoon air temperatures are great for warming up afterward. There are a number of frequented river pools, ranging from the pond on Tenaya Creek immediately below Mirror Meadow to the spacious Merced River pool beside the Cascades Picnic Area. During the summer, water temperatures tend to be in the low 60s at the east end of the Valley and in the mid 60s at its west end. By driving out of the Park and down past El Portal, you may spot some of the Merced River's roadside pools, which can warm up to 70°F or more.

During late spring and early summer high runoff, rafting on the Merced River is pro-

hibited. Later on, drifting by raft or air mattress is relatively safe from Clark Bridge down to El Capitan Bridge. Rapids or fast water will be found both above and below these structures. The drawback of this popular activity is that once you've gone downstream, you have to get back to your starting point. However, if you park your vehicle at the west end of the Yosemite Lodge parking lot (don't use the guests' spaces), you can take the shuttle bus upriver to the Clark Bridge (by the Pines Campgrounds), then inflate your raft or air mattress and make the leisurely 3¼-mile cruise down to the unnamed bridge near Yosemite Lodge. This is the seventh bridge beyond the Clark Bridge. Until the early 1990s fallen trees were removed from the river, which made rafting quite easy. However, the policy has changed, and rafters now can expect to encounter fallen trees. These snags, while upsetting to rafters, increase the diversity of river habitats, which benefits both birds and trout.

Sailing: Nonmotorized boats are allowed in Tenaya Lake, whose strong afternoon winds are great for sailing. Since the lake lacks a launching ramp, the size of the boat is limited to whatever you and your friends can carry to the lake's shore.

Tenaya Lake water sports

Bicycling: In the eastern part of Yosemite Valley there are over 8 miles of bike paths, which allow you to enjoy the scenery from about Sentinel Rock and Yosemite Falls east to Happy Isles, Half Dome and Mirror Meadow. You can rent bikes at both Yosemite Lodge and Curry Village. However, *rented* bikes are not allowed on the relatively steep road up to Mirror Meadow.

Rock Climbing: Yosemite Valley is, in the opinion of the author (a former Valley climber), the rock-climbing capital of the world. It offers over a thousand drug-free ways to get high. For the uninitiated or the novice climber, Yosemite Mountaineering School and Guide Service offers safe, affordable introductory lessons. For the more-advanced climber, it offers qualified guides. However, for the very difficult climbs (5.10 and above) the rate can be hundreds of dollars per day. During the summer, the climbing service operates out of Tuolumne Meadows, while off-season it operates out of Curry Village in Yosemite Valley. The author does not recommend rock climbing from about

On La Escuela, base of El Capitan

mid-November through mid-February due to stormy weather and/or the cold.

Skiing and Ice Skating: Both downhill and cross-country skiing are popular at Badger Pass, just off the Glacier Point Road. Lessons and rental equipment are available. The season is brief, at best from about Thanksgiving to early April. Cross-country skiing also is popular in Yosemite Valley, whose floor is typically snow-covered during January and early February. One can rent equipment in the Valley. Other cross-country ski areas with longer-lasting snow are Crane Flat and the Mariposa Grove. You might also inquire about natural-history ski trips, which go to Ostrander Lake (Hike 84). These are sponsored by the Yosemite Association. Finally you can ice skate at the Curry Village skating rink from about Thanksgiving through March. Rental skates are available.

Yosemite Association Field Seminars: The Yosemite Association offers a diverse array of courses in every season but particularly in summer. There are courses in geology, botany, zoology, history, photography, art, backpacking and cross-country skiing. Some courses involve little exercise, others a lot, and some are child-oriented. For course information, contact: Yosemite Association, P.O. Box 230, El Portal, CA 95318; phone (209) 379-2321 or 379-2646. Membership is not necessary, but is recommended, and it does give you discounts on courses and publications, thus paying for itself. Taking a course may be the only way you'll guarantee having a place to stay in the Park, since campsites and/or lodging is set aside for course participants.

Other Activities: Many scheduled activities, such as nature walks and slide shows, are held each week. Consult the Yosemite Guide, a weekly newspaper given to you at the Park entrances, or else check at the Visitor Center. The Visitor Center and the Tuolumne Meadows Information Center both have the latest weather forecasts, which may help you plan your activities.

With so many activities available at Yosemite National Park, it is unfortunate that most visitors don't stay longer to appreciate them. The Park is certainly large and varied. In Chapter 4, which is essentially about the Park's geology, we'll see just how complex its landscape can be. The Park's biology, discussed in Chapter 5, is even more intricate.

Chapter 2

Man in Yosemite

The Thursday morning had been icy and at times the horses of the Mariposa Battalion found themselves chest-deep in snow. Coaxed on by the spurs or verbal commands of their mounted riders, the horses progressed north toward the unknown-but-rumored Yosemite Valley. Descending through deep drifts, the battalion's 50-60 men suddenly emerged from forest cover on the brink of the Valley's south wall. Early rumors about the Valley had not prepared the men for the overpowering view now before them. Later recalling that profound moment of discovery, Lafayette Bunnell wrote: "The grandeur of the scene was but softened by the haze that hung over the valley—light as gossamer—and by the clouds which partially dimmed the higher cliffs and mountains. This obscurity of vision but increased the awe with which I beheld it, and as I looked, a peculiar exalted sensation seemed to fill my whole being, and I found my eyes in tears with emotion." Momentarily forgetting that he was here to round up hostile Indians, the doctor continued: "I have here seen the power and glory of a Supreme being: the majesty of His handy-work is in that 'Testimony of the Rocks.' That mute appeal—pointing to El Capitan—illustrates it, with more convincing eloquence than can the most powerful arguments of surpliced priests." The day was March 27, 1851, and though over 50 million visitors have now seen the Valley, many of today's visitors still share similar thoughts when first viewing it.

Leaving their viewpoint, which they quickly named Mt. Beatitude (today's Old Inspiration Point), the battalion descended to the floor of Yosemite Valley and, after a brief reconnoiter, set up camp near the edge of Bridalveil Meadow. That night, at the suggestion of Dr. Bunnell, the Valley was christened "Yo-sem-i-ty," which the good doctor felt was the name of the tribe of Indians living in it. Later they discovered that the Miwok Indians inhabiting it called it "Ah-wah-nee" and called themselves the "Ah-wah-ne-chee." However, the name "Yo-sem-i-ty" stuck, though its spelling was changed to "Yosemite" in the first published account of the Valley, which was written by Lieutenant Tredwell Moore for the January 20, 1854 issue of the *Mariposa Chronicle*.

The Mariposa Battalion, under the leadership of Major James D. Savage, was certainly the first group of white men to see *and* enter the Valley. Joseph Reddeford Walker, crossing the central Sierra Nevada under threatening weather during the autumn of 1833, may have *seen* the Valley, for his party came to the rim of a deep canyon whose walls appeared to be "more than a mile high." The Valley was certainly viewed and *possibly* entered by William P. Abrams and his companion on October 18, 1849, for his description accurately portrays some of the Valley's landmarks. Nevertheless, it was members of the Mariposa Battalion who first publicized its existence.

Left: **Bennettville's ruins, not far beyond the park's Tioga Pass. Had this silver-mining town reached its projected population of 50,000 instead of going bust, much of Yosemite's forests around Tuolumne Meadows would have been ravaged for the town's buildings, mine shafts and firewood.**

Chief Teneiya and the Ahwahnechee

Of course, Yosemite Valley was first discovered by the Indians. Just how many bands of Indians visited or resided in the Valley is unknown; however, the last band to live there was the Ahwahnechee, under the leadership of Chief Teneiya. Growing up with his mother's tribe, the Mono Indians, he spent much of his youth in the Mono Basin, but as a young man founded his own band and in the early 1800s moved west across the Sierra crest, probably via Mono Pass, to take up residence in Yosemite Valley. Before dying, an old "medicine man" counseled the young chief against the horsemen (Spaniards) of the lowlands, declaring that if they should enter Ahwahnee, he and his tribe would be the last Indians to live in their beloved Ahwahnee. The prophecy was self-fulfilling, for his braves attacked the outpost of James D. Savage, whose site was located along the mouth of the South Fork Merced River. Today it is passed by motorists driving east along Highway 140 up toward El Portal.

Indians gathering acorns in Yosemite Valley

Savage and his men were not driven away; rather, he returned to the area as Major Savage of the all-volunteer Mariposa Battalion, entered the Valley in spring 1851 and burned the Indian settlements (see **The Ahwahnechee** in Chapter 5 for a look at Indian life). By June, Chief Teneiya and his band were captured by troops under Captain John Bowling and were escorted to a reservation near Fresno. Life there was unpleasant for the chief, and he made it unpleasant for others, so with some relief the reservation's officials let him return to the Valley on his own recognizance. Unfortunately, a group of eight miners who entered the Valley in the spring of 1852 were attacked by the chief's braves, and hostilities were renewed. Realizing that troops would soon be sent, Teneiya and his band fled the Valley and took refuge with his blood relatives, the Mono Indians. They apparently returned to the Valley around summer or early autumn in 1853, but then his braves returned to the Mono village, stole some horses that the Monos had stolen from ranches, and returned to the Valley. Fired with anger over the way the Ahwahnechee had violated their hospitality, the Monos pursued and destroyed most of the Ahwahnechee, including Chief Teneiya. The Valley was now safe for tourists.

The Early Tourists

Few Californians believed the first accounts of Yosemite Valley. When Dr. Bunnell wrote an article describing the height of the Valley walls as 1500 feet (half of their true height), a San Francisco newspaper correspondent suggested he cut his estimates in half. Enraged, Bunnell tore up his manuscript. Lieutenant Moore, mentioned earlier, thus published the first written account in January 1854. However, local Indian trouble instilled fear in potential tourists, so the first ones did not visit the Valley until the 1855 season. Among them were three men who would contribute to the Valley's history: James Hutchings, Thomas Ayres and Galen Clark.

Word of the beauty and grandeur of Yosemite Valley spread quickly, perhaps due to James Hutchings more than anyone else. In June 1855 he organized and led the first tourist party to Yosemite Valley, bringing along artist Thomas Ayres to record their discoveries. No sooner than he had returned to Mariposa, Hutchings wrote up his adventures, which were published in the July 12 issue of the *Mariposa*

Upper House, built in 1859, later converted to Cedar Cottage

Gazette. In 1855 California as a state was but five years old and, largely due to the clamor of the Gold Rush, it was an area of interest to many persons in the eastern states. Hutchings' article was copied in one form or another in a number of journals and newspapers, which, if nothing else, diverted readers' minds from the serious, burning issue of slavery.

Hutchings was not content to sit idle after his one article, and in July 1856 he began to publish a magazine, *Hutchings' Illustrated California Magazine,* which was devoted to the scenery of California. The first issue contained a lead article on "The Yo-Ham-i-te Valley," illustrated by none other than Thomas Ayres. Later, Hutchings elaborated on this article, producing "The Great Yo-Semite Valley" in a series of four installments, from October 1859 to March 1860. These installments then immediately appeared as part of his book, *Scenes of Wonder and Curiosity in California,* which stayed in print well into the 1870s.

During 1856, when Hutchings first began his magazine, Thomas Ayres returned to Yosemite Valley to produce more sketches. These were highly detailed, though not true to form; rather, they exaggerated the angularity of the Valley's walls and the size of the Valley's falls. Nevertheless, Ayres, who also began to write about Yosemite, underestimated the height of the falls, as had most of his predecessors.

Commercialism first came to Yosemite in 1856. In that year Milton and Houston Mann— 2 of the 42 tourists to see the Valley in 1855— completed a toll path up the South Fork Merced River and over to the Valley floor. They charged $2.00 per person—a large sum in those days — but they were later bought out by Mariposa County, and the path became free. Today you can more or less parallel this historic route by first walking up the South Fork Merced River along the Alder Creek trail (Hike 82), then hiking from Wawona up to Bridalveil Creek (last half of Hike 83). Next, Hike 72, from Bridalveil Creek to Dewey Point, and Hike 71 from Dewey Point to Yosemite Valley, complete the course.

The Mann brothers needed a way station along their trail, so they convinced Galen Clark, who had just built a cabin in today's Wawona area, to tend to the needs of the tourists. He did this with kindness, and his spirit of devotion to Yosemite profoundly imbued travelers with a similar reverence for this mountain landscape. The impact Clark made on others was far greater than one would expect from a quiet mountain man.

Meanwhile, a simple structure, later called the Lower Hotel, was being completed as the first tourists rode down the Manns' still-fresh trail into Yosemite Valley. Other trails and hotels quickly followed and tourism increased.

Yosemite Becomes a Park

The Civil War began in April 1861, just months after Hutchings' *Scenes of Wonder and Curiosity in California* appeared. With America locked in Civil War, it is a wonder that anyone visited Yosemite. Nevertheless, some people did, and a few of these helped to get park status for Yosemite Valley. The highly influential Reverend Thomas Starr King, who had visited the Valley in 1860, saw that homesteading and commercial pursuits in it might be harmful, and he was the first—through his nationwide audience—to press for a public park. Photographs of the Valley were taken in 1861 by C. E. Watkins, and these, together with geographic and geologic data gathered by the Whitney Survey of California, provided legislators with favorable evidence backing King's exhortations.

The call of Yosemite eventually lured Frederick Law Olmsted—the country's foremost landscape architect—to Yosemite in 1863 and he too noted that the Valley and the Mariposa Grove of Big Trees were both being ruined by commercial interests. Though young, he was already very influential, and he convinced Senator John Conness of California to introduce a Park bill in the senate. The bill, not being controversial in the war-torn Congress, easily passed in both houses and was signed by President Abraham Lincoln on June 30, 1864. The bill deeded Yosemite Valley and the Mariposa Grove of Big Trees to the State of California "for public use, resort and recreation," and these two tracts "shall be inalienable for all time."

It is one thing to create a park on paper; it is another matter to bring it into existence. In September, California's governor proclaimed a board of Yosemite commissioners, which did not come into existence until 1866. The commissioners appointed Galen Clark as the Park's first guardian, a position he would hold on and off through 1896. However, the commissioners at first lacked authority to evict homesteaders, and an 11-year battle ensued. Josiah D. Whitney, who was the first director of the California State Geological Survey, feared that "Yosemite Valley, instead of being 'a joy forever,' will become, like Niagara Falls, a gigantic institution for fleecing the public." Expressing his concern in his 1870 *Yosemite Guide-Book*, he continued:

> Instead of having every convenience for circulation in and about the Valley,—free trails, roads, and bridges, with every facility offered for the enjoyment of Nature in the greatest of her works, unrestrained except by the requirements of decency and order,—the public will find, if the ownership of the Valley passes into private hands, that opportunity will be taken to levy toll at every point of view, on every trail, on every

bridge, and at every turning, while there will be no inducement to do anything for the public accommodation, except that which may be made immediately available as a new means of raising a tax on the unfortunate traveller.

In part he was writing against Hutchings, who like others had hoped to gain homesteading rights to 160 of the Valley floor's 2200 acres. In 1875 the claims of the early settlers were resolved. Hutchings, like three other pre-Park land owners, lost his ownership, but he was in part compensated with a State grant of $24,000 for the improvements he made on the Upper Hotel, which he had purchased just months before President Lincoln signed the Park bill. Hutchings lost his hotel, but still profited from his book, which continued to attract tourists. In 1877, just after his land loss, Hutchings published a second guide, *Hutchings' Tourist Guide to the Yo Semite Valley and the Big Tree Groves for 1877*, which, amazingly, was very factual and not vindictive toward the Park commissioners.

In 1880 the reigning Park commissioners were ousted, new ones were appointed, and James Hutchings replaced Galen Clark as the Park guardian! Hutchings was a man who could get things done—usually for the *good* of the Park, despite insinuations to the contrary. A man for all seasons, he even speculated on the origin of Yosemite Valley, a subject debated by the eminent Josiah D. Whitney and the relatively unknown John Muir (see page 241). Surprisingly, Hutchings' interpretation proved to be more accurate than either Whitney's or Muir's.

Back on May 10, 1869—prior to Hutchings' land loss—the transcontinental railroad was completed, and during the 1870s a flood of settlers poured into California. These people were potential tourists, but like the vast majority of Californians, they felt the lengthy *horseback* ride to Yosemite Valley was not worth the effort.

Horse stage on Big Oak Flat Road in 1903

However, in the mid 70s, three stagecoach roads were built to Yosemite Valley: the Coulterville Road (June 1874), the Big Oak Flat Road (July 1874) and the Mariposa (Wawona) Road (July 1875). Tourists now came in droves, and this influx resulted in the increase of hotels and services in Yosemite Valley, which were more or less regulated by the commissioners. Nevertheless, these men were concerned over the Valley's deteriorating condition, as evidenced in their 1880 report:

1. Most of the available land is under lease for pasture and garden purposes.
2. The enclosed fields are being invaded by willows, wild roses, and other growth, to the damage of their value and of the beauty of the Valley.
3. The upper portion of the Valley, which has been set apart for the convenience of campers [first camp established in 1878], is largely overgrown with willows and young pines. The views are obstructed, the pasturage destroyed, and the appearance injured.
4. There is no practicable and unobstructed carriage road around the Valley, near the base of the cliffs. At present all who attempt to make the circuit of the floor of the Valley, must pass through gates and fields, lose some of the finest views, and be subjected to annoyance and loss of time.

Creating a National Park

While Yosemite Valley was being undermined by the detrimental effects of tourism, the surrounding countryside fared no better. Although this land was supposedly protected under Federal jurisdiction, its meadows were subjected to overgrazing by sheep (and to a lesser extent by cattle) and its forests to depletion by loggers. This rape of the landscape was first noted by a young Scotsman, John Muir, who visited Yosemite Valley in 1868 and decided to stay. His exploration of the High Sierra, first while working as a shepherd, convinced him of the damage done by man and his animals. In the mid 1870s he criticized both shepherds and loggers, but to no avail. Lumber was needed to build California's growing communities, and wool export had become big business, with more than 20 million pounds produced annually.

Muir's protestations generally fell on deaf ears until 1889, when he met Robert Underwood Johnson, who was editor of the very influential *Century Magazine*. Muir took Johnson on a tour of Yosemite's highlands, including Tuolumne Meadows, and showed him the damage done by "the hooved locusts" as well as by loggers. About camping at Soda Springs in these meadows, Johnson later wrote:

> One conversation that we had beside the campfire at Soda Springs had an important sequel, for it was here that I proposed to Muir that we should set on foot the project of the Yosemite National Park. Our camp on the Tuolumne was outside the limitations of the Yosemite Valley reservation. It did not by any means include the headwaters of the streams which fed the three great falls, the Yosemite, the Nevada, and the Bridalveil. On account of the denudation by sheep the winter snows, having no underbrush to hold them, melted in torrents early in the spring, so that there was comparatively little supply for the waterfalls during the summer months. This was all explained to me by Muir, whereupon I said to him, 'Obviously the thing to do was to make a Yosemite National Park around the Valley on the plan of the Yellowstone [National Park, created in 1872].'

As any seasoned Yosemite visitor knows, Yosemite's falls greatly diminish in summer, sheep or no sheep. This is because the Sierra's soils are sparse and gravelly, not extensive, deep and clay-rich. Most of these soils are, after all, geologically young, having developed from deposits left by glaciers that retreated from about 15,000–13,000 years ago. These Tioga-age glaciers, like earlier ones, had scoured the High Sierra landscape, eradicating previous soils.

That Muir was wrong is not important. What mattered is that his sheep argument was convincing, and he wrote some articles for the *Century Magazine* which coincided, conveniently, with a Park bill introduced in Congress. The Yosemite Act of October 1, 1890 easily passed without opposition, for communications in those days were still poor—the sheep and lumber men out west probably knew little, if anything, about the Act. But even if they had known, they wouldn't have been able to organize a lobby against it—the Act was passed too quickly. This Act withdrew lands from "settlement, occupancy, or sale" and protected "all timber, mineral deposits [none in Yosemite], natural curiosities or wonders, and their retention in their natural condition." This included protection against "the wanton destruction of the fish and game and their capture or destruction for purposes of merchandise or profit."

Yosemite Under the Fourth Cavalry

What the Yosemite Act failed to stipulate was how the newly formed Yosemite National Park should be administered. Hence it was, like Yellowstone National Park before it, put under Army jurisdiction. Troops of the Fourth Cavalry, led by Captain Abram Wood, arrived in the new park on May 19, 1891, and set up camp in Wawona, *not* in Yosemite Valley, for that part of the Park still lay under state jurisdiction. Troops were allowed into the Valley, but they had to camp at its west end, in Bridalveil Meadow.

One of several major problems confronting Captain Wood and his men was the problem of sheep grazing. Each year about 100,000 sheep had been led up into Yosemite's high meadows, but now this practice was illegal. Wood lacked the legal authority to arrest the trespassing sheepmen, but he devised a technique that discouraged them: his men would escort these herders "to another part of the Park for ejectment, this march consuming four or five days; and after they are ejected it takes as long to go back to their herds. In the meantime the sheep are alone, and the forest animals are liable to destroy and scatter many of them. When the owner awakens to this fact, he takes more

interest in the doings of his herders and gives them orders not to enter the Park under any circumstances.'' The herders, however, grew more wary and took their sheep into more remote parts of Yosemite. The sheep problem, therefore, did not come under control until the late 1890s, and at least one herder drove sheep into Yosemite until the 1920s.

To aid in their pursuit of herders, the troops established a network of trails. Since these trails were faint and obscure, they were made easier to follow by blazing trailside conifers with a conspicuous T, or trail mark. Few if any of the original Ts exist today, but the symbol stuck, and even in recent years trees along Yosemite's trails have been T-blazed.

At the end of 1896, an aging Galen Clark, who had earlier been reappointed Yosemite guardian, resigned, and was replaced by an inept guardian. Yosemite Valley began to have increased problems and the Army, whose jurisdiction lay outside the Valley, could do nothing about it. John Muir had earlier seen the need to incorporate the Valley into the Park and in 1892 had organized and become first president of the Sierra Club. With 181 other charter members he pressed for this goal and others, and in 1906, after much lobbying, saw the return of Yosemite Valley and the Mariposa Grove to the Federal Government. However, a

Cavalry F Troop on the Fallen Monarch giant sequoia in 1899

price was paid: the area of Yosemite National Park was substantially reduced. (Today, however, *more* lands are protected than in the 1890 Act, due to the creation of three buffer areas around the Park: the Minarets, Hoover and Emigrant wildernesses).

The Hetch Hetchy Reservoir

Though Muir and the Sierra Club could claim partial victory with the creation of a unified, if reduced, Yosemite National Park in 1906, they had another serious problem to confront. In 1901 the city of San Francisco had applied for permission to dam Hetch Hetchy. "Dam Hetch Hetchy!" Muir exclaimed. "As well dam for water-tanks the people's cathedrals and churches, for no holier temple has ever been consecrated by the heart of man." Secretary Hitchcock of the US Department of the Interior concurred with Muir and denied permission. But the city persisted and, despite continued opposition by Muir, the Sierra Club and many others, it succeeded in obtaining water rights with the passage of the Raker Act in late 1913. The new Secretary of the Interior favored dams.

Construction began, Hetch Hetchy's granite became the dam's core, and the canyon's floor was cleared of timber. Part of this timber was used in the dam's construction, but an additional 6+ million board feet of timber logged *inside the Park*, was also used, adding insult to injury. The project was completed in 1923, but in 1938 the dam was increased by 85 feet to its present height. This reservoir could have been located down-canyon, just outside Hetch Hetchy, and many conservationists today still favor relocation of the dam. However, economics makes this project unfeasible.

Exit the Army

With the passage of the Raker Act in 1913, conservationists took a decisive defeat in their battle to save Hetch Hetchy. Muir died shortly afterward, perhaps of heartbreak, though certainly of old age. Just before he died he expressed hope that "some compensating good must follow [from the Raker Act]." It did—in the form of a new spirit of conservation, of a growing national morality that Americans must preserve the land, not exploit and destroy it. This mounting consensus probably played a significant part in the creation of the National Park Act of 1916—though in addition Europe

was already at war, America was talking war, and the Army probably wanted all its troops out of the nation's parks.

When the Fourth Cavalry left Yosemite, they left behind an impressive record. They had driven sheep and cattle from the Park, helped to settle property disputes, had laid the foundation for today's trail system, and had mapped the Park in substantial detail and had even planted trout in the Park's lakes. Many of the cavalry's troops are commemorated today by their names lent to dozens of the Park's backcountry features, such as Rodgers and Foerster peaks, Benson and Smedberg lakes, Fernandez and Isberg passes. For Yosemite, the cavalry had by and large "come to the rescue."

Dawn of the Automobile Era

While the intrusion of dammed water into Hetch Hetchy raged as an issue from 1901-1913, another intrusion faced the Park administrators. In 1900 the first automobile entered Yosemite Valley, stirring up dust and controversy, and soon proponents squared off on both sides of the automobile question. The final decision came in 1913: automobiles would be allowed in the Valley. Thus when the fledgling National Park Service took over administration in 1916, they were faced with a rising tide of tourists. America had entered the era of the automobile, the airplane, the transcontinental telephone and the Eastman (Kodak) camera.

Faced with a rapidly growing clientele, Park administrators turned most of their attention to upgrading services. New trails were built and old ones were brought up to modern standards. In 1916 Tuolumne Meadows Lodge was built, as were camps at Tenaya and Merced lakes, followed in 1924 by precursors of the rest of today's High Sierra Camps. Also in 1916 the Tioga Road was opened to the public, and that summer 600 automobiles entered the Park from its east side. Existing roads were paved, widened and realigned while others were built. The All-Year Highway (Highway 140) opened in 1926 and assured that food and supplies could be transported to Yosemite Valley year-round. Herds of dairy cows had left the Valley's meadows in 1924, only to be replaced with hordes of automobiles. This flood spelled an end to the Yosemite Valley Railroad, which had started service in 1907. Because many drivers drove their autos into the meadows, the Park

Service cut roadside ditches in 1929, thus saving the meadows by keeping autos on the proper track. Campgrounds were now in forest groves, away from the meadows that had once been so important to the previous generation of horseback tourists.

The Yosemite Museum opened in the same year as the All-Year Highway, just 4 years after the creation of Yosemite's first Park Naturalist position. The early naturalists relied heavily on extensive field work done under Joseph Grinnell and Tracy Storer of the Museum of Vertebrate Zoology at U.C.'s Berkeley campus. Their 1914-20 field work resulted in the 752-page *Animal Life in the Yosemite,* a classic, detailed natural-history study. In 1930, François Matthes produced an equally classic study of the evolution of the Yosemite landscape, with special emphasis on Yosemite Valley.

When the Yosemite Museum was opened in 1926, the "urban" center of Yosemite Valley was still in the "Old Village," between today's Sentinel Bridge and the Yosemite Chapel. Gradually the Park's headquarters and Valley's stores were moved to the area around the museum, for this site was sunnier, considerably warmer in winter, and less subject to flooding. Also in 1926, work was begun on the Ahwahnee Hotel, which opened with festivities on Bastille Day, July 14, 1927. Steven T. Mather, the National Park Service's first Director, presided over the ceremonies.

Certainly of greater importance to the Park was the end to Park logging. More than ½ *billion* board feet of timber—mostly sugar pines—had been logged from World War I until 1930, when John D. Rockefeller, Jr. and the US Government split the cost of buying out the Yosemite Lumber Company (some of the raped land can be seen along part of Hike 83).

During the Depression years, numerous persons were employed in CCC, CWA and PWA projects that added refinements to the human imprint on the Yosemite landscape. World War II temporarily put an end to future projects and during it the Park served as an R & R site for almost 90,000 battle-weary troops.

The Postwar Years

After VE and VJ days, America returned to its pursuit of the good life, and this included traveling in ever-increasing numbers. About ⅔ million tourists visited Yosemite in 1946 and by 1954 the number had grown to 1 million. In 1956 the National Park Service embarked on a 10-year "Mission 66" program, whose goal was to "assure the maximum protection of the scenic, scientific, wilderness, and historic resources of the National Park System in such ways and by such means as will make them available for the use and enjoyment of present and future generations." By the end of this program, in 1966—the 50th anniversary of the NPS, Yosemite was receiving about two million visitors a year.

Hikers and car-campers continued to inundate Yosemite in following years. On the three-day "summer" weekends—Memorial Day, Fourth of July and Labor Day—as many as 50,000+ visitors, half of them youths, crammed into Yosemite Valley. Whereas campers used to leave their belongings out on tables day after day, to do so now was to invite theft. By 1970 the Yosemite Valley scene had become ugly, with thefts, drugs, rapes, fights— even murders. It had become a mountain slum. Like Watts and other ghettos the Valley had its riot, which occurred over the 1970 Fourth of July weekend.

However, 1970 also marked the start of a series of projects based on research done in the Mission 66 program. One of these was to remove cars from the congested east end of the Valley and replace them with a free shuttle bus system. The long-term goal, still years away, is to completely ban the automobile from Yosemite Valley and return it to the tranquility it experienced in the Park's early days. Some feel that the noisy, polluting shuttle buses should also go, and perhaps they will be replaced with silent, clean-running trains that use electricity generated from solar energy.

Realizing that the auto ban was years away, the Park Service took an intermediate step to reduce the Valley's noise and violence. During the early and mid-70s it gradually converted the campgrounds over to a fixed-site plan, which reduced the camper population to several thousand instead of tens of thousands. Peace began to return to Yosemite Valley.

And what of the backcountry? It too experienced a population explosion, compounded by lightweight backpacking technology which made carrying one's food and gear into the mountains easier than ever. The backcountry, like Yosemite Valley, became overcrowded. In 1972 a group studying the pressures of the backpacking public counted 4712 fire rings in the backcountry—a real sign of overuse.

The wilderness permit came to Yosemite in that year as an initial step in dealing with this overuse. The information backpackers wrote on these permits gave the Park planners real data on who was going where, and in what numbers. In succeeding years, rangers attempted to direct hikers away from the more crowded areas, such as Little Yosemite Valley, which had become so crowded that it was like the Yosemite Valley campgrounds except for having no cars. Pit toilets became necessary.

During the 1970s the number of Yosemite visitors temporarily stabilized at about 2–2½ million per year. However, the '80s saw an upswing in visitation so that by the early '90s it had risen to about 3½ million per year—and visitation will likely increase. How can the Park Service address the needs of these all these visitors and still protect the natural integrity of the Park? A range of solutions were proposed in the 1980 *General Management Plan* (GMP), but in retrospect these may have been naive and idealistic. Jack Morehead, a Park superintendent during the '80s, called certain portions of the plan "unrealistic" and "unattainable." No matter. Soon economic reality hit—the mounting Federal deficit guaranteed that major funding to execute the plan would not be forthcoming.

Nevertheless, during the '80s, some points made in the plan were implemented. Some of these were: the asphalt parking lot in front of the Visitor Center was removed; miles of bike paths were constructed; sewage treatment was upgraded; the warehouse and reservation functions of the Yosemite Park and Curry Company were relocated to Fresno; most of the Park was given wilderness status; and bighorn sheep were introduced back into the Park. Still, most of the plan was not implemented, and in August 1989 the National Park Service produced the *Draft Yosemite GMP Examination Report,* which stated why the 1980 GMP won't work and why it should be changed. Predictably, this enraged certain environmental groups.

The Park celebrated its centennial as a national park in 1990. It was not the Park's best year. January brought a flood of letters, mostly negative, on the *Draft Yosemite GMP Examination Report.* In March a rockslide briefly closed Highway 140. The Tioga Road, opened on May 17, was twice closed by late-season snow. July 13 saw a downpour in Yosemite Valley. Then from August 7 through 21, lightning-caused fires ravaged western Park

The 1970s "John Muir Freeway," 8 lanes wide, skirting Tuolumne Meadows

lands, burning over 24,000 acres and destroying most of the homes of the private inholding known as Foresta; Yosemite Valley visitors had to be evacuated. On October 1, the Park celebrated its 100th anniversary. However, because of Federal budget uncertainties, campgrounds and visitor centers in the Park were closed for two days. Later in October an earthquake centered below Lee Vining caused rockslides, which temporarily closed several Park roads.

As part of the 1990 Centennial Celebration, three speeches were presented by noted speakers on the condition of Yosemite. They were not celebrations; rather, each speech dealt with Yosemite's problems. Mike Finley, who had recently been appointed the Park superintendent in 1989, was deluged with angry rhetoric, much of it from well-meaning environmentalists who would have liked to see the Park returned to its natural condition. Unfortunately, Yosemite—particularly Yosemite Valley—can never be returned to the pristine condition seen by its discoverers, the Indians. But one hopes it can be managed in such a way that will instill in each new visitor the same awe and reverence that were experienced by those who first laid eyes on it.

Chapter 3

One Hundred Hikes

Selecting Your Hike

There are two ways to select your hike. First, if you know what area you want to hike in, turn to the appropriate geographical section and review its hikes. The 100 hikes in this guide are divided into eight sections, and these sections are more or less arranged from northwest to southeast.

If you are unfamiliar with Yosemite's geography, then a geographical focus will be meaningless. For you, Table 1 should help you decide what hike is best for you. For each hike, certain basic information is given which should help you narrow your selection to just a few possibilities.

Recommended Hiking Time: This is the period of time that the author feels is best for a given hike walked by the *average* hiker. You may want or need more time or less time. Elevation, topography and hiking duration were taken into account in arriving at these recommended times, for a hike will be more exhausting if it is at high altitude, if it involves lots of ascent and descent, or if it is long and therefore requires a heavy pack. Generally, most of this book's backpack trips require only 8-10 miles of walking per day—a travel rate designed to give you ample time for many stops. John Muir would have found this meager distance disgraceful, and the recommended hikes in *his* 1912 guidebook generally required an output of 25 miles per day. At that rate, however, you see little more than peaks and domes, and you can't absorb the myriad sights, sounds, odors or feelings experienced by hikers conscious of their surroundings.

Grade and Difficulty: The information in this column tells you how hard your hike will be. The numbers refer to each hike's mileage, as follows: 1, 0.0-4.9 miles; 2, 5.0-9.9 miles; 3, 10.0-14.9 miles; 4, 15.0-19.9 miles; 5, 20.0-29.9 miles; 6, 30.0-49.9 miles; and 7, 50.0+ miles. The letters refer to the total elevation gain you must climb: A, 0-499 feet; B, 500-999 feet; C, 1000-1999 feet; D, 2000-3999 feet; E, 4000-6999 feet; F, 7000-9999 feet; and G, 10,000+ feet. Total gain is *not* the elevation difference between your trail's high and low points (that is net gain); rather it is the vertical distance you'll have to climb along your *entire* trip, both going and returning. The ratings are for the minimum distance and don't include any side hikes that are suggested in the hike's description—these are extra.

The words "easy," "moderate" and "strenuous" describe the difficulty of the hike, given the recommended hiking time. Of course, you can decrease the difficulty of most hikes by taking longer to do them.

Two hikers descending Half Dome's cable route

Table 1. Summary of this guide's 100 hikes

Hike	Recommended hiking time	Grade and difficulty	Hiking season	Hiker use	Can swim and fish	Exceptionally scenic
Section 1: Trails of Yosemite's Northwestern Backcountry						
A. Trails approached from the north						
1	1 day	4D-strenuous	July-mid Oct.	Light	No	Yes
2	6 days	7F-moderate	July-mid Oct.	Moderate	Yes	No
3	2 days	4D-moderate	July-October	Heavy	Yes	No
4	6 days	7F-moderate	July-mid Oct.	Moderate	Yes	Yes
5	2 days	3D-moderate	July-October	Moderate	Yes	Yes
6	3 days	5E-moderate	July-mid Oct.	Moderate	Yes	No
7	2 days	4D-moderate	July-September	Moderate	Yes	Yes
B. Trails approach from the west						
8	4 days	6E-moderate	mid June-Oct.	Moderate	Yes	No
9	2 days	4D-moderate	mid June-Oct.	Moderate	Yes	No
10	1 day	3D-moderate	May-November	Heavy	No	No
11	4 days	5E-easy	mid June-Oct.	Moderate	Yes	No
12	4 days	6F-moderate	July-mid Oct.	Light	Yes	No
13	5 days	7G-strenuous	July-mid Oct.	Light	Yes	No
14	6 days	7G-strenuous	July-mid Oct.	Light	Yes	No
Section 2: Trails of the Hetch Hetchy Area, between the Tuolumne River and Highway 120						
15	½ day	1C-moderate	April-November	Light	Yes	No
16	½ day	1B-easy	May-November	Light	No	No
17	2 days	4E-moderate	June-October	Light	No	No
18	2 days	4D-moderate	mid June-mid Nov.	Light	No	No
19	½ day	2B-easy	June-October	Heavy	Yes	No
20	2 days	5D-moderate	July-October	Light	Yes	No
21	5 days	6F-easy	mid June-Oct.	Moderate	Yes	No
22	2 days	5E-moderate	June-October	Moderate	Yes	No
23	½ day	1A-easy	July-October	Moderate	Yes	No
24	½ day	1A-easy	July-October	Light	Yes	No
25	2 days	3D-moderate	July-mid Oct.	Heavy	Yes	No
26	½ day	1B-moderate	July-October	Heavy	Yes	No
27	1 day	2D-strenuous	July-October	Heavy	Yes	Yes
28	3 days	5E-moderate	July-September	Light	Yes	Yes
Section 3: Trails of the Hetch Hetchy Area, south of Highway 120						
29	½ day	2C-strenuous	May-November	Light	Yes	No
30	½ day	1B-easy	mid June-Sept.	Light	Yes	No
31	1 day	4D-strenuous	mid June-Sept.	Light	Yes	Yes
32	1 day	3C-moderate	July-October	Moderate	Fish	No
33	1 day	2D-moderate	July-October	Light	No	Yes
34	½ day	2A-moderate	July-October	Light	Fish	No
35	1 day	3B-moderate	July-October	Light	Fish	No
36	2 hours	1A-easy	mid June-Oct.	Moderate	Yes	Yes
Section 4: Trails of the Tuolumne Meadows Area, north of Highway 120						
37	1 day	2B-easy	July-mid Oct.	Light	Yes	No
38	1 hour	1A-easy	mid June-mid Oct.	Moderate	No	Yes
39	2 days	3C-easy	July-mid Oct.	Heavy	Fish	Yes
40	6 days	7F-moderate	July-mid Oct.	Heavy	Yes	Yes
41	4 days	6F-moderate	July-October	Moderate	Yes	Yes
42	7 days	7G-strenuous	mid July-Sept.	Moderate	Yes	Yes
43	5 days	7G-strenuous	mid July-Sept.	Moderate	Yes	Yes
44	2 days	3D-moderate	July-mid Oct.	Heavy	Yes	Yes
45	½ day	1B-moderate	July-mid Oct.	Heavy	Yes	Yes
46	1 day	2C-easy	July-mid Oct.	Moderate	Yes	Yes
Section 5: Trails of the Tuolumne Meadows Area, south and east of Highway 120						
47	2 days	3D-easy	July-mid Oct.	Heavy	Yes	No
48	1 day	3D-strenuous	July-October	Moderate	No	Yes

49	2 days	5E-strenuous	July-October	Moderate	No	Yes
50	½ day	2C-moderate	July-mid Oct.	Heavy	Yes	Yes
51	2 days	5D-moderate	July-mid Oct.	Heavy	Yes	Yes
52	3 days	6D-easy	July-mid Oct.	Heavy	Yes	Yes
53	½ day	2C-moderate	July-mid Oct.	Light	Yes	Yes
54	½ day	1C-moderate	July-mid Oct.	Heavy	Yes	No
55	½ day	2A-easy	July-mid Oct.	Heavy	Fish	Yes
56	4 days	5E-moderate	July-mid Oct.	Heavy	Yes	Yes
57	2 days	5D-moderate	July-mid Oct.	Heavy	Yes	Yes
58	3 days	5D-moderate	mid July-Sept.	Moderate	Yes	Yes
59	½ day	2C-moderate	July-mid Oct.	Moderate	Yes	No
60	2 days	5D-moderate	mid July-Sept.	Light	Yes	Yes
61	½ day	2D-strenuous	July-mid Oct.	Heavy	No	Yes

Section 6: Trails of the Yosemite Valley Area

A. Valley Floor

62	½ day	2B-easy	April-December	Moderate	Yes	Yes
63	½ day	2A-easy	April-December	Moderate	Yes	Yes
64	2 hours	1A-easy	April-December	Moderate	Yes	Yes
65	2 hours	1A-easy	May-December	Moderate	Fish	No
66	2 hours	1A-easy	May-December	Moderate	Yes	Yes
67	½ day	2A-easy	April-November	Heavy	Yes	Yes

B. North Rim

68	½ day	2D-strenuous	mid May-mid Nov.	Heavy	No	Yes
69	1 day	3E-strenuous	July-October	Moderate	No	Yes
70	1 day	4E-strenuous	July-October	Moderate	Fish	Yes

C. South Rim

71	1 day	3D-moderate	mid June-mid Nov.	Light	No	Yes
72	½ day	3C-moderate	July-October	Light	No	Yes
73	2 hours	1A-easy	mid June-Oct	Moderate	No	Yes
74	2 hours	1B-moderate	mid June-Oct.	Heavy	No	Yes
75	1 day	3D-moderate	July-October	Light	Fish	Yes
76	2 hours	1A-easy	mid June-Oct.	Moderate	No	Yes

D. East of Valley

77	2 hours	1A-moderate	April-December	Very heavy	No	Yes
78	½ day	2D-strenuous	June-November	Very heavy	No	Yes
79	2 days	2D-easy	June-October	Heavy	Yes	Yes
80	1 day	4E-strenuous	mid June-Sept.	Heavy	Yes	Yes
81	3 days	5E-moderate	mid June-mid Oct.	Heavy	Yes	Yes

Section 7: Trails south and east of the Glacier Point Road

82	½ day	2C-moderate	mid April-mid Nov.	Light	No	No
83	3 days	6E-moderate	mid June-Oct.	Light	Fish	No
84	2 days	3C-easy	July-October	Heavy	Yes	No
85	2 days	4D-moderate	July-October	Moderate	Yes	No
86	4 days	6E-easy	July-mid Oct.	Moderate	Yes	No
87	1 day	2C-moderate	mid June-Oct.	Moderate	No	Yes
88	6 days	7G-moderate	July-mid Oct.	Moderate	Yes	Yes
89	5 days	6F-moderate	July-mid Oct.	Moderate	Yes	Yes
90	1 day	2D-moderate	May-November	Moderate	No	No
91	4 days	5E-easy	July-mid Oct.	Moderate	Yes	No
92	1 day	3D-moderate	June-November	Light	No	No
93	½ day	2C-moderate	June-November	Light	No	Yes

Section 8: Trails of Yosemite's Southeastern Backcountry

94	2 days	4E-moderate	July-October	Light	Yes	No
95	2 days	3D-easy	July-October	Heavy	Yes	No
96	3 days	5E-easy	July-October	Moderate	Yes	No
97	3 days	3D-easy	July-October	Heavy	Yes	Yes
98	6 days	6F-moderate	July-mid Oct.	Moderate	Yes	Yes
99	2 days	4D-moderate	July-mid Oct.	Moderate	Yes	No
100	3 days	5E-moderate	July-mid Oct.	Moderate	Yes	Yes

Hiking Season: This is the period of the year you should be able to drive to a trailhead and then hike an essentially snow-free trail. On the higher trails you may experience snow flurries, but your trail will be covered by only a few inches of snow, not a snowpack. Of course, you can hike early in the season, but then be prepared for some route-finding problems due to the trail being under snow. In Yosemite Valley you can hike year round, for it is unlikely you will get lost even with a foot of winter snow on the valley floor. You may not find the trail, but then, you won't have to, if the snowpack is firm enough for cross-country hiking or skiing.

Hiker Use: "Light," "moderate," "heavy" and "very heavy" are used to describe each trail's popularity. This gives you an idea of how many people to expect. On heavily used backpack trails, campsites may be in short supply on weekends though probably not on weekdays. Some of this book's hikes have sections that vary significantly in usage. For example, on Hike 21, you'll probably meet no one between the Harden Lake trail junction and Highway 120, but you'll probably meet hundreds of people and dozens of hikers later on in Yosemite Valley. Therefore this hike has a compromise rating: moderate.

Can Swim and Fish: This is fairly obvious. If you can do only one of these two activities, then the table says which one. Usually both are done in one or more lakes seen along the trail, but not always. You can swim in the Tuolumne River (Hike 15) or in the Merced River (Hikes 62, 63, and 79, among others). Sometimes swimming is marginal, as at Cascade Creek (Hikes 29 and 30), but at least the creek has pools deep enough to get you completely wet.

Exceptionally Scenic: Yosemite as a whole is very scenic, but some trails are more scenic than others. The criterion used for this category is that a hike is classified "exceptionally scenic" if the views alone justify taking it. Hikes that are not rated exceptionally scenic are still worth taking unless your sole concern is spectacular mountain photography.

Other Pre-Hike Information

Once you have narrowed your potential hike down to a few choices, you can turn to them and read their descriptions to see which one is best for you. At the start of each hike is certain basic information: distance, grade (already discussed), trailhead information and introduction.

Distance: Distance is given in both miles and kilometers. Eventually all trail signs may be metric, but until topographic maps have contour lines in meters, most hikers will still think in terms of feet and miles. Included with the distance is the type of hike: round trip, loop trip, semiloop trip, and one-way trip. A *round* trip is not a circular one, but rather is one on which you hike to a destination and return the way you came. A *loop* trip is one on which you wind across the terrain and return to your trailhead without having to retrace any of your route, except perhaps for a small part of it. A *semiloop* trip is a combination of the two; it has at least one significant segment on which you'll have to retrace your steps plus at least one loop. A *one-way* trip is one on which you hike in one direction, ending somewhere away from your starting point. On this kind of hike you'll usually have to be dropped off by someone who later meets you at trail's end. Or, if you and your friends have two cars, you can leave one at the start and the other one at trail's end.

Trailhead: The trailhead is where you park your car and start walking. Included in this paragraph for each trip are all the necessary driving directions to get to the trailhead. Virtually all the roads are in good-to-excellent condition except when snowbound. The few road problems that may develop are mentioned in the relevant hikes. At the end of the **Trailhead** paragraph a letter and a number give the location of the trailhead on the map in the back pocket of this book.

Introduction: This paragraph tells you briefly what you can expect. It is useful in your decision of what trail to hike.

Yosemite's trails are usually marked with "T" blazes, "i" blazes or "ducks"

Wilderness Permits, etc.: You'll need a permit to stay overnight in the backcountry of Yosemite National Park or any of the wildernesses that border it. The necessary permit information is stated on the back side of this book's topographic map. Also included on the map's back side is information on day hiking, backpacking, animal problems, weather and natural history.

Section 1

Trails of Yosemite's North
and West Backcountry

Introduction: There are so many trails leading into Yosemite's northern backcountry that their descriptions could easily fill a book. Actually, in past years they have helped to fill four books: *Pinecrest, Tower Peak, Matterhorn Peak,* and *Hetch Hetchy* High Sierra Hiking Guides, published by Wilderness Press. Of these, only *Hetch Hetchy* is still in print, though in 1990 the three others were replaced by Dr. Schifrin's *Emigrant Wilderness and Northwestern Yosemite.*

    The trail description in this section is limited to only six outside approaches, with the omission of longer and/or less desirable ones. All the trails within Yosemite's north and west backcountry are described. This area's landscape is characterized by many parallel or nearly parallel canyons, and, generally speaking, they get progressively deeper toward the east. Many of the canyons lack trails in them, and the Park's management is to be applauded for keeping them that way. In the author's opinion, this Yosemite backcountry and the adjacent Emigrant Wilderness together contain the finest assemblage of cross-country routes to be found in the Sierra Nevada—a last stronghold for the true wilderness experience.

Supplies and Services: Absolutely everything you'll need for a Yosemite outdoor experience can be purchased in the western-foothills town of Sonora. This includes full backpacking and mountaineering gear, these available at Sonora Mountaineering. Supplies in Bridgeport, on Highway 395, are also quite complete, and each of these towns has at least one hospital. Limited supplies can also be purchased in smaller settlements such as Groveland, Pinecrest, Strawberry, Dardanelle, Lee Vining, and Mono Village. Mono Village, a large resort, has one of the best backpacker-oriented stores to be found in any Sierra mountain resort.

Wilderness Permits: For Hikes 1 and 2, get your permit at the Summit Ranger Station, located at the Pinecrest "Y." For Hikes 3–7, stop at the Bridgeport Ranger Station for permits if you're coming from the north. It is on Highway 395, about ½ mile south of Bridgeport. Those driving from the south on Highway 395 may prefer to get a permit at the Lee Vining Ranger Station, on Highway 120, 1.2 miles west from the Highway 395 junction.

For Hike 7, permits are also available at the Saddlebag Lake Resort, near the trailhead. Those following Hike 8 should stop at the Groveland Ranger Station in "downtown" Groveland, about 14 miles before the Cherry Lake turnoff. For Hikes 9–14, use either the Information Station by the Park's Big Oak Flat Entrance Station, or use the Hetch Hetchy Entrance Station, by the Mather Ranger Station. The latter is open from about early April through late October.

Campgrounds: For Hike 1, if you are driving up from the west, use Baker Campground, located just off Highway 108 about 9.2 miles before Sonora Pass. If driving from the east, use Leavitt Meadow Campground, on Highway 108, 7.1 miles west of Highway 395 and 8.0 miles east of the pass. Also use this campground for Hike 2. For Hikes 3 and 4 use any of the five campgrounds along Twin Lakes Road or use the private campground in Mono Village. For Hikes 5 and 6, camp at Virginia Lakes Campground, just yards from the trailhead. Saddlebag Campground is best for Hike 7 since it is only a minute's walk from the trailhead parking area. Sawmill Walk-in and Junction campgrounds are along the Saddlebag Lake road, and five more campgrounds are found along Highway 120 between Highway 395 and Tioga Pass.

For Hike 8 use the Cherry Valley Campground. At the major intersection near the trailhead parking area go left 0.5 mile west up Road 1N04, then branch right and go 0.5 mile to the campground's entrance. For Hikes 9–14, you could spend the night at Carlon or Middle Fork campgrounds, both along Evergreen Road between Highway 120 and the Hetch Hetchy Road. However, a better place to stay is at the 1991-vintage backpackers' campground near the O'Shaughnessy Dam trailhead.

Hike 1   Sonora Pass to Kennedy Canyon Crest

Distance: 16.2 miles (26.1 km) round trip

Grade: 4D, strenuous day hike; no trailside campsites

Trailhead: Drive up Highway 108 to its summit, Sonora Pass, and park there. Trail begins in map section **H1.**

Introduction: This alpine route, an 8-mile segment of the Pacific Crest Trail completed in 1977, provides breathtaking panoramas of granitic northern Yosemite National Park and of the volcanic Sonora Pass area. Continuing southeast on the Pacific Crest Trail to Dorothy Lake Pass (reverse of Hike 42) is an extremely scenic way to enter Yosemite National Park.

Description: The Pacific Crest Trail crosses Highway 108 only 50 yards north of Sonora Pass, and on it we follow a winding course southwest up the crest of the Sierra Nevada. In only 250 feet of elevation gain the dominant lodgepole pines are mostly replaced by those harbingers of timberline, whitebark pines. We cross the crest, then dip to cross five closely spaced gullies, which contain our only perma-

nent source of water. Beyond them we circle clockwise, climbing the well-graded trail up a cirque's rubbly headwall back onto the now-alpine crest. Once on it, a panorama explodes into view, ranging from peak 10641 in the southwest to Stanislaus and Sonora peaks in the north, and down into the West Walker River canyon in the east. Our climb south stays just a few yards east of the crest, and on the upper part of this ascent the narrow trail becomes quite exposed. Although this exposure on loose volcanic rock is generally not a problem in mid or late summer, it can be one before mid-July, when it is apt to be covered by an icy snowfield. Inexperienced mountaineers should not attempt this trail during that season, for then there are also two more hazardous trail sections.

Our 400-foot climb ends above the 2-mile high level, leaving us breathless but elated, for all our major climbing is now over, and the trail ahead is generally an easy, contouring one. Its ease is certainly an added plus, for with a full ⅓ less oxygen than at sea level, the rarefied atmosphere would hinder one's enjoyment if the trail were difficult. Your enjoyment can also be hindered if you haven't dressed for windy weather and if you haven't protected yourself—with hat, glasses and lotion—from the more intense ultraviolet radiation found up here. On west slopes within Emigrant Wilderness we contour south toward Leavitt Peak, the point where three crests unite. Dense waist-high clumps of whitebark pines sporadically paint the rusty alpine landscape with patches of green both before and after a crest saddle. At a second saddle the Pacific Crest Trail crosses the crest, makes a brief, steep switchback, then descends gradually—seasonally across a lingering snowfield—to two glacial moraines at the foot of a glacial cirque. These two terminal moraines represent the extent of two advances by a glacier, probably during the last stage of the Little Ice Age. Because the volcanic rock there is so rubbly, it doesn't hold water, so we don't find a lake in the small, deep basin between the two moraines and Peak 11265.

From the moraines we climb steeply but briefly up to a cleft in a ragged ridge and are almost knocked off our feet by the overpowering view (or perhaps by a gusty wind). You can find higher passes in the Sierra Nevada, but hardly one with a view that surpasses the rugged, alpine view before us. From the cleft we skirt the base of the ridge, staying high above Latopie Lake, whose barren, rocky shore offers little consolation to the camper. The abundance of large blocks along our traverse testifies to the instability of the volcanic ridge above us, and the possibility of a rock avalanche is a real concern for early-season hikers. Their final concern will be just ahead, where this short stretch in early season could send an inexperienced hiker quickly down to—and over—the brink of a cliff above Latopie Lake. Luckily, this hazard can be avoided by first climbing southwest up to a level

area below Leavitt Peak and then heading southeast on it to the gully.

Beyond the gully our trail descends gradually across a giant scree slope—the east side of Leavitt Peak. Its instability makes plant growth on it virtually impossible, thus making the landscape an austere one. Where the slope curves from southwest to southeast, you should leave the trail if you plan to "bag" Leavitt Peak, a loose but safe 800 feet of climbing above you. Otherwise, contour ¼ mile southeast back to the crest of the Sierra Nevada—actually a double crest that has the tendency to become very blustery. Your last 2¼ miles of trail also can be likewise, though most day hikers will experience pleasant weather. The volcanic slopes here are more stable than the ones we just left, thus you may see alpine gold and other high-altitude wildflowers dotting the landscape. From us volcanic rocks extend all the way down to the shore of Kennedy Lake, 2800 feet below us. By seven million years ago, our once-granitic landscape had been buried in places to a depth of more than 3000 feet due to the outpouring of dozens of lava flows and other volcanic products. Along your volcanic-ridge traverse be sure to stop at the three main crest saddles, all only a few yards away from the trail. The changing views of glaciated Leavitt Creek canyon are well worth the small effort.

Our section of the Pacific Crest Trail ends at a switchback on a usually closed jeep road, and from here you retrace your day's course. Alternatively, if you have a nonhiking friend who has driven a car up to Leavitt Lake, you can follow the jeep road first ¼ mile northeast up to a saddle and then 1½ miles down to the lake. Before you start your hike, be sure that the 2.9-mile Leavitt Lake Road (gated at Highway 108) is open (usually by mid-July).

The Sierra crest, including Tower Peak at far right, seen from jeep road above Kennedy Canyon

Hike 2   Tower Peak Country via West Walker River

Distance: 57.3 miles (92.2 km) one way

Grade: 7F, moderate 6-day hike

Trailhead: Park one car at trip's end at Sonora Pass on Highway 108 (Hike 1 trailhead). Drive the second car 8.0 miles east down Highway 108 to Leavitt Meadow Campground. Park at the north end of the dirt campground loop road. **H1.**

Introduction: This relatively low-level route into the heart of the Yosemite north country passes some justifiably popular fishing waters, then cuts cross-country for two miles to reach Tilden Lake, possibly the epitome of the verdant, pastoral north country. Our exit, via the famous Pacific Crest Trail, provides a rugged, spectacular alpine finale.

Description: The West Walker Trail leaves Leavitt Meadow Campground and drops east a few yards to bridge the wide West Walker River under a typical east-slope volcanic-soil forest association: robust, widely spaced Jeffrey pines, squat junipers, streamside Fremont's cottonwoods, and a sagebrush understory. East of the river, our well-trod path climbs briefly east, then traverses briefly south to a west-dropping usetrail. From this junction we climb east momentarily to a low ridge and, 0.3 mile from our trailhead, reach an important junction. From it the older trail to Roosevelt Lake continues east before climbing south. This trail is 0.6 mile longer than the newer trail, and its undulating route requires quite a bit more climbing and descending.

We take the newer trail, which swings south and quickly drops to an open, sagebrush-dotted bench on the east side fo giant Leavitt Meadow. It stays along this side for 1.4 miles, keeping well above wide meanders of the West Walker River. Across it, one may hear the shouts of Marine mountain troops practicing rock-climbing techniques on a cliff near the site of Leavitt Meadows Lodge. Later, we pass the horse trail from Leavitt Pack Station, which is not a recommended route for backpackers due to a deep, dangerous ford of the river. After Leaving Leavitt Meadow, we begin to climb, and in several minutes reach a junction with another Leavitt Meadow trail, coming in on the right, and then in several more minutes our trail tops out at a diminutive pond. Immediately beyond it we encounter a long, slender pond and just past it a junction with a trail that heads northeast to Secret Lake. Ahead, we traverse about 130 yards to a junction with the last Leavitt Meadow trail—the route one would take if one were to follow the meadow's westside road.

We continue south, going through a gulch between granite bluffs. This easy walk leads quickly to the north shore of Roosevelt Lake, which, with its southern twin, Lane Lake, is usually overcrowded but makes a good lunch stop. Both of these small, shallow lakes harbor brook trout and crayfish, as well as a teeming variety of insect and attendant bird life. Lane and Roosevelt lakes are separated by a broad isthmus of wind-transported sand, possibly of glacial origin, and it is possible that wind, as well as mineral-rich lake-bottom springs, bring the nutrients to support this unusual abundance of life. Here, even some beaver-felled lakeside logs are covered with plants—a verdure more commonly seen in the wet Cascades.

The West Walker trail passes some adequate camps on the isthmus between Roosevelt and Lane lakes, then climbs gently above the latter, returning soon to camps at its southern outlet. Here a newer trail branches from the older one, which can still be followed southwest down to the West Walker to large, secluded campsites. The newer trail climbs, via switchbacks, southeast up volcanic tuffs to a rising mile-long traverse through open aspen groves and sagebrush flats on a bench east of the West Walker River. Later, we rejoin the old riverbank route and drop to a lodgepole-and-aspen grove that borders the West Walker's trench. Here, under a 400-foot bluff of solidified volcanic mud flows, we could share shaded campsites with cattle that summer throughout the upper Walker basin in accordance with the Forest Service's Multiple-Use policy.

We quickly leave this cooler haven to swing southeast across a side stream, then steeply attack an eroded trail that climbs over a chaparraled spur. Once across this obstacle, we des-

Roosevelt Lake

cend to pass the signed Red Top Lake trail, then resume a pleasant streamside stroll south past good camps under sheltering lodgepoles. After ¼ mile, the West Walker River's course becomes a 15-foot-deep gorge through jointed granodiorite, and we follow it closely on some dynamited tread. Just beyond this gorge, the old trail fords the river, but horseless backpackers will prefer to stay on the new trail on the east bank for another ½ mile, until a signed junction points back—north—across the river via an easy, sandy ford.

On the far bank we find campsites, the west-bank West Walker River trail, and the signed Fremont Lake trail, which climbs steeply northwest ¾ mile in deep sand to Fremont Lake, the best bet for our first night's camp. Fremont Lake lay directly on the route of the pioneers' Sonora Trail route to the gold fields. In fact, emigrants once had to lower the outlet level of this good-sized lake so that their wagons could pass around its lodgepole-and-juniper-lined western shore! Heavily used camps greet us at Fremont Lake's south end. Fishing for large brookies and rainbows is fair.

The next morning, ignore lateral trails south from Fremont Lake to Chain of Lakes and the Long Lakes—these trails are unpleasantly dusty, and when the latter lakes aren't nearly stagnant, they teem with mosquitos (but, in all fairness, with trout, too). Instead, return to the West Walker River. Here also ignore the longer, less-used west-bank trail, as it, too, is sandy, is mosquitoey in early summer, and later reeks of cowpies. Regain the east-bank trail, southbound, and climb moderately up a wooded gully and over a col to Long Canyon, where a trail leads southeast 4 miles up to Beartrap Lake. Leap Long Canyon's creek, then continue southward through a forested groove to a stock fence and a small pond which herald Lower Piute Meadow.

Keeping well back in the dry eastern fringe of lodgepole forest, our way turns south along that sandy grassland, then undulates over small ridges to the signed Long Lakes trail, which branches west across a small, moist meadow. After a few more minutes of easy walking, we pass the Cascade Creek trail, and continue up-canyon in pleasant lodgepole forest.

After a mile of usually easy climbing, we level off at a junction near the north end of large Upper Piute Meadow. From here the Kirkwood Pass trail continues ahead along the side of the meadow. Our route branches right, south, and momentarily we wade across—if a log's not handy—the West Walker and reach nearby the Forest Service's Piute Cabin. Beyond a corral and a stock gate, we head out into stunningly beautiful Upper Piute Meadow, backdropped by graceful, sweeping Hawksbeak Peak. We head south around the meadow's perimeter, following tread that may be discontinuous. About halfway along this stretch, blazes mark a resumption of good tread, angling slightly uphill into a lodgepole forest. This leads quickly to a small, wetter meadow, then to a nice packer camp on the edge of lovely Rainbow Meadow.

With Tower Lake as an objective, we progress south up Tower Canyon, soon crossing its creek, and in ½ mile recrossing it. You might consider spending your second night along this ½-mile stretch, for camping is poorer at Tower and Mary lakes, both near timberline. Our trail crosses a tributary, then parallels the Tower Lake outlet creek midway to the lake. It then crosses this multibranched creek and climbs steeply to very steeply, up to the lake's outlet. Taking many breather stops on this ascent, the backpacker can admire the challenging buttress of Tower Peak's north ridge, to the south, or the fine crest of Hawksbeak Peak, to the east. In early fall this landscape, like Leavitt Meadow

Upper Piute Meadow, Hawksbeak Peak above it and Ehrnbeck Peak on the right

where we started, is painted a brilliant gold as the plants—here willows—change color. Tower Lake and its northern satellite are both tightly rimmed with bedrock, talus and willows, leaving only tiny spots to camp on.

Our route from here is cross country. From the lake's south shore we climb south nearly 600 feet up to a conspicuous saddle. The climb, though fairly steep, is fairly safe for experienced backpackers, the greatest danger perhaps being a careless twist of one's ankle. From the 10,150-foot saddle between Saurian Crest and Tower Peak we can gaze southwest down the canyon of Tilden Creek, over barren, windswept Mary Lake to long, forest-girded Tilden Lake and its southern guardian dome, Chittenden Peak. Leaving this austere gap, we scramble easily down through a swale of corn lilies and willows to the clustered whitebark pines that afford the best camps above the inlet of Mary Lake, which may have some beautiful golden trout. Follow Mary Lake's rocky northwest shore to reach the outlet, then descend moderately through frost-shattered hummocks and a velvety alpine fell-field of Brewer's reed-grass, rice-grass, and red heather to about 9420 feet, about ¼ mile below the outlet, where a poor, ducked trail begins to define itself. This use trail leads southwest, always quite near the west bank of raucous,

Doe and fawn at Tilden Lake

dancing Tilden Creek, down through a step-ladder of delightful meadows and subalpine conifers. Once, at 9120 feet, Tilden Creek makes a small waterfall, and wildflowers explode onto the moist slopes, overlooked on the east by mitre-capped Craig and Snow peaks. A long hour below Mary Lake, we traverse the final lumpy meadow to the head of lovely Tilden Lake.

The trail follows the west shore of 2-mile-long Tilden Lake, which is conspicuously better clothed in lodgepole pines than the east side, which is slabby and lacking soil. Almost half-way down this narrow gem, we find a sandbar which offers the best swimming beach for miles around. Farther on, our lakeside path bends southwest and enters open subalpine meadows near the base of black-streaked Chittenden Peak. This summit, named for an early Yosemite boundary commissioner, is easily climbed and provides the best overlook of Jack Main Canyon. Rounding south of Chittenden Peak, we find some good camps under a lodgepole canopy, then reach the end of Tilden Lake's long outlet lagoon. Here we boulder-hop south to find the well-used Tahoe-Yosemite Trail. Even if you don't plan to camp at Tilden Lake, you may want to walk ¾ mile east on this trail for storybook views up-canyon, where Tilden Lake mirrors the cockscombed Saurian Crest. Excellent camps are also found here, near emerald shoreline meadows.

From the outlet of Tilden Lake, the cobbly trail drops moderately west along the slabby, boulder-strewn south banks of frolicking Tilden Creek, where a profusion of shrubs and herbs line our path: spiraea, shooting-star, willow, red heather, corn lily, rosy everlasting and ground-sel. Chittenden Peak's south face looms well above us, and we gain views west across the wooded trough of Jack Main Canyon to Scho-field and Haystack peaks. Soon switchbacks appear to smooth our way down into thickening forest, always near now-cart-wheeling, some-times free-falling Tilden Creek. Below 8400 feet we turn south through sandy lodgepole forest and trace Jack Main Canyon downstream for ½ mile before stepping through a fringe of Labrador tea to the 70-foot-wide, shallow ford of Falls Creek. This horse ford will confer wet feet most of the year. On the west bank, we find a pleasant camp, and 80 yards later reach the signed Pacific Crest Trail and turn north. To complete the next three days' spectacular hiking along the PCT, see **Hike 42.**

Hike 3

Upper Kerrick Meadow via Barney and Peeler Lakes

Distance: 18.6 mi. (29.9 km) round trip

Grade: 4D, moderate 2-day hike

Trailhead: From Highway 395 near the west side of Bridgeport, take paved Twin Lakes Road south 13.6 miles to the signed entrance to Mono Village at the west end of upper Twin Lake. Park free outside the entrance, or inside for a small fee. E1-F1.

Introduction: The Robinson Creek trail is the most popular route through the Hoover Wilderness and into the Yosemite north country, and justifiably so. This short, scenic trail leads quickly into breathtaking subalpine terrain, and glittering Peeler Lake, surrounded by frost-shattered and glaciated granite and windswept conifers, mirrors the region's grandeur. Intimate campsites beside its shore more than compensate for the day's tough climb.

Description: Mono Village, a private resort sprawling across the alluvial fan of Robinson Creek at the head of upper Twin Lake, is such a maze of dirt roads, lavatories, RVs, pipelines, beached Boston Whalers, and umbrella tents that the Robinson Creek trailhead, on the campground's western frontier, is almost impossible for the uninitiated to find on the first try. The solution: walk south from the portalled Mono Village entrance, past the store, cafe, and marina facilities to the campground entrance station, and ask directions. These should point you just south of west for 0.5 mile to a cable across a dirt road that leads west along the northern margin of a lodgepole- and willow-encroached meadow.

It would be a mistake, however, to start up the Robinson Creek trail without first spending a few minutes at the head of Twin Lakes, especially in the fall when the Kokanee salmon run and hillside aspens turn first amber, then red. Twin Lakes lie behind curving recessional moraines of the Tioga glaciation, the most recent of the Ice Age glaciations. Tioga lateral moraines form obvious bouldery, sagebrush-dotted benches high above both the north and south shores of Twin Lakes, indicating that these last glaciers filled the canyon here to a depth of about 1000 feet! Summits to the north of Twin Lakes, from Eagle Peak to Robinson Peak and Sawmill Ridge, as well as Crater Crest and Monument Ridge to the south, are composed mostly of violently erupted volcanic rocks—tuff and tuff breccia—and to a lesser extent of lava flows and sediments. All appear to have accumulated mostly during the Triassic period (about 245–208 million years ago). Starting about 163 million years ago, all underwent metamorphism during a mountain-building period caused by the collision of an offshore land mass with our area. Subsequent metamorphism occurred with the later intrusion of magma that now forms our canyon's granodiorite walls.

From the cable-gated dirt road at the west end of the Mono Village complex, tread the road 300 feet west to reach the indistinct start of the Robinson Creek trail, branching right, away from the pretty meadow and its tantalizing glimpses of granitic parapets south up Blacksmith and Horse creeks. A sign demarcating the trail now lies a few yards up the soon-defined way, in bare-floored Jeffrey-pine forest. The level path strikes west, entangled in a braid of jeep trails that wind north of Robinson Creek under a canopy of white fir, Jeffrey pine, Fremont cottonwood, and aspen. But presently, under the scarp of a small roche moutonnée, where Basque shepherds carved their names on aspen trees early in this century, these routes coalesce and the resultant path ascends gently under mixed trees, paralleling an unusual flume. A ten-minute walk reaches a persistent stream, chortling down through wild-rose shrubbery from the basin between Victoria and Eagle peaks.

Afterwards, the trail winds gently up through more-open terrain, where bouldery ground moraine and alluvium support sparse conifers, sagebrush, manzanita, and squirrel-tail barley. Soon our cobbly, dusty path comes close to Robinson Creek, where its waters veer north around a jutting granitic promontory, and here the canyon, and our vistas, open up. As our path continues on a westward course, well above dying lodgepole pines in beaver-dammed Robinson Creek, we note the sweeping aprons of avalanche-scoured slope-wash that descend south from ruddy Victoria Peak, contrasting sharply with the spidery cliffs of light-hued quartz monzonite that form the sharper crests of Hunewill and Kettle peaks, guardians of the upper Robinson Creek basin. Here, the dry surroundings are mule ears, relieved by patches of gooseberry, turkey mullein, rabbitbrush, and some curl-leaved mountain mahogany. At 7600 feet we pass though a grove of aspens, then amble through more sagebrush and boulders to a sign proclaiming the **Hoover Wilderness**. From here a use trail cuts south to the mouth of Little Slide Canyon, up which can be seen the smooth granite buttress called the Incredible Hulk, as well as other incredible, but unnamed, rock-climbing goals. Minutes later we re-enter white-fir cover, and stop for a drink beside tumbling Robinson Creek.

Now rested and ready to assault the canyon headwall, we gear down to accommodate more than a dozen well-graded switchbacks that lead north through head-high jungles of aspen, bitter cherry, serviceberry, snowberry and tobacco brush, always within earshot of invisible Robinson Creek. Above 8000 feet we step across a rivulet merrily draining the slopes of Hunewill Peak, a welcome respite that furnishes flowers of creek dogwood, giant Indian paintbrush, Parish's yampah, Labrador tea, fireweed, asters, and ligusticum to delight the eye. Still climbing, we return momentarily to the creekside, where industrious beavers have recently created a small pond, then climb rockily, bending south, in a gully under aspen shade. Half our ascent is behind us when we level out to step across a branch of Robinson Creek that drains the 10,700-foot saddle to our west. Just a yard beyond this creek, the easily-missed South Fork Buckeye Creek cutoff trail branches west through a tangle of aspens and creek dogwoods. Just a few yards later, where Robinson Creek is repeatedly plugged by small beaver dams, a level

use trail branches south along the outlet stream of Barney Lake, reaching numerous good, sandy campsites. This spur trail joins the paralleling main trail at the northwest corner of Barney Lake, where prevailing southerly winds have created a sandy swimming beach, a fine spot for a lunch break.

Fourteen-acre Barney Lake, at 8290 feet, is nestled in a narrow, glaciated trough, rimmed on the east by the broken, lichen-mottled north spur of Kettle Peak. The western shoreline, which our trail follows, is a dry talus slope mixed with glacial debris. Here, a pair of switchbacks elevate the trail to an easy upgrade some 100 feet above Barney Lake's inlet. Below, golden beavers have dammed meandering Robinson Creek, drowning the meadow and a grove of lodgepole pines. Farther southwest, cirque-girdled Crown Point dominates the horizon, with Slide Mountain behind its east shoulder, while Kettle Peak flanks to the east, topped by a gendarmed cockscomb.

A short surprise descent comes in a few minutes, in the form of three dusty switchbacks, after which the path winds through broken rock and avalance-twisted aspens, over two freshets draining Cirque Mountain, then comes to a ford of Robinson Creek. This crossing requires one to doff boots in early season, because industrious beavers have widened the ford by damming Robinson Creek in the soggy meadow just downstream. Rainbow and brook trout of handy pan size abound here, as in Barney Lake. After drying our feet, we climb easily south in a

Glacier-cleft Crown Point rises more than 3000 feet above Barney Lake

pleasant forest of lodgepole pine, red fir, western white pine, and a new addition—mountain hemlock—reflecting our higher altitude. The trail soon leads back to the west bank of Robinson Creek, which we cross (using a log if one is handy). Next the trail crosses the cascading stream from Peeler Lake, beside which one might rest before ascending a long series of switchbacks just ahead. The first set of gentle, well-engineered switchbacks traverses a till-covered slope to about 8800 feet, where we level off momentarily for a breather before darting north for another, steeper and more eroded ascent. The vistas east to stunted whitebark pines growing on rough, ice-fractured outcrops of Kettle Peak offer good excuses to stop frequently on this energetic climb. Eventually we come to a small saddle at 9195 feet, signed for the Rock Island Pass/Slide Canyon trail.

Those bound for Peeler Lake now turn northwest, walking moderately up in mixed open forest, to a small, shaded glade beside Peeler Lake creek. We step across this stream twice before switchbacking south moderately up into a narrow gully. The wind picks up as we ascend this ravine, a sure sign that we're nearing the ridgetop, and sure enough, Peeler Lake's wind-swept waters soon heave into view, behind automobile-sized quartz monzonite blocks that dam its outlet. A short descent leads us below this talus to dynamited trail tread on the lake's north shore, where its startling blue lake waters foreground rounded Acker and Wells peaks, in the west. Most of the good campsites, under mixed conifers, are found as we undulate rockily into forest pockets along the north shore—though the east shore has some fine ones too, if a bit out of the way. The lake margin, mostly rock, does have a few stretches of meadowy beach, where one can fly-cast for rainbows and brookies to 14 inches.

Leaving Peeler Lake near its northwest end, the path climbs slightly to a granite bench dotted with bonsai-stunted lodgepoles plus sedges and ocean spray, where views back across the outlet show serrated Peak 11581 rising east of Kettle Peak. Now a short descent leads to a profusion of signs designating the Yosemite National Park boundary, beyond which pocket meadows covered with bilberry and short-hair sedge gradually coalesce into the northeastern arm of Kerrick Meadow. Soon our path ends in Kerrick Meadow at a junction, from which the Buckeye Pass trail goes north and the Kerrick Canyon trail (**Hike 4**) goes south.

Hike 4 Kerrick Canyon/Matterhorn Canyon Loop

Distance: 53.9 miles (86.7 km) semiloop trip
Grade: 7F, moderate 6-day hike
Trailhead: Same as the Hike 3 trailhead. **E1-F1.**

Introduction: Matterhorn Canyon, named for 12,264-foot Matterhorn Peak, which dominates its head, is the most spectacular canyon in the Yosemite north country. Here Ice Age glaciers did their work well, and transformed the 13-mile-long trough into a dazzlingly polished array of smooth cliffs and aprons, capped with lofty, frost-riven peaks that even now support small glaciers. Cozy conifer groves make the canyon bottomlands eminently hospitable to campers. After traversing through equally interesting Kerrick Canyon, which has less relief but a marvelous assortment of canyon-side domes, this hike follows a portion of the Pacific Crest Trail to find Benson and Smedberg lakes, both with good fishing. We then traverse a major part of Matterhorn Canyon, and as a finale, walk right under the spiry Sawtooth Ridge at the head of little-visited Slide Canyon.

Description: Follow the Robinson Creek trail (described in **Hike 3**) up from Mono Village past Barney and Peeler lakes to the north arm of Kerrick Meadow, where a post marks the Kerrick Canyon trail, leading south. Kerrick Meadow, covering a vast ground moraine at the head of Rancheria Creek, is a frost-hummocked expanse of short-hair sedge, rice-grass, Brewer's reed-grass and dwarf bilberry, quite typical of Sierran subalpine meadows. Note the numerous young lodgepole pines here, encroaching upon the grassland downwind from taller, fringing lodgepoles. Many of the young trees are dead or dying, a result of their untimely exposure to freezing rime and winds when the snowpack was low first during the dry winters of 1975–76 and 1976–77 and then in subsequent dry winters.

Turn down-canyon along the path, in a rut cut sometimes two feet deep in the delicate turf, and soon cross the seasonal headwaters of Rancheria Creek to its west side. Descending easily, we amble along the west margin of the meadow, over slabs and dry terraces, typical habitat of

Rock-rimmed Peeler Lake and the Buckeye Ridge

short-hair sedge. A profusion of birds seasonally flit among the open lodgepoles near our route: yellow-rumped warblers, American robins, mountain bluebirds, white-crowned sparrows, northern flickers, dark-eyed juncos and Brewer's blackbirds. Lemmon's paintbrush and alpine gentian flower in early summer.

Soon afterward we come to the well-signed Rock Island Pass trail, an alternate route for our return trip. Still gently descending, we pass through a lodgepole grove, then emerge at the northern end of an even larger meadowed expanse, rimmed on the west by 400-foot-high glacier-quarried bluffs. Long views south down upper Kerrick Canyon are topped by Piute Mountain and other dark, rounded summits near Seavey Pass. After 1½ miles of rolling, sandy trail, our trail crosses a trio of lateral moraines, then cuts close to an oxbow in 20-foot-wide Rancheria Creek where the broad canyon pinches off above a low hillock. In this area you'll find the north-flowing outlet creek of Arndt Lake. This lake, ¾ mile south, has good campsites. Presently Rancheria Creek's banks become a broken gorge, and we drop rockily down, only to strike another sandy meadow, this one with a flanking cluster of steep domes. Our path soon leads out of this lupine-flecked flat, down through a bouldery salient of lodgepoles to yet another meadow. Down this we amble south, soon to walk muddily right along the bank of meandering Rancheria Creek. At the next curve, we cross, following a vague trail to a clump of lodgepoles on the east bank, where

good trail resumes. Presently a master joint in the Cathedral Peak granodiorite bedrock forces Rancheria Creek east, and we follow its splashing course down over broken, porphyritic slabs, then back west (another master joint) for ½ mile on a cool, shaded hillside to the signed Seavey Pass trail (Pacific Crest Trail)—**Hike 42.**

Bound for Seavey Pass, our route climbs sometimes steeply up sandy-cobbly trail, heavily used by stock, into a dome-girded ravine, at the top of which we glimpse a small pond rimmed with corn lilies and other flowers. The trail now bends southeast and ascends to the Rancheria Creek/Piute Creek divide, then drops southwest to another gap, the real Seavey Pass. From this point, our path winds its way down over open benches, soon coming upon a large tarn with vistas over the confusing array of rust-stained cliffs surrounding Piute Creek to Peak 10060 and Volunteer Peak, which form the horizon. From this pond, our route switchbacks west down a shaded draw, then turns steeply southeast, negotiating sometimes brushy slopes first north of, then south of a cascading stream. Glimpsing our day's goal, Benson Lake, we finally reach the valley bottom, a sometimes-swamped tangle of willows and bracken ferns under lodgepoles and firs, then reach the signed Benson Lake spur trail at the flood plain's south end.

The short spur to Benson Lake ends at a broad, sandy beach with campsites sitting just back from the sand's edge. Heavily used camps are all along the shore, giving vistas over the frequently choppy waters to brushy domes at the outlet. Angling here is sometimes excellent for large rainbow and brown trout.

Our third morning should find us retracing our steps to the PCT, where we turn southeast across wide Piute Creek via fallen logs, then climb up into the morning sunlight to a brushy saddle. A short distance later our route strikes the creek that drains Smedberg Lake, which poses a difficult fording problem in early summer, usually best solved in the thicket of aspens just upstream. South of that stream the path climbs rockily up, often at a steep gradient, before crossing the creek twice more, in easier spots, along a more moderate ascent in a tight canyon walled by tremendous bluffs. Once again south of the creek, our route tackles a steep hillside, via moderate switchbacks under increasing numbers of mountain hemlocks. Red heather forms a discontinuous, showy understory here. Almost 700 feet higher, but still under the stony gazes of precipitous Peak 10060 and Volunteer Peak, we find a trail branching southwest to Murdock Lake, only 10 minutes away, where the impressive profile of Volunteer Peak forms a startling backdrop to that grass-fringed lakelet. At this junction, our route turns east to the Rodgers Lake trail, ¼ mile away, a recommended sidehike for those desiring seclusion, not often found at populous Smedberg Lake.

To reach Smedberg, the PCT switchbacks down, then up, to a slabby, polished bench overlooking the south shore of the lake. Named for an Army cartographer who, with Lieutenants Benson and McClure, mapped the Yosemite backcountry in the early 1900s, Smedberg Lake (30 acres) is dotted with low, grassy islets and rimmed with light granite, strips of sedge and bilberry meadow, and pockets of conifers. Pan-sized rainbow trout are common in its shallow waters, which reflect a sweeping face of streaked granite over the east shore, and the brooding vertical profile of Volunteer Peak on the south. Most camps are found on the west and north shores. We leave Smedberg Lake by curving south into a hummocky, boulder-and-meadow vale, then step across its draining creeklet to climb northeast toward Benson Pass. The first rise is moderate, under open mixed conifers; then we level out in a small meadow before the last, earnest climb to the pass. Near the top, some of the sandy, eroded trail must be classified as very steep, but it is soon behind us, and we stand in rotting granite sand, sparingly inhabited

by whitebark pines, catching our breath to views west to Volunteer Peak and northeast over Doghead and Quarry peaks and beyond to Whorl Mountain and Twin and Virginia peaks.

A steep trail rapidly leads us from Benson Pass down to a gravelly flat; then it becomes a switchbacking descent, under pleasant shade, to the hop-across ford of Wilson Creek in a steep-walled glacial trough. Turning down-canyon, the path alternately traverses dry openings and lodgepole forests as we cross Wilson Creek twice more. Soon the gentle-to-moderate descent resolves itself into some two dozen tight, rocky switchbacks as hanging-valley Wilson Creek canyon debouches itself into deeper Matterhorn Canyon. Bottoming out a few minutes later, the trail turns up Matterhorn Canyon through dry, sandy, lodgepole-filled flats and passes a large camping complex just before the wide, cobbly ford of slow-moving Matterhorn Canyon creek.

On the east bank, we choose the signed Matterhorn Canyon trail, which climbs imperceptibly north, past some good camps, keeping near the large creek, over sandy meadowland colored with senecio, goldenrod and bilberry. Views within this steep-walled trench are dominated by soaring Peak 10400+, on the west canyon slope. In about 1½ miles we pass into an open, bouldery stretch, then cross Matterhorn Canyon creek via boulders to a small, lush meadow, later recrossing the stream at a horseshoe bend. Just one-tenth mile of streamside ambling later, we see that the surrounding lodgepoles and hemlocks are topped eastward, away from the river, or are broken off at the 8-foot level, and are stripped of west-facing branches to a height of 20 feet. These facts attest to the magnitude of winter avalances that sweep from the tremendous heights of Quarry Peak across Matterhorn Canyon. This massive apron offers rock climbs up to 10 pitches long in the summer months.

About ¾ mile farther upstream, we ford again to the west side, then wind into a boulder-strewn, talus-footed meadow. Willows line the streamside, intermittently making way for rapidly thinning forest patches. Our gently ascending sandy path passes a few very nice camps, after which it's pretty much open going, with Burro Pass clearly in sight. It is the low point on a light ridge, with Finger Peaks on the west and massive Matterhorn Peak on the east. Standing behind Burro Pass, the jagged Sawtooth Ridge slices into blue skies and billowing afternoon

Finger Peaks (left) and Sawtooth Ridge (center), from 9300 feet in Matterhorn Canyon

cumulonimbus clouds. Above 9800 feet, under an arc of jagged peaks that stretches from Matterhorn Peak to Whorl Mountain and its unnamed overhanging outlier, the tread becomes steeper, trenching a delicate alpine fell-field replete with Lemmon's paintbrush, Sierra penstemon, and pussy paws. Soon the cobbly, rip-rapped trail becomes steeper still, and resolves into a chaos of eroded, miniature switchbacks through the broken granite forming the final slope of Burro Pass. Gasping, we clamber the last yards to the sign BURRO PASS, then rest while taking in the magnificent 360-degree panorama. To the north, aptly named Sawtooth Ridge throws up a picket line of fractured granite gendarmes, culminating in 12,264-foot Matterhorn Peak. East of us, massive Twin Peaks loom beyond an unnamed peak, dwarfing Whorl Mountain and its 11920-foot outlier, which together spawn a textbook rock glacier. Vistas back down the golden trough of Matterhorn Canyon stop at the exfoliating slopes of Quarry Peak, save for a real treat on a clear day, when over its east flank peek Clouds Rest, Quarter Domes and Half Dome, all near Yosemite Valley. Before our view southwest is blocked by the shoulder of Finger Peaks, we see Doghead Peak, the tip of Volunteer Peak, and distant Central Valley smog. West of Burro Pass, Slide Canyon curves down into timber from a pair of beautiful, little-visited alpine lakelets occupying a bench under the gaze of Finger Peaks.

Leaving Burro Pass, our trail drops steeply via rocky switchbacks, often obscured by long-lasting snowfields, to hop across infant Piute Creek in spongy alpine-meadow turf. It then follows that raucous, bubbling stream west on a sometimes steep descent into clustered white-

bark pines, which soon become an open forest. Soon we hop to the south bank of Piute Creek, then wind through a delicate, boggy meadow before recrossing just above an excellent campsite, complete with small waterfall, in mixed conifers. Leaving this camp, the trail stays farther from the creekside and descends, sometimes via moderate switchbacks, into heavier forest. Fair camps are found all the way down to campsites in willow-understoried forest beside a sign proclaiming SLIDE CANYON and marking our trail's low point along Piute Creek.

Now the trail begins to go gently up in sun-dappled forest, and soon finds itself switchbacking moderately near a small branch of Piute Creek. Here we can look down-canyon to view the feature that gave the names to this canyon and the mountain south of us—the Slide. This feature was first noted by Lieutenant Nathaniel F. McClure, while mapping the Yosemite north country:

> After traveling three and one half miles down the canyon, I came to the most wonderful natural object that I ever beheld. A vast granite cliff, two thousand feet in height, had literally tumbled from the bluff on the right-hand side of the stream with such force that it not only made a mighty dam across the canyon, but many large stones had rolled far up the opposite side.

McClure somewhat overestimated Slide Mountain's 1400-foot wall, but he understated the magnitude of the landslide—boulders the size of small houses cut a swath across Piute Creek some ¼ mile wide, and rolled almost 200 vertical feet up the far bank!

After a few switchbacks we find ourselves atop the rim of Slide Canyon, on a sloping subalpine bench. Here we step across the small stream we've been paralleling, then ascend more steeply west into a rocky gulch. This climb presents ever-improving panoramas east to Burro Pass and the headwaters of Slide Canyon. Our trail climbs north up the gully, then descends gently south into a spongy, boulder-rimmed stepladder meadow. The final rise from this vale to the 10460-foot saddle dividing the Piute and Robinson creek drainages proceeds on frequently steep, always cobbly and eroded trail tread. Possibly the most interesting view from this windy col is to the northeast, over the head of Little Slide Canyon, guarded by the Incredible Hulk and north beyond to the ruddy metamorphic caps of Buckeye and Flatiron ridges.

Leaving behind the Yosemite Park boundary signs, our Robinson Creek trail negotiates six or seven moderate switchbacks down to a stream-braided, marshy terrace fed by an unmapped snowfield in the hollow north of Slide Mountain. At the lower end of this flat lies a small tarn, which we skirt to the south, and then we descend rockily in a maze of head-high whitebark pines and talus blocks east of the lake's outlet stream. Soon the way becomes even steeper, plunging north 500 feet down excruciating rocky switchbacks to another pocket meadow, where our path hops to the west stream bank. Below, we trace the sharp western lateral-moraine crest of the Slide Mountain glacier down to Robinson Creek, in another sandy, willowed flat that contains the signed junction of the Rock Island Pass trail.

Here anglers and hikers who desire a more secluded alpine campsite may turn southwest toward Rock Island Pass. Their route up along the steep southern slope of Crown Point succumbs to gentle switchbacks and rewards one eventually with a grassy knoll at 10260 feet, affording a breather and views over the Sierra crest to the Sawtooth Ridge. Then the trail angles easily down past snug, sandy camps to sedge-rimmed Snow Lake, containing both rainbow and rare golden trout, 8-14 inches long. Almost everyone who reaches here, especially photographers, will want to ascend the short, meadowed distance from Snow Lake's inlet to broad Rock Island Pass, for lake-reflected vistas of frost-fractured Kettle Peak. Some hikers may decide to descend the moderate trail west from Rock Island Pass, down through quiet subalpine forest, to meet the Kerrick Canyon trail at the lower end of Kerrick Meadow, then exit Yosemite National Park via Peeler Lake, adding an extra half day to their journey.

Back at the Rock Island Pass trail junction, the Robinson Creek trail turns downstream, through talus boulders and willows. Across the stream, 100 yards east, sits a large, pretty tarn,

Evening view from Rock Island Pass: Kettle Peak above Snow Lake

well worth the side trip for the ecological lessons, views, and secluded alternative camping to often-crowded Crown Lake. This lakelet sits on a meadowed bench between granite hillocks. Its outlet stream used to flow northeast, directly down to the head of Crown Lake, but it now starts northwest down into the willow-choked meadow traversed by the Robinson Creek trail, then goes around a rocky knob, before heading down-canyon. Possibly, rapid growth of the thick bilberry, sedge and rush turf surrounding the pond blocked the original outlet and elevated the lake level until the water found the northwest outlet. Also, frost-heaving of the dense sod during spring months may have closed off the old outlet and further elevated the lake rim—note that it is markedly higher than the surrounding meadow.

Leaving this interesting lakelet, we return to the Robinson Creek trail and descend east via gentle switchbacks to the sodden meadow on the west shore of Crown Lake. The path circumvents the meadow to reach Crown Lake's north outlet, from where use trails lead to the only legal campsites, in grouped whitebarks and hemlocks above the lake's rocky east shore. Anglers will be pleased to find a self-sustaining fishery of large rainbow trout.

The next leg of our descent leads to the two small Robinson Lakes, on a 9200-foot bench under towering Crown Point. First we hop Robinson Creek just a minute north of Crown Lake, then descend more and more steeply under open coniferous shade. One-half mile below our first ford, we jump back to the west bank, just above the larger Robinson Lake, where we get nice views north over its shallow, rainbow-breeding waters to Hunewill and Victoria peaks. Meager camps are located on the isthmus between the two Robinson Lakes, but they are even less appealing since a thoughtless camper left his fire unattended and caused a small forest fire.

Leaving this blackened area, our trail swings west along the north shore of the swampy, grassy western lakelet, then climbs through a chaos of mammoth talus blocks—the terminal moraine of the Crown Point cirque-glacier. One-third mile of dynamited trail through this bad-land ends under the quiet shade of a pure mountain hemlock grove that lines a gully containing a seasonal creek. We hop the creek here, turn northeast, and soon climb to a sunny col to meet the signed Peeler Lake trail. From here we retrace our first day's steps downhill all the way to Mono Village on upper Twin Lake.

Hike 5   Virginia Lakes and Green Creek Basin

Distance: 14.8 miles (23.8 km) with side trip to West Lake; one way

Grade: 3D, moderate 2-day hike

Trailhead: Turn west off Highway 395 at Conway Summit, 12.3 miles north of Lee Vining or 12.8 miles south of Bridgeport, onto paved Virginia Lakes Road. Follow it 5¾ miles to dirt Virginia Lakes Campground road. Keep left on the branching road, not entering the campground proper, then turn right on the next, unsigned side road through a low thicket of aspens. If you reach Big Virginia Lake you've gone ¼ mile too far. Park off the road at some unofficial campsites under lodgepole pines. F2.

Green Creek roadend is reached by dirt Green Creek Road, which meets 395 4.4 miles south of Bridgeport or 8.4 miles north of Conway Summit. Follow it 8.9 miles west to Green Creek Campground, then another bumpy ½ mile to the signed parking area. **F2.**

Introduction: Between them, the Virginia Lakes and Green Creek basins hold over 20 assorted, sparkling, trout-abundant lakes that are easily visited. In addition, this area provides interesting geological lessons, multihued panoramas of crumbling peaks, and an unmatched parade of wildflowers.

Description: From the parking area, the Blue Lake trail climbs easily west into a stand of pines. Under this sparse subalpine shade, we parallel an unused mining flume in a narrow ravine, quckly pass north of first one and then a second small tarn, and reach the Hoover Wilderness boundary. Moments later Blue Lake comes into view, cupped in steep slopes of ruddy-brown hornfels—a metamorphic rock that lacks foliation. Where our path nears the outlet of Blue Lake, there is a small grove of pines, an adequate camp and a profusion of wildflowers. Elsewhere, as we see while climbing gently above the north shore of Blue Lake, the terrain is composed of talus or moraines, supporting a sparse but lively ground cover of Eastwood paintbrush, buckwheat, antelope brush and penstemon. Rickety spires of rusty-weathered Dunderberg Peak loom high to our north, spalling talus that is home for numerous yellow-bellied marmots that study our ascent.

At Blue Lake's western headwall, our way climbs steeply, stopping for a moment at a 9950-foot overlook, then rounds an immense talus fan to the verdant banks of Moat Lake's outlet stream, which descends merrily from the north together with a steeply clambering use trail. Now under the prow of a light-colored crag guarding Moat Lake, our trail switchbacks southwest up a forested hillside, presently to find the still-active Gold Start Mine, with a rock-shingle-roofed cabin and prospect pits. One more switchback brings us to the outlet of Cooney Lake, which occupies a low bench in this austere timberline upland. Good camps are found south of the inlet in wind-tortured knots of whitebark pines. Here views open to our trip's high point as barren Burro Pass (a local name), 11,110 feet, saddles the western horizon, its metamorphosed tuffs looking cream-colored against the surrounding darker metalavas, such as Black Mountain, to our south.

We leave windy Cooney Lake and ascend gently west into a rocky-meadowed draw. Here we easily step across infant Virginia Creek via rocks and logs to find a second, rolling bench, harboring a clutch of small lakelets—the Frog Lakes—aptly named for mountain yellow-legged frogs that share the cold, shallow waters with small eastern brook and rainbow trout. We swing south of the meadowy lowest Frog Lake, then ascend on lush alpine turf to the largest and highest lake, where good camps are found in scattered whitebark pines.

The next riser on our staircase ascent is steeper than those before, and has even less tree cover. Finally, the trail resolves into red-sandy switchbacks, reaches an overlook of the highest Frog Lake, then leaves the last whitebark pines behind for a true alpine ascent along the north cirque wall. The warm, mineral-rich, easily weathered, water-holding metavolcanic soil here supports an abundance of alpine wildflowers rarely seen elsewhere in such numbers: robust, blue-bugled Davidson's penstemon, sour-leaved sorrel, furry-leaved alpine hulsea, showy polemonium, and ubiquitous sulfur flower. At the cirque's talused head, after a burst of switchbacks, we gain 11,110-foot Burro Pass, then gaze back down Virginia Creek over our day's toil. By walking north just a minute from the trail's high point, we can also view pleasures to come: north of us the Green Creek basin spreads ruggedly below our feet. There, we can make out the Hoover Lakes and East Lake, flanked by the summit of Epidote and Gabbro peaks. In the northwest, Summit Lake occupies the saddle under Camiaca Peak's avalance chutes, backdropped by the dark, brooding temple of Virginia Peak.

From the barren, dark, windswept crest, we make an initial descent south, then momentarily switchback northwest toward Summit Lake. Beside the trail you'll see tight clusters of whitebark pines, the largest cluster offering emergency shelter if you're caught in a blizzard. Our trail switchbacks 400 feet northwest down through a small, stark side canyon to a sloping subalpine bench, which gives our knees a rest before we hit the third set of switchbacks. On a small bench at the base of these we reach a signed trail junction. From here the Virginia Canyon trail drops west before climbing to Summit Lake (see **Hike 6**).

Blue Lake trail and Frog Lakes, view northeast from near Burro Pass

Hoover Lakes, view down-canyon

The Green Creek trail turns northeast, down over gravelly slopewash past a small tarn (look for dainty, violet alpine speedwell) to an excellent overlook down-canyon to the Hoover Lakes. Beyond, light-granitic Kavanaugh Ridge shows over the massive shoulder of Dunderberg Peak. We drop to step north across East Fork Green Creek, then gently descend over orange, cobbly schist around the north shore of the larger upper Hoover Lake. The 50-foot-wide rocky outlet stream poses only minor difficulties, below which we find lower Hoover Lake and an old trail going southwest to windy camps on the upper lake's east shore. Lower Hoover Lake, which our trail traverses via the talus-strewn south shore, has no camping, but like the upper lake, is attractively stocked with rainbow, brook and brown trout 8-10 inches long. Below it, we drop easily over willowed benches, then circle above less-visited Gilman Lake to cross East Fork and Green Creek once again, via logs, in a stand of hemlocks and whitebark pines. Soon afterward, our descent ends and our route rises gently past easily recognized outcrops of conglomerate rocks. Soon we pass the spur trail to Gilman Lake, followed closely by small, green Nutter Lake. Camps are found below our trail in subalpine conifers at Nutter Lake's west end.

A short northwest climb away from Nutter Lake on a dry, mat-manzanita-patched hillside next presents East Lake, largest of the Green Creek lakes, spread 100 feet below us under the iron-stained talus skirts of crumbly Epidote Peak, Page Peaks, and Gabbro Peak. We round above East Lake's rocky, open-lodgepole-forested east shore on a descent past two small ponds to the extensive camping complex at the rock-dammed north outlet. Fishing is good here for large rainbow trout.

Departing East Lake, we step across the small outlet stream, then drop gently through dry, open lodgepole cover, taking a few switchbacks, to recross East Lake creek some 140 vertical feet lower. A short dogleg leads from this rockhop to another one across the same stream, in a lusher assemblage of lupine, monkshood, alumroot, meadow-rue and columbine. Regaining the west bank, we stay near the stream's dull roar all the way down a chain of short switchbacks, ending finally near shaded camps clustered beside West Fork Green Creek. These camps are just yards east of Green Lake's log-strewn outlet, where fishing is good for large rainbow and brook trout.

A log bridge leads us north across the stream and past an old log mining-cabin to a signed junction, where our route turns right, down Green Creek, and a not-to-be-missed side trail to the north shore of Green Lake, Virginia Pass, and West Lake climbs west, back into forest cover.

From the signed East Lake/West Lake trail junction on the brushy, morainal shoulder northeast of Green Lake, the Green Creek trail drops northeast on dusty tread through low aspens and tobacco brush past unexpected mariposa lilies. Some 200 feet lower, in pleasantly shaded lodgepole and aspen groves, we come to parallel West Fork Green Creek in fantasy-jungles of early-season wildflowers: tiger lily, rein orchid, checkerbloom, giant paintbrush, columbine, larkspur, sweet-cecily, monkshood and blue-eyed grass. This damp, gently descending path crosses numerous streams, some of them mapped, and then we leave the Hoover Wilderness and descend more steeply on a moraine hillside via 12 open switchbacks. Below them, we tread through another quiet forest grove, then climb a small juniper-clad ridge where an old mine-shaft lies 50 feet north of our sandy path. We quickly leave this dry saddle and descend steeply down to Green Creek and the meadowed parking area, just 160 feet after a rocky turnaround.

Hike 6   Virginia Canyon

Distance: 21.9 miles (35.3 km) by shortest (round trip) route

Grade: 5E, moderate 3-day hike

Trailhead: Same as the Hike 5 trailhead. **F2.**

Introduction: Virginia Canyon is the easiest-to-reach classic glacier-scoured subalpine gorge of the Yosemite north country. As well as its own pleasant, sunny lodgepole forests and ever-changing Return Creek, it offers a variety of more rugged alpine options to avoid retracing one's steps on the return trip.

Description: Follow the trail described in **Hike 5** up past the Virginia Lakes, over 11,110-foot Burro Pass, and steeply down a long procession of switchbacks to the Green Creek trail, on a gravelly, whitebark-pine-dotted bench just above 10,000 feet near East Fork Green Creek. Our route here turns southwest and drops momentarily to cross four small freshets in a verdant meadow where tiny yellow club-moss ivesia, daisies, Lemmon's paintbrush, and monkey flowers all float in a sea of purple-mist grass and alpine timothy. A steep, cobbly ascent ensues, paralleling Summit Lake's outlet stream. Soon the climb moderates, and we see the avalance slopes of Camiaca Peak straight on as our ascent over dry sedge flats and benches passes numerous good hemlock-bower campsites. Nearing Summit Lake's usually windswept outlet, we level off. Campsites are few here, and a tent is advisable, for the scattered whitebark pines offer little wind protection. Sunset views, however, are quite spectacular. Angling for 6-8 inch brookies is fair.

Continuing on, we curve west near Summit Lake's north shore, alarming "picketpin" ground squirrels in dry flats of Brewer's reed-grass and sagebrush. Signed Summit Pass, on the Yosemite Park boundary, rises only a man's height above the 10,205-foot-high lake. As recently as 14,000 years ago, a glacier flowed from the lake basin both east and west. A future Summit Lake *might* drain into Yosemite instead of the Hoover Wilderness. Today the lake is slowly diminishing in size as winter avalanches carry loose rocks and detritus down into it. Standing at the pass, you can readily identify the pointed metamorphic summit, Virginia Peak, that rises above the summits of Stanton Peak and Gray Butte, both south of it. Broad, deep Virginia Canyon, below us, has been considerably smoothed by repeated episodes of glaciation over the last 2

million years. On a clear morning, vistas down Virginia Canyon frame distant Mount Hoffmann.

As we descend into Yosemite, Summit Lake's stunted whitebark pines quickly give way to well-formed lodgepoles and a sagebrush ground cover. After a mile's descent, we meet a junction with the Virginia Pass trail, a highly recommended return route that will be described after the description of Virginia Canyon. From this junction, the down-canyon trail immediately crosses Return Creek and descends moderately-to-gently through a lodgepole forest for 4 miles before reaching the Pacific Crest Trail at 8540 feet. Most of this canyon, like much of the Park's granitic terrain north of Tuolumne Meadows, is composed of an igneous rock called quartz monzonite, which solidified in the earth's crust mostly 80-90 million years ago. Marking our down-canyon progress is an ever-changing view of Shepherd Crest, on our left, whose steep-sided north slopes harbored glacierettes during cold periods of the Little Ice Age. Near the junction of the Pacific Crest Trail (**Hike 42**) you'll find quite a number of campsites above both banks of Return Creek. In early season Return Creek is dangerous to cross, and you had best camp on the west bank. Due to its popularity, this camping area has attracted hungry bears, so before you go to bed, make sure all your food is bear-proof.

One recommended exit route, so as not to retrace one's steps, is to link this hike with **Hike 7**, for an enjoyable subalpine sojourn at McCabe Lakes.

The Virginia Pass trail, which branches from the descending Virginia Canyon trail at 9340 feet, is initially on the east bank of Return Creek, but crosses that stream thrice on its northbound ascent. It finally peters out at 9850 feet, in 1.2 miles, in a thick meadow turf where a stream falls down from an unnamed lake under the red pyramid of Virginia Peak, to our west. One could ascend easily to this lake for nice, secluded camping.

From where the trail dies out, it is but another 700 feet north up steep, open timberline slopes of sagebrush and whitebark pines to 10,540-foot Virginia Pass. Views here are breathtaking. South down timbered Virginia Canyon, the spiry western Cathedral Range, Half Dome and Clouds Rest can be seen, bordered on the east by the tips of Mt. Conness and North Peak and the north scarp of Shepherd Crest. More to the west,

From Park boundary, view east across Summit Lake to Dunderberg Peak, on left

the upper cirque is guarded by Gray Butte, Stanton Peak, Virginia Peak, and the towering, gendarme-bristled south slope of Twin Peaks. In the northeast, Glines Canyon slopes to forested Green Lake, while the rolling sageland around Bodie marks the horizon. Spend a few minutes examining the metamorphosed volcanic schists that make up windy Virginia Pass. Note that glacial striae, or grooves, in this hard rock indicate that a glacier flowed from west to east *over* this col. This fact must mean that a massive glacier, originating between Virginia and Twin Peaks, had a high enough surface to flow both south down Virginia Canyon and northeast into Glines Canyon.

Leaving this instructional gap, a well-ducked use trail on the right side of the pass makes its way steeply north down into Glines Canyon. Poor switchbacks soon come into play over a slope of moraine and talus, and then we level off momentarily in a rocky meadow at 10,230 feet. Here *southbound* hikers will want to look for the vague path along the left-hand margin of the meadow, near the first cluster of whitebark pines. Everyone should look for the hexagonally-patterned rock rings that have been heaved up by repeated frost action in this soggy flat. Down-canyon hikers will find a resumption of trail along the east side of West Fork Green Creek, which tumbles musically down through Sierra willows, dwarfed pines, red and white heather, and little elephant's heads. Next, we veer away from the stream for a short while and then drop steeply to a marshy flat, where we rejoin the creek. Here lies a mammoth boulder of marble that is slowly dissolving, and its minerals are precipitating on all the cobbles downstream, causing the stream bed to appear ghostly white. Across this meadow, we turn momentarily up along Green Creek, then hop north over it just below eye level with another meadow. Our steep descent continues, now under scattered-to-

moderate mountain hemlocks that frame vistas of Peak 10880, on the north canyon wall. Soon a thicker, steeper hemlock forest blocks all views, and we come to the wood-and-iron ruins of an old stamp mill, in a lush herbaceous jungle. An upward jog a minute later finds a ruined log cabin in a field of fireweed capping a viewful promontory; yards behind it is a collapsed adit, on the contact between two differing schists. From this cabin we switchback north down to cross two streams, the second being the outlet from Par Value Lakes, in a patch of swamp onions, yarrow and horkelia. Just above us lie the ruins of a water-powered, eight-crucible, rocker-arm "Ideal Stamp Mill pat. Oct 8 1899," with rusted hydraulic pipe, a Pelton water wheel, and a "No. 3 Dodge Rock Brkr" from the Parke and Lacy Co. Old prospect pits dot both hillsides.

Below this amazing testament to strong backs and hopeful, ingenious minds, our trail sidehills down near scattered lodgepoles, then enters a deeper, Cascadian forest that frequently forces us to duck where unpruned hemlocks drape the route. The creek stays within easy earshot, and we eventually walk along an old wagon road that supplied the mine. Near the head of Green Lake, our path finally becomes gentle and reaches some excellent campsites, in duff-floored lodgepole-and-hemlock forest. To reach the east end of Green Lake, from where the Green Creek trail may be followed north for an easy exit, or the East Lake trail may be climbed back to Summit Lake (see **Hike 6**), our trail heads north around the west side of 50-acre Green Lake. Numerous creeks create a boggy path. Look for Brewer's bittercress and great polemonium in the wetter places. From Green Lake's north shore, our overgrown path climbs up some 50 feet to a dry, mule-ears-and-sagebrush bench, where we meet the descending West Lake trail (see the last part of **Hike 5**).

Hike 7

McCabe Lakes via the
Saddlebag Lake Hinterlands

Distance: 16.7 miles (26.9 km), semiloop trip to Lower McCabe Lake; only 8.1 miles (13.1 km) if cross-country hike to Secret and McCabe lakes is omitted

Grade: 4D, moderate 2-day hike, or moderate 2B hike if the cross-country hike is omitted

Trailhead: Drive 2.1 miles north on Highway 120 from Tioga Pass, then 2.4 miles northwest to Saddlebag Lake. **F3.**

Introduction: By adhering to official trails you won't find a quick way in to the McCabe lakes. Knowledgeable hikers, however, reach Upper McCabe Lake in only three hours by taking this described partly cross-country route. Since the crest route above Secret Lake can be dangerous, hikers inexperienced at mountaineering should not attempt to climb it. Even if you stick to the basic semiloop—Saddlebag Lake to Helen Lake and back—you will absorb some of the Sierra's finest scenery and will do so without any climbing risks. Those who go to the McCabe Lakes should be prepared for a sudden summer snowstorm. If you're caught in one, *don't* attempt to return to Secret Lake and *don't* attempt to hike cross country to Roosevelt Lake. Rather, do as the rangers suggest and take the trail from Lower McCabe Lake west 2⅓ miles to the Pacific Crest Trail, then south 7 miles to Glen Aulin High Sierra Camp, where aid, if necessary, can be secured.

Description: Just before Saddlebag Campground is a fairly large trailhead parking area for those hiking north into the Hoover Wilderness. You can get both a wilderness permit and fishing license at close-by Saddlebag Lake Resort. The resort's store sells fishing supplies and a few groceries, and its cafe serves breakfast and lunch, but not dinner. The resort also rents small boats, and on weekdays as well as weekends Saddlebag Lake often has quite a population of anglers in hot pursuit of the lake's brook, rainbow and Kamloops trout. If you want to fish here, great, but get off this large lake in a hurry if a thunderstorm approaches—lightning kills. The resort also provides scenic trips on the lake plus water-taxi service to the lake's far end. The water taxi will pick you up at your own pre-arranged time.

To get to the lake's far end, you could hike along the closed road that parallels the east shore, but a better, shorter alternative is to hike on a trail that parallels the west shore. From the trailhead parking entrance you can see a road descending to the base of the lake's dam, then climbing to the dam's west end. Here the trail begins—a blocky tread cutting across open, equally blocky talus slopes. This metamorphic-rock talus may be uncomfortable to walk on, but from an alpine plant's perspective it is better than granitic-rock talus. Metamorphic bedrock fractures into smaller pieces than granitic bedrock does, thus creating a greater water-storage capacity for plants. Furthermore, it is much richer in dark minerals, so it makes a more nutrient-rich soil. And, being darker in color than their granitic counterparts, metamorphic-derived soils absorb heat—very important to plants at these alpine altitudes.

About ½ mile north of the dam, our trail bends northwest and Mt. Dana, in the southeast, disappears from view. Shepherd Crest, straight ahead, now captivates our attention, in tranquil reflection across the early morning waters of Saddlebag Lake. Among willows and a seasonally fiery field of Pierson's paintbrush, our trail dies out near the lake's north end, and we climb west to the east shore of Greenstone Lake. In the early morning a breathtaking reflection of North Peak mirrors across the placid waters, providing some of the best color-photography potential in this quadrangle. Following the lake's shore north, we quickly meet the closed mining road that water-taxi riders will be hiking west on. Above the lake's north shore, our narrow road enters the Hoover Wilderness, an area of 47,916 acres flanking the northeast boundary of Yosemite National Park. It serves as a buffer for the Park wilderness and is itself a beautiful, if not more spectacular, piece of wilderness. Southwest across Greenstone Lake a granite wall sweeps up to a crest at Mt. Conness, in whose shade lies the Conness Glacier. Our main tread, complicated by two short jeep-road segments, climbs northwest, and then at the "Z" Lake outlet creek bends west over to relatively warm Wasco Lake.

Beyond the first tarn north of Wasco Lake, our trail enters the drainage of northeast-flowing Mill Creek. Then just past the second tarn we come to a junction with a jeep trail—the start of interesting side trips. We take this trail, which descends north to the south shore of Steelhead Lake, bends west, then starts a climb south up a linear gully. Growing in its moist confines are dense clusters of Suksdorf's monkey flowers. Typical of many alpine plants, their stems are greatly reduced, thereby making their one-inch-long yellow flowers seem greatly oversized. You could continue up the gully, then branch southwest to easily reached snowfields below North Peak, but we climb west from the gully to nearby Potter Lake. Its outlet creek immediately cascades noisily into deep Steelhead Lake, and near the cascade are ledges from which brave souls can high-dive into that lake's chilly depths.

Our route to the McCabe Lakes is now essentially cross country, although we'll be following a faint *de facto* trail for most of the way. Just northwest of Potter Lake is a low, broad bedrock ridge that separates Towser Lake from larger Cascade Lake. Start north up this bedrock, and soon you'll be climbing a faint trail up beside a Cascade Lake inlet creeklet. Eventually this trail crosses the creeklet and then parallels its west bank up to a granite bench that holds icy, barren Secret Lake. Hardly a secret, it sometimes attracts dozens of day-hikers on weekends.

Pausing at Secret Lake to survey your route up the headwall, you have three choices. Adept mountaineers can attack the wall directly, preferably keeping just to the right of the black, lichen-stained vertical streak on the headwall. Hikers who want to put out some extra effort to achieve certainty and lack of steep exposure can

View southeast from crest: Secret Lake, Steelhead Lake, Saddlebag Lake and pointed Mt. Dana

arduously pick their way up the scree north of Secret Lake to the lip of what looks like—but isn't—a lake basin. From there, they will traverse slightly upward to their left, under the solid face of the east end of Shepherd Crest, to the low point on the headwall divide. Probably most people choose the third way: From the south side of Secret Lake walk directly up the increasingly steep headwall until, about halfway up, you come to a long ledge that slopes slightly up to the south. Many ducks mark this route, but they are not always easy to see. About 200 yards south up this ledge, you leave it and follow ducks almost directly up to the ridgecrest. Once on it, follow it north to the low point of the divide to find the ducked route descending on the west side of the ridgecrest. From the crest's saddle—a shallow gap—you can see that an ascent up Shepherd Crest would be tedious but not really dangerous. While you're looking at it, note how icy winds have reduced the whitebark pines on its lower slopes to a knee-high ground cover. To the southeast, pointed Mt. Dana stands high on the horizon above Saddlebag Lake.

The descent from the saddle is easier and safer than the ascent. A ducked route starts among cropped whitebark pines and bush cinquefoils, then descends steeply southwest toward a large, seasonal pond on a flat bench. There are several primitive paths down to this pond, and many incorrect routes. The greatest danger—assuming you don't get way off route— is that of knocking loose rock down on your traveling companions. Beyond the pond you'll come to large, deep, wind-blown Upper McCabe Lake. Along its north shore are several cramped campsites among stunted whitebark pines—not much protection from wind or from lightning storms. Better campsites lie ahead, but if you decide to stay here, please don't vandalize the modest supply of whitebark pines, as a few others have done.

Boulder hop the lake's wide outlet, climb due west ¼ mile up to a shallow gap on a glaciated spur ridge, then descend south a short ¼ mile to a shallow pond that has been dammed behind a low lateral moraine. Beyond the moraine's crest you drop steeply southwest through an ever-increasing forest that boasts sizable lodgepole pines by the time you reach the north shore of deep Middle McCabe Lake. Since it lacks campsites, we follow its outlet creek down to shallower Lower McCabe Lake, perhaps the most photogenic of all three. Good campsites are found beneath lodgepole and whitebark

North Peak and more distant Mt. Conness (center), from Steelhead Lake

pines, which grow on the moraine that dams this bouldery lake. However, the added presence of red heather and Labrador tea warns us that mosquitoes will be a pesky problem until late July.

After your stay, return to Secret Lake and then descend to the south shore of Steelhead Lake to begin the last part of the Saddlebag Lake hinterlands. From the shore of Steelhead Lake follow the closed jeep road north alongside deep blue Steelhead Lake to its outlet. The road continues west above the lake's north shore to the Hess Mine, blocked with boulders. Higher up the road, however, is an unblocked mine that goes 50 yards into the mountainside. Just beyond it the road ends and there you have a commanding view of this "20 Lakes Basin," as it is sometimes called. The large, white horizontal dikes on North Peak stand out well, and pointed Mt. Dana pokes its summit just into view on the southeast skyline. On the west side of Steelhead Lake's outlet—Mill Creek—we go a few yards downstream, then scramble over a low knoll as we follow a faint trail that quickly descends to the west shore of tiny Excelsior Lake. At the north end we go through a notch just west of a low metamorphic-rock knoll that is strewn with granitic glacial erratics. A long, narrow pond quickly comes into view which, like many of the lakes, contains trout. Our trail skirts its west shore, then swings east to the north shore of adjacent, many-armed Shamrock Lake, back-dropped by Mt. Conness.

Our ducked route—more cross country than trail—now continues northeast over a low ridge, then goes past two Mill Creek ponds down to the west shore of Lake Helen. On a trail across talus we round this lake's north shore to Mill Creek, where our trail dies out just below the lake's outlet—which flows through a tunnel. We go 30 yards up to the tunnel, walk across it, and begin an east-shore traverse south across blocky talus. Don't follow the tantalizing trail that follows the lake's outlet creek north; it quickly becomes very dangerous.

Adding warm colors to the dark metamorphic blocks are crimson columbines, white Coville's columbines and their pink hybrids. Two creeks empty into the lake's southeast end, and we follow the eastern one up a straight, narrow gully that in early season is a snow chute rather than a wildflower garden. Soon reaching the outlet of Odell Lake, we cross it and parallel the west shore southward while observing the lobes of talus just east of the lake. Like some other metamorphic-rock talus slopes in this glaciated basin, these developed lobes through solifluc-tion—a slow downslope flowage of unstable, water-saturated rock masses.

Near the lake's south end our trail forks, and the older route climbs slightly before dying out while the newer route drops to water's edge before climbing from the south shore up to Lundy Pass. At this gap our path quickly disappears, but by heading south down toward a pond, we soon reach the outlet of Hummingbird Lake and here our trail resumes. This tread parallels the east side of the outlet creek ½ mile down to the closed mining road. Here you can descend to the water-taxi dock and wait for the boat if you made reservations for a return trip, or you can retrace your steps on the west-shore trail. Of course, for variety you can take the closed road back to the lake's south end.

Hike 8   Boundary Lake Loop

Distance: 30.2 miles (48.6 km) round trip, including two visits to Kibbie Lake and one to Boundary Lake

Grade: 6D, moderate 4-day hike

Trailhead: From Groveland drive east 13.6 miles on Highway 120 to paved Cherry Oil Road 1N07, starting just beyond the highway bridge over South Fork Tuolumne River. Follow it 5.3 miles to a junction with paved Hetch Hetchy Road, branch left and go 17.6 miles to Cottonwood Road 1N04. The signed Cherry Dam parking area is just yards down Road 1N04 to the east. While you could start your hike from here, most people would prefer to save 4.3 trail miles and a 1200-foot ascent by starting at a newer trailhead. To reach it, drive across Cherry Valley Dam, then head ½ mile up Road 1N14 to a T, where you branch left, north, onto Road 1N45Y. Drive up this good dirt road, then down 2 miles to a succession of signed trailhead parking areas for, respectively, the Lake Eleanor, Kibbie Creek-Flora Lake, and Kibbie Ridge trails. Three switchbacks and another 2¼ miles lead to an abrupt deadend at 5880 feet. Here you'll find a metal corral and a sign that indicates the way to the Kibbie Ridge trail.

Introduction: The lower, less-trammeled Kibbie Ridge region of Yosemite is the favorite among knowledgeable backpackers for early- and late-season weekenders. Deep forests and some little-fished subalpine lakes are their rewards. For the more adventuresome, the Kibbie Ridge trail is the fastest way in to Huckleberry Lake, in the heart of one of the most lake-blessed areas of the Sierra Nevada. At 4 miles distance, Kibbie Lake, the goal of the first day of backpacking, is close enough for comfortable day hiking.

Description: From the road's end, we start up a spur trail that leads east-northeast uphill to the nearby Kibbie Ridge trail. Just about a minute's walk down this trail is Shingle Spring, with beautiful dogwoods and nearby camps. However, our route goes north, gaining about 400 feet in elevation as it first climbs to a descending ridge and then curves east into cool, forested Deadhorse Gulch. Just past its upper end we reach the main ridge and, in a conifer grove beside a small grass-choked pond, meet the Kibbie Lake trail—our route.

Skirting this pond, we near a ridgetop open space freckled by silver-haired Dana's lupine, streptanthus, buckwheat and golden brodiaea,

used by the Miwok Indians for food. Quickly our trail enters Yosemite National Park and drops on rocky tread surrounded by chaparral, lightly treed with Jeffrey pines, into a small canyon. We amble north through a sodden bottom land, passing the first lodgepole pines of our trip, which here, accompanied by white firs, form a dense canopy. Indian hemp, branched Solomon's seal, bracken fern, Parish's yampah, violets, shooting stars and deadly bleeding heart thrive in the shadows, enticing the traveler to linger in coolness. But mosquitoes, far and away the most numerous inhabitants of damp early-season forests, will no doubt urge you on!

The trail leaves the forest, climbing northeast onto granitic slabs mottled by huckleberry oaks, to a 6500-foot saddle. The rocky route next descends to cross a tributary of Kibbie Creek under a south-facing dome that offers good rock climbing on its peeling skin. After the step-across ford, we closely parallel smooth, green pools on Kibbie Creek, which is lined by western azaleas, willows and tall conifers. We pass a good camp on the right, then, just yards later, before a poorer trail climbs up amid huckleberry oak to the right of a granitic outcrop to continue over slabs to the west shore of Kibbie Lake, our route angles down to a 30-foot rock-hop of Kibbie Creek. Across the ford, among lodgepoles, is a very good camp. Our trail turns upstream, climbing over blasted granitic ledges, the route copiously indicated by rock ducks.

After passing ice-scoured lagoons presaging 106-acre Kibbie Lake, we reach its south shore, where camps are found in a lodgepole-and-Labrador-tea fringe. Kibbie Lake is named for pioneer H. G. Kibbie, who traveled throughout the Yosemite north country and constructed small cabins at Frog Creek in the Lake Eleanor vicinity, at Tiltill Meadow, and on Rancheria Mountain. Kibbie Lake is bounded on the west by gently sloping granite, while the east shore is characterized by steep, broken bluffs and polished bosses. The lake is shallow, with an algae-coated sandy bottom, where distinctively orange-colored California newts may take your bait if a rainbow trout doesn't.

The next day, retrace your steps to the Kibbie Ridge trail, and turn north on its duff tread. After dropping past signed Sand Canyon, you pass, in quick succession, a marshy flat, a creek with a good camp (at the Emigrant Wilderness boundary) and a switchback that leads up onto sparsely forested granitic slabs covered with "gruss," or weathered granite. Note how the massive roots of the Jeffrey pines loosen and fracture the peeling rock, hastening the development of soil.

Soon re-entering red-fir forest, we climb steadily to signed Lookout Point, with vistas west of the deep cleft of Cherry Creek canyon. Next we pass Swede's Camp—a corn-lily-filled meadow—and ascend to a large, warm, shallow pond. After skirting its sandy north shore, we climb under sparse mixed trees, often at a steep incline, to an open-ridgetop sand flat where we find the Yosemite National Park boundary. A steep, vague path straight up the sandy ridge, blessed with fine panoramas southeast to Mount Conness, leads to the muddy, marsh-marigold-dotted vicinity of Sachse Spring, where there is a good camp.

Somewhere along your ridge route to here, you might stop and consider the ecology of the mule deer which make this area their home in the summer and fall months. Biologists studying the mule-deer herd in this area named it the "Jawbone Herd" after its winter range on Jawbone Ridge and Jawbone Creek, some 12 miles below Cherry Lake. The mammologists separated the herd into two distinct groups— Clavey Unit deer, occupying the rich, brushy, volcanic-earthed Clavey River basin, and Cherry Unit deer, ranging throughout the Cherry Creek drainage. Mule deer of the Cherry Unit must

subsist in poorer conditions than Clavey deer, owing to the prevalence of forage-poor glacier-polished-granite terrain and lack of food-rich fire- or logging-caused brushy areas in the Cherry Creek basin. When springtime snows begin to melt, Cherry mule deer begin to drift from their winter range, following budding plants upward, keeping generally 1000 feet below the receding snowline. By contouring along canyon slopes that are first to sprout new vegetation, most of the deer reach the prime summer range by late June. Once on the summer range, the deer fawn and fatten themselves on forbs and shrubbery. Deer populations are most dense between 6000 and 7500 feet, in forest fringes near meadows and brush. In this habitat, moderate summer deer populations are found below Lookout Point and Kibbie Lake, while deer are rare in higher elevations in the open, soil-deficient granite terrain. On Kibbie Ridge, as elsewhere, deer prefer the open, brush-floored Jeffrey-pine community, and are less common in the shadier red-fir community. The most preferred browse species for Jawbone deer in summer months is snow bush, and huckleberry oak is also favored. Aspen and willows are desired foods for pregnant or lactating does, as well as young black-oak leaves and mountain misery.

In fall, prompted by the first snowstorms, deer in the Cherry drainage begin a downward migra-

Granite cliffs provide high-diving opportunities at Kibbie Lake

tion, the highest deer moving first, and finally reach their winter range by early December. There are two main travel corridors followed by Cherry deer heading south to the winter range. One begins west of Emigrant Lake, heads north of Hyatt Lake to West Fork Cherry Creek and then down Hells Mountain, passing along the ridge west of Cherry Lake. The second migration route begins south of Emigrant Lake and bisects the region visited in this hike by traversing to Lord Meadow, then going east of Many Island and Kibbie lakes to lower Kibbie Ridge, between Cherry Lake and Lake Eleanor. Other Park deer have similar migratory routes.

East of Sachse Spring the trail undulates on morainal material in well-spaced western white pine and red fir. A large lakelet almost 0.2 mile off the trail offers good, but sometimes littered campsites along its south shore. Beyond a seasonal creek our route begins to descend onto open granitic slabs, a harbinger of typical Emigrant Basin terrain to come. Mercur Peak, at over 8080 feet elevation, is a prominent dome in the northeast, and it is a good showpiece of the results of the two dominant erosional processes operating in this part of the Sierra—exfoliation ("onion-skin" rock peeling) and glaciation. Coming off the slabs into a small lodgepole forest surrounding a murky tarn, we keep right, following blazes and ducks, then continue over sandy slabs on a bearing straight for Mercur Peak. Its summit, reached by an easy scramble up its south slope, provides a fine vantage point for examining the southern Emigrant Basin. In a lodgepole forest south of the peak, our trail passes a large tarn, quite wet in early season, which marks the turnoff point for Many Island Lake. You can camp here, although the ground is quite wet in early season.

To reach this aptly named lake, proceed due south from this tarn through lodgepoles and around numerous early-season ponds to low-angle slabs bounding the north part of the cirque that contains this glacial lake. By keeping one's feet flat on the sloping rock and pointed downhill, one should have no difficulty descending in a total of ½ mile, to the campsites flanking its warm, shallow waters, which harbor rainbow trout.

East of the Many Island Lake cross-country route, the Kibbie Ridge trail passes through a narrow, joint-controlled gully to unsigned Styx Pass, where it leaves Yosemite National Park. We descend to better views of the North and East Fork Cherry Creek drainages, flanked by soaring domes and smooth aprons. Eight tight,

rocky switchbacks decorated by clumps of sedge and red Sierra onion bring us to a long traverse east to the Boundary Lake trail, 0.6 mile from Styx Pass. This easily missed junction is encountered on a steep, broken slope of exfoliating granite right before one makes two small switchbacks and starts a traverse northwest down to Lord Meadow. On the vague Boundary Lake trail we make a switchbacking ascent east-southeast toward a low point on the nearby crest. The ascent presently becomes less steep as it climbs through a jumble of lodgepoles and rocks to a forested tarn. From it a final rise takes us into Yosemite National Park where we immediately confront a pair of seasonal ponds that in early season connect with Boundary Lake's north shore. Sandy flats with sparse conifers make for good camping on this side of the lake; the east shore is composed of high bluffs. The trail around Boundary Lake's west side winds over granitic outcrops, through patches of huckleberry oak and stands of fir and pine. The undulating path keeps generally away from the irregular rocky shore, but sometimes we near the shore to find a snug camp near clumps of willows or Labrador tea. Visitors can expect good fishing for rainbow trout.

At Boundary Lake's south end, we steer through a notched dome, then descend to a step-across ford of the outlet. On the south bank for a moment, we have telescoped views across the lake's slate-gray entirety to Gillett Mountain before we turn south down a joint gully to the marshy north end of Little Bear Lake. Heading east of this islet-speckled, 25-acre rainbow-trout fishery, we pass a fine packer camp on the north shore, then turn south behind a red-fir-and-lodgepole grove entangled in a marshy maze of bracken and manzanita, where the trail peters out. From the south end of Little Bear Lake you could extend your trip by descending ½ mile southeast to granite-cupped Spotted Fawn Lake, which has adequate camping in its north-shore lodgepole curtain and, like all the lakes of this area, has angling for rainbow trout.

For your third day retrace your steps along Kibbie Ridge and then back to Kibbie Lake. This lake can also be reached by cross-country routes from either Many Island Lake or Little Bear Lake—both routes being shorter than retracing the trail. Since Many Island Lake drains into Kibbie Lake via Kibbie Creek, the cross-country route along that creek is easy to follow until the lake, where you will likely have to surmount cliffs regardless of which way you go around the lake. To end your hike, retrace your steps to the trailhead. However, you can take an alternate way back to it, which is about 4 miles longer.

Rather than leave Kibbie Lake the way you came, you can start at the camps on the lake's south shore and follow a little-used path. This path strikes southwest, ascending gently to moderately through pleasant pocket meadows, then goes out onto pine-dotted slabs that give vistas southwest down Kibbie Creek. Above 6800 feet, the way becomes steeper, and we clamber south up rough switchbacks to the ridgetop—a pleasant, dry, red-fir forest floored with mat manzanita. Here we quickly cross the crests of three glacial moraines before our faint trail strikes a slightly more visible trail. This gradually disappearing trail climbs about 2 miles northeast before completely vanishing about one mile west of Flora Lake. At this junction we leave the morainal crest and follow now-better trail south, the way becoming very steep, bouldery and open. In the southwest, clearcuts spread over the rolling topography above Cherry Lake, the result of California's ever-growing demand for lumber. As our descent becomes more moderate, once again in forest cover, we approach a seasonal creek, entrenched below us, angle southwest, and then descend often-brushy, glaciated terrain for about a mile before we cross the creek. To avoid a smooth whaleback ridge, our trail skirts around its brushy base and then enters another shady forest. We walk southwest down the slopes of a large terminal moraine and then, at its base, angle south and reach a ford of wide, potholed Kibbie Creek—a wet crossing until late summer. Beside the crossing large-leaved umbrella plant, or Indian rhubarb, whose stalks the Miwoks ate raw, grows along or in the creek.

Across the creek you'll discover several small, gravelly campsites.

Beyond the wide ford, conifers gradually give way to gold-cup oaks as we descend gradually southwest, but they reappear as the dominant plant form after a mile, where our bouldery trail veers south to begin a saddle-crest traverse of Kibbie Ridge, along the border of Yosemite National Park. At the saddle's lowest point, we reach a junction with the prominent Lake Eleanor trail, marked by metal signs.

Those who want to spend one more night in the back country can drop east to the west shore of large Lake Eleanor, visible through the pine-and-black-oak cover atop Kibbie Ridge. From here, a good trail leads moderately down for ¼ mile to a signed trail junction, from where the left fork drops east to a shaded peninsula on 27,000-acre-foot Lake Eleanor. This reservoir was created by the City of San Francisco in 1918 to raise, by 35 feet, an existing lake. Travelers may desire to follow the right-hand trail south to the 60-foot-high, 20-caisson concrete dam. At its east end lies the Lake Eleanor NPS Station and a road that follows a part of the south shore of Lake Eleanor, then climbs south and east to Miguel Meadow, where the trail to Laurel Lake begins (see **Hike 9**).

When you want to return to your trailhead from the Lake Eleanor environs, go to the ridgetop junction above the lake and then start northwest down the Lake Eleanor trail to soon strike the trailhead's road. This you could follow north about 3¼ miles back up to the trailhead. However, if you go but 0.1 mile north on it, you'll intersect a lower part of the Kibbie Ridge trail, which you can take 1¾ miles up to the trailhead.

Hike 9   Laurel Lake Loop

Distance: 15.5 miles (25.0 km) by shortest (round trip) route

Grade: 4D, moderate 2-day hike

Trailhead: Just 1.1 miles outside the Park's Big Oak Flat entrance station, leave Highway 120 and drive north 7.4 miles on Evergreen Road to its junction with the Hetch Hetchy Road. Turn right and go 9.1 miles to the large parking area at O'Shaughnessy Dam. **B3.**

Introduction: Large, forest-nestled Laurel Lake sits somewhat off the beaten path to Jack Main Canyon. Its 6485-foot elevation, lowest of any

large natural lake in Yosemite, places it in the hospitable fir belt, providing warm swimming and secluded camping. It's a great early- or late-season overnighter.

Description: This hike is best started early in the morning, before the sun heats the ½-mile-high south-facing slopes ahead. Walk down to chain-gated Lake Eleanor Road, atop O'Shaughnessy Dam (3814 feet) at Hetch Hetchy Reservoir. Halfway across this curving monolith, named for the Hetch Hetchy Project's chief engineer, we find a water fountain where the

City of San Francisco graciously "shares" some of its precious drinking water, and we fill our canteens in anticipation of an arid ascent. Bronze plaques posted here commemorate the back-room politicos who made possible this blasphemous inroad on a national park, back in 1914, along with similar structures on Lake Eleanor and Cherry Lake. Visitors today can look, but not touch (to protect San Francisco's hygiene, one must assume), so we can only gaze east over the choppy, 8-mile-long reservoir. The soaring canyon walls that remain standing above the inundation are good reminders of what Hetch Hetchy Valley once was—a less-spectacular sibling of Yosemite Valley. On the south wall, the prow of Kolana Rock soars 2000 feet up from the water, while to the north, tiered Hetch Hetchy Dome rises about 400 feet higher. In a shaded cleft on the dome's west flank, two-stepped Wapama Falls plunges an aggregate 1400 feet. In early summer its gossamer companion, Tueeulala Falls, glides down steep slabs farther west.

Across the 600-foot-long dam, we enter a 500-foot-tunnel blasted through solid granite when the original dam was raised 85 feet in 1938. Emerging from this bat haven, the pot-holed, discontinuously paved road climbs steadily above the rocky west shore of Hetch Hetchy Reservoir in a pleasant grove of Douglas-fir, Digger pine, big-leaf maple, and bay trees. Sour, blue-blushed California grape, shiny poison oak, and palmlike giant chain ferns grow in the trees' shadows. Each one of these plants was utilized by the Miwok Indians that visited in Hetch Hetchy. Soon we reach the signed junction with the Rancheria Falls trail (see **Hike 10**), but keep to the road and attack the steep north-canyon wall. Eight cobble-paved switchbacks take our route inexorably north to better views up the reservoir of LeConte Point and the Grand Canyon of the Tuolumne River.

Our switchbacking road finally swings north to a trail junction on a small flat. The road curves west, but we continue north, climbing briefly to a small meadow, by which we spy this hike's first sugar pines, with their long, pendulous cones. Beyond the meadow we cross a usually dry gully whose shady confines harbor bracken ferns and thimbleberries. Then our generally viewless trail climbs in earnest, ascending 1000 feet of forest slope—steep at times—to the low crest of a moraine that dams a linear, knee-deep pond. After rounding this seasonal pond's east end, we exit over a low morainal crest, then climb easily north, being thoroughly shaded by a dense white-fir canopy in our half-mile hike up to a trail junction. Laurel Lake, though only ¾ mile northwest of us, is at least 2½ *trail* miles away by either trail we can take, and one wonders why a trail was not built directly to it. On our return from Laurel Lake, we may choose to hike up the narrow, little-used trail that descends southwest from this junction. If your throat is really parched, you can descend ¼ mile on it to ever-flowing Frog Creek.

From the junction we follow the shady trail northeast, dip to cross a bracken-bordered creeklet, then soon hike alongside a linear meadow that in season is profuse with arrowhead butterweed and Bigelow's sneezeweed, two kinds of sunflowers. The meadow pinches off at a low pass, beyond which we quickly find ourselves in the southwest corner of a triangular meadow. Staying within the shady cover of white firs and lodgepole pines, we parallel the meadow's edge past snow-survey equipment, over to its east corner, called Beehive, where there is a signed trail junction. Here the Laurel Lake trail veers northwest, while the Jack Main Canyon trail starts east (see **Hikes 11 and 12**). Beehive was the site of an 1880s cattlemen's camp, and a log cabin once stood north of the trail junction, where a popular camp is now

Evening comes to Laurel Lake

found. A small spring lies 20 yards west of the junction, protected by a wooden box.

By walking north only a minute on the Laurel Lake trail, we reach another trail junction. Here a signed path that loops around Laurel Lake's north shore branches north, while a shorter trail to Laurel Lake's outlet strikes west. Following this latter route, we drop easily down into a white-fir-shaded gully and then cross 40-foot-wide Frog Creek via large cobbles. On its west bank, we contour for a bit, then pantingly ascend to a heavily forested ridge before gently dropping to good camps at Laurel Lake's outlet. Another fraction of a mile brings us to a signed junction with the north-shore loop trail, branching northwest to the best campsites. At shallow 60-acre Laurel Lake, western azalea grows thickly just back of the grassy lakeshore, a fragrant accompaniment to huckleberry and thimbleberry. Fishing is fair for largish rainbow trout.

By continuing north around Laurel Lake, one will encounter a large packer campsite on the northwest shore. There the trail turns east through a bracken-overgrown deadfall, negotiates an easy ridge, and drops to a camp beside Frog Creek, here running through cobbles and tall creek dogwood shrubs. Across that stream, our way turns southeast, ascending easily to a junction with the southern Laurel Lake trail, just north of Beehive.

Leaving Laurel Lake near its outlet, we pick up the Frog Creek trail, heading southwest, and wind under a dense canopy of white fir. Within ½ mile this walk becomes a gradually steepening descent, down an open nose of fire-damaged conifers. A trail junction is reached midway down the nose, where we must make a choice of return routes. The first contours 1¼ miles east to Frog Creek, then another ¼ mile up to the trail we came in on, leaving us with 5.3 miles of backtracking to Hetch Hetchy. The second—straight ahead—descends to Miguel Meadow.

Should we choose the longer route via Miguel Meadow, we head west from the trail junction and drop steeply on sandy tread, with views west over Lake Eleanor and down on conifer-shaded Frog Creek. Beyond an emergency campsite, we easily hop cobbles to the south bank and climb a short switchback. Now a traverse leads southwest through dry forest to a ridge saddle clothed in manzanita. The disused Beehive trail once dropped west from here to the shores of Lake Eleanor. We turn south from this saddle, gently descending into the basin of Miguel Creek, where we walk under a pleasant canopy of Jeffrey pines and black oaks where flickers and white-headed woodpeckers dwell. Below 5400 feet our path comes out into the open on a bouldery, hot hillside. Lower down, we pass north of unseen Gravel Pit Lake, then traverse southwest to an intersection of the dirt Lake Eleanor Road.

From this junction Miguel Meadow, with a NPS ranger and pleasant camping under large black oaks, is just ⅓ mile southwest along the road. However, to return to Hetch Hetchy, turn southeast on Lake Eleanor Road, cross nearby Miguel Creek, wind east for 3.2 miles up a shallow, open-floored canyon, top a mile-high saddle, drop a few hundred yards to the Laurel Lake trail, which we climbed the first morning, and finally descend the switchbacking road back to O'Shaughnessy Dam.

Hike 10   Rancheria Falls

Distance: 12.7 miles (20.4 km) round trip

Grade: 3D, moderate day-hike

Trailhead: Same as the Hike 9 trailhead. **B3.**

Introduction: A stately grove of Jeffrey pines and incense-cedars harboring a spacious camping area near 25-foot-high Rancheria Falls marks the terminus of this easy hike, but the real rewards are inspirational vistas of the awesome cliffs and early-summer waterfalls which line our precipitous path along the north wall of unique Hetch Hetchy Reservoir.

Description: Follow the Lake Eleanor Road as described in **Hike 9** across O'Shaughnessy

Dam, through a tunnel, and along the west shore of Hetch Hetchy Reservoir to the signed Rancheria Falls trail, at the road's first switchback. From here we descend gently first south and then east across an exfoliating granitic nose, then switchback once down to a broad, sloping ledge, sparingly shaded by Digger pines and mountain mahogany. Odd-appearing bird's beak and lavender Sierra lessingia grow here, amid boulders splotched with mosslike selaginella, actually a relative of ferns. We follow this shelf ½ mile to an unnamed stream that cascades hundreds of feet down some brushy slabs as Tueeulala Falls—but only in the spring and early summer. Beyond its step-across ford, we wind down along the north shore of Hetch Hetchy Reservoir to a bridge over a steep ravine, where our views east to the lake's head expand impressively. On the north wall stands multifaceted Hetch Hetchy Dome, guarding thundering, split-level Wapama Falls. Opposite this monolith towers the obdurate, warshiplike prow of Kolana Rock, which forces a constriction in the 8-mile-long reservoir's tadpole shape.

A few minutes of easy traverse east from here end at a steep, dynamited descent through a field of huge talus blocks under a tremendous unnamed precipice. Soon, if we're passing this way in early summer, flecks of spray dampen our cobbly path, as we come to the first of four bridges under two-stepped Wapama Falls. During some high-runoff years, even these high, sturdy steel bridges are inundated by tumultuous Falls Creek.

East of Wapama Falls, our rocky path leads up around the base of a steep bulge of glacier-polished and striated granite under a fly-infested canopy of gold-cup oak and California laurel, or bay tree. Four switchbacks eventually raise our route 500 feet to a 100-foot-wide ledge, formed along a master joint, that slopes across the mind-boggling face of Hetch Hetchy Dome. Looking south across the lake to Kolana Rock, we see that an extension of the same joint plane has formed a similar terrace, with the same shady collection of Digger pines, scrub and gold-cup oaks, laurel, poison oak and wild-grape vines.

Huge flakes of shattered granite also dot this bench, spalled from the walls above. After the terrace we're on tapers off, our frequently dynamited trail undulates along a steep hillside in a hot, open chaparral of yerba santa and mountain mahogany, making switchbacks on occasion to circumvent some cliffy spots.

Eventually our path descends to the oak-and-pine-shaded gorge cut by Tiltill Creek and crosses two steel bridges, the second over the named stream's 60-foot-deep, inaccessible cleft. Beyond the second span, our route climbs the canyon's east slope via a set of tight switchbacks to emerge 250 feet higher on a gentle hillside of sunny, gray-lichened slabs, Digger pines, and Mariposa manzanita. Soon our way levels off, and we spy Rancheria Creek as it slides invitingly over a broad rock trough, superb for skinny-dipping. Just a minute later we pass the first of dozens of good campsites south of the trail in spreading black oaks, dense incense-cedars and tall Jeffrey pines along the cobbly north bank of wide Rancheria Creek. The duff-floored forest stretches to within 100 yards of 25-foot-high Rancheria Falls, which shoot off a ledge of resistant dark intrusive rock. Fishing below the falls might yield pan-sized rainbow trout. Be warned that these popular camps are often shared with marauding black bears, and bearbag your provisions accordingly. After side hikes to Tiltill Valley (**Hike 11**) or to panoramic LeConte Point (**Hike 13**), retrace your steps to O'Shaughnessy Dam.

Hike 11   Lake Vernon and Tiltill Valley Loop

Distance: 29.8 miles (47.9 km) loop trip

Grade: 5E, easy 4-day hike

Trailhead: Same as the Hike 9 trailhead. **B3.**

Introduction: This relatively low-country loop, a good early-summer conditioner, winds through gently rolling forest stands to two large lakes—Laurel Lake and Lake Vernon—both good rainbow-trout fisheries, then visits meadowed Tiltill Valley, an interesting pocket of spring wildflowers and grasses. For the finale, our return route undulates among the cliffs and waterfalls surrounding the magnificent Hetch Hetchy gorge.

Description: Follow **Hike 9** to the Beehive junction, then west 1.3 miles to Laurel Lake, and camp there. This lake is too close to your route to bypass. Next day, backtrack to Beehive

and take the eastbound trail that winds up through a forest of white firs and lodgepole pines to a moraine-crest junction with the Jack Main Canyon trail, just below the higher crest of Moraine Ridge. From the junction we descend to an open, granite bench. Now on bedrock, we follow a well-ducked trail past excellent examples of glacier-smoothed rock—glacial polish—and glacier-transported boulders—glacial erratics. Scattered Jeffrey pines lend occasional shade along our northeast traverse, their roots seeking out cracks in the granite in which they might take hold and help form a soil. On drier, more inhospitable sites grow rugged western junipers, which manage to survive where the Jeffreys don't because their scalelike leaves lose less water to the atmosphere than do the Jeffrey's long needles.

Along this section we can look across the far wall of Falls Creek canyon until a nearby minor outlier, ½ mile southwest of Lake Vernon, obstructs our view. Just after this happens, we angle southeast and follow a winding, ducked route up toward the point, but cross a low ridge just north of it. Now below us lies large but shallow Lake Vernon, flooding part of a broad, flat-floored canyon. During colder times, glaciers occupied this canyon and buried it under as much as 1600 feet of glacier ice. When the last glacier retreated from the canyon about 14,000 years ago, it left minor depressions in the bedrock floor, which quickly filled to become Lake Vernon and its satellite lakes.

From this view-packed ridge we descend generally northeast—the trend of this area's master joints—and in ⅓ mile reach a junction with the Lake Vernon trail. Leaving a small flat with a few nearby aspens, this trail shoots northeast, at first staying close to the base of a similar-trending wall. After ¼ mile of walking, you'll be close to the shore of the unseen lake, and you can head southeast to it. A popular horsemen's campsite lies by the lodgepole-lined lakeshore, just out of sight. More campsites will be found as you approach Lake Vernon's north corner, a few minutes distant. Just beyond that corner, the trail is best described as cross-country, for it quickly fades into the bedrock landscape.

After your pleasant stay at shallow, fairly warm Lake Vernon, backtrack to the main trail, head southeast to a quick bridging of Falls Creek, then round a bedrock slope back to the lake's southwest corner. More campsites will be found along the lake's south shore. Our next objective, a descent to Tiltill Valley, *first* involves a thousand-foot climb, accomplished with the aid of about three dozen short switchbacks. The view improves as we climb higher, and the spreading panorama gives us good excuses to take plenty of rests. The views disappear when we enter a tiny hanging valley high above Lake Vernon. Now under a cover of firs, we make a short climb up past several moraines until we top the last of them.

With easy hiking ahead, we first dip into a gully, then contour south, passing above two small meadows before crossing another moraine and gently descending to the lower end of a long meadow. The grove of aspens at its upper end may hide a few deer, for aspen leaves are part of their summer diet. Leaving the meadow, we arc southwest up to the crest of a nearby moraine, which from our vantage point is only a low ridge, though it stands a full 4,000 feet above the inundated floor of the Grand Canyon of the Tuolumne River. About 75,000 years ago, when the Tahoe glaciation was at its maximum, this canyon was completely buried by a tremendously large glacier—a glacier so thick that it overflowed the canyon in several places. Smith Peak, the high point of the canyon wall south of us, stood only 800 feet above the glacier back then, and during a considerably older glaciation it stood only 150 feet above the ice.

The moraine we stand on is littered with red-fir snags, their destruction probably due to violent winds along this exposed ridge (see wind-downed white firs near Dewey Point, along **Hike 71**). After the forest canopy was downed, the soil was once again exposed to sunlight, and thorny snow bushes now crowd the moraine, making it "deer heaven." Indeed, this area is one of the best browsing areas for deer in the entire Park. In addition to snow bush—a favorite food—deer have nearby supplies of

Near Lake Vernon, glacier-transported boulders rest on barren, glacier-polished rock

aspen, huckleberry oak, scrubby black oak, gooseberry and willow. Our descent along the brushy hillside provides grand views, but the flanking shrubs at times present thorny problems to hikers in shorts. After an initial brief descent, our trail contours for about a mile, then steepens and on well-built switchbacks descends southeast toward distant Tiltill Valley.

Our descent ends where thirst-quenching Tiltill Creek spills out onto flat-floored Tiltill Valley. On its west bank is a small campsite under incense-cedars and pines, which is enjoyable once the mosquitos abate, usually after mid-July. A cluster of Miwok Indian bedrock mortars lies nearby, under some large black oaks. Our trail leaves the creek and hugs the base of the valley's towering north wall. At times the trail seems too close to it, for it wanders among large blocks of rockfall-deposited talus; however, a trail built in the meadow would often be waterlogged. We soon pass an unmarked junction with the Tiltill Canyon trail, and go south across the seasonally boggy meadow, our trail being protected by levees and ditches. The thigh-high bunchgrasses forming the meadow teem with life—grasshoppers and Brewer's and red-winged blackbirds are constantly active by daylight hours, while mule deer and black bears forage timidly in the morning and evening. The meadow's dry hummocks and sodden drainage channels themselves offer an ever-changing display of a unique Transition Zone meadow flora, including 8-foot high mountain helenium, a close relative of sneezeweed, giant umbrella-topped cow-parsnip, elephant's heads, yellow evening primrose, square-stemmed horse mint and fireweed, to name but a few of the showier blooms. Presently we strike an old signed trail junction at the meadow's center. From it a disused trail heads toward the valley's east end, but fades away just yards from the Tiltill Canyon trail.

From this junction we continue south to the base of some steep bluffs that bound Tiltill Valley on the south and enter a lush stand of aspens, alders and willows surrounding a small spring. Both the treelike mountain dogwood and the shrubbier, red-barked creek dogwood thrive here, shading lady-fern, bracken, thimbleberry, raspberry and currant. A few Douglas-firs hug the hillside's shade here, sharing the coolness with mountain-maple shrubs. Upon reaching the canyon wall, our path immediately begins to climb, taking some well-engineered switchbacks southwest to a large joint-controlled rift. This we follow gently up, southwest, past a small, linear pond decked with yellow pond lilies. Overhead, staircased black cliffs fall from Peak 6595, overlooking our progress through a thick forest of white fir and incense-cedar. Fragrant western azalea is the dominant understory shrub, joined in sunnier spots by uncommon white-bugled Washington's lily. Straight as an arrow our trail zooms up through a narrow saddle and then gently down into another straight-sided canyon, this one also trending southwest.

After ½ mile we angle west out of this canyon onto open slabs, where we have views south over brushy LeConte Point to somber-cliffed Smith Peak. Now the route begins to descend in earnest, high above the forested coolness below. The trail twists itself into numerous sandy, moderate switchbacks, soon dropping to the 5300-foot level, where the hillside is too hot for Transition Zone species, and Digger pines and gold-cup oaks take over, offering meager shade. Here, too, we perceive some blue slivers of Hetch Hetchy Reservoir, bent around sentinel Kolana Rock to the west. Six hundred feet more of occasionally furnace-hot switchbacking descent follow, depositing us, finally, at a signed junction with the Rancheria Mountain trail on a manzanita-cloaked sandy hillside. Here we turn right, down some easy switchbacks, and soon bend south to find the cool haven of a large, thick conifer grove along the north bank of Rancheria Creek. Good camps are found here, described at the end of **Hike 10**.

Later, follow the trail along the north side of Hetch Hetchy Reservoir, the reverse of **Hike 10**, back to O'Shaughnessy Dam.

Hike 12   Jack Main Canyon Loop

Distance: 40.9 miles (65.8 km) loop trip

Grade: 6F, moderate 4-day hike

Trailhead: Same as the Hike 9 trailhead. **B3.**

Introduction: Following a route used around the turn of the century by both illegal sheep-

herders and their US Army pursuers, the Jack Main Canyon trail (named for one of the early sheepmen) visits a succession of small subalpine meadows along the course of delightful, cascading Falls Creek. Wilma Lake, the gem of Jack Main Canyon, marks our northernmost point in that glacier-scoured trough, and offers pastoral camping with the opportunity to visit over 20 fishing and swimming lakes or climb to more than a dozen viewful mountaintops, each within an easy day's hiking!

Description: Follow **Hike 9** from Hetch Hetchy Reservoir up to Beehive, then west 1.3 miles to Laurel Lake, and camp there the first night. The next morning, retrace your steps to Beehive and pick up the Jack Main Canyon trail, which ascends gently northeast through a forested glade. Soon we bend eastward on a more moderate forested ascent, which later becomes rocky and dusty on more open slopes, to reach a morainal crest, where we pass the Lake Vernon trail (see **Hike 11**).

Here our Jack Main Canyon trail veers north to begin a long, sandy, dry ascent of Moraine Ridge. This bedrock ridge is mantled with Tahoe- and Tioga-age moraines of broad, 500-foot-deep Frog Creek glaciers on the north and 1200-foot-deep Falls Creek glaciers south of the ridge. Knowing this, we can easily predict the nature of our surroundings along this 3-mile, gentle-to-moderate ascent: our trail is mostly in deep, glacial sand, paralleled by narrow ridges topped with large, rounded boulders. A sparse ground cover of drought-tolerant species includes silver-hairy Brewer's lupine, pussy paws, snow bush, squirrel-tail barley and delicate whisker-brush. Overhead, sun-loving Jeffrey pines dominate the conifers until supplanted above 7500 feet by wind-damaged red firs. Higher still, we can look down into Falls Creek's canyon to the lily-pad lakes above shallow Lake Vernon, and glimpse the outlet of rockbound Branigan Lake. When on Moraine Ridge we finally reach the trail's sandy high point—about 8110 feet— panoramas explode to the north and east, stretching from the broken, water-streaked summits of Richardson, Mahan and Andrews peaks in the foreground to distant Saurian Crest, Piute Mountain, Sawtooth Ridge and Mount Conness.

Leaving this viewful height, our path begins a descent of the "Golden Stairs" northeast toward Falls Creek. These moderate switchbacks lead through an open conifer stand to a dogleg in a seasonal stream, where a pleasant campsite has views to the east. Beyond this flat, our staircase is more demanding—very steep, tight switchbacks of riprapped and dynamited granite plunge down along a joint-controlled ravine amid a sun-drenched tangle of western chokecherry, mountain maple and Indian hemp. After hopping the small creek that drains this gorge, we come

alongside pooling Falls Creek and begin our ascent of Jack Main Canyon.

Our first mile of walking along Falls Creek sets the tone for the rest of our journey: the trail undulates moderately, alternately visiting benches of sunny, glaciated granite dotted with huckleberry-oak thickets and precariously rooted western junipers, and pocket stands of lodgepoles and stately red firs, their canopy shading twinberry, mountain ash and red elderberry. We pass above a triad of sand-banked pools, then descend slightly to a horseshoe bend in Falls Creek that has a grove of red firs with good camping nearby. East of this bend our still-undulating trail winds among open slabs and up to a piney bench. Here one may choose to leave the trail and strike south across Falls Creek and up through a gap west of striated Andrews Peak to Andrews and Branigan lakes. Our path turns north, dropping to the largest and most beautiful of a number of unnamed lakelets in lower Jack Main Canyon. Shaped somewhat like a horseshoe, this shallow lakelet reflects the broken south face of Mahan Peak while supporting a shoreline garden of Parish's yampah and Bigelow's sneezeweed. Our route skirts its north shore, then veers south around another pond following "T" blazes back to the north bank of slow-moving, tepid Falls Creek. Here we turn east, on a 30-foot-wide isthmus between the stream and an aspen-bordered pond that lies just north of the trail, fed only by ground water.

From the head of this pond, we climb north to a gap, then drop easily to a large meadow known as Paradise Valley. Here our path keeps near the screen of infringing lodgepole pines, leaps the outlet stream of Mahan Lake, and comes to a large complex of streamside campsites surrounding a signed junction with a cut-off east to Tilden Canyon. This hot, unworthy route is recommended only for those headed for the Branigan Lakes. To take it, wade across sandy Falls Creek just below a wide pool and find the vague trail as it swings east around the south side of a grassy mosquito pond. The little-used route then climbs tortuously southeast through pockets of mat manzanita and open lodgepole pines to a viewful knoll. Next, this route drops east, then turns southwest up a narrow rock corridor. Near the head of this herbaceously floored ravine, where further progress seems blocked by lady-fern and rare baneberry near a talus slide, the path turns abruptly and steeply up to the east. Then the trail bends back to the northeast and climbs easily to a tarn-dotted flat. From here you switchback steeply east over gneissicbanded intrusive rocks into a forested canyon. Lodgepoles and hemlocks shade the way as the drainage heads northeast, then south, to 8575 feet, where the route tops out in a narrow gap. From this pass you drop southeast to find the signed Tilden Canyon trail.

To finish our hike up Jack Main Canyon to Wilmer Lake, we slog through sand beyond the Tilden Canyon cutoff, quickly reaching the lodgepole-shaded shores of a glacial lake that is picturesquely backdropped by a lichen-covered cliff. Beyond it, we're led back throuqh a gap to Falls Creek, now a wide lagoon, and we walk north near its meanders, which are hidden by tall willows. Above us, the ancient Falls Creek glacier sculptured the resistant rock of Peak 8280 into some fantastic fins which today provide excellent multipitch rock climbs. Later, Sybol Lake, now reduced to a seasonal lily pond by a fast-encroaching meadow, is passed with only a glimpse of it through a screen of lodgepoles and aspens.

North of Sybol Lake, Falls Creek, true to its name, tumbles through a narrow gorge of mafic rock and slides over some smooth slabs that are ideal for bathers, and our path takes some rocky, dynamited switchbacks up along it. Above the gorge our streamside way is more gentle as it winds northeast over slabs dotted with erratic boulders, mat manzanita, and hummocks bearing dense stands of lodgepoles. Note that many of the lodgepoles hereabouts have prominent "witches brooms"—bizarrely twisted branches of too-dense needles—that are caused by a virus which disrupts their growth pattern. Presently we spy turf-bounded Wilma Lake lying across the stream, in a pleasant mixed-conifer forest. Now our route ascends a final shoulder and drops to a large, dry flat from where the signed

Pacific Crest Trail leads up Jack Main Canyon (see **Hike 42**). On it we turn east, to wade broad Falls Creek near some heavily used camps.

Striking southeast, we soon reach Wilma Lake, which has rainbow trout. In this vicinity you may see a cabin that is occasionally occupied by a seasonal ranger. An earlier cabin had been destroyed in an avalanche. The PCT skirts close along the lake's south shore, past lodgepoles and hemlocks. We then wind moderately up a canyon past two pleasant tarns to a junction with the Tilden Lake trail, which ascends north to its namesake.

At this junction we turn south down the PCT for 110 yards to the Tilden Canyon trail, and take it southwest down along Tilden Canyon Creek under a mosquitoey lodgepole canopy. This shady walk soon reaches a pear-shaped, grassy tarn rimmed with Labrador tea and bilberry. From its west end, we bend south, following blazes and ducks in open lodgepole stands interspersed with erratics and glaciated slabs. In about a mile we again come close to Tilden Canyon Creek—here a wide lagoon cut deep through meadow turf—where one might disturb a family of mallard ducks. Pressing on, we negotiate a small rise, then ascend once more, this time via steep, eroded, rocky switchbacks, past a junction with the cut-off route to Paradise Valley. The grind abates minutes later, when we level off just below the summit of Peak 8778. The summit of this small roche moutonnée is well worth the minute it takes to reach it, for its presents sweeping panoramas of northern Yosemite. We can look all the way up Jack Main canyon to Bond Pass; then, swinging our gaze east, we spot Tower Peak, Matterhorn Peak, Piute Mountain, and the Cathedral Range from Fairview Dome to Mt. Lyell.

Wilma Lake, from the Pacific Crest Trail

Resuming our trek, we walk south along a low, broad ridge, then drop on a switchback to an easy traverse that is shaded by red firs, mountain hemlocks and western white pines. Uncommon bleeding-heart and common pine-woods lousewort grow in the shade here. Presently we ascend to a broad, forested saddle, then descend to a diminishing lakelet, our last permanent water source for almost 8 miles. Below it, we walk for a while beside the meadowed outlet creek, then veer away on a rocky descent around a steep bluff before resuming a creekside route under moderate forest cover. We walk easily for a mile down through an understory of yarrow, meadow rue, aster, senecio and corn lily to small Tiltill Meadow, which has the ruins of a cabin built by H. G. Kibbie.

South of Tiltill Meadow, we continue in the same easy manner for a ½ mile, then turn southwest down a dry morainal slope to a red-fir grove beside a small meadow drained by a step-across branch of Rancheria Creek. Now begins a 2300-foot descent to Tiltill Valley. Chaparral areas allow views south and east over the bluffs of Smith Peak and Rancheria Mountain. Moderate switchbacks ease our descent to 7300 feet, and then we drop more gently southwest down a sandy canyon and look west to a brush-covered Mount Gibson. Next we work south along a bouldery, brushy bench, and then begin the final 1300-foot plunge. At first, we stay on the north side of a small ridge, descending steeply on sand in the relative shade of high huckleberry-oak

brush and scattered Jeffrey pines. But below 6600 feet we swing onto the ridge's south face, which allows our first views of lush Tiltill Valley and, beyond it, Hetch Hetchy Reservoir, but also subjects us to the full heat of the midday sun. Woe betide anyone climbing *up* this slope! Eventually, at 6330 feet, we reach a gap on the ridge, which affords some shade and a good spot to study the effects that the mammoth Rancheria Creek and Tuolumne River glaciers had on the country below us. At this elevation, during the Ice Age's height, we would have been buried under about 1200 feet of glacier ice, since the Tiltill Creek glacier had a trimline near 7500 feet on Mount Gibson and the Rancheria Creek glacier rose to the level of the last small meadow that we passed at 7900 feet, at the start of this steep descent! At Hetch Hetchy, the Tuolumne glacier filled the 2-mile-wide canyon to well over the 7500-foot elevation.

Below this instructional rest stop, more steep, rocky, exposed switchbacks ensue, this time leading east through gold-cup-oak scrub. Eventually the trail bends south and lowers us to the long-awaited shade of a grove of incense-cedars, black oaks and Jeffrey pines at the eastern corner of Tiltill Valley. We turn west onto the flats and emerge into a hummocky, open grassland, then follow its edge to join the Lake Vernon trail, which turns south across the meadow. To continue your journey, follow **Hike 11** to Rancheria Falls, then the reverse of **Hike 10** out to O'Shaughnessy Dam.

Hike 13   Rancheria Mountain and Bear Valley Loop

Distance: 52.4 miles (84.3 km) semiloop trip

Grade: 7G, strenuous 5-day hike

Trailhead: Same as the Hike 9 trailhead. **B3.**

Introduction: The broad, conifer-robed massif of Rancheria Mountain affords a snow-free early-summer route into the Yosemite north country. Hikers who don't demand a spectacular, high-level trail will find that the floral gardens and the serene forests on this north rim of the Grand Canyon of the Tuolumne, coupled with secluded hemlock-bower camping beside Bear Valley Lake, more than compensate for the prolonged climb in.

Description: Follow **Hike 10** from Hetch Hetchy Reservoir to Rancheria Falls, about 6 miles, and camp there the first night. The next morning, ascend easily past the Tiltill Valley

trail (see **Hike 11**) to a 40-foot-long bridge over Rancheria Creek, which bumps and slides frothily below us through a series of well-worn potholes and slabs, inviting divers and sunbathers. Tank up on water here—your next source will be a hot 3000 feet higher, on the west slope of Rancheria Mountain. Marching south from the streamside, we contour under shadeless, bedraggled Digger pines into a broad ravine draining the north slope of brushy LeConte Point.

Now we start the first, 1400-foot leg of our 4000-foot climb over Rancheria Mountain. The trail switchbacks methodically up on a moderate ascent under some forest cover. As we progress higher, vistas west over the reservoir and Kolana Rock improve. We finally top a sandy nose at 6225 feet, east of a saddle on LeConte Point, then lose a bit of elevation while traversing east along a sandy chaparral hillside. In a side canyon at the end of this traverse, we encounter the first white firs of our journey. The ascent resumes, on dusty switchbacks up past some fire-cleared forest openings that now support a thriving population of deer, flickers and chickarees. At 6800 feet we swing onto a south-facing chaparral slope and can look south across the Grand Canyon of the Tuolumne River to the rolling upland region around the Tioga Pass Road. From a bench our path ascends north-east on a comfortable gradient and returns to forest cover. The way resolves to switchbacks after ½ mile, so we tediously zigzag up on the dusty, dry forest litter to our first honest respite, at 7700 feet. Here, near an adequate camp, an unnamed tributary of the Tuolumne River cuts a sandy swath throuqh a dry flat and offers the first almost-permanent water source since Rancheria Creek.

After quenching our thirst and topping off our canteens, we continue up the duff-treaded path, now under sun-dappled lodgepoles and red firs, to another creek draining the west flank of Rancheria Mountain. In a pleasant glade on its north bank we find a small, ruined log cabin, constructed, like the one in Tiltill Meadow, by pioneer fish-propagator H. G. Kibbie. Beyond this relict we wander for a moment up along the stream, then angle northeast away from it, ascending up over a morainal divide back to the first creek that we met. A fallen conifer may facilitate your crossing to the north bank, where one may linger for some time to observe the shoulder-to-shoulder ranks of wildflowers spread under the scattered timber here. Standing almost head-high are stalks of blue-bonnet larkspur, slender lupine, umbrella-leaved cow parsnip, red elderberry and four-petalled green gentian. Reaching between our knees and waists are lacy meadow rue, purple asters, white yarrow, yellow senecio, aromatic pennyroyal, and leather-leaved mule ears. Under all there at times can be a mat of Jacob's ladder, rarely seen in such large numbers.

From this flower garden, our path turns northeast up the shallow canyon and soon leaves lush surroundings behind as it climbs easily along a dry volcanic hillside. This volcanic-mud-flow material and the overlying darker cap layer of harder andesite (it forms the summits of Peaks 8772 and 8995) are one of the most southern remnants of the Mehrten Formation, an assemblage of lava and pyroclastic flows that inundated the entire northern Sierra area during

and just before the present-day Sierra's upheaval. After a mile our way becomes a ridgetop amble, eventually bringing us to our high point (8650 feet) on Rancheria Mountain. To reach the 8015-foot saddle north of us, our path makes a moderate northward descent in deep duff. Five switchbacks spare our knees on the steep hillside, then the trees disperse momentarily, and we look northeast to the Sawtooth Ridge and closer Volunteer Peak. A short distance later, we reach a signed junction with the Pleasant Valley trail (see **Hike 14**).

The Bear Valley trail drops north across the timbered saddle, then climbs up a steep, shaded pitch to a small, grassy pond. This knee-deep lakelet does have a fair campsite just behind the fringe of Labrador tea, but the water is tepid and bears are frequent nuisances. We climb gently north from this pond along a sandy ridge to the willowy east bank of an unnamed creek. In ½ mile, a big leap takes us across this stream so that we can climb northwest through a meadow of dry wheat-grass and squirrel-tail barley to top a lateral moraine and find yet another unnamed creek. After jumping to its west bank we ascend gently north on a hard gruss tread on a sparsely timbered hillside. Soon our little-traveled trail fades to a faint depression in the meadow turf. Small cairns and ducks guide us, however, right on course to a windy saddle, flanked by huddled whitebark pines, lying just under 9500 feet. Beyond, 700 feet below us, is pastoral Bear Valley, overshadowed by knife-edged Bear Valley peak. Farther north, the Yosemite north country rears its shining ivory summits and red-volcanic Relief Peak, near Sonora Pass, touches the horizon.

Raucous Clark's nutcrackers supervise our knee-jarring plummet north down the cirque wall of Bear Valley. At first our path is contorted into short, tight, rocky switchbacks, but later the legs lengthen as we descend a wet route through a lush thicket of willows, mountain maple, meadow-rue and seasonal forbs. After rapidly losing 500 feet of altitude, the descent becomes gentler and turns northwest down to the south side of meadowed Bear Valley. The path is lost for some 150 yards north across the hummocky, frequently soggy grassland, but we can pick it up again easily enough beside a metal sign. We then climb easily over a forested medial moraine and drop to the east end of a small, hospitable lakelet circled by lodgepoles and western white pines. Just a minute north of this tarn we hop across Breeze Creek, then ascend northeast along it over open, slabby terrain. Soon the trail

Bear Valley lake

ling for his wide-angled lens. Excellent camps are found in conifers back from the north shore.

The next morning we walk a short distance northwest from the lake's outlet to a small gap between two low domes. Here we gird ourselves for a 1200-foot descent north into Kerrick Canyon, involving the better part of 100 moderate-to-steep switchbacks. For the first 400 feet of this direct descent, our way is shaded by hemlocks and western white pines, and we can survey north over intervening ridges to Snow Peak and ragged Tower Peak. Lower down, however, the views are hidden by a rising horizon and a thick growth of hemlocks and lodgepoles. Finally reaching morainal till re-arranged by sometimes-raging Rancheria Creek, our descent abates and we turn east through dry lodgepole flats to join the Pacific Crest Trail where it bends north at an over-signed junction to cross Rancheria Creek.

levels off through a delightful open stand of pines and hemlocks and arrives at the outlet of long-awaited Bear Valley lake. This shallow gem sits in a washboard-bottomed glacial trough, and numerous reefs of polished quartz-monzonite push up through the lake's mirror-surface. These picturesque islets, combined with a shore line of closely cropped grasses, red heather, and dwarf bilberry, provide a stunning foreground for soaring Bear Valley Peak. The total scene will send even the most jaded photographer scramb-

Take the Pacific Crest Trail north and then west as described in **Hike 42**, 7.3 miles to Wilmer Lake and camp there. The following day, retrace your steps 1.5 miles to the Tilden Canyon trail, described in **Hike 12**. Proceed down it about 10 miles to Tiltill Valley, your best campsite. Walk out to O'Shaughnessy Dam the next day by following **Hike 11** down to Rancheria Falls and then reversing your first day's course.

Hike 14   Pleasant Valley and Rodgers Canyon

Distance: 69.5 miles (111.8 km) loop trip

Grade: 7G, strenuous 6-day hike

Trailhead: Same as the Hike 9 trailhead. **B3.**

Introduction: This is the longest trip described through the Yosemite north country, and it also visits the greatest variety of subalpine settings to be found anywhere in the Park. Our little-traveled path through Pleasant Valley to sub-alpine Rodgers Meadow is a nicer alternative to using the Pacific Crest Trail to reach the Benson Lake region.

Description: Take the trail described in **Hike 10** to Rancheria Falls and camp there the first night. The next day, follow **Hike 13** to the Pleasant Valley trail at 8015 feet on a broad, dusty, red-fir-forested saddle north of Rancheria Mountain. Here we branch southeast, then head more eastward down a shallow draw to the rim of Piute Creek canyon's 1200-foot western scarp. Emerging from a thick stand of young

aspens, we are treated with superb vistas north-east over sparsely forested Pleasant Valley to a rolling landscape of dark exfoliating domes and hillsides above Piute Creek, terminating this side of spiry Sawtooth Ridge. A part of little-visited Irwin Bright Lake, one of several shallow, granite-rimmed lakes arcing around Pleasant Valley, can be seen on a forested bench below. As we switchback down moderately-to-steeply east, we can also look southeast across the Grand Canyon of the Tuolumne River to the flying buttresses on Double Rock and Colby Mountain. Below 7500 feet our path swings northeast to angle down a hillside overgrown with huckleberry oak, scattered conifers and black oaks. Soon we reach a hanging-valley aspen grove and walk in the seasonal creekbed that drains it, then descend down along the stream in a narrow chute. A few short switch-backs lead us north from this ravine down to the floor of Pleasant Valley, at 6860 feet. Here we find an interesting heterogeneous forest of red and white firs, Jeffrey pines, incense-cedars, junipers, and dominant lodgepole pines, growing on a sparsely meadowed alluvial floor. A few minutes' amble through these woods brings us to a signed trail branching northeast 0.2 mile to large packer camps beside a pool on Piute Creek. Campers should beware of persistent black bears that forage here seasonally.

From the Pleasant Valley camping spur trail, our path veers south to momentarily reach shaded Piute Creek, incised deeply in cobbly alluvium. This ford could be a 50-foot-long wade in early summer. On the east bank another spur trail heads upstream to more camps, but we turn downstream. Just past a stock-drift fence our route leaves shading conifers and begins to ascend moderately on an open hillside of friable dark diorite. The rocky climb does have one very steep pitch, to reach the south shoulder of a low ridge, and then it dips easily to a log crossing of Table Lake's outlet stream. The best campsites on Table Lake are reached by ascending north along the open bench just before crossing this stream. A dry peninsula, sparsely forested with Jeffrey pines, lies between the main lake, which is ringed with low, broken bluffs and shrubbery, and its southern arm, which is shallow and dotted with pond lilies. This rocky peninsula holds the best campsites. Angling for rainbow trout in Table, Irwin Bright and Saddle Horse lakes is good due to a scarcity of fishermen.

Now we pass south of Table Lake under a canopy of aspens. The herbaceous understory of this damp-floored flat is so dense that it has obliterated the mapped trail that once started here, bound north for Irwin Bright Lake. Near this old junction we hop a stream, and then ascend rapidly out of the shade and mosquitos onto a brushy hillside. Soon we pant up the inevitable rocky switchbacks and are partly consoled by an improving picture of Pleasant Valley. Our zigzag course persists until 7600 feet, where we top a bench to find, in another stand of aspens, the stream we crossed lower down. Now our climb moderates, proceeding southeast through alternately well-watered and dry-rocky plant associations, to a ridgetop just under 8000 feet. This open spot lets us look south down Piute Creek's gorge to Double Rock, and marks the start of the path's undulating traverse south to the Pate Valley trail. Numerous small, steep gullies are crossed while we contour pleasantly, usually shaded, above Piute Creek's gaping canyon. A mile later we find a sloping glade, some clustered, quivering aspens, and a sign pointing out the Pate Valley trail, which descends southwest (see **Hike 22**).

Our route curves southeast from the trail junction and climbs across an open volcanic hillside where a small spring trickles across the path. Excellent views and myriad wildflowers recommend this spot for a lunch break. Afterward, we gear down for a short but steep ascent east to the crest of a bouldery medial moraine robed in dark conifers. Our way descends east from the ridge crest across a hillside on rich volcanic tread. Twenty minutes later we reach our low point along the north rim of the Grand Canyon of the Tuolumne River. Here we are face-to-face with cliff-girded Colby Mountain while we stand in a field of mixed intrusive and extrusive glacial erratics. Just a few minutes later we enter Rodgers Canyon, then abruptly turn uphill.

The trail ascends a series of well-forested glacial steps to come alongside seasonally large Rodgers Canyon creek just under 8000 feet, then actually follows its bed for a moment. For

Murdock Lake and imposing Volunteer Peak

the next 1½ miles our gentle-to-moderate climbing trail keeps on Rodgers Canyon's west side, passing through typical subalpine pockets of lodgepoles that cluster near the cascading stream. After one cobbly pitch, we find a stock-drift fence, then emerge moments later on the south edge of Rodgers Meadow. Here Rodgers Canyon creek cuts a broad, lazy snake through the sedge turf, overshadowed by a small dome near Neall Lake, above the meadow's north end. Staying near the forest that demarcates the west side of Rodgers Meadow, we amble north to find a very good campsite, complete with stump-tables, in sun-dappled lodgepoles. A few yards north of this camp we leave the meadow and walk over a log to the east bank of Rodgers Canyon creek, only to cross back moments later, this time via a long boulder-hop. Now we come abruptly to a trail junction, at 8800 feet. By continuing north you can take a shorter route to the PCT, via Murdock Lake, to be described later.

Most hikers will branch right on the longer, far more scenic trail to Neall and Rodgers lakes. This route heads east to Neall Lake's unnamed outlet creek, then climbs pleasantly east along its north bank. Less than a mile from the Murdock Lake junction, we find a short spur trail going south to Neall Lake, which has fine campsites nestled by its outlet. Cupped by a terminal-moraine loop under the sharp crest of West Peak, small Neall Lake reflects surrounding cliffs, blue sky, fringing conifers and willowy fell-fields. Secluded campsites are found everywhere but on the talus of the south shore. Fishing for rainbow trout to 14 inches is excellent.

Pushing on toward Rodgers Lake, our trail steeply ascends a cobbly ridge under a western outlier of Regulation Peak. Soon we swing north, wind over terraced short-hair-sedge flats, and come to the south shore of long, subalpine Rodgers Lake. Named for the second Superintendent of Yosemite Park, it is divided into two bodies by a low granitic isthmus; the larger, eastern portion is more open and rockier. Our way rounds Rodgers Lake to a handsome grove of lodgepoles and hemlocks on the north shore. Here lie some good camps that afford excellent panoramas over the shallow waters to the ruddy north faces of Regulation and West peaks. Farther east we pass another group of camps, then begin to switchback north over metasediments that have been intruded by a netlike swarm of quartz veins.

Presently we arrive atop a grassy saddle at 9790 feet, where the stunning sheer profile of nearby Volunteer Peak completely dominates a horizon of greater summits throughout the north country—Piute Mountain, Price and Tower peaks, and Crown Point. Descending north from this gap via short switchbacks, we soon re-enter timber and wind past huge talus blocks, seasonal willow-fringed tarns and hummocky meadows to a well-signed junction with the Pacific Crest Trail. Here, under the brooding face of Volunteer Peak, which has been frost-riven into thousands of vertically oriented flakes, we may decide to strike northeast one mile on the PCT to Smedberg Lake, or continue west 3.6 miles along the PCT (see **Hike 42**) to spend the night at large Benson Lake. Within ⅓ mile along our way to Benson Lake, we strike the Murdock Lake trail, the shortcut from upper Rodgers Canyon.

If you don't take the scenic longer route, then from the trail junction at 8800 feet in Rodgers Canyon, take the Murdock Lake trail northward moderately up along a hillside, quickly leaving behind the canyon-floor forest. Soon you tackle a set of very steep, sandy switchbacks, then angle northeast, passing below a small spring. The remainder of this ascent ends abruptly on a level subalpine meadow at 9530 feet. Shallow Murdock Lake is cupped in a depression in this rolling grassland. Some adequate camps lie in lodgepoles above its west shore and offer interesting views of Volunteer Peak, Matterhorn Peak and Sawtooth Ridge. Leaving the ridgetop meadowland, our trail descends back into mixed conifers and soon reaches the Pacific Crest Trail.

To complete your hike, follow **Hike 42** west to Wilma Lake, the best camping area in Jack Main Canyon. Then reverse the steps of **Hike 12** out Moraine Ridge, take a trail to Laurel Lake, and spend your last evening there. On the last day, descend the path described in **Hike 9** to Hetch Hetchy Reservoir.

The north-facing cliff of Mt. Hoffmann's highest summit

Section 2

Trails of the Hetch Hetchy Area, between the Tuolumne River and Highway 120

Introduction: The land explored in this section is one of contrasts. Some of the trails in its low, western section are seldom used, while those in its high, eastern section are extremely popular. The reason for this is obvious: the lower areas tend to be hot, dry and devoid of spectacular scenery; they are best hiked in spring or early summer, when snow still buries the upper trails. The trails of this section cover a great altitude span, from 3330 feet (1015 m) at the bottom of the Poopenaut Valley trail to 10,850 feet (3307 m) at the summit of Mt. Hoffmann. Between these elevations you'll find all of the Park's seven plant communities, from Foothill Woodland to Alpine Fell-Fields. Only Section 7 has a greater altitude span, and that is only if you include all of the Alder Creek Trail, most of which is outside the Park.

Supplies and Services: Absolutely everything you'll need for a Yosemite outdoor experience can be obtained in Sonora, on Highway 108, about 50 miles from the Big Oak Flat entrance station. This includes full backpacking and mountaineering gear, available at Sonora Mountaineering. This town also has several large grocery stores, numerous dining places, and two hospitals.

Groveland, about 24 miles from the Park entrance, is the last town you'll pass on Highway 120; however, several resorts and gas stations are found closer to the park. Gas, meals and lodging are found at Evergreen Lodge, on the Evergreen Road just 0.6 mile before it ends at the Hetch Hetchy Road.

Once inside the Park you can find virtually anything you'll need down in Yosemite Valley, but this is out of your way. Gas, food and other supplies are best obtained at the store at Crane Flat. Fewer supplies are at White Wolf Lodge, the center for Hikes 19-23, though lunch and dinner are served at it. The lodge also offers horse rides.

Wilderness Permits: If you are driving east up Highway 120, get a permit at the Big Oak Flat Information Station, which is immediately past the Park's entrance station. Note that from about early April through late October you can get a permit at the Hetch Hetchy Entrance Station (by the Mather Ranger Station). You cannot get a permit in the White Wolf area. If you are driving up Highway 140 or 41, get your permit at the Visitor Center in Yosemite Valley, and if you are driving west down Highway 120, stop in Tuolumne Meadows (see "Wilderness Permits" in Section 4, on page 96).

Campgrounds: For Hikes 15–18, you could spend the night at Carlon or Middle Fork campgrounds, both outside the Park along Evergreen Road between Highway 120 and the Hetch Hetchy Road. However, a better place to stay may be at the Park's 1991-vintage backpackers' campground near the O'Shaughnessy Dam trailhead. Within the Park you can stay at Hodgdon Meadow Campground, reached by turning left immediately after passing through the Big Oak Flat entrance station. Driving east on Highway 120, you'll reach another possibility, the Crane Flat Campground, ¼ mile before Crane Flat. Both these campgrounds are on a reservation system—see page 2. After turning left at the flat's junction, you then drive 14.5 miles to the White Wolf road. Opposite this road's White

Wolf Lodge is the entrance to the White Wolf Campground, an ideal place for those taking Hikes 19–24. Those taking Hikes 25–28 can also stay here or at Porcupine Flat Campground, on Highway 120 9.2 miles past the White Wolf road junction. During the summer season all these campgrounds can be full, so plan to find a campsite early in the day. Finding a campsite on weekends may be impossible.

Hike 15   Poopenaut Valley

Distance: 2.1 miles (3.3 km) round trip

Grade: 1C, Moderate half-day hike; no camping allowed

Trailhead: Just 1.1 miles outside the Park's Big Oak Flat entrance station, leave Highway 120 and drive north 7.4 miles on Evergreen Road to its junction with the Hetch Hetchy Road. Turn right and follow it 1.3 miles to the Mather Ranger Station, then an additional 3.9 miles to a clockwise turn in the road. On the road's right side you'll find limited parking for two cars. If you're driving from the O'Schaughnessy Dam parking area, then go 3.7 miles to this curve. **B3.**

Introduction: You can't swim in Hetch Hetchy Reservoir, so if you've just returned from a hot, sweaty backcountry hike in this area, you might want to take this trail down to the Tuolumne River for an invigorating swim. In spring it is a good training hike.

Description: The signed trail begins about 10 yards down the road, beside a shoulder-high pointed flake. The trail starts across an open expanse of granodiorite that supports a drought-tolerant growth of manzanita and incense-cedar,

then drops steeply down a shady slope. As you descend just over 1000 feet of steep trail, the forest cover of white fir and sugar pine becomes one of incense-cedar, black oak, Douglas-fir and ponderosa pine. Because oak leaves cover the trail on its lower sections, rattlesnakes could lie hiding under them, so don't bring along any children.

The steep trail approaches a cascading, seasonal creek before it veers west, eases its gradient, and soon reaches a large, grassy meadow. Paths go in several directions, but you'll probably want to traverse west through the meadow, heading for the base of a granodiorite ridge—hosting Digger pines—that plunges to the river. Since this resistant ridge constricts the river, it has cut a deep channel, unlike the shallow, willow-lined channel in spacious Poopenaut Valley. The ridge has ledges that permit you to dive from heights of 25 feet or more into the river. Because the river drains from Hetch Hetchy's cold waters, the swimming hole stays cold even on the hottest day. To avoid working up a sweat and pooping out on the steep ascent back to your car, plan to return in the late afternoon.

A rock-lined swimming hole at the lower end of Poopenaut Valley

A lone Jeffrey pine and glacial chatter marks atop Lookout Point

Hike 16   Lookout Point

Distance: 3.0 miles (4.8 km) round trip

Grade: 1B, easy half-day hike

Trailhead: Just 1.1 miles outside the Park's Big Oak Flat entrance station, leave Highway 120 and drive north 7.4 miles on Evergreen Road to its junction with the Hetch Hetchy Road. Turn right and follow it 1.3 miles to the Mather Ranger Station. **B3.**

Introduction: For a good view of the lower Tuolumne River canyon, the hike to Lookout Point can't be beat. It is particularly enjoyable in springtime, when water is present and temperatures are mild.

Description: This hike is best done in the morning, when temperatures are still fairly cool and shadows are good for photography. Our starting point, Mather Ranger Station, sits on a broad, glaciated granite bench that has a shady, fairly dense cover of ponderosa pines, incense-cedars and black oaks. From the station's east side we follow a trail south along the border of its pasture, meet a trail intersection, turn left, and parallel the Hetch Hetchy Road east. Our trail rollercoasters across rocky slopes, partly covered with gold-cup oak and Mariposa manzanita, then climbs steeply but briefly up a gully. At its

top we level off and parallel its springtime creeklet northeast to a quick junction with the Lookout Point spur trail.

Beneath shady white firs, sugar pines, ponderosa pines and incense-cedars, we walk north for a minute, skirt around a seasonal pond, then circle counterclockwise up the northeast side of a largely barren, glacier-smoothed knoll. As you start your last 100 yards to the summit, note how the granitic rock gradually decomposes from fresh, angular, joint-controlled rocks to weathered, rounded ones. A few Jeffrey pines—more drought-tolerant than their nearby look-alikes, ponerosa pines—struggle to survive on its summit, but they don't obstruct our view. In the northeast, wispy Tueeulala Falls adds accent to the springtime landscape while adjacent, voluminous Wapama Falls usually flows the year around.

This summit has been glaciated, probably as recently as 15,000 years ago. Faint striations left by glaciers, together with glacier-cut gouge marks, make up the evidence here. Additional evidence is found on the barren knoll just northeast of us, best reached from the Hetch Hetchy Road, which has large, glacier-transported boulders strewn over its surface.

Hike 17   Mather Ranger Station to Smith Peak

Distance: 19.6 miles (31.6 km) semiloop trip

Grade: 4E, moderate 2-day hike

Trailhead: Same as the Hike 16 trailhead. **B3.**

Introduction: Smith Peak, with its all-encompassing view of the northwest half of Yosemite National Park, can be reached from White Wolf or from Mather Ranger Station. If you are hiking in May, June, October or November, then take this hike, the Mather route, to avoid snow problems. If you are hiking in July, August or September, then take Hike 20, the White Wolf route.

Description: From the east side of the Mather Ranger Station our trail starts south and quickly intersects the Camp Mather-Lookout Point trail (**Hike 16**), on which we'll be returning. Continuing ahead, we skirt across slopes with Mariposa and greenleaf manzanitas and pass several trails descending to Camp Mather before we duck into a conifer-shaded gully, dominated by white firs. Its shade plus the presence of gray squirrels and song birds make the 500-foot ascent up its trickling creeklet a fairly pleasant one, despite the steepness of the trail. Amid a forest of ponderosa pine, sugar pine, incense-cedar and black oak, we level off on a broad saddle that has a trail junction. From it a possibly vague half-mile trail winds northwest down to our return-route trail. We continue east, traversing across manzanita slopes before briefly climbing to a junction, nestled between two lateral moraines, with the Base Line Camp road. Remember this

junction if you plan to return this way, for if it's unsigned, it's easy to miss. After dropping from the junction, our road parallels the crest of a lateral moraine, on our left, as it contours toward Base Line Camp. Where the road bends left to go 170 yards to the camp, we go but 90 yards southeast on a trail to a quick trail fork. If you are following **Hike 18,** you veer right.

To get to Smith Peak we veer left, traverse above the two water tanks of Base Line Camp—a generally abandoned building—then climb up the blazed trail ½ mile east to the crest of a large moraine. This lateral moraine, 2500 feet above Poopenaut Valley, represents the thickness of a glacier that plowed down the Tuolumne River canyon, retreating from this locality perhaps as recently as 15,000 years ago. At one time Cottonwood Creek may have drained west into Poopenaut Valley, but today the moraine forces the creek southwest into the Middle Tuolumne River. At this higher elevation Jeffrey pines now replace ponderosa pines, and lodgepole pines appear as we approach lower Cottonwood Meadow. Once we leave this meadow the lodgepoles disappear, for conditions are now drier, and about ½ mile beyond it the sharp-eyed hiker will notice about a dozen trailside mortar holes. Sugar pines, known as *hi 'ymachi* by the local Indians, grow in this vicinity, and the Indians ate the seeds probably after grinding them here. They also made use of the tree's whitish sugar, which they considered a delicacy. About a mile northwest of this mortar site are

First-year cones hang at the ends of a sugar pine's long branches

black oaks, whose acorns were a major part of the Indians' diet, in ground form providing them with bread, mush and even soup.

A mile farther we enter upper Cottonwood Meadow, wetter than the lower one, and in it we are forced to cross wide Cottonwood Creek, which is generally a wet ford before mid-June. Continuing northeast, we climb rather steeply up the outer side of a glacial moraine, and on its low inner side jump across Cottonwood Creek, which flows along the edge of relatively dry Smith Meadow. Like the nearby peak, this meadow is named for a sheep rancher who claimed that this part of Yosemite belonged to him. Ignoring the land's Park status, he grazed his sheep in its meadows well into the 1920s. We continue northeast across this meadow and come to an intersection with the westbound trail from White Wolf (**Hike 20**).

The trail to the summit of Smith Peak is direct and steep, so before you start, you might want to get some water at a trickling creeklet a few yards west on the White Wolf-Mather trail. We start our climb in a forest of white firs, sugar pines and incense-cedars, and by the time we reach the first of three wet meadows—all of them rich in summer wildflowers—we have left the incense-cedars behind. If you're hiking this trail before late June, you're liable to run into snow patches from here on. Although you may lose the trail beneath them, you won't lose your way as long as you keep heading northeast upslope. A second wet meadow, marking the halfway point, is quickly passed; then we pass a third one midway between it and the Tuolumne River canyon crest. By the time we reach the crest, red fir has become the dominant forest tree, with Jeffrey pines occupying the drier, sunnier spots and white firs in between. If you came up on horses, leave them at the canyon-crest saddle, for the footpaths ahead are steep and narrow.

The final 250-foot gain can be made by any of several brush-lined paths. Perhaps the safest and most frequently used path is the one that climbs the west slope, then traverses along the south slope. To reach the best viewpoint, atop pitted granitic rocks, you'll have to plow through a dense cover of huckleberry oaks. The solution pockets—some of them filled with water after recent rains—represent an extremely slow type of weathering often found on unglaciated, gentle-sloped surfaces of granitic rock. If the surfaces are recently glaciated, are steep-sloped, or are metamorphic or volcanic rock, then solution pockets will not form. From these

Solution pockets on Smith Peak's summit

pocketed rocks you can gaze down into the deep Grand Canyon of the Tuolumne River and see the Hetch Hetchy Reservoir, about 4000 feet below you. During the time of the Tahoe glaciation, a glacier filled the canyon below us to a depth of 3500 feet or more. About five miles upstream, near the end of Hetch Hetchy Reservoir, this glacier was 4000 feet thick. Being so thick, the glacier ice exerted a force of about 100 tons per square foot along the canyon's bottom; nevertheless, the shape and depth of the canyon haven't changed all that much despite repeated glaciation. As you can see, the canyon is distinctly **V**-shaped in cross section. You can also see that much of the Yosemite landscape north, south and west of the canyon is a gentle, rolling topography. It is expected to remain so for millions of years into the future. In contrast to this old surface is the younger Grand Canyon of the Tuolumne River and the even younger Sierra crest, which appears to be no more than four million years old. Scanning the northeast skyline, keen map users should be able to identify, from east to northeast, Mt. Hoffmann

Tiltill Creek canyon, left of Tower Peak (center horizon), cascades down to Hetch Hetchy Reservoir

plus the prominent crest summits of Mt. Conness, Matterhorn Peak and Tower Peak.

Unless a storm is approaching, don't be in a hurry to leave this view-packed summit. Scarcity of water prevents tall conifers from overpowering the summit and blocking our views. The shallow dry soils, however, are the perfect medium for the densely packed, shrubby huckleberry oaks, whose small, evergreen leaves keep the plant's water loss at a minimum. On the more snowbound slopes of Smith Peak grows the giant chinquapin, a distant cousin of the huckleberry oak. Also found here are a few California black oaks, which stand hardly more than knee-high, though in Yosemite Valley they grow up to 80 feet tall. This oak prefers sunny slopes, and in the absence of conifers it has managed to survive. At about 7750 feet in elevation, this patch of black oaks may be the highest one in Yosemite; only in a few other parts of the Park are they seen at the 7500-7600 foot level. This oak together with whitebark pine are the only two Yosemite trees that reduce to shrub height as they approach the upper limit of their ranges. A final bush worth noting is the snow bush, a spiny *Ceanothus* that prefers *deep, dry* granitic soils. We've seen it along drier sections of the Cottonwood Creek drainage and we'll see it again on our return route.

Returning to Smith Meadow, you might look for a place to camp under shady conifers along the meadow's edge. Along this stretch of Cottonwood Creek there are actually at least six meadows, not one, and as we hike west on the White Wolf-Mather trail, we quickly pass through three small ones. About 300 yards beyond the last one we meet the bank of Cottonwood Creek and then parallel it for more than ½ mile before a brushy moraine forces its course southeast. Before leaving the creek be sure you have enough water to last to the trailhead. Generally hiking under conifer shade, we drop to a flat with tree-size California black oaks, then proceed northwest across several low, brushy moraine crests to a lily-pad lakelet—frog heaven. Beyond it we cross more low moraine crests, then make a major winding descent to a junction with the Hetch Hetchy Trail, an old, little-used trail that dies out just above the Hetch Hetchy Road at a point about 1½ trail miles north of here. On the lower part of our descent to this junction, Douglas-firs have appeared, but they soon disappear as we climb south up drier slopes. On a bedrock bench near the top of a 250-foot climb, incense-cedars, ponderosa pines, black oaks and gold-cup oaks have given way to greenleaf manzanita. As we contour southeast across benches that are similar to those seen on the west side of the Tuolumne River canyon, numerous mice and ground squirrels thrive, generally unseen, and they make abundant prey for this dry area's rattlesnakes.

(If you'd rather not risk meeting a rattler, you can return from Smith Meadow the way you went to it.)

About 250 yards before a seasonal creek you enter a 30-yard-long meadow in which the tread can momentarily disappear, but you can find it again by just walking straight ahead. Beyond the creek our route becomes shadier, and it gradually descends ¼ mile to the edge of a fairly large meadow. Here the tread may disappear once again. Follow the meadow's edge about 60 yards to a usually dry creeklet, then cross it and go west-southwest across the upper part of the meadow. Soon the tread should become obvious, and you follow it to the meadow's south corner. Under conifer cover you now walk ¼ mile southwest to a junction from which a lateral trail descends in less than ½ mile to the Hetch Hetchy Road. Our route, however, makes a

short, moderate ascent, enters a trough, and in ½ mile nears the south shore of a long, shallow lakelet. With abundant pond vegetation and a flourishing insect life, it too is frog heaven. A lateral moraine, left by a glacier as recently as 15,000 years ago, stands above the pond's north shore and is largely responsible for damming up this body of water. After walking west for a few minutes, we pass by the partly hidden trail, on our left, that winds up to the Cottonwood Creek trail, the route we took earlier. In a few more minutes we come to a junction with the Lookout Point trail, on our right, which is too short, scenic and instructive to forego, so we walk up to the point, return to our main trail, and then descend southwest to our trailhead at the Mather Ranger Station. The last part of our hike, from Lookout Point onward, is described in **Hike 16** in reverse.

Hike 18   Mather Ranger Station to Long Gulch

Distance: 16.5 miles (26.5 km) round trip

Grade: 4D, moderate 2-day hike

Trailhead: Same as the Hike 16 trailhead. **B3.**

Introduction: If you're looking for solitude, hoping to avoid the summertime crowds, you might consider this hike. There are a number of reasons for its pronounced absence of hikers. Few people know about it and those who do know that it is a very *un*spectacular, viewless, lakeless trail going from one road to another.

Description: Follow **Hike 17**'s description up to the trail junction in the neighborhood of Base Line Camp. Where the Cottonwood Creek trail veers left, we veer right and momentarily climb over the crest of a low lateral moraine. We had seen two of them earlier, crossing one of them just after starting east down the Base Line Camp road. Beyond the third moraine we confront a steep slope and labor up past snow bush, green manzanita and chinquapin. Finally our slope gives way to a broad summit area, shaded mainly by white firs, and on it we cross three more moraine crests before dropping to willow-lined Middle Tuolumne River. In early season you're almost certain to find it deep and wide. Locate the trail among azaleas on its south bank and start to climb again. In 200 yards you'll meet a junction from which an abandoned trail climbs southwest toward Ackerson Meadow, just outside the Park boundary. We angle

left, make a short climb to another morainal crest, traverse east almost to a small meadow, then cross our last low morainal crest—eight in all, if you've been counting. The last two are probably left from the Tahoe glaciation while the lower ones are probably left from the more recent Tioga glaciation. As the Tioga-age Tuolumne River canyon glacier began to diminish, perhaps 12,000 years ago or earlier, it left these moraines, one below another, as it sporadically shrank in size. Had it shrunk at an even rate, we should have seen one continuous moraine.

Just beyond moraine number eight we encounter a jump-across creek whose headwaters originate on the slopes of Bald Mountain. We start across a small meadow, then begin a cool, shady climb in a predominantly white-fir forest, staying with the creek for about 1½ miles before crossing it at the lower end of a boggy meadow. If you diagonal southeast while crossing the meadow, you should quickly locate the trail along the east edge. Soon we leave the meadow's edge and its many dogwoods and few aspens in order to make a steep climb up to a saddle east of Bald Mountain. Unless you're really looking for this low mountain, you won't even know it's there.

Jeffrey pines locally dominate on the south slopes just beyond the saddle, and across these slopes we traverse to a small aspen-bearing flat,

Before the *new* Big Oak Flat Road opened in 1940, you entered Yosemite via Aspen Valley

then go 200 yards southeast to the edge of a lodgepole-pine-fringed meadow. You can lose the trail here if you are not careful, but as long as you hike along the meadow's southwest edge, you should quickly find it again. Beyond the meadow we cross two low summits, then drop moderately to steeply more than 550 feet to the upper north end of a fairly dry meadow. In it the trail disappears, but it resumes again along its east edge. On it we have a short pleasant descent to the Old Tioga Road, along which visitors traveled before Highway 120 was built. This closed fire road traverses one mile southwest to Aspen Valley, an area of private homes within the Park. Please respect their property; it is of historic value. Other residences are in Wawona and a few in largely burned-over Foresta.

You can either return the way you came or else head northeast up the Old Tioga Road to the Harden Lake trail, follow **Hike 20** over to Smith Peak, climb it, and then follow the second half of **Hike 17** back to your trailhead. This suggestion is a pleasant four-day, 35-mile, rarely taken excursion.

Hike 19   Harden Lake

Distance: 5.6 miles (9.0 km) round trip

Grade: 2B, easy half-day hike; no camping allowed

Trailhead: From Crane Flat drive northeast 14½ miles up Highway 120 to the White Wolf turnoff and follow that road down to where it is closed to motor vehicles, about ¼ mile beyond the White Wolf Campground. **C4.**

Introduction: Only an hour's hike from White Wolf Campground, this lake attracts quite a number of summer visitors. In late July the water level usually begins to fall and the lake warms up to the low and mid 70s—ideal for swimming. Before the lake drops in late summer, photography and wildflower identification can be quite rewarding.

Description: Our route, a closed fire road, immediately bridges the infant Middle Tuolumne River then parallels its sometimes splashing course down an unglaciated granitic terrain that sustains a healthy stand of lodgepole pines. After a mile of easy descent, we come to a spur

Harden Lake greatly diminishes in late summer, exposing its bouldery lake bed

road that goes to a sewage-treatment pond, constructed in the mid-1970s as part of a Park-wide program to upgrade treatment plants to tougher environmental standards. The spur road is closed to visitors (you wouldn't want to smell the sewage anyway), so continue on the main road—a favorite for horseback riders—and climb over a low ridge of glacial deposits before dipping into a shady alcove of lodgepole pines and red firs. A primitive campground used to be here before the construction of the sewage pond, but today only a trail junction exists.

Those hikers taking **Hike 21** keep to the road while those taking **Hikes 19** and **20** take the trail, which traverses the slope of a large glacial moraine. The well-drained sediments of this moraine support a different plant community than our generally rocky-road descent, and on this moraine grows a forest of Jeffrey pines together with some white firs and aspens. Thousands of bracken ferns seek the forest shade together with chinquapins, the bushes with spiny, seed-bearing spheres. Seeking the sun are snow bushes, which have spine-tipped branches. In ⅔ mile our trail ends and we follow Harden Lake road across relatively flat glacial sediments. After a few minutes of walking, we reach

a gravelly junction with a trail to Pate Valley (the return route of **Hike 22**), but adhere to the road as it bends left and goes almost to the southwest corner of Harden Lake. Here, beside a corral and a fenced-in pasture, **Hike 20** continues northwest on a trail. If you've traveled here on horseback, please leave the horse at the corral, not at the lake.

Harden Lake has a rather uncommon origin, for it occupies a small depression that formed between two lateral moraines. This shallow, nine-acre lake has no surface inlet or outlet, and not long after adjacent snow patches melt, the lake's level begins to drop. In the drought year of 1977 this lake dwindled to barely a pond by summer's end, and its stocked rainbow trout died. The lake's diminishing size not only reduced food and oxygen available to these trout, but it also raised the water temperature into the mid-70s—great for swimming but fatal for trout. Swimmers, if they are careless, could scrape their feet on the lake's many buried, glacier-transported boulders. With no incoming stream to carry in sand and gravel, the lake is only very slowly being filled in, mostly by organic matter, which mantles the lakebed's boulders with a soft layer of ooze.

Hike 20   White Wolf to Smith Peak

Distance: 20.0 miles (32.1 km) round trip
Grade: 5D, moderate 2-day hike
Trailhead: Same as the Hike 19 trailhead. **C4.**
Introduction: Looking for a nice weekend hike without the summer crowds? Then take this hike. Its elevation range is perfect for summer hiking—not too cold, hot, windy or sunny. Near the end of your hike you can enjoy a refreshing swim at Harden Lake—that is, before it drops substantially in late summer.

Description: For the first 2.8 miles follow the route description of **Hike 19**, which directs you to a corral near the southwest shore of Harden Lake. From the corral a trail starts northwest, hemmed in by a meadow on the left and a bouldery moraine on the right. Soon we cross the crest of the moraine, which sits almost 4000 feet above the unseen east end of Hetch Hetchy Reservoir. On slopes we now traverse west through a red-fir forest, crossing two small meadows before briefly descending to a larger one atop a broad saddle. Meadows, being often damp, support all too many mosquitoes, but usually by late July most of the insects have died as the meadow's soils have dried out, and then this meadow is particularly enjoyable for botanizing. Here you may find a rainbow of colors in the flower blossoms: white-flowered cow parsnip and Richardson's geranium, creamy corn lily and bistort, yellow senecio and monkey flower, orange alpine lily, red columbine, maroon shooting star, blue-violet lupine and blue Leichtlin's camas. On the nearby drab forest floor bits of color may be seen in the whitish-yellow stemmed coral root and the brilliantly red snow plant. Both plants are *saprophytes,* that is, they thrive on organic components in the soil rather than utilizing sunlight to make their own food.

Beyond the lodgepole-fringed meadow and the low crest just north of it, red firs yield to white firs and Jeffrey pines as we make a diagonal descent across south-facing slopes. Bracken ferns and snow bushes also thrive on the forest slopes, and scrubby black oaks make a showing just before we reach the crest of a moraine, likely left by a Sherwin-age glacier. As we traverse west down this crest we can see Smith Peak, to the northwest, through the trees. Eventually we abandon the crest, and by descending shady slopes we exchange the company of Jeffrey pines for that of red firs, then white firs, and by the time we reach a creeklet,

Life-size photo of western dwarf mistletoe, a joint-stemmed parasite growing, in this case, on a red-fir branch

incense-cedars join us. Soon we cross the creeklet, which is lined with alders, azaleas, thimbleberries, bracken ferns and water-loving wildflowers, and we follow it down to a seasonally wet meadow. Just beyond the meadow you'll cross Cottonwood Creek and arrive at eastern Smith Meadow. This little-used trail can be hard to follow through it, but it generally goes northwest, re-entering forest cover near the meadow's north edge. To avoid damp soils, the trail stays close to the base of Smith Peak as it traverses northwest to western Smith Meadow, by which you'll find a junction with the Smith Peak trail. A detailed description of this trail and the Smith Peak environs is given in **Hike 17**. After climbing the peak, return the way you came, perhaps stopping at Harden Lake for a refreshing swim—when the lake is full. If someone is willing to drive to Mather Ranger Station, you can follow **Hike 17** down to it, which is easier than climbing back up to White Wolf.

Hike 21   The Western Yosemite Loop

Distance: 44.4 miles (71.4 km) loop trip

Grade: 6F, easy 5-day hike

Trailhead: Same as the Hike 19 trailhead. **C4.**

Introduction: Each year thousands of visitors hike or ride the High Sierra Camps loop trail. Until this book was published, no one ever heard of the western Yosemite loop trail. Half its length is along little-known trails, part of it is along the Old Tioga Road, and the rest is along moderate to heavily used trails. Being a loop, it can be started from any of a number of points, but by starting from White Wolf, most of your first day's hiking—when your pack is heaviest—is downhill. In short, the route leaves White Wolf, eventually reaches Tamarack Flat Campground, descends to Yosemite Valley, climbs up Yosemite Creek, then returns to White Wolf via Lukens Lake.

Description: The first 9.4 miles of this loop trip is down the Old Tioga Road, now only a fire road closed to traffic. About 1⅔ miles down this historic road you come to the Harden Lake trail junction, then in ½ mile pass the Harden Lake road junction. From this junction to Tamarack Flat Campground, 14½ miles ahead, you'll probably have the whole country to yourself.

Lodgepole pines, red firs and white firs generally shade our descent, but on drier slopes grow Jeffrey pines and on wetter ones, groves of aspens. From about one mile before you cross the Middle Tuolumne River, the old Tioga Road hugs this stream, giving you close access to water should you decide to camp along the road. Where the road finally does cross the river, 6.4 miles from the trailhead, you'll find evidence of campsites.

About a mile beyond the bridge, the Middle Tuolumne River angles northwest through a small, bedrock gorge of granodiorite while our southwest-trending road tops a low, flat, weathered divide. Long Gulch creek takes over where the Middle Tuolumne left off, and starting along it we descend into aptly named *long* Long Gulch. Our canyon has been straight for 5 miles, probably due to erosion along a major fracture in the granitic bedrock, but soon Long Gulch curves south, and we descend into a vegetation zone that contains sugar pines. As our road levels out, we approach Long Gulch creek, then contour west and soon reach a trail (**Hike 18**) climbing north up the gully. In 40 yards, just

beyond the gully's creeklet, this trail resumes and we take it down-canyon. Had we stayed on the Old Tioga Road, we would have reached Aspen Valley in another mile.

In its first half mile our old trail goes through two meadows. Then it sticks to Long Gulch creek for another mile, until that creek begins its plunge to the South Fork Tuolumne River. Along this part of the trail you could make a small camp. You won't have another acceptable camping opportunity until Tamarack Flat Campground, about 6-7 miles farther. Our trail stays high in order to avoid steep slopes, and on this traverse we meet mountain misery, a low, scented shrub with sticky, finely divided leaves. Soon our trail makes a plunge south toward the South Fork, descending well-weathered granitic slopes. Just before reaching the South Fork, we come to a junction, from where an abortive trail strikes west. We turn east and descend quickly to alder-choked Long Gulch creek, which has a curious plant association of chinquapin together with umbrella plant.

No sooner have we crossed this creek than we are confronted with the South Fork, a seasonal torrent with bedrock banks that offer no camping. After a ford of the South Fork, we start a long climb under the shady cover of sugar pines, white firs and other conifers, with chinquapin and greenleaf manzanita growing beneath them. After a mile the trail eases its grade, and after another mile—this one of easy climbing—we top a flat ridge that boasts a mature stand of giant sugar pines. Now only ½ mile from Highway 120, we scurry up to this busy road, quickly cross it at a saddle, then once more return to seclusion. The climb up to the road and down from it toward Tamarack Flat Campground is partly through a forest of lodgepole pines ("tamaracks") badly charred in an August 1990 lightning fire.

Our hike from the road is now downhill virtually the entire distance to the floor of Yosemite Valley. Our little-used trail quickly touches the north end of a linear meadow, descends along its east side to a second meadow, and from its lower end soon approaches Tamarack Creek. Our trail hugs the west bank of this tranquil creek for 1¼ miles before re-entering civilization at the northernmost tables of Tamarack Flat Campground. The Old Big Oak Flat Road is about 90 yards west of us, and on it we walk south about ¼ mile to its crossing of

Tamarack Creek. The campground is certainly a logical place to spend the night. The next morning you then continue 2⅓ miles down the road to Cascade Creek. This short stretch is described as **Hike 30.** Beyond the Cascade Creek bridge, the Old Big Oak Flat Road essentially dwindles to a trail and in about ½ mile it reaches Yosemite Valley's north-rim trail. Should you decide not to enter Yosemite Valley, you can shorten your hike by about 4 miles if you take this trail east past El Capitan and Eagle Peak to Yosemite Creek. However, the old section of trail between El Capitan and the Eagle Peak lateral trail is not all that enjoyable, for it was poorly routed, resulting in unnecessary gains and losses.

This guide's proposed route descends along the increasingly dry, abandoned Old Big Oak Flat Road. Due to lack of permanent water and the dryness of the vegetation, no camping and no fires are allowed along it. White firs and sugar pines are joined by and then gradually replaced by incense-cedars and ponderosa pines, which in turn yield to Douglas-firs along the shadier parts, such as near Fireplace Creek, lined with azaleas and alders. In some years this creek runs until late July, but don't depend on it. Beyond this creek gold-cup oaks gradually take over as the dominant tree. Soon you'll spy the old railings of Rainbow View, from where you get your first good views of *anything* along this shady old road. In the Park's early days this viewpoint gave travelers their first glimpse down into Yosemite Valley, a view framed by El Capitan and the Cathedral Rocks. To the south you'll see the much newer Discovery View, on the Wawona Road, situated below you on the opposite wall of the start of the Merced Gorge.

Beyond the viewpoint you'll quickly come to a major gully, and just beyond it the old road switchbacks. Rather than descend a brush-choked switchback leg, descend the east side of the gully, then continue your descent east, which is sometimes brushy but sometimes has gold-cup oaks and bay trees to lend some shade. The road through the unstable Rockslides is choked with boulders, and spraining an ankle is more of a potential hazard than meeting with a rattle-snake. Past the Rockslides, views of Yosemite Valley gradually disappear as we once again enter forest cover. An indistinct, abandoned road descends from our road just before ours winds down to a trail junction.

Hiking east on the trail, we quickly cross two channels of Ribbon Creek, both of them usually dry in summer, and then begin our last segment

Crocker Point, across Yosemite Valley

of the Old Big Flat Road. Continuing east on this blocked-off road we soon reach a small hollow from whose north end a *de facto* trail climbs up to the nose of El Capitan. About ⅓ mile beyond this depression our road ends at a bend in the westbound valley road. You might walk an additional ⅛ mile east to the Devils Elbow Picnic Area, perhaps the best swimming spot along the Merced River's entire course through Yosemite Valley.

The rest of this hike is mostly described in detail in several other hikes. Starting from the bend in the valley road, we follow the last two thirds of **Hike 63** as it goes south to El Capitan Bridge, southeast to the Cathedral Picnic Area entrance, then east along the valley floor's south trail to a crossing of the eastbound valley road. Here you walk northwest past roadside picnic tables, descend to a long footbridge and start across it. From it you get good views of Yosemite Falls, Royal Arches, Washington Column, North Dome, Clouds Rest, Sentinel Rock, the Cathedral Rocks and the Three Brothers. Beyond the bridge and the Merced River you follow a trail north to the west end of Yosemite Lodge—the place to go if you want hot meals—

then you cross the westbound valley road near a gas station. Immediately west of the gas station is Sunnyside Walk-in Campground, where you might spend the night. This campground is one of two Valley campgrounds that are not on the reservation system during the summer. Hopefully, you'll find a vacant site in it, since getting a site during the summer at the Valley's other campgrounds is a nearly impossible task.

Along the east side of the gas station is the start of the Yosemite Falls trail, **Hike 68,** which you take all the way up to the lip of Upper Yosemite Fall. Camping is illegal within ½ mile of the Valley's brink, so continue north and search for secluded sites that are found upstream. From these campsites return to the Yosemite Falls trail, which always stays west of Yosemite Creek. In ½ mile of northward travel you'll meet a junction with the Eagle Peak trail, **Hike 69.** Leaving this junction atop a ridge that separates two in-line gullies, we now start on the Hetch Hetchy trail, which descends the northern gully ¼ mile to Yosemite Creek. Found here is a medium-sized campsite, and since you've got most of the climbing behind you and you have only 11 miles left to hike, you might consider it as a possible place to spend your last night on the trail.

Leaving the campsite, our lodgepole-shaded trail curves west, then makes an almost imperceptible climb to usually flowing Bluejay Creek, no doubt named after the Park's very common Steller's jay. The trail's gradient remains a gentle one for the next ½ mile; then it makes a short, moderately steep ascent up a ridge, along which we can see a series of small, potholed pools in Yosemite Creek, below us. Just above these the creek runs across granite slabs, and here, nine miles from the hike's end, you'll find a small campsite. Pools and slabs continue to be our trailside companions for another mile; then we veer away from Yosemite Creek and climb ½ mile to three closely spaced ephemeral creeks of a tributary canyon. Between the second and third is a trail junction, and here we fork left for a viewless climb 2⅔ miles up the glaciated canyon to the Yosemite Creek Campground road—part of the Old Tioga Road.

An alternate route, 1¾ miles longer, is to hike two miles up the Yosemite Creek trail to the Yosemite Creek Campground, just seven miles from trail's end, then next morning head 2½ miles northwest up the road to a reunion with the main route. This reunion can be easily missed. After this road has climbed for almost two miles, it bends west, soon passes a meadow on your left, then in ¼ mile tops a low crest. Here the road levels off and about 80 yards northwest from the crest, the road curves west and our faint trail climbs north.

Shaded by red firs and western white pines we make a moderate climb ¾ mile up to a turnout at a bend on Highway 120, then follow **Hike 24** up to shallow Lukens Lake, where no camping is allowed. From the lake follow the **Hike 23** description in reverse, descending a trail north to the upper Middle Tuolumne River, then west along it to White Wolf and your starting point.

Hike 22　　　　White Wolf to Pate Valley

Distance: 21.3 miles (34.3 km) semiloop trip

Grade: 5E, moderate 2-day hike

Trailhead: From Crane Flat drive northeast 14½ miles up Highway 120 to the White Wolf turnoff and follow that road one mile down to the trailhead opposite White Wolf Lodge. **C4.**

Introduction: Pate Valley is sort of a miniature Yosemite Valley without the automobiles and tourists. It therefore attracts quite a number of backpackers, who in turn attract a few bears. Nevertheless, if you want to have a warm, spacious camp along the Tuolumne River, Pate Valley may be just for you.

Description: This hike is described as a semiloop trip since we feel that both trails leading to the Pate Valley trail are worth taking. However, if mosquitoes in the White Wolf area are intolerable, often until mid July, you should first follow **Hike 19** to Harden Lake, then take the Pate Valley trail northeast. Our recommended route, however, first skirts the south edge of White Wolf Campground, and then traverses east about a mile through a lodgepole-pine forest. Then we cross the upper Middle Tuolumne River just a few minutes before we reach a junction. The trail to Lukens Lake goes right (**Hike 23**) but we go left and continue a traverse across the flat, forested floor. A short climb soon follows, which ends on a broad, shallow gap. The well-eroded rocks seen here indicate that the course we have just traversed hasn't been glaciated in a long time, if ever.

Leaving the crest we descend northwest down a gully to the east edge of a meadow, beyond which we enter level terrain strewn with sediments probably left by a Sherwin-age glacier. Only one significant creek drains this terrain, seasonally rich in ground water, and by late summer it is dry. Just beyond the creek we climb to the crest of an old lateral moraine left by a Tahoe-age glacier. Amid red firs we now start the long descent to Pate Valley, hiking over or past the crests of four more moraines. The three lower ones show much less weathering and contain far more boulders than the uppermost one, and therefore are likely to have been deposited by a Tioga-age glacier, which finally retreated from this area about 14,000 years ago. By the time our 1⅓-mile descent with its dozen-plus switchbacks ends at a junction with the Pate Valley trail, our forest cover has changed from one of red fir and western white pine to one of white fir, Jeffrey pine and incense-cedar. Bushy black oaks, which are tall trees in Pate Valley, are also found near the junction.

Our return route goes west to Harden Lake, but we strike east on a sympathetic trail that drops only very gently, thus giving our knees a chance to recover from our first switchbacking descent. In ½ mile you'll cross a spring-fed creeklet whose banks are hidden among a luxuriant growth of water-loving vegetation, in particular, alder, aspen, creek dogwood, bracken fern, thimbleberry and currant. In late summer this is your last reliable source of water until you reach the floor of the Grand Canyon of the Tuolumne River. In a few minutes we cut through a flat-floored notch high on this canyon's south wall, then after a few more minutes of gentle descent reach seasonal Morrison Creek. After paralleling it for ¼ mile we come to a low, rocky knoll, on our left. Here you may be scolded by Steller's jays—avian indicators of a warmer plant community. Onward we start our second set of short switchbacks—about four dozen of them—which lead us on a descent to a crossing of Morrison Creek.

Along this descent through a white-fir forest, note that sugar pines appear, incense-cedars grow in numbers, and black oaks now have tree stature. On the dry, rocky ridge paralleling our descent grow scraggly western junipers and pervasive huckleberry oaks. Finally we come to a crossing of Morrison Creek, which in late summer can be bone dry, and then flies can be a nuisance. During this season they can become almost unbearable on the canyon floor way below us.

Our last set of switchbacks—about 55 of them down to the river—begins just past Morrison

Black bears, adept at climbing trees, are common in Pate Valley

Creek. Along this descent you'll get numerous views of the Grand Canyon of the Tuolumne River, whose distant floor gradually draws nearer. Black oaks tend to be our dominant shade tree at first, but half way down, after we cross a dramatic water-polished gully that descends the canyon's south wall, our vegetation soon changes. Gold-cup oaks and bay trees slowly put in an appearance. Afternoon temperatures are hot, even under the gold-cup oaks, by the time we cross a granite gap. Greenleaf manzanita, seen higher up, is now replaced with Mariposa manzanita.

After the gap comes a grassy pond, which can dry up in late season but before then makes a warm swimming hole. At the pond's east end we cross the crest of the low moraine that has dammed this pond, then negotiate the few remaining switchbacks down to the flat floor of this great river canyon. Here the forest composition is nearly identical to that of Yosemite Valley, it being dominated by ponderosa pines, black oaks and incense-cedars. Over the next two miles of fairly level hiking you'll pass several near-river campsites, and isolated ones could be set up in a number of places.

Only several hundred yards before two bridges across the Tuolumne River, you'll enter Pate Valley proper and pass through a very large riverside camping area, recognized by the tables, stools and benches, which makes it a popular site with horsemen. Its popularity can be judged by the over-abundance of toilet paper to be found under almost any moveable log or rock. Please burn or carry out yours. Backpackers can find cleaner sites by crossing the two bridges over the chilly Tuolumne River, then climbing through a narrow bedrock notch and arriving at the north bank of the river's main branch. Bear cables are supposedly set up in Pate Valley, but

don't count on them being there—bears are already devising means to bring them down. You might place your food in a rodent-proof stuff sack, then perch it on an inaccessible rock ledge, for bears are poor rock climbers. About a minute's walk beyond the north-bank camps you'll come to a trail junction. The hot dry climb up to the Pleasant Valley trail is not worth the toil and sweat.

To return to your trailhead, retrace your steps 6 miles southwest back up to the trail junction one mile west of Morrison Creek. On this ascent be sure to have an adequate supply of water (a quart isn't too much) and be sure to take it easy. If you start late on a hot summer day you can lose a lot of water *and* salt if you overexert yourself, and you therefore can run the risk of heat stroke. We want you to survive, so start early and make many rest stops. When you reach the mentioned junction, don't retrace your steps, but rather head for Harden Lake on a trail whose first mile is a comfortable cool contour. Many aspens are passed along the second half of this contour, which fill their thirsty appetites by tapping the large "reservoir" of water stored within the morainal sediments we traverse across. One source of this "reservoir" is our immediate goal, Harden Lake, which has no surface outlet, but rather loses some of its water via percolation through the morainal sediments.

To reach Harden Lake we climb moderately to steeply up about 20 switchbacks, entering a forest of lodgepole pines, then of red firs and western white pines. When you arrive at Harden Lake you'll need a rest and probably a refreshing dip in the lake. From the lake your trail quickly ends at a road which you follow southeast for ¼ mile, then take a short trail over to the Old Tioga Road, which heads up to White Wolf. This hike from Harden Lake is described in detail (in the reverse direction) in **Hike 19**.

Hike 23   White Wolf to Lukens Lake

Distance: 4.6 miles (7.4 km) round trip

Grade: 1A, easy half-day hike; no camping allowed

Trailhead: Same as the Hike 22 trailhead. **C4.**

Introduction: This is the longer, yet more popular route to Lukens Lake. The second route, Hike 24, would be more popular if its trailhead were better signed. Since Lukens Lake

is already heavily visited, however, it is perhaps best that the shorter route's trailhead is not that conspicuous. Lukens Lake is very similar to Harden Lake (Hike 19), and if you enjoy one, you'll enjoy the other.

Description: If you stay at White Wolf Campground and rise early in the morning, you just might be fortunate enough to see a great gray owl perched on the trailhead sign or on a small

A peaceful afternoon spent fishing at Lukens Lake

lodgepole that has invaded White Wolf meadow. With keen, alert senses, this largest species of the North American owls waits for one of the meadow's many rodents to make a move. In this mid-elevation meadow, the likely prey would be one of the following: a shrew, deer mouse, meadow mouse, western jumping mouse, Belding ground squirrel or perhaps even a pocket gopher. Also preying on these rodents is the more-abundant coyote, a predator that is found in all of Yosemite's plant communities except the alpine one. Coyotes and great gray owls may also be seen in another similar habitat, Crane Flat meadow.

Our trail to Lukens Lake skirts the south edge of White Wolf Campground and traverses about a mile through a shady lodgepole-pine forest, crossing the upper Middle Tuolumne River—maybe a wet ford in early season—just a few minutes before arriving at a junction with a trail north to Pate Valley (**Hike 22**). Until mid July the mosquitos can be particularly abundant along this level stretch, for the ground is nearly saturated with water. During this time horses' hooves can turn the trail into a mire, but in late season, hikers will find little evidence of this, for once the trail dries out, the multitude of ensuing hikers plow it smooth again.

From the junction we hike east upstream for a nearly level, shady, short mile and come to our second junction. The trail climbing east up-

canyon continues 3.8 miles to a junction with the Ten Lakes trail. Not many hikers backpack to Ten Lakes via this trail, for it is considerably longer than the Ten Lakes trail, described in **Hike 25**. Leaving the junction, we head south 20 yards, jump across the infant Middle Tuolumne River, then begin a continuous, generally moderate, half-mile ascent to Lukens Lake. Climbing this trail segment, the observant hiker will note that we cross at least four glacial moraines, the final one forming a dam along the north shore of Lukens Lake. Along this shore we now find a well-mixed conifer forest, with red firs, western white pines and mountain hemlocks joining the lodgepole pines, which have dominated so much of our route.

Like Harden Lake, Lukens Lake is a 9-acre, moraine-dammed lake, and it is also shallow, warm and viewless—no peaks in sight. Unlike Harden, Lukens has trout—rainbow, brook and brown—and it tends to have a grassy bottom, not a bouldery one, though both have a lot of soft, organic-derived sediments, since stream-transported gravels are nonexistent. Since it is illegal to camp at this lake, try White Wolf Campground or more-secluded Yosemite Creek Campground. The latter is reached by driving on Highway 120⅓ mile east past the White Wolf turnoff to a junction with the Old Tioga Road, on your right. Follow it 4¾ miles to Yosemite Creek.

Hike 24   Highway 120 to Lukens Lake

Distance: 2.2 miles (3.6 km) round trip

Grade: 1A, easy half-day hike; no camping allowed

Trailhead: From Crane Flat drive northeast 14½ miles up Highway 120 to the White Wolf turnoff, then continue an additional 1.9 miles to a paved turnout on the highway's south side. **D4.**

Introduction: This is the shorter approach to Lukens Lake (see Hike 23).

Description: From the Highway 120 turnout, located in a shady gully near a curve in the highway, look for a signed trailhead on the north side of the road. Among red firs and lesser amounts of western white pines, make an easy ⅓-mile climb to a viewless saddle. As is usually the case, chinquapin bushes are found associated with the firs. Leaving the viewless saddle, you make an equally easy descent to the southeast end of a sedge-dominated meadow that also contains conspicuous corn lilies and, of course, willows. From this meadow's corner the main trail strikes northwest toward the lake's north shore and a lesser trail—one of use—strikes west toward its south shore. For more information on this lake see the last part of **Hike 23**.

Hike 25   Ten Lakes Basin

Distance: 12.6 miles (20.3 km) round trip distance from first lake; side trips to other lakes extra

Grade: 3D, moderate 2-day hike

Trailhead: From Crane Flat drive northeast 19⅔ miles up Highway 120 to the trailhead parking area, on *both* sides of the highway, immediately before the highway bridges signed Yosemite Creek. **D4.**

Introduction: The Ten Lakes basin is extremely popular with weekend backpackers, for with only a few hours' hiking effort you can attain any of its seven lakes.

Description: From the west end of the road's north parking lot a spur trail goes 90 yards northwest to the main trail, the Ten Lakes trail. On it we hike up canyon, first through a lodgepole-pine flat, then soon climb away from unseen Yosemite Creek and encounter Jeffrey pines and huckleberry oaks as we do so. Shaggy-barked western junipers are next met as we climb, seemingly too much, up to drier granitic slopes. This ascent, however, takes us above most of the lodgepoles, which tend to be a haven for mosquitoes. The climb also gives us views of Yosemite Creek canyon, Mt. Hoffmann and the county-line crest north of it. Soon after we get these views the trail levels, enters a forest of red firs and lodgepoles, then arrives at a creekside junction with a trail from White Wolf.

From the junction we boulder-hop the creek and leave its north-bank campsite to begin a moderate climb up a well-forested moraine left after the retreat of a large glacier about 14,000 years ago. Our climbing ends momentarily and we descend to and cross three seasonal creeklets. Then we climb, steeply at times, in a forest of red fir and western white pine to the top of a moraine. Behind it lies crescentic, wet Half Moon Meadow, which probably exists because the moraine impedes the meadow's drainage. The trail cuts across the meadow's relatively dry north edge, which nevertheless contains enough water to support a healthy crop of corn lilies. By its northeast corner is a campsite, nestled under lodgepoles and close to a creek. The next stretch of ascent is steep and dry, so rest here and take a small drink.

Roughly three dozen short, steep switchbacks guide us up almost to the Tuolumne/Mariposa county-line crest, from which we veer away to a trail junction. From it a poorly designed trail drops hundreds of feet in its 1.2-mile length to lower Grant Lake. A far better route, at least for cross-country hikers, is to start from the south corner of Half Moon Meadow and climb southeast cross-country up to this lake. There is no maintained trail to upper Grant Lake, but rather just a faint, discontinuous use trail up to it. The more popular lower lake has better campsites than the upper lake, though fishing for rainbow trout may be better at the less visited upper lake.

Leaving the Grant Lakes trail junction, the Ten Lakes trail climbs gently across a gravelly slope that is covered in midsummer with large,

Hikers resting at pass above Ten Lakes Basin; Sierra crest on skyline

deliciously scented lupines. These taper off just before we cross the county-line crest, which here is a broad, level, unglaciated surface that has eroded very little over many millions of years. Here at the pass are two kinds of granitic rock, a gray quartz diorite, at our feet, and a cream-to-buff quartz monzonite, on the low knolls to the east and west. Just north of the pass we cross two long dikes that have intruded the quartz diorite. Since these dikes are younger than the rock they intrude, their source, the quartz-monzonite granitic body, or *pluton,* is also younger than the quartz-diorite pluton. As you hike about Yosemite you can see other instances where one granitic rock intrudes another rock, and you can be certain that the rock that does the intruding is the younger of the two.

Leaving the Merced River drainage system, we enter the Tuolumne River drainage as we descend briefly north to a shallow saddle. Just beyond it is a small summit and to the left of it is flat-topped Colby Mountain, which crowns the west rim of the Ten Lakes Basin. This undistinguished summit is named for a very distinguished man, William Colby, the third president of the Sierra Club—just after John Muir and Professor Joseph LeConte. Colby served the club for nearly half a century and was truly one of the greatest conservationists in the early days of Yosemite National Park.

As we start a descent from the shallow saddle, a panorama of steep-sided, severely glaciated Ten Lakes Basin opens all around us, and three of the western deep-blue lakes are clearly evident. Our descent, which started close to some windblown whitebark pines growing on the county-line crest, ends near the largest of the western Ten Lakes, in a forest of mountain hemlocks and lodgepole and western white pines. The presence of hemlock and lodgepole together with lakeside red heather and Labrador tea indicates you have entered prime mosquito country—at least before August—and until then you should bring along a tent to escape their

Lower Grant Lake

10 Lake Basin's large western lake

bloodthirsty attacks. However, camping is quite enjoyable during August, when the lakes are at their warmest temperatures, and during September, after most hikers have left. It is then that a common, rarely noticed plant, the dwarf bilberry, makes its presence known by turning to a blazing crimson color. Around the largest of the western lakes you'll find at least half a dozen campsites, most of them along its western shore. Swimming is best at the lake's sunnier, shallower, island-dotted north end, and just beyond its nearby outlet are first-rate examples of glacier polish. From the north end you can hike cross-country ¼ mile northeast over a low ridge to one of the basin's more isolated lakes.

Other lakes can be reached by starting at the large lake's southwest corner and following its inlet creek upstream. A path goes up each of its banks to the first lake, which has a large north-shore campsite with a view of towering cliffs. Beyond this popular lake only the east-bank path continues, and it climbs ½ mile to a campsite at the outlet of the next lake, then ends at a campsite at its inlet. Few hikers climb cross country to the steep-sided uppermost lake basin.

To get to the eastern basin lakes, you must start from the large western lake's south shore. Draining into the lake's south end is a creeklet, and on its east bank you'll find your trail climbing southeast up to a sedge-filled meadow, then northeast from it up a bedrock ridge. The trail is steep in places, but the view improves with height, urging us on. Nearing the top of the crest, the trail enters a shady forest of hemlocks and lodgepoles, then soon makes a half-mile traverse southeast to the outlet of the large eastern lake. Although it lacks the photo esthetics of its western counterpart, it has almost as many campsites but not as many campers. The best sites are along the west and north shores. If you want secluded camping, then start a down-canyon hike from the north shore, soon following a creek that goes ½ mile down to the basin's northeastern lake, the most isolated lake in the Ten Lakes area.

After visiting one or more of the basin's sparkling gems, hike back out the way you came—or from the large eastern lake follow the long trail out to May Lake (the reverse of **Hike 28**).

Hike 26

May Lake

Distance: 2.4 miles (4.0 km) round trip

Grade: 1B, moderate half-day hike

Trailhead: From the Tenaya Lake Walk-in Campground parking area, drive west 3.7 miles on Highway 120 to the Old Tioga Road, then drive northeast up it 1.7 miles to the trailhead, just before the road is blocked off. **E4.**

Introduction: May Lake is a very popular destination because its shores provide good base-camp sites for the ascent of Mt. Hoffmann.

Description: Although this walk is treated here as a day hike, there is no reason, really, save inability to make a reservation, that one should not stay overnight at the May Lake High Sierra Camp. If you don't have reservations, you can camp out in the hikers' camp just above the lake's south shore.

The trail begins by a small pond on Snow Flat in a moderately dense stand of hemlock, red fir, and western white and lodgepole pines. To the northwest is the peak which is at the geographic center of the park, Mt. Hoffmann. In a little vale to the east of the trail, water lies late in the

season, permitting corn lilies to bloom into August. Our sandy trail ascends gently through forest cover, where we recognize the western white pine by its long, narrow cones and checkerboard bark pattern, and we notice how the red-fir cones, near the tops of these trees, stand upright on the branches, unlike the hanging cones of pines and spruces.

The initial ascent leads up open granite slabs dotted with lodgepoles. Then, as we switchback west up a short, steep slope, we have fine views of Cathedral Peak in the east, Mt. Clark in the southeast, and Half Dome and Clouds Rest in the south. Near the top of the slope, the forest cover thickens and the western white pines become larger and more handsome. Just beyond the crest, we find ourselves in a flat beneath a half-dozen superb, large hemlocks by deep-blue May Lake. Swimming is not allowed, but you may try your luck at catching the lake's brook trout or rainbow trout while contemplating the lake's beautiful backdrop of the east slopes of massive Mt. Hoffmann. The steep but safe, popular and relatively easy climb to its summit is described in the next hike.

Hike 27   Mt. Hoffmann

Distance: 6.0 miles (9.8 km) round trip

Grade: 2D, strenuous day hike

Trailhead: Same as the Hike 26 trailhead. **E4.**

Introduction: Mt. Hoffmann, centrally located in Yosemite National Park, provides the best all-around views of this park's varied landscapes. Perhaps more hikers ascend it than any other high peak in the Park, with only Mt. Lyell and Mt. Dana challenging its popularity. As with any 2-mile-high peak ascent, wear dark glasses and lots of sunscreen, for there's ⅓ less air on the summit, and the ultraviolet rays come on strong. Also, avoid altitude sickness, which is brought on by overexerting yourself, particularly after a large breakfast. If you are not in shape, camp overnight at May Lake to get partly acclimatized, then climb the peak the next day. Take it easy, for the route is short. However, abandon your attempt if a thunderstorm is approaching.

Description: Follow **Hike 26** to May Lake, above whose southeast corner you'll see a trail striking west. This immediately passes the camping area, then traverses across metamorphic rocks cropping out above the lake's southwest shore. You now follow it south, first through a small gap, then through a boulder-strewn wildflower garden. You might lose the trail here, but the route south—up a shallow gully to a small, linear meadow—is quite obvious.

From the meadow's south end, near a saddle, the trail goes 100 yards southwest, leaves the quadrangle, and climbs northwest up to the broad, lupine-decked summit plateau. Unsuspecting hikers may end up going several hundred yards past the meadow, an erroneous route taken by predecessors.

Numerous summits exist; all should be visited. The western summit is the highest, and you have an easy, safe scramble to its top. Having lunch here, you'll almost certainly attract marmots, begging a meal. Please don't feed them. Since your book comes with a map of the Park, you should be able to identify almost every major peak in or bordering it, since most are visible from here. Note how Mt. Hoffmann's nearly flat summit plateau contrasts with the mountain's steep sides. Glaciers have eaten back into all sides of this mountain, almost destroying this plateau, which like those on Mt. Conness, Dana Plateau, Dore Pass, and a few other spots was once part of an extensive, rolling landscape that existed as much as 50 million years ago. When you return, take the beaten path you ascended. Other routes are steeper, have loose rock and are potentially dangerous.

A summit view east: May Lake, Tenaya Lake and Sierra crest from Tioga Pass to Mt. Lyell complex

Hike 28   Ten Lakes Basin via May Lake

Distance: 14.6 miles (23.5 km) one way to the easternmost lake in the Ten Lakes Basin.

Grade: 3D, moderate 3-day hike

Trailhead: Same as the Hike 26 trailhead. **E4.**

Introduction: The "back door" into the Ten Lakes Basin is along this route. Since it is more than twice as long as the regular route, Hike 25, few hikers take it. Therefore, it is a route by which a backpacker escapes from the crowds. Virtually no one, however, takes this long route to the basin and then returns on it, rather, they exit west along the regular route. The total distance along it, not counting any side trips, is 22.2 miles (35.7 km)—a 5E hike.

Description: Follow **Hike 26** to May Lake, then continue along its east shore to its north shore, both of them with potential—but illegal—campsites. Stay only in the official south-shore camping area. Leaving the lake, you climb to a quickly reached shallow pass that seasonally is painted bluish purple with a field of aromatic, waist-high lupines. From the pass the trail soon begins a switchbacking descent that provides views of Cathedral Peak, standing high above Polly Dome. After about a dozen switchbacks, our descending trail's gradient eases, and in forest shade we wind southeast, crossing four seasonal creeklets before sighting Raisin Lake. Being shallow and having no icy creeks to feed it, this lakelet is one of the warmest swimming holes to be found in the Park. Being just off the trail, it is not visited all that often, which makes it even more attractive. However, should you decide to camp above its east shore before late July, be prepared to bring a tent to fend off hordes of mosquitoes.

Beyond Raisin Lake our eastbound trail soon runs into the flank of a low knoll, and heads up beside it to our second shallow pass. At it, a panorama of the High Sierra unfolds, with Mt. Conness dominating the Sierra crest. Note that Polly Dome is very *un*-domelike and rather is basically rectangular. You'll see long, straight fractures—*joints*—which govern the dome's shape and along which rows of conifers grow. Leaving the pass and its southward view of Clouds Rest, we descend some rocky switchbacks, then traverse north for ¾ mile, staying high on the slopes above Murphy Creek and its largely hidden trail (**Hike 37**). At the end of the traverse, we cross our third shallow pass in a stand of lodgepoles that obstruct a backward view of Tenaya Lake. As our trail descends north-facing slopes for ¼ mile to a junction, the forest cover becomes increasingly dominated by mountain hemlocks—trees that do well in areas of long-lasting snow cover.

At the trail junction we leave the popular High Sierra Camps loop trail (**Hike 40**), and start southwest on the seldom-used eastern part of the Ten Lakes trail. After ¼ mile the trail veers north, and as we hike in that direction, lodgepole pines, red firs and western white pines increase in numbers but then diminish as we gain altitude, giving us fair views east toward the Cathedral Range. Moderately graded switchbacks take us up to a crest saddle—a good breather stop—and then we continue up a ridge to a higher crest. A twisting traverse now confronts us as we first drop immediately to a sparkling pond—a good lunch spot—drop some more, then climb and drop and wind westward to a good overlook point high above the South Fork canyon.

Short rocky switchbacks carry you down toward the canyon floor, and then you veer south on a long contour just below a low-angle cliff, only to resume more switchbacks. The South Fork is reached in minutes, and hiking down along it, one can find suitable campsites on either side of this creek. After two miles of near-creek winding trail, you cross this creek—a wet ford in early season—go briefly downstream, then prepare for a two-dozen-switchback climb of a generally open, juniper-dotted slope. Your last chance for secluded camping is in this vicinity, just downstream from the trail.

As you perspire up the switchbacks, stop and rest and take in the ever-expanding views of northern Yosemite, from Mt. Gibbs westward, with the north wall of the mighty gorge of the Tuolumne River dominating the foreground. As the switchbacks abate, the trail enters forest shade and then climbs a mile to a seasonal pond. Beyond it, about 150 feet below us, is the large eastern lake of the Ten Lakes Basin—an area with abundant potential for camping and exploration. See **Hike 25** for a description of this basin and the trail west out from it.

From erratic boulders atop a crest in Hike 35, you can make an easy, mile-long, cross-country crest traverse south to this view of Pywiack Cascade in Tenaya Canyon. From this viewpoint, one-half mile east of Mt. Watkins, you see most of Tenaya Canyon and all of Clouds Rest.

Section 3

Trails of the Hetch Hetchy Area,
south of Highway 120

Introduction: Of all this guide's sections, this is the only one that lacks a prominent, nearby peak. It is chiefly a heavily forested uplands landscape of rolling, gentle topography. However, along this land's southern perimeter, the slopes end in steep-walled cliffs that make up the north wall of Yosemite Valley. Lacking alpine scenery, the trails in this section get only light-to-moderate use except for the stretch of trail that descends from the brink of Upper Yosemite Fall to the valley floor. Compensating for the alpine deficiencies are five spectacular viewpoints along the valley's north rim: El Capitan, Eagle Peak, the Upper Yosemite Fall brink, Yosemite Point and North Dome. Furthermore, one can study the ever-changing perspective of Half Dome along his descent into Tenaya Canyon (Hikes 34 and 35).

Two possible hiking areas not included in this chapter nevertheless deserve mention: the Tuolumne and Merced giant-sequoia groves. Most folks drive rather than hike along the one-way road through the Tuolumne grove, north of Crane Flat. In contrast, the less popular Merced grove is reached via a closed road. The trailhead is along Highway 120 some 3.7 miles west of the Crane Flat junction.

Supplies and Services: See "Supplies and Services" in Section 2.

Wilderness Permits: See "Wilderness Permits" in Section 2.

Campgrounds: All the campgrounds mentioned in the "Campgrounds" of Section 2 can be used plus the three following ones. After driving east 3⅔ miles up Highway 120 from Crane Flat, branch right immediately before Gin Flat and follow the Old Big Oak Flat Road 3 winding miles to Tamarack Flat Campground, the first of these campgrounds. This camp is best for Hikes 30 and 31. The second campground is also off the highway. Just ⅓ mile past the White Wolf road junction is a junction with the easily missed Old Tioga Road, on your right. Follow it 4¾ miles to the Yosemite Creek Campground, best for Hike 32. The last additional campground is on Highway 120 at this area's only lake, Tenaya Lake. The Tenaya Lake Walk-in Campground is 30½ miles northeast of Crane Flat and 8½ miles southwest of the Tuolumne Meadows Campground. This campground is ideal for Hikes 35 and 36 and for Section 5's Hikes 47–49. Half of its campsites are reserved through MISTIX. Porcupine Flat Campground, mentioned in the previous section, is best for Hikes 33 and 34. At all campgrounds look for a site early in the day.

Hike 29   New Big Oak Flat Road to Cascade Creek

Distance: 7.8 miles (12.6 km) round trip
Grade: 2C, strenuous half-day hike
Trailhead: From Crane Flat drive east 6 miles toward Yosemite Valley down the new Big Oak Flat Road to the Foresta turnoff, on your left, then an additional ¼ mile to the first turnout with

a Yosemite Valley view. Park there and walk back up to the Foresta road junction. **C5.**

Introduction: During the late spring, when most of Yosemite's trails are under snow, this trail is at its best. Views are few and lakes are nonexistent, so it will appeal only to those who want an invigorating yet not exhausting walk and to those who appreciate the finer details of mid-Sierran ecology.

Description: Our signed trail begins about 50 yards west of the Foresta road junction, and during spring you're likely to find a field of Stiver's lupines blooming somewhere around here. With their yellow- and pink-colored flowers, they are hard to miss. Later on, these flowers will be replaced with pea pods—typical of legumes—and the abundant nearby Mariposa manzanitas, with their gray-green leaves, will have produced berries.

The first part of our route is a climb past burned snags resulting from an August 1990 lightning-caused fire. This destroyed most of the homes in Foresta, a settlement on a granite bench below us. Originally, gold-cup oaks grew at the trailhead but they were quickly replaced up-slope by incense-cedars, ponderosa pines and black oaks. Over the ensuing years the forest will grow back, although manzanita and other fire-loving shrubs are likely to at first dominate the slopes. After a 400-foot gain we top a ridge and see El Capitan and Half Dome east of it. We climb up the ridge and then enter a white-fir forest, leaving the fire scars behind as we traverse north across slopes with deep, moist soils. About 1½ miles from the trailhead we descend to step-across Wildcat Creek, which generally flows only through spring. Next we descend to hop two of its tributaries before climbing again.

About a mile past Wildcat Creek we reach a small ridge, see the Wawona Road on the flanks of Turtleback Dome to the southeast, then immediately descend to long-lasting, fairly wide Tamarack Creek, which has room on its west bank for a small camp. Springtime visitors may find the crossing of this creek a difficult boulder-hop and may prefer to wade across it. In the next mile we climb 500 feet, mostly under the shade of white firs, sugar pines and ponderosa pines, each species locally dominating the slopes where environmental conditions are best suited to it. You might look around to see what conditions are best for each.

After your trail finally levels out, it makes a brief drop to a Cascade Creek tributary, which is boulder hopped only yards away from the Old Big Oak Flat Road. At this creek crossing, serviceberries hug the bank of a small pool fed by a splashing cascade. Once on the road, we have a brief walk down to the bridge across Cascade Creek—a good spot for a lunch break (camping prohibited). In late summer the flow of Cascade Creek is slow and warm enough for safe and enjoyable splashing around in the small pools immediately downstream. During the summer, when the road to Tamarack Flat Campground is open, you'll want to take the much shorter **Hike 30** down to Cascade Creek.

Hike 30   Tamarack Flat C.G. to Cascade Creek

Distance: 4.4 miles (7.1 km) round trip

Grade: 1B, easy half-day hike

Trailhead: From Crane Flat drive northeast 3¾ miles up Highway 120 to the Tamarack Flat Campground turnoff, immediately before the Gin Flat scenic turnout. Drive southeast down the Old Big Oak Flat Road to the east end of Tamarack Flat Campground, 3¼ miles from Highway 120. **C4.**

Introduction: Around mid-morning, Tamarack Flat Campground becomes temporarily abandoned, only to receive another flood of motorized campers in late afternoon. Take the time to enjoy the campground during the tranquil part of day, and while you're in the vicinity, you might take a few hours to make this pleasant, easy hike.

Description: Until the mid-1970s you could drive from Tamarack Flat Campground down to Cascade Creek, but now that the road is closed to motor vehicles, this stretch is a relaxing hike, one that is ideal for appreciating the peaceful forest and for reflecting on your role in nature. *Homo sapiens* is an integral part of the total biosphere, planet Earth, yet too often he tries to isolate himself from it and to dominate or destroy it. Early visitors travelling to Yosemite Valley by this road from 1874 onward thought little about man's role in nature, at least not while in their stagecoaches, which were crowded and uncomfortable. They had already traveled about 100 miles or more just to reach Tamarack Flat and still had a few more anxious miles to go.

Tamarack Flat derives its name from its extreme predominance of tamaracks, known

Cascade Creek's northwest tributary

today as lodgepole pines. However, as you leave the flats and hike across slopes on the Old Big Oak Flat Road, white firs become dominant. Along both sides of the road you'll see large, partly buried granitic boulders. These were not carried here by glaciers, as John Muir once supposed, for this local terrain was never glaciated. Instead, they developed right where you see them, being resistant enough to subsurface weathering that they finally emerged on the surface quite intact, while the adjacent, less resistant, more fractured bedrock was chemically broken down and slowly stripped away by erosion. Thus these boulders did not "grow" out of the ground, but rather, the ground around them was slowly removed—a process that took millions of years.

Just before you reach a prominent cluster of rocks—ideal for rock-climbing practice—your road begins a steady descent to Cascade Creek. At a road switchback just 240 yards before the bridge across this creek, you'll see a junction with a trail to the New Big Oak Flat Road, **Hike 29**. Down at this lower, warmer, drier elevation you'll find Jeffrey and sugar pines intermingled with the firs. Along the first 200 yards below its bridge, Cascade Creek splashes down low cascades into small pools, and in late season these make nice "swimming holes." Before then the creek is likely to be too swift for safe frolicking, particularly since the water-polished rock can be quite slippery. Rooted in this creek are large-leaved umbrella plants, and growing just beside the water's edge are creek dogwoods, willows, western azaleas and serviceberries. Huckleberry oaks crowd the dry rocks above the banks. Your day hike can be rounded out with a creekside picnic, under shady, spacious conifers, before you return to the campground.

Hike 31 El Capitan

Distance: 15.4 miles (24.8 km) round trip

Grade: 4D, strenuous day hike

Trailhead: Same as the Hike 30 trailhead. **C4.**

Introduction: The vertical walls of 3000-foot-high El Capitan attract rock climbers from all over the world, and more than five dozen extremely difficult routes ascend it. For nonclimbers this hike provides a much easier, safer way to attain El Capitan's summit, which stands only 15 feet above the north-side approach.

Description: Descend to Cascade Creek, as directed in **Hike 30**, then continue ½ mile down the Old Big Oak Flat Road—now more like a trail—to a junction with Yosemite Valley's north rim trail. Here a major climb of almost 2000 feet confronts us. Starting in a summer-warm forest of incense-cedar, ponderosa and sugar pines, and white fir, we climb hundreds of feet—steeply at times—up to drier slopes with clusters of greenleaf manzanita and huckleberry oak. Also growing in the gravelly soils are some common drought-tolerant wildflowers—streptanthus, spreading phlox, pussy paws and mat lupine. When we do re-enter the forest, it is one of white firs and Jeffrey pines. Occasionally black oaks are seen, but these diminish to shrub height as we climb higher, disappearing altogether by the time we reach a small drop on a ridge. In this vicinity chinquapins compete with huckleberry oaks, and they herald the imminent

Panorama from El Capitan: Clouds Rest and Quarter Domes, below it, above Tenaya Canyon; Half Dome; twin summits of Mts. Maclure and Lyell above Bunnell Point cliff; Little Yosemite Valley below it; Glacier Point ridge in foreground; finlike Mt. Clark above rounded Sentinel Dome, which is above and right of top of Sentinel Rock; Gray Peak above Mt. Starr King, which is just right of Sentinel Dome; Red and Merced Peaks on far right skyline.

encounter with red firs, which we find growing near the top of the crest. Lodgepoles joint in the ranks as we make a short descent from it down to a sedge-filled damp meadow that sprouts short-blooming shooting stars, marsh marigolds and other water-loving wildflowers. The meadow guides us to a crossing of a Ribbon Creek tributary, which we parallel east 1 mile down to Ribbon Creek. Ribbon Meadow, which we traverse on the first part of this descent, is more forest than meadow, and on the bark of lodge-poles you'll see blazes to guide you where the route becomes a little vague. Along the banks of Ribbon Creek are the trail's only acceptable campsites, for water runs down the creek until midsummer. Now only 1¼ miles from our goal, we make a brief climb, an equally brief descent, then an ascending traverse east to the top of El Capitan Gully. One of Yosemite Valley's first mountaineering tragedies occurred in the upper part of this gully when on June 5, 1905, Charles Bailey fell to his death. His partner, J. L. Staats, became the first known person to ascend the gully successfully. Every year a few climbers are killed on the walls of Yosemite Valley. This shouldn't happen, for rock climbing has the potential to be a very safe sport. All too often, however, it attracts reckless individuals who spurn safety precautions.

Your first views of El Capitan and the south wall of Yosemite Valley appear on this traverse to El Capitan Gully, and views continue through the sparse stand of Jeffrey pines as you climb south from the gully past dense shrubbery to a junction with the El Capitan spur trail. If you are hiking this trail in late summer, after Ribbon Creek has dried up, you may want to continue on the main trail ½ mile northeast to two trickling springs. The trail beyond them is not all that interesting, but it does get you to Eagle Peak (the long way) and to Yosemite Creek (see **Hikes 32** and **69**).

Along the spur trail south to El Capitan's broad, rounded summit, you can gaze up-canyon and identify unmistakable Half Dome, at the valley's end, barely protruding Sentinel Dome, above the valley's south wall, and fin-shaped Mt. Clark, on the skyline above the dome. Take your time exploring El Capitan's large, domed summit area, but don't stray too far from it. The summit's slopes gradually get steeper and you just might descend a little too far, then slip on loose, weathered crystals, giving you a one-way trip to the bottom. Remember that many climbing deaths occur after the triumphant party has reached the summit.

Hike 32   Highway 120 to Yosemite Valley
via Yosemite Creek

Distance: 12.8 miles (20.6 km) one way

Grade: 3C, moderate day hike

Trailhead: Same as the Hike 25 trailhead. **D4.**

Introduction: This is perhaps the best hike along which to observe the differences between two distinct landforms: steep-walled Yosemite Valley and the rolling uplands of Yosemite Creek. This route also takes you to the dramatic viewpoint at the brink of Upper Yosemite Fall with only one-third the climbing effort of Hike 68, which starts from the floor of the valley. Unfortunately, when the waterfall is at its best—before late June—snow patches and mosquitoes are prevalent along the Yosemite Creek trail.

Description: Yosemite's trails are generally so well marked that the hiker rarely needs a map or guidebook for reference. Many hikers, however, miss this trailhead and start directly south from the parking area. The correct start is to walk on the highway 120 yards west from the parking area to the signed, though easily missed, trailhead. Except perhaps for snow patches your route ahead is quite clear. Being a mid-elevation, near-creek hike, the route is dominated by lodgepoles, though red firs thrive on shady slopes and junipers and Jeffrey pines on dry, rocky ones. After a mile of rambling trail we reach and boulder hop wide Yosemite Creek.

An additional mile of walking, this one close to the creek's east bank, gets us to the north end of Yosemite Creek Campground.

Along the campground's east sites we follow a dirt road south several minutes to a junction with the Old Tioga Road, and then tread its rutted surface southwest down-canyon for ½ mile to a faltering bridge. Beyond it we soon enter the campground proper, with a telephone booth, then cross an often-sluggish tributary and in 25 yards come to a resumption of our trail. You could drive to this point and start here, saving 2¾ miles of walking. To get to it by car, start from Crane Flat and drive northeast 14½ miles up Highway 120 to the White Wolf turnoff, then an additional ⅓ mile on the highway to the easily missed junction with the Old Tioga Road. Turn right and follow its rambling course 5 miles to this Yosemite Creek Campground trailhead.

From the campground we hike south through a fairly open forest on a trail that stays a short distance from the creek, then, after 1½ miles, climbs up a ridge away from it. Glaciers advancing from Mt. Hoffmann scoured this countryside, and our route up across the bedrock ridge could be hard to follow were it not for arrows painted on the granite slabs here. Large boulders resting atop polished slabs constitutes evidence of this glaciation. From our ridge we

View down mildly glaciated Yosemite Creek canyon; the gentle topography gives no hint of the dropoff to come

can look across the canyon and see a low dome that is exfoliating—shedding slabs of granite as a giant onion might shed its layers.

Short switchbacks guide us down from the ridge, and then the trail shoots west over to three closely spaced creeks of a tributary canyon. Between the first and second is a junction with a faint trail climbing north up it (**Hike 21**). About ½ mile southeast from this junction we join the west bank of Yosemite Creek at a spot where the creek's course has migrated laterally west to abut against granitic bedrock. Small pools soon appear in the creekbed as we descend south; then, farther downstream, the pools are interspersed with water-polished slabs. None of the pools is large enough for a swim, though many are suitable for a refreshing dip. Along this section of creek you are apt to see a small campsite; then, just past it, the trail makes a short, winding drop down a low ridge, touches the creek, ducks into a small cluster of aspens, and in ¼ mile leaves all evidence of late-Pleistocene glaciation behind. Now our almost level trail hugs the creek for ⅔ mile before temporarily veering away from it to skirt around a large gravel bar. Beyond it the trail winds southeast for ½ mile, then comes to seasonal Eagle Peak Creek. A moderate-sized campsite lies between it and Yosemite Creek—worth considering since camping is illegal within ½ mile of the valley's brink.

Climbing from the shady campsite, we hike south up a gully to a divide and on it meet the Eagle Peak Trail, **Hike 69**, striking west. If you've got the time, you might make the 7-mile round trip to Eagle Peak and back. It involves only about 1000 feet of climbing, and the peak's panoramic views are certainly worth the effort. Beyond this trail junction we descend into a second gully, climb out of a third and descend to another trail junction in the fourth. All four lie in a straight line, which probably represents a major fracture in the bedrock. From this last junction, among mature Jeffrey pines, we follow the description of **Hike 68** in reverse, first climbing east, then descending south to the fenced-in viewpoint near the brink of Upper Yosemite Fall, then retracing our steps to this junction and finally descending 3 miles to the floor of Yosemite Valley.

Hike 33   North Dome

Distance: 9.6 miles (15.4 km) round trip

Grade: 2D, moderate day hike

Trailhead: From Crane Flat drive northeast 23.7 miles up Highway 120 to the Porcupine Flat Campground, then an additional 1.1 miles to a closed road, on your right, which is signed PORCUPINE CREEK. The trailhead is 2.1 miles west of the May Lake turnoff. **D4.**

Introduction: North Dome, which looks so inaccessible from the Yosemite Valley floor, can be reached in a couple of hours by this little-known route. From the dome you get perhaps the best views of the expansive faces of Half Dome and Clouds Rest, as well as excellent views of Yosemite Valley. Along this hike you can also visit one of Yosemite's few known natural arches. Another one is, surprisingly, underwater, near Tuolumne Meadows Lodge (Hike 55).

Description: Through 1976 you could drive to Porcupine Creek Campground, a primitive campground with rutted roads and overused sites, but now the road to it is closed, and down to it we walk. Just ¼ mile from Highway 120 our road becomes dirt, and here you'll notice the faint, abandoned Old Tioga Road crossing it. To the east this road goes 1.0 mile to a highway turnout that is 1.1 miles short of the May Lake turnoff, a continuation of this historic road. To the west it goes 1.2 miles to Highway 120 and the entrance to Porcupine Flat Campground, continues west through the campground and recrosses the highway in 1.0 mile, then descends 2.6 miles to the east campsites in Yosemite Creek Campground. Armed with this knowledge you can plan hiking routes that link up with May Lake and Yosemite Creek. Our obvious dirt road descends to the former site of Porcupine Creek Campground, and in the westernmost part of this site, a signed trail begins at Porcupine Creek.

Porcupine Creek and Porcupine Flat are well named, for they are located in a nearly pure stand of lodgepole pines—the favorite food of the Park's porcupines. They seem to prefer lodgepoles among all conifers because of this tree's thin bark, and they usually attack the tree's upper section, where the bark is especially thin. What they relish is the tree's soft growing tissues immediately beneath the bark. The porcupine's chief enemy is the fisher, a minklike carnivore only one fourth its size, which can swiftly attack its vulnerable, unprotected belly. Today, however, very few fishers exist in the Park, and we should expect the porcupine population to get way out of hand. Coyotes, mountain lions and bobcats are less adept at killing porcupines, and they often receive a good share of quills in their attempts. The porcupine population may be controlled by diseases and internal parasites.

From the west bank of Porcupine Creek our trail contours for a little over a mile to a junction atop a shady saddle dominated by red firs. From here a trail leads east, then south, descending 2¾ miles to a junction with the Tenaya Lake and Tuolumne Meadows trail (**Hike 35**). Just 20 yards beyond the crest of our saddle, we reach a second junction, and here a trail forking right descends 1.6 miles down along Lehamite Creek to the North Dome trail (**Hike 70**). We fork left and traverse ⅓ mile to a spur ridge with a large boulder on it, from whose top you can see Sentinel Dome. Past it we contour an equal distance, then drop to a gully before climbing steeply to a junction located only yards short of a second red-fir saddle. Veering left on a trail signed for Indian Rock, we steeply ascend it ¼ mile up brushy slopes to a delicate arch. Just over a foot thick at the thinnest part of its span, this 20-foot arch came into existence when the highly fractured rock beneath it broke away.

After investigating this curious feature, which is quite easily climbed from the west, return to the near-saddle junction, top the saddle, and head south a mile along Indian Ridge. Red firs and western white pines yield to Jeffrey pines;

The delicate arch on Indian Ridge

then, about ¼ mile from a trail junction, these pines give way to huckleberry oaks and other shrubs, and you have superb views of nearby North Dome and more distant Half Dome. Just before your descending trail comes to a junction, you'll note a large dike, composed of resistant *aplite,* standing several feet above its adjacent bedrock. At the junction with **Hike 70**, from the west, we turn left and take the ½-mile spur trail out to the bald, rounded summit of North Dome. Be careful on the first part of this trail, for a slip on loose gravel could send you sliding down a dangerously steep slope.

From the North Dome summit area, you can probably see more of Yosemite Valley and its adjacent uplands than can be seen from any other summit except Half Dome. Note how severely glaciated Tenaya Canyon, to the east, is distinctly **V**-shaped in cross section, not **U**-shaped as glaciated canyons are supposed to be. The enormous 4000-foot-high face of Clouds Rest dominates the canyon's east side, and to

Bald, exfoliating North Dome, from Indian Ridge

the south and west of it stands mighty Half Dome, perhaps Yosemite's best-remembered feature. Continuing our clockwise scan, we next recognize Mt. Starr King, a steep-sided dome above Little Yosemite Valley. West of this unseen valley is joint-controlled Panorama Cliff, which bears the scar of a large rockfall near Panorama Point, close to Illilouette Fall. Extremely popular Glacier Point stands west of the fall's gorge, and above and right of the point, Sentinel Dome bulges up into the sky. Looking down Yosemite Valley we see Sentinel Rock, with its near-vertical north face, which is due to

the unloading of slabs along the rock's near-vertical joint planes. Opposite the rock stand the Three Brothers, also shaped by joint planes, and beyond them protrudes the brow of El Capitan, opposite the Cathedral Rocks. Note the broad, gentle surface north of El Capitan, a surface that has changed but little in at least the last 50 million years. It and the other upland surfaces strongly contrast with Yosemite Valley, which has undergone considerable excavation in the last few million years. Before leaving North Dome, investigate some of its exfoliating slabs—features common to all of Yosemite's domes.

Hike 34   Highway 120 to Mirror Meadow via Snow Creek

Distance: 8.2 miles (13.1 km) one way

Grade: 2A, moderate half-day hike

Trailhead: At a Highway 120 parking area immediately east of a roadcut through a signed glacial moraine, 0.6 mile east of the May Lake turnoff and 3.1 miles west of the Tenaya Lake Walk-in Campground. **D4.**

Introduction: Three trails converge in Snow Creek canyon before uniting to descend to Mirror Meadow: one comes from Porcupine Creek and North Dome (Hikes 33 and 70), another from Tenaya Lake (Hike 35), and this one, which is the shortest, from Highway 120. Hikers who want to descend from Tuolumne Meadows to Yosemite Valley via May Lake and Mirror Meadow can follow Hike 40 past Glen Aulin to May Lake, then follow Hike 26 in reverse to the May Lake trailhead. Opposite this trailhead a little-used trail descends southwest for 2¼ miles to Highway 120, from where you follow this route, Hike 34, down to Mirror Meadow (total length: 25.6 miles, or 41.2 km).

Description: You can't ask for a better glacial moraine to examine than the one immediately east of our trailhead, where Highway 120 cuts through the crest of a lateral moraine. Note its characteristic composition, a gravelly, unsorted matrix containing boulders of all sizes. Were these combined sediments stream-laid, then we would see sorting, or layering, of gravels and boulders.

With a rating of only 2A you might expect this hike to be an easy one, but it is rated moderate because of its 4000+ foot descent. The trail, a continuation of one from May Lake, starts from Highway 120 just by the west side of a nearby

closed road that goes 250 yards south to a heliport. From this dirt road our trail climbs west to the crest of the lateral moraine, turns south on it and goes past red firs and western white pines that bear "blazes" in the form of old license plates. After about a half-mile crest traverse we come to a giant trailside boulder, called an *erratic,* which was dropped on this moraine's crest by an even higher glacier. The glacier, descending the canyon immediately east of us, must have been at least 700 feet thick, and we can appreciate its power by marveling at the size of this particular erratic, which weighs at least 100 tons.

Before leaving the boulder you might note unmistakable Cathedral Peak, to the east, and the Echo Peaks, just south of it. After hiking a couple of minutes past the boulder, our route begins a wandering, 2-mile, 1000-foot drop to a junction with a trail from Tenaya Lake. The remaining 5.4 miles (8.6 km) coincide with **Hike 35** and are described in it.

A large erratic; clipboard indicates size

Hike 35   Tenaya Lake to Mirror Meadow
via Snow Creek

Distance: 11.3 miles (18.1 km) one way

Grade: 3B, moderate day hike

Trailhead: On Highway 120 at the Tenaya Lake Walk-in Campground entrance, which is 30½ miles northeast of Crane Flat and 8½ miles southwest of the Tuolumne Meadows Campground. **E4.**

Introduction: When linked with the Highway 120 trail (see Hike 50), this hike provides the shortest route from Tuolumne Meadows to Yosemite Valley, only 19.8 miles (31.9 km). Though not nearly as scenic as Hike 49, Hike 35 is shorter and considerably easier, making it best for an unacclimated hiker.

Description: From the southern, larger entrance to the Tenaya Lake Walk-in Campground, start east on the camp's short road and take the first spur trail you see that heads south through the lodgepoles to the edge of a nearby meadow. Along its edge is the main trail, which goes to the Sunrise Lakes and Sunrise High Sierra Camp, and connects with other trails to Clouds Rest, Happy Isles, Tuolumne Meadows and other destinations. On this main trail we make a traverse southwest across the sometimes boggy meadow for ½ mile before coming to a junction with a little-used spur trail that goes ¼ mile north to Highway 120. Along this meadow traverse we get backward glances of Polly Dome, rising above the dense lodgepoles that ring our meadow. Few wildflowers are seen in this typical Sierran meadow; rather, it is dominated by sedges and dwarf bilberries. The latter aren't obvious until

Clouds Rest in late afternoon

late August, when they turn a blazing crimson color.

From the spur-trail junction we walk south ¼ mile along the west edge of a meadow; then, after another ¼ mile past lodgepoles, we cross a head-high glacial moraine and momentarily spy a knee-deep pond, with no legal or desirable camping, just 60 yards east of us. Beyond it our trail begins to climb, and in a small clearing we can look back and see distant Mt. Conness between Polly and Medlicott "domes," neither of them domes, and steep-sided Tenaya Peak, rising high above the east shore of Tenaya Lake.

Beyond this clearing we enter a forest, now containing numerous mountain hemlocks, and climb, ultimately by short switchbacks, up to a gap that lies immediately below perhaps the most popular scenic turnout along Highway 120. The turnout, Olmsted Point, is 130 yards north of us, and it provides a view northeast toward stirring Tenaya Lake, and a view south towards Clouds Rest and Half Dome. At the turnout Clark's nutcrackers—oversized jays— are often seen begging tourists for handouts. South from our gap a little-used nature trail goes 170 yards to the top of a low, glaciated knoll that offers a better view of Clouds Rest and Half Dome than that obtained from the scenic turnout. Atop this low knoll, partly clothed with scattered lodgepole, western white and Jeffrey pines, are erratic boulders left behind as a glacier retreated up-canyon 14,000 years ago.

The next ½ mile of trail west from the gap is an incredibly winding one, for the trail avoids many bedrock protruberances and one overhanging cliff. Beyond these our erratic-strewn course tops a low crest, then begins to veer away from nearby Highway 120 as we switchback down into a forested, damp-floored canyon with plenty of corn lilies, arrowhead butterweeds, lupines and moisture-loving wildflowers. Our westbound trail crosses two ephemeral creeks, then angles southwest and descends this glaciated canyon—rich in mosquitoes before August—for a mile before climbing 300 feet up to a crest. Erratic boulders atop it testify to the presence of a past glacier, and the huge, ice-smoothed southeast wall of Tenaya Canyon, opposite us, adds further evidence. Following our trail's painted metal markers—nailed high on conifers for snowbound travelers—we switchback down into a forested side canyon, traversing below two smooth-sloped domes before arriving at a junction with a trail from May Lake (**Hike 34**). Around this junction white firs begin to compete with red firs for space, and Jeffrey pines, with us for some time now, become more numerous.

Switchbacks drop us well into Snow Creek canyon and then we head south for a mile, dropping 500 feet to campsites under white firs along the banks of Snow Creek. While chick-arees (Douglas squirrels) live in red firs higher up, down here western gray squirrels are more likely, living in white firs. About 1987, a fire raged through the creek's drainage basin. However, most firs survived even though many trunks were blackened. From the several camp-sites the trail bridges the reliable creek, starts down-canyon, and in 140 yards comes to a junc-tion with a trail. This trail first follows the west bank of Snow Creek before veering west to meet the Porcupine Creek-North Dome trail (**Hike 33**). From the junction our southbound trail traverses for ⅓ mile through a forest of white firs, Jeffrey pines and—surprisingly—ponderosa pines before emerging on more-open slopes to begin a nine-dozen switchback descent to the floor of Tenaya Canyon, ½ mile below us. Our first views of course include the massive north-west face of Half Dome plus short-lived views of Watkins Pinnacles, to the east, and the top of Mt. Clark, behind Half Dome.

About a dozen switchbacks down, we enter a gully and encounter a small community of trees that include—surprisingly again—Douglas-firs, which usually aren't found up at this elevation (6300 feet) and particularly not on south-facing slopes. Our trail continues down this gully for another 40 switchbacks, many of them oblit-erated in an April 1987 rockslide, then rebuilt. We then strike across a dry slope that provides ground for Mariposa manzanitas and season-ally blooming wildflowers such as the brilliantly colored wavy-leaved paintbrush and the equally colorful showy penstemon. Among rocks here is bird's foot fern, specially adapted—unlike most ferns—to this hot, dry environment.

Clouds Rest and Half Dome continue to dominate our views as we switchback down even lower, and we also take note of Tenaya Creek plunging over a long vertical wall. Near the canyon's bottom our trail passes by a cliff that has a blocky, fractured aplite dike running along it. Similar dikes are all-important to climbers ascending certain routes on Half Dome and Pywiack Dome. Beneath this cliff our trail enters a forest dominated by gold-cup oaks. Also in it, however, are bay trees, easily identi-fied by the aroma given off from the crushed leaves. On the floor of Tenaya Canyon, near the wide, bouldery bed of Tenaya Creek, our trail meets the Tenaya Canyon loop trail (**Hike 67**), and on it we walk a fairly level 1.1 miles west to our trail's end, beside a parking area of a now-closed road, just above the west edge of Mirror Meadow (formerly it existed as Mirror Lake—see **Hike 66**). Be aware that there is no trail-head parking here; the closest is a large lot at Camp Curry, about 1½ miles away.

Hike 36   Tenaya Lake Loop

Distance: 3.1 miles (4.9 km) loop trip

Grade: 1A, easy 2-hour hike

Trailhead: Same as the Hike 35 trailhead. **E4.**

Introduction: This is an easy hike around Yose-mite's most popular glacial lake, scenic Tenaya Lake. Here you'll find swimming, sunbathing, fishing and, surprisingly, sailing.

Description: A road heads east from the south-western Walk-in Campground entrance, and walking along it we soon cross the usually flowing outlet of Tenaya Lake. Immediately beyond this crossing a trail forks right, heading to a nearby trail junction (**Hike 47**), but we keep to the road and walk over to the lake's bouldery southwest shore. The boulders were left here by a Tioga-age glacier that retreated up-canyon about 14,000 years ago. Along with preceding glaciers, it helped carve the bedrock basin now occupied by the lake. The surrounding land-scape has acquired its soils and vegetative cover only since the last glacier left the area. It used to be thought that since that time, incoming sedi-ments had filled in up to ¼ of the lake's original surface area, creating the gently sloping lands just northeast of the lake. However, as one can observe, the rate of sediment influx is very minor and so the lake's size has diminished very little in the last 14,000 years. One can also conclude from the minor amount of talus at the base of Polly Dome that it too has changed very little during this time.

If you plan to go swimming in chilly Tenaya Lake, do so at the bouldery southwest shore. The sandy beach of the northeast shore is lacking here, but so too are the strong up-canyon

Mammoth Polly Dome, seen from Tenaya Lake's outlet, looms over the lake and dwarfs
Pywiack Dome, just right of it. From near the lake's north shore, Pywiack Dome (below)
seems quite large.

winds that were needed to form it. Besides, here
you'll find a few small boulder islands worth
swimming or wading to—something lacking
near the northeast shore.

From the lake's southeast corner head a few
yards upslope to a trail and walk northeast one
mile on it to the sandy beach at the north shore.
On this stretch of trail you'll have, as at the south
shore, great views of massive Polly Dome and
small Pywiack Dome, and you'll also have
several opportunities to descend to Tenaya
Lake's little-used east shore. Climbers have
divided what is commonly called Polly Dome
into four domes, from south to north: Stately
Pleasure, Harlequin, Mountaineer's and Polly
domes. None of these four is a true dome, and
only from certain angles does any appear domelike. Skirting the bases of these domes is the
rather new Highway 120, which was opened to
the public in June 1961. Although the road
made the domes' climbing routes readily accessible, climbers avoided them, for they were too
busy with their "gold mine" on the walls of
Yosemite Valley, which provided fame—though
not fortune—to those who could tally an impressive number of first ascents. By the late 1960s,
however, most of the Valley's "easier" climbs
had been done, and climbers concentrated for a
few years on the "Tuolumne Domes," which
include domes of the Tenaya Lake area.

If you were to continue north on the trail
rather than cut across the beach toward Stately
Pleasure Dome, you would reach a junction with
the John Muir Trail (**Hike 50**) in about 6.9 miles
(11.1 km). This stretch of generally viewless,
lodgepole-shaded trail is little used, but when it
is combined with **Hike 35**, it provides the
shortest route from Tuolumne Meadows to
Yosemite Valley, only 19.8 miles (31.9 km).

The Mirror Meadow-Tenaya Lake trail section
approximates the route taken by Captain Bowling
and his 35 men in search of Chief Ten-ie-ya's
band. In early June 1852 they surprised this
band at Py-wi-ack—"Lake of the Glistening
(glacier-polished) Rocks." This lake was named
by Lafayette Bunnell in memory of the old chief,
and before departing for an Indian reservation,
both Indians and troops spent the night in what is
now the west side of today's Walk-in Campground.

Whereas the south shore is best for swimming,
the north shore, with its broad, sandy beach, is
best for sunbathing. On a hot summer afternoon
it is crowded with people, and the parking lot,
picnic tables and restrooms just north of it are all
full. Leaving the beach we walk southwest along
Highway 120, which cuts across the base of
glacier-polished Stately Pleasure Dome. On
this dome you're likely to see climbers inching
upward hundreds of feet above you. The highway
curves west to Murphy Creek, which has a trail
ascending beside it (**Hike 37**). Then we continue southwest, passing many day-use picnic
sites before reaching the spot where we began.

Calm before the storm: The Cathedral Range "rises" out of Middle Gaylor Lake

Section 4

Trails of the Tuolumne Meadows
Area, north of Highway 120

Introduction: Although this section generally describes trails lying north and west of Tuolumne Meadows, it also describes two that extend beyond this regional area. Hike 40, the High Sierra Camps Loop trail, wanders more than half of its length in the country south of the highway and Hike 42, the northbound Pacific Crest Trail, goes through the Park and then winds over to Sonora Pass. Hike 42, at 72 miles, is the longest one described in this guide; Hike 38, at about ½ mile, is the shortest. Between these two extremes you'll find a hiking length ideal for you as you explore this subalpine wonderland. This section's highlights are too numerous to mention. Of all its hikes, only Hike 37 would not receive a spectacular rating. Ragged peaks, crystal-clear lakes, glaciated domes, long canyons and roaring cascades await the High Sierra hiker here.

Supplies and Services: Information, guide books, natural-history books and topographic maps are available at the Tuolumne Meadows Information Center, which is 7½ miles northeast up Highway 120 from the Tenaya Lake Walk-in Campground and an even 8 miles southwest down it from Tioga Pass. About one mile east of the center is the Tuolumne Meadows store, which has a well-stocked supply of food and camping gear. Fishing needs are also met. Also here are a small cafe, a post office, and the Mountain Sports Center, where climbing gear can be bought and lessons arranged for. The Tuolumne Meadows Stable provides sightseeing for those wanting to stay closer to the ground. Rides available are ½ day, full day, 4 day and 6 day. You'll find the stable at the end of a spur road starting west from the base of Lembert Dome, just east of the highway bridge over the river. This road angles right at a closed gate.

Those wanting to stay in the Tuolumne Meadows area in a rustic style should stay at Tuolumne Meadows Lodge. To reach it, drive 0.6 mile northeast on Highway 120 from the campground entrance, then turn right on the lodge's spur road and follow it to its end. Accommodations at the lodge consist of canvas tents on wooden platforms. Breakfast and dinner are served here, and you can get them without being a guest. On weekends, however, reserve your spot at the dinner table early in the day. Showers are also available; inquire at the office.

Just 2 miles outside the Park, you'll find the Tioga Pass Resort, with some supplies, meals and lodging—an alternative to the crowded Tuolumne Meadows area. This resort is usually open from late May until mid-October. Most of the Tuolumne Meadows facilities are open for a shorter duration, usually from mid-June until mid-September. The Tuolumne Meadows Campground and the Information Center stay open a few weeks longer. All-year services are available in Lee Vining, just north of Highway 120's junction with Highway 395. This town is about 19½ miles from the Tuolumne Meadows Campground.

Wilderness Permits: Get your permit at a booth in the parking lot a short way down the Tuolumne Meadows Lodge spur road. From late June through the Labor Day weekend this booth is open on Friday nights, and it opens as early as 6 a.m. on Saturdays. After the Labor Day weekend, get your permits at the Information Center.

Campgrounds: For Hike 37, camp at the Tenaya Lake Walk-in Campground, on Highway 120, 8.5 miles southwest from Tuolumne Meadows Campground. This walk-in camp is also ideal for Section 5's Hikes 47-49. For the remaining hikes, camp at large Tuolumne Meadows Campground, whose entrance is just southwest of the Tuolumne River bridge. You may also want to try Tioga Lake and Junction campgrounds, just outside the Park below Tioga Pass, but these are small and usually full.

Hike 37   Polly Dome Lakes

Distance: 6.2 miles (10.0 km) round trip to the largest lake

Grade: 2B, easy day hike

Trailhead: Across from a picnic area midway along Tenaya Lake. Driving northeast on Highway 120 you come to this trailhead just 0.6 mile northeast of the lake's walk-in campground. **E4.**

Introduction: This hike is for those who want to visit a readily accessible lake that isn't being visited by everyone else. A small amount of cross-country hiking is required, but you don't have to be an expert to do it. As long as you don't cross over any divide, you can't really get lost, for if you can't find this fairly large lake, you can always head back down-canyon—back toward Tenaya Lake—and find your trail again.

Description: Our trail, up seasonally flowing Murphy Creek, climbs three miles north to a junction with the High Sierra Camps Loop Trail (**Hike 40**). We take this uneventful trail most of

the way, passing a bridge across Murphy Creek early on our hike. The trail south from it descends to within a few yards of the western of the two Tenaya Lake Walk-in Campgrounds.

Midway along our hike is ample evidence of glacier action: glacier-transported boulders and glacier-polished bedrock slabs. Across these slabs the trail can disappear, so watch for ducks (man-made stone piles). Near the divide at the head of Murphy Creek you'll reach a trailside pond, on your right. Leave the trail here and progress cross-country ½ mile southeast to the north shore of the largest of the Polly Dome Lakes. Any cross-country route you might take will tend to get a little damp and/or brushy, but the distance is short and the lake is almost impossible to miss, particularly since it lies at the base of Polly Dome. The best campsites are along the west shore of this warm, shallow, boulder-dotted lake. The small lakes northeast of it aren't worth your effort unless you happen to like mosquitoes.

Mt. Hoffmann, right, pokes above lodgepoles encircling the largest of the Polly Dome Lakes

Hike 38   Pothole Dome

Distance: Approximately 0.5 mile (0.8 km) round trip

Grade: 1A, easy one-hour hike

Trailhead: Turnout at west end of Tuolumne Meadows, 1½ miles west from the Tuolumne Meadows Information Center. **E3.**

Introduction: Pothole Dome is Yosemite's most accessible dome, and its upper slopes provide outstanding views of Tuolumne Meadows and the surrounding peaks and domes.

Description: More people climb this dome than any other in the Park except perhaps Lembert Dome (**Hike 45**) or Sentinel Dome (**Hike 74**). Because the dome's slopes aren't very steep and don't look very high, some High Sierra novices are tempted to run up them. This usually results in altitude sickness, due to the rarified air found at this elevation. Take your time.

Like Lembert Dome and most other Yosemite domes, Pothole Dome has gentle up-canyon slopes and steep down-canyon slopes. On this dome, glaciers repeatedly planed down the east slopes but plucked away at the west ones. Glacial evidence includes slopes of highly polished bedrock plus anomalous boulders—*erratics*—resting on them, which could have reached their present locations only by glacier transport. Pothole Dome differs from other domes in the great number of potholes it has, particularly on its south slopes. Potholes are usually found in streams, where boulders swirl around in a bedrock depression and gradually drill out a hole. Obviously, streams did not flow up over Pothole Dome, but glaciers did. Richard Balogh, studying these potholes in 1975, concluded that the potholes were formed by flowing watercourses trapped beneath a glacier, and these courses did flow uphill over the dome.

Another interesting geologic feature is the presence of large, blocky crystals of potassium feldspar that are so characteristic of this hiking section's landscape. About 80-85 million years ago these crystals solidified just before the molten matrix surrounding them solidified. The resulting large-scale granite body that formed is known as the Cathedral Peak pluton, and it covers much of the Yosemite landscape in Sections 4 and 5.

Author in large pothole on Pothole Dome

From Pothole Dome: Clouds build over Tuolumne Meadows and the Sierra crest

Hike 39   Tuolumne Meadows to Glen Aulin

Distance: 11.4 miles (18.3 km) round trip

Grade: 3C, easy 2-day hike

Trailhead: At the base of Lembert Dome, at the east end of Tuolumne Meadows, leave Highway 120 and drive ⅓ mile west on a dirt road to a gate that bars it. If no space is available here, park at the base of Lembert Dome. Mileage is counted from the start of the closed road. **F3.**

Introduction: Scenically, this popular hike is noted for the many beautiful cascades it passes. Because the hike is virtually all downhill, it is ideal for hikers unaccustomed to high elevations. Spending a night at Glen Aulin gets you partly acclimated, preparing you for the hike back up to your trailhead. This trail comprises the easiest section of the High Sierra Camps loop trail (**Hike 40**). It is also a section of the Pacific Crest and Tahoe-Yosemite trails.

Description: From the locked gate we continue west along the lodgepole-dotted flank of Tuolumne Meadows, with fine views south across the meadows of Unicorn Peak, Cathedral Peak and some of the knobby Echo Peaks. Approaching a boulder-rimmed old parking loop, we veer right and climb slightly past the old Soda Springs Campground, which once surrounded the still-bubbling natural soda springs. From here the sandy trail undulates through a forest of sparse, small lodgepole pines, and then descends to a boulder ford of Delaney Creek. Just before the ford, the stock trail from the stables back in the meadows comes in on the right. Immediately beyond the ford we hop a branch of Delaney Creek, hop another in 1/6 mile, and in 1/6 mile more pass the Young Lakes trail (**Hike 44**).

White Cascade plunges into a churning pool

At this junction our route goes left, and after more winding through scattered lodgepoles, it descends some bare granite slabs and enters level, cool forest. A half mile's pleasant walking in this shade brings us to the bank of the Tuolumne River, just before three branches of Dingley Creek, near the west end of the huge meadows. From here, the nearly level trail often runs along the river, and in these stretches by the stream, there are numerous glacier-smoothed granite slabs on which to take a sunny break.

After a mile-long winding contour, we climb briefly up a granite outcrop to get around the river's gorge. On the south side of the gorge below you is Little Devils Postpile, a dark plug of basalt that was forced up through the adjacent Cathedral Peak granodiorite 9.4 million years ago. Despite repeated attacks by glaciers, this intrusion remains. Now we descend on individual stones carefully fitted together, down toward a sturdy bridge over the river. There is camping space on the south side of the river here, but to camp here is illegal, since you are within 4 trail miles of Tuolumne Meadows. From this locale, however, you can hike upriver to Little Devils Postpile.

Immediately beyond the bridge we can look north up long Cold Canyon to Matterhorn Peak and Whorl Mountain, and, to their right, Mt. Conness. The trail then dips through several glades brightened by Labrador-tea flowers and corn lilies. As the river approaches Tuolumne Falls, it flows down a series of sparkling rapids separated by large pools and wide sheets of water spread out across slightly inclined granite slopes. Beyond this beautiful stretch of river the trail descends, steeply at times, past Tuolumne Falls and the White Cascade to a junction with the trail to May Lake (**Hike 40**). From here it is only a few minutes' walk to Glen Aulin Camp, reached by crossing the river on a bridge below roaring White Cascade. In early season, you may have to wade just to reach this bridge!

Just north of the camp is the heavily used Glen Aulin backpackers' campground. Only 15 yards beyond the spur trail across Conness Creek to Glen Aulin High Sierra Camp is the Tuolumne Canyon trail, going left, and ⅓ mile down it are less-used campsites. Bears, however, can be more of a problem here, since it is easier to protect your food at the Glen Aulin site, because the hikers' camp has a "bearproof goalpost" and the High Sierra Camp stores food for a fee. **Hike 41** continues westward.

Hike 40   High Sierra Camps Loop

Distance: 50.4 miles (81.2 km) loop trip

Grade: 7F, moderate 6-day hike

Trailhead: Several possibilities. We recommend the large parking lot just beyond the start of the Tuolumne Meadows Lodge spur road. This road is reached by driving ½ mile northeast from the Tuolumne Meadows Campground entrance. During *most* of the summer this large lot, immediately west of the spur road, has a small booth that dispenses wilderness permits. **F3.**

Introduction: This hike has become very popular, and quota to limit the number of hikers using it is often filled. Therefore, if you plan to hike it, make reservations well in advance or do it out of season, such as after the Labor Day weekend. However, if you are hiking it then, don't expect to find the High Sierra Camps open, and do plan for the possibility of sudden snow storms and know what to do if you're caught in one.

Description: Along this loop are six High Sierra Camps, each spaced a convenient day's hike from the next. Many visitors make this loop on horseback. Others hike the trail carrying little more than a day pack, for by making advanced reservations—best done in January—they can get all their meals and sleep at the camps.

From your parking lot a wide trail—an abandoned road—heads west to Highway 120 and its westside Lembert Dome parking lot. Now follow **Hike 39** west 6 miles down the Tuolumne River to campsites at Glen Aulin, the place most hikers spend their first night.

The second day's hike will be from the Glen Aulin High Sierra Camp to the May Lake High Sierra Camp, about 8½ miles. From the junction immediately south of and above Glen Aulin's bridge across the Tuolumne River, you curve northwest through a notch and then your duff trail ascends gently southwest, soon crossing and recrossing McGee Lake's *northeast*-flowing outlet, which dries up by late summer. Where the trail levels off, McGee Lake, long and narrow and bordered on the southwest by a granite cliff, comes into view through the lodgepole trees. The dead snags along the shallow margin, and the fallen limbs and downed trees make fishing difficult, and in late summer the lake may dwindle to a stale pond. Camping is best at its south end.

Beyond the lake our trail descends along its *southwest*-flowing outlet for ¾ mile, crosses this stream, and in ¼ mile reaches a tributary of Cathedral Creek. From here we have a view down the shallow granite canyon to hulking Falls Ridge, which this creek has to detour around in order to join the Tuolumne River. A few hundred yards beyond this ford is a boulder-hop ford of 20-foot-wide Cathedral Creek, which runs all year. On the moderate ascent beyond the creek, we soon reach a stand of tall, healthy red firs, and the contrast with the small, overcrowded lodgepole pines earlier on the trail is inescapable.

Higher on the trail, there are good views, and after three miles of walking through moderate and dense forest, the panorama seems especially welcome. In the distant northeast stand Sheep Peak, North Peak and Mt. Conness, guarding the basin of Roosevelt Lake. In the near north, Falls Ridge is a mountain of pinkish granite that challenges the white and gray granite of the other peaks. When we look back toward McGee Lake, the route appears to be entirely carpeted with lodgepole pines.

Our trail continues up a moderate slope on gravel and granite shelves, through a forest cover of hemlock, red fir and lodgepole. After arriving at a branch of Cathedral Creek, we cross it, then more or less parallel it for almost a mile to a junction shaded under some tall hemlocks. A trail departs from this junction to go down Murphy Creek to Tenaya Lake (**Hike 37**). Down this trail, a short ½ mile before the lake, a lateral trail departs southwest, parallels Highway 120, and ends at a bend in the highway between the two Tenaya Lake Walk-in Campgrounds.

Mt. Conness reflected in McGee Lake

Polly Dome and Tenaya Peak hem in Tenaya Lake

A half mile from the hemlock-shaded junction, we pass a trail (**Hike 28**) to Ten Lakes that climbs slopes beneath the very steep east face of Tuolumne Peak. Here we branch left and ascend briefly to a long, narrow, shallow, forested saddle beyond which large Tenaya Lake is visible in the south. After traversing somewhat open slopes of sagebrush, huckleberry oak and lupine, we reach a spring with a manmade water basin, then momentarily come to a series of switchbacks. Our progress up the long, gentle gradient of these zigzags is distinguished by the striking views of Mt. Conness, Mt. Dana and the other giants on the Sierra crest/Yosemite border. The trail then passes through a little saddle just north of a glacier-smoothed peak, and ahead, suddenly, is another Yosemite landmark, Clouds Rest, rising grandly in the south: we are looking at part of the largest expanse of bare granite in the Park.

Now our trail descends gradually over fairly open granite to a forested flat and bends west above the north shore of Raisin Lake, which is one of the warmest "swimming holes" in this section. It also has pleasant campsites, and some hikers might want to purify the water. From the lake view, we walk beside a flower-lined runoff stream bed under a sparse forest cover of mountain hemlock and western white and lodgepole pines, and then swing west to ford three unnamed streams (if it's still early season; otherwise they will be dry).

Finally our trail makes the last ½-mile steep ascent to May Lake up a slope sparsely dotted with red firs, western white pines and other conifers. Views improve constantly as we breathe more heavily, and presently we have a panorama of the peaks on the Sierra crest from North Peak to Mt. Gibbs. The Tioga Pass notch is clearly visible. At the top of this climb is a gentle upland where several small meadows are strung along the trail, with turgid corn lilies growing at an almost perceptible rate in early season, while aromatic lupine commands our attention later on. In the west, Mt. Hoffmann is entirely dominant. A little awed by it, we swing south past the backpackers' campsites at the northeast corner of May Lake and down along the east shore to the High Sierra Camp, where we meet the trail of **Hike 26**.

From the lake you follow **Hike 26**, described in the opposite direction, south to the May Lake trailhead. From here you follow the paved road northeast for two minutes to where it is blocked off, then descend the abandoned dirt road southeast to Highway 120. Cross the highway and follow a trail which parallels this noisy route to the Tenaya Lake Walk-in Campground. Now follow **Hike 47** up to Sunrise High Sierra Camp, where you spend your third night. This leg of the loop is about 9 miles long. Leaving the camp, tread the John Muir Trail a short mile, first east and then north to the Echo Creek trail, described in **Hike 52**. Take this lateral trail 6½ miles down Echo Creek to a trail junction, from which you descend ¾ mile to the Merced Lake trail, in Echo Valley. Now you first pass through a burned-but-boggy area, then climb east past the Merced River's largely unseen but enjoyable pools to Merced Lake's west shore. Don't camp here, but rather continue past the north shore to Merced Lake High Sierra Camp and the adjacent riverside campground, a little less than 10 miles from Sunrise High Sierra Camp. The bear population here is high, but there are bearproof boxes in which you can store your food.

Begin day five by hiking an early level mile east to the Merced Lake Ranger Station and an adjacent trail junction. From it you struggle 1¼ miles in a 1000-foot climb northeast up to another trail junction, from where you follow the second half of **Hike 56** back to your trailhead. If at the end of day five you plan to camp at or near Vogelsang High Sierra Camp rather than at Boothe Lake, turn right at the scissors junction near Emeric Lake and hike 2⅓ miles northeast up to the camp. Emeric Lake also makes a good last night's stay.

Hike 41   Tuolumne Meadows to Pate Valley

Distance: 40.4 miles (65.0 km) round trip

Grade: 6F, moderate 4-day hike

Trailhead: Same as the Hike 39 trailhead. **F3.**

Introduction: Rather than take Hike 22 to Pate Valley, you can take this route, which is longer but more spectacular. On it a lot of hikers go no farther than Waterwheel Falls, which at 3½ trail miles from Glen Aulin is the westernmost of the Tuolumne River's five major cascades. Go before mid-July to see the "waterwheels" at their best. Horseback riders should check with rangers if they intend to travel beyond Waterwheel Falls; there may be an early-season high-water problem.

Description: Follow **Hike 39** to Glen Aulin, which is the usual first-night's camp even though it is only ⅓ the distance to Pate Valley. Then, starting from Glen Aulin High Sierra Camp, we see the White Cascade, which tumultuously splashes into a swirling pool. The camp's sandy beach bordering the pool is periodically built up with fresh sand and gravel at times of very high runoff. Just 15 yards past the entrance to the camp, our lateral trail leaves the northbound Cold Canyon trail and climbs over a low knoll that sports rust-stained metamorphic rocks. From it we get an excellent view west down the flat-floored, steep-walled canyon. It looks like a glaciated canyon should look: U-shaped in cross section. However, the flat, broad Tuolumne Meadows vicinity upstream and the V-shaped Grand Canyon of the Tuolumne River downstream were also glaciated and are certainly not U-shaped. In Yosemite it is the joint (fracture) pattern of the resistant granitic bedrock that determines the canyon's shape, not the process of glaciation, which in weaker rocks determines the shape.

Leaving the knoll, we switchback quickly down into Glen Aulin proper. Paralleling the Tuolumne River through a lodgepole-pine forest, we soon reach a backpackers' camp that has a "bearproof goalpost" on which you can hang your food. Also, you might store your food at the High Sierra Camp even though they charge you for this service. We tread the gravelly flat floor of the glen for more than a mile, and then, on bedrock, quickly arrive at the brink of cascading California Falls, perched at the base of a towering cliff. Keep your distance from these falls and from any part of the falls you'll see downstream. Even the lower part of a cascade is

dangerous, and just because the adjacent bedrock is dry, that doesn't mean it is safe—the bedrock is polished to a very high degree. Don't lose your life as too many others have.

Switchbacking down beside the cascade, we leave behind the glen's thick forest of predominantly lodgepole pines with associated red firs and descend past scattered Jeffrey pines and junipers and through lots of brush. At the base of the cascade, lodgepoles, western white pines and red firs return once more as we make a gentle descent north. Near the end of this short stretch we parallel a long pool, which is a good spot to break for lunch or perhaps take a swim. However, stay away from the pool's outlet, where the Tuolumne River plunges over a brink.

Our trail parallels this second cascade as it generally descends through brush and open forest. On this descent we notice that red firs have yielded to white firs. Sugar pines also put in their first appearance as we reach the brink of broad LeConte Falls, which cascades down fairly open granite slabs. On the flat-floored section of canyon, incense-cedar joins the ranks of white fir, Jeffrey pine and sugar pine, with few, if any, lodgepoles to be found. In this forest we reach our fifth and final cascade, extensive Waterwheel Falls. This cascade gets its name from the curving sprays of water thrown up into the air, which occur when the river is flowing with sufficient force. It is worth the trip in early season to see the white water turning to rainbow as it sprays the canyon full of light and color. The cascade's classic views are not from its brink but rather from near its base, about 300 feet lower. Starting on a trail segment recommended by John Muir and completed in 1925, we follow switchbacks down to the cascade's base, then continue to descend past a smaller set of cascades, beyond which you reach a small campsite beside a Tuolumne River pool. About 200 yards past it a larger campsite is reached, this one located by the east bank of Return Creek. On the map Return Creek up Virginia Canyon looks like a good cross-country tour, but in reality it is overgrown with huckleberry oak and other shrubs, making an ascent up it a hot, dusty experience.

Just past Return Creek you'll note a swimming hole between two low cascades—one of many possible swimming holes you'll see before reaching Pate Valley. Unfortunately, these pools are best in August, but if you go then, the river's

Waterwheel Falls reaches its full glory in early summer

flow has diminished sufficiently to make Waterwheel Falls just an ordinary cascade. Upon descending to lower elevations—now characterized largely by incense-cedars, black oaks and gold-cup oaks—late-season hikers in particular face pesky hordes of flies. Continuing down-canyon, we pass a massive south-wall cliff before coming to a fair campsite, and then in ½ mile we cross a low ridge. During most of the summer the afternoon temperature at our now-lower elevations is distinctly warm, if not hot, but most of our route is shaded and the Tuolumne River is usually close by for dipping. At these elevations ground squirrels and other rodents abound, so rattlesnakes are likely too. At first our route is along a shady, flat-floored valley into which only a minimal amount of talus has fallen in about the last 14,000 years—the time when the last glacier retreated up this canyon. After a mile, we begin a curve north around the base of a half-mile-high buttress, and here see, to the southwest, the twin-ribbed buttress of Colby Mountain, standing on the west rim of the Ten Lakes Basin. Experienced climbers have successfully descended from that basin to our trail, but others have been less fortunate.

Beyond this buttress the Tuolumne River trail begins a climb up and around the Muir Gorge. Under shade it climbs 400 feet to a viewless subsidiary ridge, arcs counterclockwise across fairly open slabs to a larger ridge, and then switchbacks up to its crest. On that crest the trail surprisingly encounters a low, joint-controlled trough, which obstructs views, although imme-

diately east, west and south of it are excellent ones. You can now look south straight up the deeply glaciated, plunging Ten Lakes canyon. Our climb down-canyon is not yet over, for we descend two dozen switchbacks—a 500-foot drop—only to climb again. This climb, however, is short-lived, and we very quickly pass through a notch, which has been cleft straight as an arrow. It, like so many other geomorphic features, lies along a straight fracture in the granitic bedrock. Now we switchback down Register Creek, bridge it near its 60-foot plunge into a walled-in pool, and immediately bridge smaller Rodgers Canyon creek. Both may be dry after Labor Day. Just beyond them you can peer through the gold-cup and black oaks and look straight "down the throat" of linear Muir Gorge—a product of the Tuolumne River's cutting down along a major fracture. John Muir was probably the first white man to descend the gorge, and in 1931 two Sierra Club parties became the first successful groups to duplicate this feat. Even in times of low water, this hike/swim feat can be dangerous, and yet each year hikers attempt it—at great peril to their lives.

After a few descending switchbacks our trail leaves the mouth of the Muir Gorge behind and traverses a very level mile before presenting the hiker with views of an incredible section of the canyon's north wall. Above you towers a giant wall, with fresh polish and striations, which looks like glaciers left it only yesterday. Mottled in dark gray and pale orange, it presents an opportunity for good early-morning color photography. The gray color is not the color of the bedrock, but rather of the lichens growing on it.

Continuing your descent west down the Grand Canyon of the Tuolumne River, you might see wild grapes growing along the trail. The river is forced south by a "mountain"—a large, glacier-defying bedrock mass within the canyon—and across its lower slopes our trail parallels the river to shadier, easier terrain. The last mile of trail to the Pate Valley junction is nearly flat, and along it you'll see burned snags—evidence of careless campers. From the Pate Valley junction, head for riverside campsites, about 100-200 yards west, or continue beyond the two Tuolumne River bridges to even more campsites.

A glacier-polished wall, east of Muir Gorge

Hike 42   Tuolumne Meadows to Sonora Pass

Distance: 77.2 miles (124.2 km) one way

Grade: 7G, strenuous 7-day hike

Trailhead: Same as the Hike 39 trailhead. **F3.**

Introduction: Deep, spectacular glaciated canyons, crossed one after another, characterize this hike. The backpacker here sometimes feels he's doing more vertical climbing than horizontal walking. Nearing the north end of this hike, you leave the expansive granitic domain behind and enter Vulcan's realm—thick floods of volcanic flows and sediments that buried most of the northern Sierra Nevada before it rose to its present height. By hiking these 77 miles you will have completed almost 3% of the entire Pacific Crest Trail, which extends from the Mexican border north to the Canadian border. The popularity of this hike is attested to by bears, who have become attracted to most of the good Yosemite campsites along this trail.

Description: Follow **Hike 39** to Glen Aulin, a good place to spend the night if you're taking seven or more days to do this hike. Leaving Glen Aulin, our trail—the Pacific Crest Trail, or PCT—climbs north, sometimes along Cold Canyon creek, 3 miles to a forested gap, then descends ½ mile to the south edge of a large, usually soggy meadow. Midway across it you'll notice a huge boulder, just west. Its overhanging sides have been used as an emergency shelter,

but in a lightning storm it is a prime strike target. Beyond it our multitracked route continues north, first for a mile through meadow, then on a gradual ascent through forest to a crest junction with the McCabe Lakes trail. A long-half-mile walk northeast up it will get you to a small campsite just above McCabe Creek; an hour's walk up it will get you to larger, better campsites at scenic Lower McCabe Lake. If you took **Hike**

Sunrise over Lower McCabe Lake

7's mountaineer route to the McCabe Lakes and you are caught in a snow storm, exit via this route, *not* by the route you came in on, for the Secret Lake pass is far too treacherous when snowbound.

If you're trying to do this hike in six days, however, your first night's goal should be campsites along Return Creek or lower McCabe Creek, both down in Virginia Canyon—a *long* 14 miles from the trailhead if you're carrying a heavy pack. We switchback down to this canyon's floor, cross McCabe Creek—a wet ford before July—and quickly come to a junction. A spur trail continues briefly up-canyon past campsites, but we turn left to ford powerful Return Creek, which usually is a wet ford and in early season can be a dangerous one. At times of high water, look up to ½ mile up-canyon for slower-flowing water rather than attempting to cross here. Don't rope up since hikers have been known to drown before they could untie their rope after they slipped.

On the west bank we walk but a few steps southwest before our trail veers right and meets the Virginia Canyon trail (**Hike 6**). On the PCT we start down-canyon, climb west up into Spiller Creek canyon, and then, halfway to a pass, cross the canyon's high-volume creek. A favorite route among mountaineers is to hike from Twin Lakes up Horse Creek canyon to the Park's boundary—a *de facto* trail most of the way—then descend Spiller Creek canyon to this PCT crossing.

Beyond Spiller Creek we soon start up two dozen switchbacks that transport us 2 miles up to a forested pass, which offers fair camps when there is enough snow to provide water. But even up here, bears roam the land. Most hikers continue 1½ miles southwest down to shallow Miller Lake, with good campsites along its forested west shore. From the lake we parallel a meadow north up to a low gap, then execute over two dozen often steep switchbacks down to a canyon floor and a junction with the northbound Matterhorn Canyon trail. **Hike 4** goes north up-canyon, but our hike descends southwest, reaching this majestic canyon's broad creek in 80 yards. Immediately beyond the often-wet foot ford lies a large, lodgepole-shaded campsite with ample space to stretch out and dry your toes.

Heading down-canyon for a mile, we pass less obvious and more secluded campsites, then soon leave the glaciated canyon to begin the usual two dozen, short steep switchbacks—this time west up into Wilson Creek canyon, a typical glaciated side canyon that hangs above the main canyon partly because its smaller glacier couldn't erode the landscape as rapidly as the trunk-canyon glacier did. We twice ford Wilson Creek, then ford it a last time and start a switchbacking climb up to windy, gravelly Benson Pass, registering a breath-taking height of 10,140 feet.

As the passes have become steadily higher, so too have the canyons become deeper, and our

Evening calm comes to Smedberg Lake

multistage descent to and then ascent up from Benson Lake can best be described as "Whew!" We begin uneventfully with an easy descent to a large meadow, reaching its peaceful creeklet just before a dropoff. Veering away from the creeklet, we soon begin a switchbacking descent that in 2 miles ends at a south-shore peninsula on Smedberg Lake. Most of the campsites, however, lie along the lake's west and north shores.

From the lake's south-shore peninsula—below the steep-walled sentinel, Volunteer Peak—we continue west, passing a spur trail to the west-shore campsites before winding southwest up a poorly defined slab-rock trail to a close-by, well-defined gap. From it the trail switchbacks down joint-controlled granite slabs, only to climb south high up to a meadowy junction with a trail to Rodgers Lake. **Hike 43**, which has coincided with the PCT to this junction now leaves our route, departing in that direction and eventually descending to Pate Valley before climbing east back up to the Tuolumne Meadows trailhead.

At this junction **Hike 14** joins the PCT as it starts southwest, crosses a low moraine and briefly descends northwest to a junction with a trail climbing southwest to a broad saddle that harbors shallow, mosquito-haunted Murdock Lake, and thence down Rodgers Canyon. Our next step down to Benson Lake is a typical two-dozen-short-switchbacks descent to a ford of Smedberg Lake's outlet creek. The PCT from that lake to here will be virtually impossible to follow in the snowbound early season. Hikers then will want to make a steep cross-country descent west down to this spot on an almost level canyon floor.

Now on the creek's north bank, we pass a small pond before commencing a steady, moderate creekside descent to a second ford—a slight problem in early season. Back on the south bank, we make a winding, switchbacking descent over metamorphic rock down to our last, sometimes tricky ford of the creek. The next ⅓ mile sees us climbing up to a brushy saddle just east of a conspicuous knoll, then descending into a shady forest of giant firs before crossing wide Piute Creek and reaching the Benson Lake spur trail. Piute Creek—almost always a wet ford—can usually be crossed via one or more large, fallen logs. No one—but no one—makes this long descent from Benson Pass without visiting the "Benson Riviera"—the long, sandy beach along the north shore of Benson Lake. Our spur trail winds southwest along the shady, often damp forest floor a short ½ mile to a section of beach near Piute Creek's inlet. *Remember this*

spot, for otherwise this route back can be hard to locate. Numerous campsites just within the forest's edge testify to the popularity of this broad, sandy beach. And if you've brought in a portable folding boat or raft, you'll probably have the whole lake to yourself. Swimming in this large, deep lake is brisk at best, but sunning on the beach can be superb—in late summer, after the water line drops. However, strong, up-canyon afternoon winds can quell both activities. Anglers can anticipate a meal of rainbow or brook trout.

After your stay, return to the PCT and prepare for a gruelling climb north to Seavey Pass. At first brushy, the ascent northwest provides views of pointed Volunteer Peak and closer, two-crowned Peak 10060. We cross the creek, continue switchbacking northwest along the base of spectacular Peak 10368, then climb north briefly, only to be confronted with a steep 400-foot-climb east. On it we are eventually funneled through a narrow, steep-walled, minor gap which rewards our climbing efforts with the sight of a relatively wind-free, sparkling pond. Just past its outlet you'll find a trailside rock from which you can dive into its reasonably warm waters. The PCT parallels the pond's shore, curves east around a miniscule pond, then climbs northeast through wet meadows before switchbacking up to a second gap. At its north base lies a shallow, rockbound pond, immediately beyond which we meet gap No. 3—signed SEAVEY PASS. A small meadow separates it from gap No. 4, beyond which we reach a more noteworthy—and the highest—gap. Now we bend northwest, travel past the head of a linear lake to gap No. 6, and switchback quickly down into a southwest-trending trough, spying a shallow pond 200 yards off in that direction. We turn right and immediately top our last gap, from which we descend northeast ¼ mile to a junction in Kerrick Canyon. **Hike 4**, descending south to this junction, follows the PCT east to Matterhorn Canyon before turning back north.

A cursory glance at the map suggests to the hiker that he now has an easy 3-mile down-canyon walk to the Bear Valley trail junction. Closer scrutiny, however, reveals a longer, winding, too-often-ascending route. After 1½ miles of hiking on it, we parallel glacial deposits, on our right, which die out in outwash around the 8350-foot elevation. The glacier that left this debris as it retreated up-canyon about 13,500 years ago.

A short northward jog of our Kerrick Canyon trail segment ends at the Bear Valley trail junction. From it **Hike 13** climbs south to Bear Valley before starting its long descent to Hetch Hetchy Reservoir. Immediately beyond this junction we cross voluminous Kerrick Canyon's erratic-coursed Rancheria Creek. Major joints cut across this area's canyons and this creek has eroded along some of them, so that now it has an angular, joint-controlled course. After crossing this creek, which can be a rough ford through mid-July, we find a north-bank spur trail striking east up to campsites that are popular with both backpackers and black bears. The PCT, however, climbs west, affording dramatic cross-canyon views of Bear Valley peak and Piute Mountain. The PCT eventually climbs north to a shallow gap, and just east of it you'll find a sometimes bear-free campsite near the west end of a small lakelet. Proceeding north from the gap, we have the usual knee-shocking descent on a multitude of short, steep switchbacks down to the mouth of Thompson Canyon. Here we make a shady, easy descent west to a large camp beside Stubblefield Canyon creek. The main trail meets the creek just below the camp, and across from it a spur trail up the opposite bank quickly meets the main trail. (If you hike this route in reverse, you probably won't see this spur trail, rather, you'll walk past it and end in a large creekside camp. From it you can rock hop—in late season only—to the north end of *our* large camp.) Cross where you will, locate the main trail near the opposite bank, and start down-canyon. In ¼ mile we leave the shady floor for slabs and slopes, in an hour arriving at a false pass. A short, steep descent west drops us into a corn-lily meadow, from which we wind ¼ mile northwest up to the true Macomb Ridge pass.

With the deep canyons at last behind us, the 500-foot descent northwest into Tilden Canyon seems like child's play. Just beyond the west bank of Tilden Canyon Creek, we meet the Tilden Canyon trail, on which **Hike 12**, from Wilma Lake, heads south. **Hikes 13** and **14**, coming west on our trail, also turn south here. From this junction we hike up-canyon north on the Tilden Lake trail just 110 yards to a second junction. From here the PCT heads west to Wilma Lake and then goes up Jack Main Canyon. A slightly longer alternate route continues north gently up to huge, linear Tilden Lake, which has many near-shore campsites and a healthy population of rainbow trout. From the lake's outlet this route then descends west to Falls Creek and the adjacent PCT.

Our main route, however, adheres to the PCT, which goes left at this junction and winds northwest past several ponds, nestled on a broad gap, before descending west to large, shallow Wilma Lake, which, like so many of Yosemite's High Sierra lakes, contains rainbow trout. Good campsites are found just beyond it, along broad, tantalizing Falls Creek. A few minutes' walk northwest up-canyon takes us to a shallow, broad ford of the creek, then past spacious campsites to a junction with the Jack Main Canyon trail. **Hike 12** comes north up this canyon to our junction, while **Hike 14** descends from it, and those looking for an isolated spot to spend a layover day can follow the trail several miles southwest, then go cross country to one or more of the dozen or so easily reached lakes of the Andrews Peak-Mahan Peak area.

From our junction, which is near a seasonal ranger's cabin, the PCT first winds northward up-canyon, touching the east bank of Falls Creek only several times before reaching a junction with a trail east to Tilden Lake. At the creek's bank, 80 yards down this trail, is a good campsite. Chittenden Peak and its north satellite serve as impressive reference points as we gauge our progress northward, passing two substantial meadows before arriving at the south end of even larger Grace Meadow. Here the upper canyon explodes into plain view, with—east to west—Forsyth Peak, Dorothy Lake Pass and Bond Pass being our guiding landmarks. Under lodgepole cover along the meadow's edge you can set up camp.

Leaving Grace Meadow, we soon pass through a small meadow before the ever-increasing gradient becomes noticeable. People have camped at small sites along this stretch, perhaps hoping to avoid bears, which are usually found lower down, but alas, no such luck. Our upward climb meets the first of two trails that quickly unite to climb to nearby Bond Pass, on the Park's boundary, the route of the Tahoe-Yosemite Trail. Just beyond these junctions volcanic sediments and exposures are noticed in ever-increasing amounts—a taste of what's to come—before we reach large, exposed Dorothy Lake. Clumps of lodgepoles here provide minimal campsite protection from the winds that often rush up-canyon. A short climb above the lake's east end takes us up to Dorothy Lake Pass, with our last good view of the perennial snowfields that grace the north slopes of Forsyth Peak.

Bond Pass, Dorothy Lake Pass and Forsyth Peak, from Grace Meadow

Leaving Yosemite National Park, we enter Toiyabe National Forest, pass rocky Stella Lake, approach tempting Bonnie Lake, and then switchback east down to campsites along the west shore of Lake Harriet. Larger, more-isolated camps are on the east shore. The PCT crosses Cascade Creek just below the lake, and then it makes short switchbacks down confining terrain, reaching a large campsite in about ½ mile. Just 50 yards beyond it, we cross the creek on a footbridge. Ahead, the way is still winding, but it is nearly level, and we soon reach—just past a pair of ponds—a junction with a trail that descends 1.5 miles to the West Walker River trail. Onward, we start north, then bend west and pass three ponds before winding down to a creek that has a junction just past it. West, the original, more desirable PCT route contorts 1.0 mile over to Cinko Lake, with adequate camp-sites. The former PCT route then descends 0.5 mile to the West Fork West Walker River trail and follows the river, making fords, 1.5 miles down to a junction with the newer route.

On this official, lackluster segment, we first parallel the creek we've just crossed, and soon pass several gray outcrops of marble, which differ significantly in color and texture from the other metamorphic rocks we've been passing. Beyond them we curve left into a small bowl, then make a short, steep climb through a granitic notch before dropping west to a seasonal creeklet. After winding briefly northwest from it, our trail turns northward, taking almost ½ mile to descend to the West Fork West Walker River trail. On it we descend just ¼ mile down-river to

a nearby junction by paltry, sedge-choked Lower Long Lake. Here we take a steel bridge across a small gorge that confines the river, and we find a large, lodgepole-shaded campsite immediately past it—the best one this side of Sonora Pass. If you're lucky, you've left Yosemite's bears behind by now, though bear-bagging might not be a bad idea here.

A few mountain hemlocks are seen as we wind westward ¼ mile in and out of small gullies, then lodgepoles take over for another ¼ mile to the west edge of the southernmost Walker Meadow. Between meadow and granite our trail passes through a lodgepole corridor to a crossing of a wide but ephemeral creek, whose water flows mostly underground through the porous volcanic sediments. About ½ mile north from this ephemeral creek is another one, this one splashing in a two-stage drop into a volcanic alcove—an ideal lunch stop. Our traverse north continues for another ½ mile, and you can leave the trail at any point to descend to the flat-floored forest just below you and make camp.

By the time our trail turns northwest up Kennedy Canyon, granitic bedrock has re-appeared, but ½ mile up-canyon, not far beyond a potential campsite, it disappears for good. Continuing up this brown-walled, volcanic can-yon, we have an easy uphill hike for a mile, cross the canyon's creek, then labor up an increasingly steeper trail to a junction with a jeep road not far north of a broad saddle. We have now left behind all reasonable campsites; none lie between here and Sonora Pass, almost 10 miles away. Ahead, water in frozen form is usually too

Last view of Tower Peak (left), from a crest notch above Latopie Lake

plentiful, but if snowfall has been scarce, then late-season hikers should fill up before climbing to this jeep road, for they may have to hike almost to Sonora Pass to encounter a permanent creek.

Switchbacking northward up the usually closed jeep road, we have ever-improving views of Kennedy Canyon and the adjacent volcanic landscape. Whitebark pines, which have been with us since upper Kennedy Canyon, are now wind-cropped down to stunted forms. Trees disappear altogether by the time we reach a high crest that gives us views westward. Leaving the crest and its expansive views over the northwest Yosemite boundary area, our jeep road climbs quickly up to a tight switchback, and here we leave the road to follow **Hike 1,** partly in Emigrant Wilderness, 8 miles to Sonora Pass.

Hike 43   Tuolumne Meadows to Pate Valley via Smedberg Lake

Distance: 54.9 miles (88.3 km) semiloop trip

Grade: 7G, strenuous 5-day hike

Trailhead: Same as the Hike 39 trailhead. **F3.**

Introduction: This rugged hike is for canyon lovers. Heading west on the Pacific Crest Trail, you cross one scenic canyon after another. Then, returning on the Tuolumne River trail, you hike up through Yosemite's largest canyon, passing many gorgeous pools and cascades.

Description: Follow **Hike 42**'s description, backpacking 26 miles to Smedberg Lake. One mile beyond it leave the Pacific Crest Trail, climb over a nearby ridge and descend to Rodgers Lake. The route from the PCT past this lake down to the Pate Valley lateral is described in reverse direction in part of **Hike 14.** Essentially your route goes from Rodgers Lake 1 mile south down to Neall Lake—both lakes having rainbow trout—then drops west into Rodgers Canyon proper. This you descend for several miles before veering west 2 miles to a junction with the Pate Valley lateral. Before leaving Rodgers Canyon, fill up on water, for the rest of the hike down to Pate Valley can be dry in late season.

The Pate Valley lateral starts at a small patch of volcanic-mudflow deposits, which represents a remnant of what was once a continuous deposit extending east up an ancient canyon to about the Sierra crest. The age of this deposit is

Rodgers Lake

about 10 million years, and since that time most of the volcanic deposits have been removed by stream and glacier action. Throughout the Park south of the Tuolumne River, granitic rocks were only infrequently buried by volcanic deposits; the Park's north country is an exception to the rule.

Our 3¾-mile-long lateral starts among aspens, junipers, Jeffrey pines and white firs and descends nine dozen switchbacks before reaching spacious Pate Valley, shaded mostly by ponderosa pines, black oaks and incense-cedars. Bears frequent this area, so hang your food sacks

properly or place them in hard-to-reach rock ledges. (Bears are excellent tree climbers but poor rock climbers.) From the valley's trail junction you go west 100-200 yards to find good-to-excellent riverside campsites. Additional campsites can be found across the Tuolumne River.

From Pate Valley you follow the Tuolumne River trail east 20 miles back up to your trailhead. This route is described in the opposite direction in **Hike 41** (from Glen Aulin to Pate Valley) and in **Hike 39** (from Tuolumne Meadows to Glen Aulin).

Hike 44   Young Lakes

Distance: 14.5 miles (23.3 km) semiloop to and from the lowest lake's outlet

Grade: 3D, moderate 2-day hike

Trailhead: Same as the Hike 39 trailhead. **F3.**

Introduction: The Young Lakes are the only reasonably accessible lakes north of Tuolumne Meadows at which camping is allowed. This isolated cluster of lakes, backdropped by the scenic Ragged Peak crest, is quite popular, though not overcrowded like the Cathedral Lakes and the lakes near Vogelsang High Sierra Camp.

Description: The first part of this trip follows the Glen Aulin "highway," a heavily traveled path from Tuolumne Meadows to the High Sierra Camp down the Tuolumne River. From the Lembert Dome parking area west of Highway 120 we stroll down a dirt road, pass a locked gate that bars autos, and continue west along the lodgepole-dotted flank of Tuolumne Meadows, with fine views south across the meadows of Unicorn Peak, Cathedral Peak and some of the Echo Peaks. Approaching a boulder-rimmed old parking loop, we veer right and climb slightly to the now-closed Soda Springs Campground. Once this campground was the private holding of John Lembert, namesake of Lembert Dome. His brothers, who survived him, sold it to the Sierra Club in 1912, and for 60 years Club members enjoyed a private campground in this marvelous subalpine meadow. In 1972 the Club deeded the property to the National Park Service so that everyone could use it, but in 1976 the Service closed the campground.

From the effervescent Soda Springs, the sandy trail undulates through a forest of sparse, small lodgepole pines, and then descends to a ford of multibranched Delaney Creek. Beyond the creek, our trail almost touches the northwest arm of Tuolumne Meadows before ascending to the signed Young Lakes trail. Turning right, we ascend slightly and cross a broad expanse of boulder-strewn, grass-pocketed glaciated sheet granite. An open spot affords a look south across broad Tuolumne Meadows to the line of peaks from Fairview Dome to the steeplelike spires of the Cathedral Range. After crossing the open, glacier-polished granite, our trail climbs a tree-clothed slope to a ridge and turns up the ridge for several hundred yards before veering down into the bouldery, shallow valley of Dingley Creek, an easy ford except in early season. The reason for the creek's boulders and our trail's gravels is that this ascent route we are following was glacier-covered until about 14,000 years ago; then this area's glaciers retreated and dropped their loads of boulders, gravels and sand. About ¼ mile beyond this small creek, we jump across its west fork and then wind moderately upward in shady pine forest carpeted with a flower display even into late season. Senecio, daisies, lupine, squawroot and gooseberries all are colorful, but one's admiration for floral beauty concentrates on the delicate cream flower cups of Mariposa lily, with one rich brown spot in the throat of each petal. Near the ridgetop, breaks in the lodgepole forest allow us glimpses of the whole Cathedral Range, a foretaste of the magnificent panorama we will see on the return route.

Cathedral Range summits, from Unicorn Peak to Fairview Dome, rise high above Tuolumne Meadows

On the other side of the ridge a new panoply of peaks appears in the north—majestic Tower Peak, Doghead and Quarry peaks, the Finger Peaks, Matterhorn Peak, Sheep Peak, Mt. Conness, and the Shepherd Crest. From this high viewpoint a moderate descent leads to a ford of a tributary of Conness Creek, where more varieties of flowers decorate the green banks of this icy, dashing stream. Immediately beyond it the Dog Lake trail meets ours, and we start a rollercoaster traverse northeast through a forest of hemlock and pine. On a level stretch of trail we cross a diminutive branch of Conness Creek, and then switchback ¼ mile up to a plateau from where the view is fine of the steep northwest face of Ragged Peak. After rounding the edge of a meadow, we descend to the west shore of lower Young Lake. There are both primitive and well-developed campsites along the north shore of this lake. At the lake's northwest corner you can hop its outlet creek—a wet ford in early season—and climb ¼ mile east to a junction. Here a short lateral veers right to the only good campsite at small middle Young Lake. If you keep left, you'll climb ⅓ mile up to a broad, open crest, from where you can start cross country to Mt. Conness or Roosevelt Lake. Most likely, however, you'll want to make an easy, nearly level, open traverse southeast to upper Young Lake.

After exploring this area, retrace your steps about 2 miles to the Dog Lake trail junction. Turn left and ascend a boulder-dotted slope under a lodgepole-and-hemlock forest cover. As the trail ascends, the trees diminish in density and change in species, to a predominance of whitebark pine, the highest-dwelling of Yosemite's trees. From the southwest shoulder of Ragged Peak the trail descends through a very large, gently sloping meadow. This broad, well-watered

expanse is a wildflower garden in season, laced with meandering brooks. Species of paintbrush, lupine, and monkey flower in the foreground set off the marvelous views of the entire Cathedral Range, strung out on the southern horizon.

Near the lower edge of the meadow we cross the headwaters of Dingley Creek and then descend, steeply at times, some 300 feet past exfoliating Peak 10410 through a moderately dense forest of lodgepoles and a few hemlocks to a seasonal creek. Another seasonal creek is crossed in ⅓ mile, and then we make a short but noticeable climb up to the crest of a large, bouldery lateral moraine. Down its gravelly slopes we descend to a very large, level meadow above which the reddish peaks of Mt. Dana and Mt. Gibbs loom in the east. Here Delaney Creek meanders lazily through the sedges and grasses, and Belding ground squirrels pipe away. The Delaney Creek ford is difficult in early season, but shallower fords may be found upstream from the main ford.

After climbing over the crest of a second moraine, our route drops once more toward Tuolumne Meadows. Lembert Dome, the "first ascent" of so many visitors to Tuolumne Meadows, can be glimpsed through the trees along this stretch of trail. The trail levels off slightly before it meets the 400-yard lateral to Dog Lake (**Hike 45**), a worthwhile side trip. In a few minutes our route passes a junction with a trail that leads east along the north side of Dog Dome, the lower adjunct of Lembert Dome. We keep southwest, parallel a creek from Dog Lake, and begin a 450-foot switchbacking descent that is terribly dusty due to the braking efforts of descending hikers on this overly steep section. At the bottom of the deep dust, the trail splits into two paths. The right one leads to the stables, the left one to the Lembert Dome parking area.

Hike 45   Lembert Dome-Dog Lake Loop

Distance: 4.2 miles (6.7 km) semiloop trip; 2.6 miles (4.2 km) round trip to Dog Lake only; 2.8 miles (4.5 km) round trip to Lembert Dome only

Grade: 1B, moderate half-day hike

Trailhead: Large parking lot ⅓ mile west of the Tuolumne Meadows Lodge parking lot. To reach this lot from Tuolumne Meadows Campground, drive 0.6 mile northeast on Highway 120, turn right on the Tuolumne Lodge spur road and follow it 0.4 mile to the lot, on your left. **F3.**

Introduction: This is perhaps the finest day hike you can take in the Tuolumne Meadows area. If you have only a few hours to spare, then hike only to the top of Lembert Dome. However, don't overexert yourself, for at this area's elevations you can easily get altitude sickness.

Description: From our parking lot, we walk briefly east toward the lodge, finding our trailhead immediately before a dirt road forks left from the lodge's paved road. A three-minute climb northwest on the trail gets us to a crossing of Highway 120, beyond which we climb more steeply up to a broad, lodgepole-forested saddle. To climb Lembert Dome, leave the trail and contour westward cross country, staying just below the crest. Dog Dome, with its precipitous north face, is reached in about ⅓ mile and is certainly worth the short climb up to its summit. Like all domes in the Tuolumne Meadows area, this one is domelike in appearance only from a certain angle, and generally un-domelike from most other angles. On this dome you'll see several large boulders left behind by a former glacier. Like the rock of Dog Dome, they are

granitic, but unlike it, they lack the large, blocky feldspar crystals. They originally came from an eastern pluton (body of granitic rock).

Glaciers also left other evidence of their presence. In some places the bedrock has been polished by the fine layer of sediment trapped at the base of the glacier, and on the dome's polished surface you might note some parallel striations gouged by rocks within the sediment. These striations mark the direction the glacier traveled—generally westward. Another feature you might note is the presence of chatter marks. These may be due to erratic gouges made by large boulders or may be due solely to the enormous force of the thick, moving glacier acting against irregularities in the bedrock. Whereas a glacier smooths and polishes the stoss, or up-canyon, side of a dome, it quarries and steepens the lee, or down-canyon, side. Thus Lembert Dome is not really a dome but rather it is, like most of Yosemite's domes, a *roche moutonnée.* Other prominent examples of roches moutonneés are Fairview Dome and Pywiack Dome, both seen along the way from Tenaya Lake. In Yosemite Valley, Liberty Cap and Mt. Broderick are examples. However, Sentinel Dome and Mt. Starr King, both essentially unglaciated, are true domes. After exploring the Lembert Dome summit, return to the trail.

Just 130 yards beyond the Lembert Dome saddle we reach a trail fork. We'll be returning on the left trail, but for now we take the right one and wander northward on easy terrain, arcing along the east end of a shallow, sedge-filled pond

Dog Dome presents hikers with a panoramic view of the Tuolumne Meadows area

Mts. Dana, Gibbs and Lewis, together with Mono Pass, backdrop placid Dog Lake

before reaching a trail fork just above the south shore of Dog Lake. We go left, toward the lake's outlet, but we could go right on another trail and make a long loop around Dog Lake. At the lake's east end, this trail temporarily dies out in a wet meadow.

Having gone left, we cross the lake's outlet and from the lake's west shore obtain some-times-reflected views of Mt. Dana, Mt. Gibbs, and also Mt. Lewis. A long peninsula extends east into the lake from our shoreline, and on it you can walk—usually in knee-deep water—well out into the middle of this large but shallow lake. Because it is shallow and it also receives no direct snowmelt, it is one of the high country's warmest lakes, suitable for swimming and for just plain relaxing. Camping, however, is pro-hibited. Like many High Sierra lakes, this one is visited in the summer by spotted sandpipers, who usually nest close to the lake's shore. Among the shore boulders you may find meta-

morphic ones—rocks that could have got here via glacier transport from their source area, the Gaylor Peak/Tioga Hill area. Today no stream connects this area with Dog Lake, which lies in a purely granitic watershed.

Leaving Dog Lake at the trail junction just west of its outlet, you descend southwest a few minutes to the Young Lakes trail, follow it a few more minutes to another trail, branching south-east, and take it. You now cross the outlet creek, then head ½ mile east back to the broad saddle you crossed earlier. On this east traverse, you pass a pond that seasonally has wild onions growing in wet ground near its shore. Rather than traverse east past this point, you can stay on the Young Lakes trail, a longer route, which descends in deep dust southwest to a parking lot at the foot of Lembert Dome, then cross High-way 120 and follow the John Muir Trail—mostly an abandoned road—back to your start-ing point.

Hike 46   Gaylor and Granite Lakes

Distance: 5.7 miles (9.1 km) or longer—mileage variable; semiloop trip

Grade: 2C, easy day hike

Trailhead: On Highway 120 at Tioga Pass—the Park's east entrance. F3.

Introduction: Five subalpine lakes await those who take this hike, part of which is easy cross country. You can also reach these glistening gems from Tuolumne Meadows Lodge by first taking a trail 2 miles east from it up the Dana Fork to Highway 120, crossing the highway, and going 2½ miles up to Lower Gaylor Lake (see start of Hike 56). However, the route description that follows is about 8 miles shorter, round trip.

Description: By the restrooms of the Tioga Pass entrance station a sign informs us that

Camping is not allowed in the Gaylor Lakes area, which includes the Granite Lakes. As the rocky trail ascends steeply through lodgepole forest, we pass a profusion of flowers in season: single-stemmed senecio, Sierra penstemon, Gray's lovage, daisy, pussytoes, little elephant's head, lupine, monkey flower, Sierra wallflower, columbine and corn lily. After hiking ½ mile we come to a lone whitebark pine, a conifer that in maturity can range from a 50-foot-high tree down to a knee-high bush. The bark of young lodgepoles and whitebarks looks very similar; however, the former has two needles per bunch while the latter has five.

Our steep trail begins to level off near the top of the ridge, and on this stretch the flower "collector" may add spreading phlox, red mountain heather, buckwheat and pennyroyal to

Gaylor Peak and Gaylor Lakes, from Great Sierra Mine

his day's journal. Atop the ridge, the well-earned view includes, clockwise from north, Gaylor Peak, Tioga Peak, Mt. Dana, Mt. Gibbs, the canyon of the Dana Fork, Kuna Peak, Mammoth Peak, Lyell Canyon, and the peaks of the Cathedral Range. From our vantage point we can see where red metamorphic rocks to the northeast are in contact with gray granites to the southwest. This division extends north to where we are standing.

As we move west on the ridgetop, the rocks underfoot become quite purplish, a hue shared by the flowers of penstemon and lupine that obtain their mineral requirements from these rocks. Now our trail descends steeply past clumps of whitebark pine to Middle Gaylor Lake, and skirts the lake's north shore. Across the lake, the peaks of the Cathedral Range seem to be sinking into the lake, for their summits barely poke above the water.

Taking the trail up the inlet stream, we begin a short, gradual ascent to Upper Gaylor Lake. Surveying the Gaylor Lakes basin, we can see that campsites are so few and wood so scarce that only a few summers of camping, were it allowed, would finish off the environment here. From the upper lake we can see a rock cabin, which bespeaks the activities of a mining company that sought to tap the silver veins that run somewhere under Tioga Hill, directly north of the lake. After picking our way up to the cabin, we marvel at the skill of the dryrock mason who built this long-lasting house near the Sierra

crest. Farther up the hill are other works—including one dangerous hole—left by the miners, in various states of return to nature. This was once the "city" of Dana.

Atop Tioga Hill we have all the earlier views plus a view down into Lee Vining Canyon. A scant mile northeast of us another "city," Bennettville, sprang up near the mouth of a tunnel being dug to exploit the silver lodes. Its founder projected a population of 50,000! The white and lavender columbines and other living things around the summit may owe their lives to the absence of these hordes.

From this general area, we make our way west cross country across a ridge and down to the easily found Granite Lakes, blue gems backed by steep granite heights. Like the upper lake with its near-shore island, lower Granite Lake is coldly swimmable in mid-to-late season. In any event, its grassy eastern shore is a fine place to sun oneself.

Finally we curve southwest, down toward Lower Gaylor Lake. In this meadowy upland we are sure to see many marmots and Belding ground squirrels. At Lower Gaylor Lake we are also likely to see a few California gulls on the spit. Spotted sandpipers, identified by their bobbing walk, are also common summer visitors to High Sierra lakes. After a pleasant rest, we make an easy, generally open, cross-country climb northeast back to Middle Gaylor Lake, then follow the trail back to Tioga Pass.

Telephoto of Cathedral Peak, from upper Cathedral Lake

Section 5
Trails of the Tuolumne Meadows Area, south and east of Highway 120

Introduction: Except for Little Yosemite Valley, an outlier of Yosemite Valley, no other area in the Park receives such an intensive backpacker use. Consequently, it is very important that you get a wilderness permit before starting your *overnight* hike. Otherwise you might discover on reaching your night's camping area that it is filled to capacity.

The extreme popularity of this area is due in part to its unbeatable scenery, which is dominated by the Cathedral Range and the Sierra crest. In part its popularity is also due to its accessibility, for in a few hours' hiking time you can easily reach crest passes and subalpine lakes. How can one forget the alpenglow on the metamorphic Sierra crest? the form of twin-towered Cathedral Peak? the expansive panorama from Mt. Dana? the beauty of an alpine wildflower garden? the enormous granite wall below Clouds Rest? These and many other sights continue to lure backpackers and dayhikers to this area year after year.

Supplies and Services: See "Supplies and Services" in Section 4.

Wilderness Permits: See "Wilderness Permits" in Section 4.

Campgrounds: See "Campgrounds" in Section 4.

Hike 47 Tenaya Lake to Sunrise High Sierra Camp

Distance: 11.4 miles (18.2 km) round trip

Grade: 3D, easy 2-day hike

Trailhead: Same as the Hike 35 trailhead. **E4.**

Introduction: Considerable climbing at fairly high elevations would normally make this hike a moderate one, but its distance is so short for a backpack trip that we've rated it easy. Some hikers go only as far as upper Sunrise Lake, only an 8-mile round trip and a good, moderate day hike. However, if you camp near Sunrise High Sierra Camp you are rewarded with a beautiful sunrise—the reason for the camp's being situated where it is.

Description: From the campground parking lot, we follow a closed road that quickly crosses the outlet of Tenaya Lake via a ford, narrows to a trail, and then parallels this stream southwestward. In 150 yards we meet a trail that parallels Highway 120 northeast to Tuolumne Meadows.

Our trail continues south for ¼ mile along the stream, then in sparse forest ascends southeast over a little rise and drops to a ford of Mildred Lake's outlet, which is dry in late season—like the other streams shown on the Park's topo map between Tenaya Lake and the Sunrise trail junction.

Beyond the Mildred Lake stream our trail undulates and winds generally south, passing several pocket meadows where the quiet early-morning hiker may see mule deer browsing. The trail then begins to climb in earnest, through a thinning cover of lodgepole pine and occasional red fir, western white pine and mountain hemlock. As our trail rises above Tenaya Canyon, we pass several vantage points from which we can look back upon its polished granite walls, though we never see the lake. To the east the canyon is bounded by Tenaya Peak; in the northwest are the cliffs of Mt. Hoffmann and Tuolumne Peak.

Above: **Matthes Crest, from Sunrise High Sierra Camp**
Below: **Exfoliation slabs and talus slope above lower Sunrise Lake**

Now on switchbacks, we can see the highway across the canyon and can even hear passing cars, but these annoyances are infinitesimal compared to the pleasures of polished granite expanses all around. These switchbacks are mercifully shaded, and where they become steepest, requiring a great output of energy, they give us back the beauty of the finest flower displays on this trail, including lupine, penstemon, paintbrush, larkspur, buttercup and sunflowers such as aster and senecio. Finally the switchbacks end and the trail levels off as it arrives at a junction on a shallow, forested saddle.

Here we turn left (**Hikes 48** and **49** go straight ahead), contour east, cross a low gap and descend north to lower Sunrise Lake, above whose east shore you'll see excellent examples of exfoliating granite slabs. The large talus slope beneath them testifies to the slabs' instability. Climbing from this lake and its small campsites, we reach a crest in several minutes, and from it one could descend an equally short distance north to more isolated, island-dotted middle Sunrise Lake. The trail, however, veers east and gains a very noticeable 150 feet in elevation as it climbs to upper Sunrise Lake, the largest and most popular lake of the trio. Campsites are plentiful along its north shore, away from the trail.

Leaving this lake, the trail climbs south up a gully, crosses it, then soon climbs up a second gully to the east side of a broad gap, from which we see the Clark Range head-on, piercing the southern sky. From the gap, which is sparsely clothed with mountain hemlocks, whitebark pines and western white pines, we descend south into denser cover, and veer east and then north to make a steep descent to Sunrise High Sierra Camp. This has an adjacent backpackers' camp complete with metal poles on which to bearbag your food. An overnight stay here gives you an inspiring sunrise over Matthes Crest and the Cathedral Range.

Hike 48   Clouds Rest

Distance: 14.0 miles (22.4 km) round trip

Grade: 3D, strenuous day hike

Trailhead: Same as the Hike 35 trailhead. **E4.**

Introduction: Although Clouds Rest is higher than Half Dome, it is easier and safer to climb, and it provides far better views of the Park than does popular, sometimes overcrowded Half Dome. Except for its last 300 yards, the Clouds Rest trail lacks the terrifying, potentially lethal drop-offs found along Half Dome's shoulder and back side, thereby making it a good trail for acrophobic photographers.

Description: Follow **Hike 47** 3 miles up to the Sunrise Lakes trail junction. Then, with all the hard climbing behind you, descend south along the Forsyth trail. This switchbacks down to a shady, sometimes damp flat, then climbs up to a block-strewn ridge that sprouts dense clumps of chinquapin and aspen. Beyond it the trail descends briefly to a tree-fringed pond—adequate for camping—then wanders south for ½ mile before veering west to cross three creeklets, which will be your last reliable sources of water. After you cross the first creeklet, follow the trail—sometimes hard to find—briefly downstream, then veer left to cross the second creeklet before climbing up to the third. Beyond it the trail rapidly eases its gradient and soon reaches the Clouds Rest trail junction.

The Forsyth trail—not worth taking—forks left, but we keep right, ascend the Clouds Rest trail west to a forested, gravelly crest and follow

it down to a shallow saddle. Our final ascent begins here. After a moderate ascent of ¼ mile, we emerge from the forest cover to get our first excellent views of Tenaya Canyon and the country west and north of it. After another ¼ mile along the crest we come to a junction with a horse trail, which can be missed if it's unsigned. If you're riding a horse from Tenaya Lake to Yosemite Valley via the Clouds Rest trail—the most scenic of the possible routes to the Valley—you'll want to take this trail after first walking to the summit. It starts at a fairly large western white pine that is 80 yards past a good view. The Clouds Rest trail essentially dies out here, so scramble 15 feet up to the narrow crest. Acrophobics may not want to continue, but they can get some spectacular views of Tenaya Canyon, Half Dome and Yosemite Valley which are nearly identical with those seen from the summit. Spreading below is the expansive 4500-foot-high face of Clouds Rest—the largest granite face in the Park.

Those who follow the now steeper, narrow, almost trailless crest 300 yards to the summit are further rewarded with views of the Clark Range and the Merced River Canyon. Growing on the rocky summit are a few knee-high Jeffrey pines and whitebark pines plus assorted bushes and wildflowers. Some hikers like to spend a waterless night on the summit in order to experience the matchless sunrise. If you do this, pack out your litter and make your latrine off the summit—it is too small to withstand pollution.

From Clouds Rest, Half Dome and Yosemite Valley captivate your attention

Hike 49   Tenaya Lake to Happy Isles
via Clouds Rest and Half Dome

Distance: 21.2 miles (34.1 km) one way, including side trip

Grade: 5E, strenuous 2-day hike

Trailhead: Same as the Hike 35 trailhead. **E4.**

Introduction: Yosemite Valley's two loftiest, most scenic viewpoints—Clouds Rest and Half Dome—are visited along this hike. The energy expended attaining the two summits is equivalent to that of Hike 81, which starts at the valley floor and climbs only to Half Dome. Good judgment is required for this hike, for both summit routes have potentially fatal drop-offs and both summits are prime lightning targets.

Description: Hike 48 describes the 7-mile trek up to Clouds Rest and the views seen from it. If you're an avid photographer, you'll want to start this trek at the crack of dawn in order to reach this summit before shadows become poor for photography. All hikers should strive to reach this summit by noon or thereabouts, for lightning storms are a real possibility in the mid-to-late afternoon.

Leaving Clouds Rest—an exfoliating high crest on the Tenaya Canyon rim—we first negotiate short switchbacks south down through a dense growth of chinquapin bushes, then descend longer ones past western white pines and a few Jeffrey pines to a junction with the Clouds Rest horse trail, which starts east. Red firs join the pines as we descend southwest from the junction, and chinquapins compete with pinemat manzanita, snow bush and even sagebrush. Our trail descends past the back sides of the two Clouds Rest "pinnacles," both broken with an abundance of horizontal fractures. Just beyond these we reach a spur ridge with several bedrock knobs that are similarly fractured. Most geologists interpret these fractures as the result of pressure release. These granitic rocks, which are a part of the 84-million-year-old Half Dome granodiorite solidified several miles beneath the earth's surface at pressures a *few thousand times* the atmospheric pressure they are exposed to today. Hence the granitic rock tends to expand, cracking in the process, and eventually it unloads slabs.

From the low knobs and their adjacent western junipers, an initially steep descent yields to a more moderate one as we pass beneath the overhanging south wall of the southern Clouds Rest pinnacle. More domelike, from our trail's vantage points, the two Clouds Rest pinnacles were certainly named by someone who viewed them from the northwest. Our west-descending trail almost touches the rim of Tenaya Canyon before it begins about one dozen moderately long switchbacks, which drop us into a vegetation zone that now includes huckleberry oaks and white firs. On this descent we pass a trickling spring, flowing near Labrador tea, a water-loving bush that is easily identified by the turpentine smell of its crushed leaves. Don't be misled by its name; it leaves will not produce a suitable tea. Instead, they can produce convulsions and paralysis.

Another set of switchbacks drops us into sufficient forest cover to obstruct our recently plentiful views of towering Half Dome. Our moderate-to-steep descent soon leaves red firs behind, and through a forest of white firs and Jeffrey pines we drop eventually to a junction with the John Muir Trail (**Hike 51**). Here, close to a tributary of Sunrise Creek, you'll find two west-bank campsites. Just east on the John Muir Trail, between this tributary and Sunrise Creek, you'll find a third, larger campsite. Any of these sites makes a logical place to spend the night, for there are no more flat, desirable, near-water sites between here and the summit of Half Dome, about 2⅔ miles farther.

From the campsite junction we descend ½ mile west along the John Muir Trail to a junction with the Half Dome trail. Now we follow the last part of **Hike 80** up to that dome's summit. Rather than carry your backpack all the way to the summit, hide it in some bushes and carry only a day pack up this strenuous section. Like Clouds Rest, Half Dome should not be climbed in threatening weather. After your exploration of the dome's expansive summit, descend to Happy Isles on the floor of Yosemite Valley, following the description of **Hike 80** in reverse.

On Half Dome's cables

Hike 50   Lower Cathedral Lake

Distance: 7.8 miles (12.5 km) round trip

Grade: 2C, moderate half-day hike

Trailhead: In Tuolumne Meadows, 1.5 miles west on Highway 120 from the Tuolumne Meadows Campground entrance. **E4.**

Introduction: If you are making this hike only and are not going any farther on the John Muir Trail, then you should make this excursion as a day hike. Lower Cathedral Lake receives so much backpacker use that those who can visit this scenic lake in only one day—an easy task— should do so. The popularity of this lake is confirmed by the presence of black bears, lured there by the tempting prospect of backpackers' food supplies.

Description: From our trailhead beside Budd Creek, we walk southwest 120 yards to a junction with the Tuolumne Meadows-Tenaya Lake trail. Starting from the east side of Tuolumne Meadows Campground, this trail traverses west to our junction, then continues for a generally viewless 8.1 miles (13.5 km) down to the entrance to the Tenaya Lake Walk-in Campground. By continuing on **Hike 35**, you can descend to Mirror Meadow, a hike that is the shortest route from Tuolumne Meadows to Yosemite Valley—only 19.8 miles (31.9 km).

Now on the John Muir Trail, we climb moderately up a stretch of trail that can at times be objectionably dusty due to humus mixing with the abundance of glacial deposits. Lodgepoles dominate our ¾-mile ascent to the crest of a lateral moraine, from which our trail briefly

Bedrock-lined lower Cathedral Lake

descends west before turning southwest. From this spot you can hike cross country ½ mile northwest to the lower slopes of Fairview Dome. During glacial periods the Tuolumne Meadows glacier was so thick that it buried this dome under as much as 700 feet of glacier ice, which then overflowed the river basin to descend into Yosemite Valley via Tenaya Canyon. Non-climbers should not attempt to climb to its summit.

Our trail traverses southwest ½ mile to a creeklet, which we cross, and then we ascend short, moderate-to-steep switchbacks beneath the shady cover of lodgepole pines and mountain hemlocks. After 300 feet of climbing, our trail's gradient eases and we traverse along the base of largely unseen Cathedral Peak, a mass of granodiorite towering 1400 feet above us. Repeated attacks by glaciers have successfully chiseled away on all of the peak's sides to create a steep-walled monolith that is the realm of the mountain climber.

Our traverse leaves the Tuolumne River drainage for that of the Merced River and soon, after a brief descent, we come to a junction with the lower Cathedral Lake trail. This spur trail descends ⅔ mile to the lake's bedrock east shore. A rust-stained waterline on the meadow side of the bedrock marks the high-water level when the meadow floods in early season. The iron from the rust is derived from the meadow's soil, not from the iron-deficient granitic bedrock. Bear-frequented campsites abound on both the north and south shores, the northern ones being roomier. Campfires are not allowed. Due to high angler use, fishing for brook trout is likely to be poor. Because of the relative shallowness of this fairly large lake, swimming in it is tolerable despite its 9300+ foot altitude.

From the lake's outlet you can look across to Polly Dome, standing high above Pywiack Dome. Also seen are Mt. Hoffmann and a bit of Tenaya Lake, nestled between Tenaya Peak and Polly Dome. By hiking cross country ¾ mile north from our lake's outlet, you can follow the rim of Tenaya Canyon to a seldom seen lakelet near the summit of Medlicott Dome. Seen from this lakelet, the dome in no way resembles a dome, but Mariuolumne Dome, ½ mile northeast of it, bears a striking resemblance to Lembert Dome and was sculptured just like it (**Hike 45**). Mariuolumne Dome gets its name from the nearby drainage divide, which separates *Mari*posa country from T*uolumne* county.

Hike 51   Tuolumne Meadows to Happy Isles via
John Muir Trail

Distance: 21.7 miles (34.8 km) one way

Grade: 5D, moderate 2-day hike

Trailhead: Same as the Hike 50 trailhead. **E4.**

Introduction: This section of the John Muir Trail is perhaps the most popular route from Tuolumne Meadows to Yosemite Valley. For those who have done the first 190 miles of this famous trail, which originates at the summit of Mt. Whitney, these final scenic miles—most of them downhill—make a perfect ending.

Description: Follow **Hike 50** about 3 miles up to the junction with the lower Cathedral Lake spur trail. Visiting this lake adds about 1½ miles to your hike's length. From this junction make an easy mile-long climb to the southeast corner of very shallow upper Cathedral Lake. Although camping is discouraged here, you may enjoy a stop for a snack on the south-shore peninsula, from which you can at times get good mirrored-image photos of two-towered Cathedral Peak.

Cathedral Peak and upper Cathedral Lake

Our trail then climbs ¼ mile to broad Cathedral Pass, where the excellent views include Tresidder Peak, Cathedral Peak, Echo Peaks, Matthes Crest, the Clark Range farther south, and Matterhorn Peak far to the north.

Beyond the pass is a long, beautiful swale, the headwaters of Echo Creek, where the midseason flower show is alone worth the trip. Our path traverses up the east flank of Tresidder Peak on a gentle climb to the actual high point of this trail, at a marvelous viewpoint overlooking most of southern Yosemite Park. The inspiring panorama here includes the peaks around Vogelsang High Sierra Camp in the southeast, the whole Clark Range in the south, and the peaks on the Park border in both those directions farther away. Our high trail soon traverses under steep-walled Columbia Finger, then switchbacks quickly down to the head of the upper lobe of Long Meadow. Here it levels off and leads down to a gradually sloping valley dotted with little lodgepole pines to the head of the second, lower lobe of l-o-n-g Long Meadow. After passing a junction with a trail down Echo Creek (**Hike 52**), the route heads south ½ mile before bending west ¼ mile to pass below Sunrise High Sierra Camp, perched on a granite bench just above the trail. South of the camp are some backpacker campsites from where you can take in the next morning's glorious sunrise.

For variation you can head west over to the Sunrise Lakes, then down to a junction with the Forsyth trail (the reverse of the second half of **Hike 47**), then follow **Hikes 48** and **49** to Clouds Rest and Half Dome. By taking this variation, you'll be taking perhaps the most scenic route of a dozen or so that go from Tuolumne Meadows to Yosemite Valley.

From the camp the John Muir Trail continues through the south arm of Long Meadow, then soon starts to climb up the east slopes of Sunrise Mountain. You top a broad southeast-trending ridge, and then, paralleling the headwaters of Sunrise Creek, descend steeply by switchbacks down a rocky canyon. At the foot of this descent you cross a trickling creek, then climb a low moraine to another creek, and in a short ½ mile top the linear crest of a giant lateral moraine. This moraine is the largest of a series of ridgelike glacial deposits in this area, and the gigantic granite boulders along its sides testify to the power of the glacier that once filled Little Yosemite Valley and its tributary valleys. Most

Tresidder Peak and pointed Columbia Finger

of the rocks have decomposed to soil because this is a Tahoe-age moraine. Lower down, additional morainal crests of the younger Tioga age appear on both sides of the trail, and we see Half Dome through the trees before our route reaches a junction with the Forsyth trail. The steep hike up it to the Clouds Rest trail is not worth taking. Look for fair campsites along Sunrise Creek about 150 yards north of this junction.

Here we turn south and in a moment reach the "High Trail" (**Hike 81**) coming in on the left. We turn right and descend southwest, our path being bounded first on the north by the south buttress of the Clouds Rest eminence and then on the south by Moraine Dome. Where our trail bends west, hikers may see a shallow saddle ¼ mile south of them, which lies at the foot of the dome. From this saddle they can follow the crest of a lateral moraine northeast up to the dome's summit. This moraine, hanging on the south side of Moraine Dome about 1750 feet above the

floor of Little Yosemite Valley, represents the approximate thickness of the Tioga-age glacier when it reached its maximum size some 20,000 years ago. Atop Moraine Dome you'll see—besides an utterly fantastic panorama—two geologically interesting features. One is a seven-foot-high dike of resistant aplite, which stands above the rest of the dome's surface because it weathers more slowly. Nearby just downslope is a large erratic boulder which, unlike the rock of Moraine Dome, is composed of Cathedral Peak granodiorite, easily identified by its large feldspar crystals. The ancient glacier that left this erratic here perhaps about 800,000 years ago had planed down the aplite dike to the dome's surface, but in the eons of ensuing time the dome has eroded around both the slowly weathering dike and the erratic, leaving the latter perched precariously atop a three-foot-high pedestal.

A mile from the last junction, the John Muir Trail fords Sunrise Creek in a red-fir forest whose stillness is broken by the creek's gurgling and by the occasional screams of Steller's jays. In ¾ mile from the ford we see a good campsite on a large, shady creekside flat, then curve northeast to quickly cross the creek's tributary, which has two west-bank campsites. Immediately past these is a trail to Clouds Rest (**Hike 48**), and ½ mile west from this junction we meet the trail to Half Dome (**Hike 80**—about 4 miles round trip—an incredible hike that shouldn't be missed). From this junction our shady path switchbacks down through a changing forest cover that includes some stately incense-cedars, with their burnt-orange, fibrous bark. At the foot of this descent we reach the floor of Little Yosemite Valley. Due to the area's popularity, the Park Service now directs camping activity hereabouts. A seasonal ranger stationed here answers questions, such as where to camp and where to find bearproof food-storage boxes. The route down to Yosemite Valley is described in the reverse direction in **Hike 79**.

Hike 52   Tuolumne Meadows to Happy Isles via Echo Creek and Merced Lake

Distance: 32.2 miles (48.9 km) one way

Grade: 6D, easy 3-day hike

Trailhead: Same as the Hike 50 trailhead. **E4.**

Introduction: In the first 2 miles of hiking you'll master half of this hike's climbing, and this accomplishment leaves you with a remaining 30

miles of very easy hiking. This hike is an excellent one for novice backpackers who want to try a multi-day wilderness experience. By ending your hiking days first at Sunrise High Sierra Camp and then at Merced Lake Camp, you can store your food at the camps. Although they charge a modest fee, you'll sleep better knowing that your food is safe from bears.

Description: Follow **Hike 51** to Sunrise High Sierra Camp, spend the night, experience the glorious sunrise, and then backtrack a short mile up Long Meadow to a junction with the Echo Creek trail, on which you will immediately ford the meadow's creek on boulders. The trail quickly switchbacks up to the top of a forested ridge and then descends through dense hemlock-and-lodgepole forest to a tributary of Echo Creek. Cross this, descend along it for ⅓ mile, recross, then momentarily reach the west bank of Echo Creek's Cathedral Fork. From Cathedral Pass, above and south of the Cathedral Lakes, experienced backpackers can hike easy cross country down-canyon to this fork. By contouring south from Echo Lake they can also meet Matthes Lake's outlet creek, trace it up to that lake and explore fascinating, serrated Matthes Crest—a mountaineer's paradise. Future glaciers descending south past it will trim it down, and at a distant time may eliminate it completely. The same fate holds true at an even sooner date for the crest immediately east of it, which is already significantly destroyed.

From the trail beside the Cathedral Fork we have fine views of the creek's water gliding down a series of granite slabs, and then the trail veers away from the creek and descends gently above it for more than a mile. Even in late season this shady hillside is watered by numerous rills that are bordered by still-blooming flowers. On this downgrade the trail crosses the Long Meadow creek, which has found an escape from that meadow through a gap between two large domes high above our trail.

Our route then levels out in a mile-long flat section of this valley where the wet ground yields a plus of wildflowers all summer but a minus of many mosquitos in early season. Beyond this flat "park" the trail descends a more open hillside, and where it passes the confluence of the two forks of Echo Creek, we can see across the valley the steep course of the east fork plunging down to its rendezvous with the west fork.

A fine cross-country route starting at Nelson Lake (**Hike 54**) descends 4 miles along the east fork to this confluence. In this area our trail levels off and passes good campsites immediately before crossing a metal bridge over Echo Creek.

Beyond the bridge, our trail leads down the forested valley and easily fords a tributary stream, staying well above the main creek. This pleasant, shaded descent soon becomes more open and steep, and it encounters fibrous-barked juniper trees and butterscotch-scented Jeffrey pines as it drops to another metal bridge 1⅓ miles from the last one. Beyond this sturdy span, the trail rises slightly and the creek drops precipitously, so that we are soon far above it. Then our sandy tread swings west away from Echo Creek and diagonals down a brushy hillside. There the views are excellent of Echo Valley, which is a wide place in the great Merced River canyon below. On this hillside we arrive at a junction with the High trail, which goes 3 miles west to a junction with the John Muir Trail. Leaving the dense growth of huckleberry oak, chinquapin, greenleaf manzanita and snow bush behind, we leave our junction and drop 450 feet into Echo Valley, shaded by lodgepoles and white firs. In it we quickly arrive at another junction, this one near an adequate camping area. Here we meet the Merced Lake trail, which is described in **Hike 81**. On it we go east, immediately bridging Echo Creek, pass through a burned-but-boggy area, then climb east past the Merced River's largely unseen, but enjoyable, pools to Merced Lake's west shore. Don't camp here, but rather continue past the north shore to Merced Lake High Sierra Camp and the adjacent riverside campground, a little under 10 miles from the Sunrise High Sierra Camp. You can count on seeing bears here, so store your food with the camp or string it high on a steel cable.

On your third day you hike almost 14 miles to the floor of Yosemite Valley, which isn't that hard because it is mostly downhill and you've gotten sufficient exercise and acclimation to handle it. First retrace your steps to Echo Valley, then continue on the Merced Lake trail as it descends to Little Yosemite Valley, referring to the first part of **Hike 81**, which describes this stretch in the opposite direction. **Hike 79** describes Little Yosemite Valley and **Hike 78** describes your possible routes down to Happy Isles.

Echo Peaks, from John Muir Trail

Hike 53   Budd Lake

Distance: 5.4 miles (8.6 km) round trip

Grade: 2C, moderate half-day hike

Trailhead: Same as the Hike 50 trailhead. **E4.**

Introduction: Mountaineers take the unmaintained, *de facto* trail to Budd Lake, for it provides the fastest access to climbing routes on Cathedral Peak, Echo Peaks, the Cockscomb and Unicorn Peak—all encircling the lake, and on Matthes Crest, south of the Cockscomb. We would not describe this unmaintained trail were it not for significant geological features found around chilly Budd Lake, which are worth investigation.

Description: The unsigned trail up Budd Creek can be hard to find. From the Budd Creek trailhead walk 120 yards southwest to a junction with the John Muir Trail, then start southwest up it toward the Cathedral Lakes. After a long ¼ mile, a use trail starts south from a point where the John Muir Trail curves northwest—the only place it does so on the lower part of its ascent. The use trail quickly becomes more obvious and its first mile is easy to follow. However, it then levels off and forks. One branch makes a brief, gentle descent, but you should stay on the right branch, which first climbs up to a granitic bench and then heads south along its brink. In about ⅓ mile this branch rejoins the lower one; then the path can become vague just before crossing Budd Creek. Once on the east bank of Budd Creek, you may see a third branch, one that had split from the lower one. From the crossing a single tread climbs a short mile up Budd Creek, crossing it again just before reaching Budd Lake.

Along your ascent of this trail you'll note that Unicorn Peak, to the east, has three summits, not one, as you might assume from the name. Although the peak is mentioned in *The Climber's Guide to the High Sierra,* no mention is made of the better climbing on the long cliff below and northwest of the peak.

At Budd Lake camping is no longer allowed to humans, but perhaps you will find an overly friendly marmot waiting to empty your pack while you're off exploring the area. Budd Lake is perhaps unique in Yosemite in that it contains two geologically recent moraines. The older moraine, perhaps formed about 2500 years ago, dams 10,050-foot-high Budd Lake. The younger one, perhaps only a few hundred years old, arcs across the lake's south end.

While you're admiring Cathedral Peak, the Echo Peaks and the Cockscomb, which rim this basin, you might take a close look at the granitic rock that composes them. Dated between 85 and 90 million years old, it was originally classified as a true granite, then briefly as a quartz monzonite, and now—by international standards—as granodiorite. The mineral and chemical composition of this Cathedral Peak pluton varies from place to place, but it generally becomes richer in feldspar and quartz toward the center, and this variation complicates the classification. Regardless of its classification, this pluton is easy to identify in Yosemite, for it contains large, blocky, protruding crystals of potassium feldspar. Climbers new to the Tuolumne Meadows area quickly discover that these make good holds. In addition to the mountaineers, fishermen are found around Budd Lake, for it contains brook trout.

A young moraine arcs across Budd Lake; Cathedral Peak in background

Hike 54   Elizabeth Lake

Distance: 4.8 miles (7.6 km) round trip

Grade: 1C, moderate half-day hike

Trailhead: Near road's end in the Tuolumne Meadows Campground. Walk up to the Group Camping Section and find the trailhead across from a masonry building. **F4.**

Introduction: Due to its accessibility this lake ranks with Dog Lake (Hike 45) in popularity. Dog Lake is certainly better for swimming, Elizabeth Lake for scenery. Fairly isolated Nelson Lake can be reached by a *de facto* trail from Elizabeth Lake.

Description: The signed trail to Elizabeth Lake begins across a road from a masonry building just before the turn-around in the Group Camping Section of the Tuolumne Meadows Campground. Because it starts at the Group Camping Section, this trail is heavily used.

Only 50 yards from the trailhead our **T**-blazed trail crosses the Tenaya Lake/Lyell Canyon trail, and then it continues a steady southward ascent. The shade-giving forest cover along this climb is almost entirely lodgepole pine as the trail crosses several runoff streams that dry up by late summer. More than a mile out, the trail veers near Unicorn Creek, and the music of this dashing, gurgling, cold-water stream makes the climbing easier.

After rising 800 feet, the trail levels off, the stunted lodgepole pines are farther spaced, and the hiker emerges at the foot of a long meadow. Partway through the meadow a short spur trail leads southwest to Elizabeth Lake. Few places in Yosemite give so much for so little effort as this lovely subalpine lake. Backdropped by Unicorn Peak, the lake faces the snow-topped peaks of the Sierra crest north of Tuolumne Meadows. From the east and north sides of the lake, the views across the waters to Unicorn Peak are classic, and one can see why this is a traditional lunch spot for people climbing this glacier-trimmed, knife-edge crest. The glacier-carved lake basin is indeed one of the most beautiful in the Tuolumne Meadows area.

From the lake's spur trail junction a *de facto* trail climbs one mile to a notch in the Cathedral Range, then descends 2 miles past the spectacular Cockscomb crest before veering ½ mile east up to Nelson Lake. Because this trail is unofficial, we're not describing it in detail, but rather are leaving it for competent backpackers to explore. From Nelson Lake and its population of brook trout, these backpackers can head cross-country down Echo Creek for 4 relatively easy miles to the creek's confluence with its Cathedral Fork (see **Hike 52**).

Hike 55   Tuolumne Meadows Loop

Distance: 5.7 miles (9.2 km) for the complete loop

Grade: 2A, easy half-day hike

Trailhead: At or just west of Lembert Dome; essentially the same as the Hike 39 trailhead. **F3.**

Introduction: A good way to get acclimatized to this area's high elevation is to take this almost level loop trip through and around Tuolumne Meadows. Parts of this trail are favorite spots for fishermen and photographers.

Description: You can start the loop at any of a number of points, but we'll start our description at the parking lot at the foot of the meadow's prominent landmark, Lembert Dome. Walk west to where the road turns north up to the Tuolumne Meadows Stable, then continue west on a closed dirt road—part of the John Muir

Trail. After a pleasant walk with views south of the western Cathedral Range peaks, you go through a low gap and the road forks. Keep right, then in a few paces leave the road and take a short trail to the rust-stained, iron-rich Soda Springs. Being effervescent, they act like tonic water and can be added to any powdered drink you may have brought along.

From the springs and the adjacent Parsons Memorial Lodge—once the property of the Sierra Club—head south to the large bridge across the Tuolumne River. Lembert Dome, a ridge that looks more like a half dome, is plainly seen from the bridge. The dome's north-west face, being laced with vertical fractures, was quarried away by repeated glaciation.

During glaciation the top of the dome was buried under about 2000 feet of glacier ice. When the last major glacier retreated up-canyon about 14,000 years ago, primeval Tuolumne

Meadows came into existence. At first it was nearly lifeless—just a large accumulation of recently deposited sands, gravels and boulders. Quite likely a braided stream—one with several dividing and reuniting channels—flowed through it. Small, shallow ponds may also have existed, but never a large lake, such as Tenaya. Sedges eventually encroached upon the sediments; then they were followed by willows and finally by lodgepoles. Until about 2500 years ago a lodgepole forest may have dominated; then came two or more little ice ages. (The feeble Sierran glaciers we see today are remnants of the last of these.) It was during these wetter times that Tuolumne Meadows and many other High Sierra meadows formed—due to rises in groundwater tables which killed the trees. We can be thankful for this event, for without Tuolumne Meadows, the rugged peaks surrounding it would be largely unnoticed by most Park visitors and certainly they would be less photogenic.

Leaving the bridge, the John Muir Trail crosses the open meadow, aiming first at Unicorn Peak, with only its northernmost summit showing, then aiming gradually westward at the Cockscomb, the Echo Peaks and finally, near Highway 120, at Cathedral Peak. We cross the highway and, starting by the east end of a trailer-sewage disposal site built in 1976, walk a few minutes south up into a lodgepole forest to meet an east-west trail. The John Muir Trail goes west but we go east, skirt the south border of large Tuolumne Meadows Campground, and at its east end reach a trail junction above the south bank of the Lyell Fork of the Tuolumne River. Now we parallel the Lyell Fork east ¾ mile to a junction, turn left and cross a small meadow to reach two bridges over the Lyell Fork. Note the north-south fracture pattern of the granite here and how it forces the river, when low, to take a tortuous path. When free of such fracture, or joints, granite is almost immune to erosion and even massive glaciers can at best shave away only a few yards. Try visiting this spot in the evening, as the day's cumulonimbus clouds start breaking up and then turn a fiery red to match the alpenglow on Mt. Dana and Mt. Gibbs.

A short, winding climb north, followed by an equal descent, brings us to the Dana Fork of the Tuolumne River, only 150 yards past a junction with an east-climbing trail to the Gaylor Lakes. Immediately beyond the bridge we meet a short spur trail to the Tuolumne Meadows Lodge. Beyond it we hear the Dana Fork as it makes a small drop into a clear pool, almost cut in two by a protruding granite finger. At the base of this finger, about eight to ten feet down, is an underwater arch—an extremely rare feature in any kind of rock. If you feel like braving the cold water, 50°F at best, you can dive under and swim through it.

Just beyond the pool we approach the Lodge's road, where a short path climbs a few yards up to it and takes one to the entrance of a large parking lot for backpackers. Now we parallel the paved camp road westward, passing the Tuolumne Meadows Ranger Station and quickly reaching a junction. The main road curves north to the sometimes-noisy highway, but we follow the spur road west, to where it curves into a second large parking lot for backpackers. Our road past the lot becomes a closed dirt road and diminishes to a wide trail by the time we arrive at our loop's end, Highway 120, at Lembert Dome.

Glacier-smoothed Lembert Dome and the placid Tuolumne River

Hike 56

Tuolumne Meadows-
Merced Lake Semiloop

Distance: 33.3 miles (53.6 km) without any side trips; semiloop

Grade: 5E, moderate 4-day hike

Trailhead: Same as the Hike 45 trailhead. **F3.**

Introduction: Although this hike can be made in two days, four are recommended because it is too scenic to hurry through. At this leisurely pace you have time for most if not all of the side trips.

Description: We start on the John Muir Trail, which runs beside the Dana Fork of the Tuolumne River just yards south of the Tuolomne Meadows Lodge road. On the trail we hike ⅓ mile up the Dana Fork to a junction with a spur trail that goes to the west end of the lodge's parking lot. From this junction we cross the Dana Fork on sturdy bridge and after a brief walk of 150 yards upstream reach a junction with a trail to the Gaylor Lakes. Unless you are riding a horse, you'll want to reach these lakes from Tioga Pass, via a much shorter route (**Hike 46**).

Veering right, the John Muir Trail leads over a slight rise and descends to the Lyell Fork, where there are two substantial bridges. The meadows above these bridges are among the most delightful in all the Sierra, and anytime you happen to be staying all night at the lodge or nearby, the bridges are a wonderful place to spend the last hour before dinner, something you might consider for your hike out. Mts. Dana and Gibbs glow on the eastern horizon, catching the late sun, while trout dart along the wide Lyell Fork.

About 70 yards past the bridges we meet a trail that comes up the river from the east end of the Tuolumne Meadows Campground (**Hike 55**), then turn left (east) onto it, and skirt around a long, lovely section of the meadow. This re-routed trail section was established because of extensive wear and ensuing erosion of the old route. Re-routing is one of several far-sighted Park Service policies that have been adopted to allow areas in wilderness a chance to recover from overuse. Going through a dense forest cover of lodgepole pine, our route reaches a junction on the west bank of Rafferty Creek. The John Muir Trail (**Hike 58**) continues east, crossing the creek's two major branches, but our route turns right and immediately begins one of the toughest climbs of this entire trip. Even so,

the grade is moderate as often as it is steep, the trail is fairly well shaded by lodgepole pines, and the length of the climb is well under a mile. Then, as the ascent decreases to a gentle grade, we pass through high, boulder-strewn meadows that offer good views eastward to reddish-brown Mt. Dana and Mt. Gibbs, and gray-white Mammoth Peak. Soon the trail dips close to Rafferty Creek, and since this stream flows all year you can count on refreshment here. After 2 miles of near-creek hiking, the gently climbing trail passes above an orange snowcourse marker—one of several—near the edge of a large meadow and continues its long, gentle ascent through a sparse forest of lodgepole pines unmixed with a single tree of any other species.

In the next mile we cross several seasonal creeks, reach an even larger meadow, and immediately veer right at a junction where the abandoned old trail up the meadow veers left. Our relocated trail up a cobbly hillside was built to allow the damaged meadow below to recover from the pounding of too many feet—people's and, especially, horses'. Finally the exclusive lodgepole pines allow a few whitebark pines to join their company, and these trees diminish the force of the winds that often sweep through Tuolumne Pass. Through breaks in this forest one has intermittent southward views of cliff-bound, dark-banded Fletcher Peak and of Peak 11799 just one mile to its southeast. Then our path leaves the green-floored forest and enters an area of granitic outcrops speckled with a few trees. Around this bedrock and past these trees we meander down to the west side of saucer-shaped Tuolumne Pass, a major gap in the Cathedral Range. Taking the signed trail to Vogelsang from the junction here, we follow a rocky, dusty path along a moderately steep hillside below which Boothe Lake and its surrounding meadows—part of our return route—lie serene in the west.

Finally our trail makes a short climb, and we see the tents of Vogelsang High Sierra Camp spread out before us at the foot of Fletcher Peak's rock glacier. This rock glacier likely has a complex origin. The author believes that during the "Little Ice Age," a large snowfield rather than a glacier built up at the base of Fletcher Peak and large granite blocks, falling from the peak's very fractured face, slid down the snowfield to its base. The accumulated blocks thus formed a crescentic ring. Later, when conditions warmed and the snowfield melted back, additional blocks fell, and these came to rest behind the crescentic "dam" of earlier blocks, gradually filling in the void once occupied by the Little Ice Age snowfield.

At Vogelsang High Sierra Camp a few snacks may be bought, or dinner or breakfast if you have a reservation. Dispersed camping is not allowed. Rather, use a designated camping area just to the northeast up at Upper Fletcher Lake. Here you can find cables on which to bearbag your food. If you camp in this area you might also take the time to explore Townsley and Hanging Basket lakes, in basins above Upper Fletcher Lake.

Taking the Vogelsang Pass trail from the camp, we descend slightly to ford Fletcher Creek on boulders and then begin a 600-foot ascent to the pass. The panting hiker is rewarded, as always in the Sierra, with increasingly good views. Fletcher Peak, with its dozens of good climbing routes, rises grandly on the left, far north is Mt. Conness, and Clouds Rest and then Half Dome come into view in the west-southwest. The trail skirts above the west shore of Vogelsang Lake as we look down on the turfy margins and the large rock island of this timberline lake. Nearer the pass, views to the north are occluded somewhat, but expansive new views appear in the south: from left to right are Parsons Peak, Simmons Peak, Mt. Maclure,

the tip of Mt. Lyell behind Maclure, Mt. Florence, and, in the south, the entire Clark Range, from Triple Divide Peak on the left to Mt. Clark on the right.

From Vogelsang Pass, which has clumps of windswept whitebark pines, the trail rises briefly northeast before it switchbacks steeply down into sparse lodgepole forest. Many small streams provide moisture for thousands of lupine plants, with their light blue, pea-family flowers. The singing of the unnamed outlet stream from bleak Gallison Lake becomes clear as the trail begins to level off, and then we reach a flat meadow, through which the stream slowly meanders. There is a fine campsite beside this meadow, though wood fires are illegal here. After proceeding down a rutted, grassy trail for several hundred yards, we cross the Gallison outlet, top a low ridge, and make a brief, steep, rocky descent that swoops down to the meadowed valley of multibraided Lewis Creek. In this little valley in quick succession we boulder-hop the Gallison outlet and then cross Lewis Creek on a log. In a few minutes we reach a lateral trail that makes a steep half-mile climb to Bernice Lake. At the lake, among dwarf bilberry, red mountain heather and stunted lodgepole and whitebark pines, you can find small marginal campsites. Perhaps the lake's best use is as a treeline base camp for those who want to explore the snowfields and alpine lakes

Rafferty and Johnson peaks backdrop Vogelsang Lake while Fletcher Peak rises from its shore

between here and Simmons Peak. The lake is also well-located for enjoying the sight of alpenglow on the Sierra crest.

In a short ½ mile from the Bernice Lake trail junction, we cross a little stream, then descend to another equally small one as we wind a quarter mile through dense hemlock forest to a good campsite beside Florence Creek. This year-round creek cascades spectacularly down to the camping area over steep granite sheets, and the water sounds are a fine sleeping potion if you should choose to camp here.

Leaving the densely shaded hemlock forest floor, our trail descends a series of lodgepole-dotted granite slabs, and Lewis Creek makes pleasant noises in a string of chutes not far away on the right. Then, where the creek's channel narrows, the traveler will find on his left a lesson in exfoliation: granite layers peeling like an onion. One is more used to seeing this kind of peeling on Yosemite's domes, but this fine example is located on a canyon slope. As the bed of Lewis Creek steepens to deliver the stream's water to the Merced River far below, so does the trail steepen, and our descent to middle altitudes reaches the zone of red firs and western white pines. After dipping beside the creek, the trail climbs away from it to a junction with the High trail (**Hike 88**), which climbs south up to the east rim of the Merced River canyon. From here the Lewis Creek trail, now out of earshot of the creek, switchbacks down moderately, sometimes steeply, under a sparse cover of fir, juniper and pine for one mile to a junction with the Fletcher Creek trail. We'll be returning on this trail.

First, however, we'll hike to Merced Lake, which is visible on part of our descent toward it. Because cascading Lewis Creek is entrenched in a small gorge, our switchbacking trail keeps a short distance away from it, reaching a small flat with large Jeffrey pines before passing a small point with an excellent lake view. Half Dome stands on the distant down-canyon skyline. Sunny switchbacks lined with brush give way to ones with junipers and Jeffrey pines, and then, near the valley floor, to ones with white firs. Among lodgepoles on the valley floor we come to a junction that is just 40 yards north of the Merced Lake Ranger Station. You could hike 2¼ miles up-canyon to Washburn Lake (**Hike 88**), which is more scenic than Merced Lake, but the route Hike 56 takes is to the Merced Lake High Sierra Camp. A level, viewless mile walk west gets us to this camp and its adjacent riverside backpackers' campground. Here you will find bearproof boxes in which to store your food. Merced Lake, which is quite photogenic in late evening or in early morning, lies ¼ mile west of the High Sierra Camp. Some hikers prefer to continue from here down to Happy Isles (**Hike 81**), about 14 miles farther and a total distance of 30.8 miles (49.6 km) from our trailhead.

After your stay climb back up to the Fletcher Creek trail junction. Here you turn left onto this path and descend on short switchbacks to a wooden bridge over Lewis Creek. Just 50 yards past it we reach a good campsite, and then the trail enters more open hillside as it climbs moderately on a cobbled path bordered with proliferating bushes of snow bush and huckleberry oak. Just past a tributary ½ mile from Lewis Creek, we have fine views of cataracts and waterfalls on Fletcher Creek where it rushes down open granite slopes, while sparsely vegetated Babcock Lake dome presents a dramatic backdrop. We then come very close to the creek before veering northeast and climbing, steeply at times, up dozens of short switchbacks composed of cobbling placed by trail crews. Here one has more good views of Fletcher Creek chuting and cascading down from the notch at the base of the granite dome before it leaps off a ledge in free fall. The few solitary pine trees on this otherwise blank dome testify to nature's extraordinary persistence.

At the notch our trail levels off and reaches the side trail to Babcock Lake. This optional ½-mile trail arcs west to nearby Fletcher Creek, where the old trail used to cross. You, however, now go 30 yards downstream to a bedrock slab, cross there, and follow the trail northwest up to a low ridge. From it the trail goes southwest, crosses a second low ridge, then reaches the lake's northeast end. Among fair lodgepole-shaded campsites by the southeast shore, the trail dies out roughly 70 yards short of the lake's tiny island. Better campsites are on the opposite shore. Suitable diving slabs are along both shores of this fairly warm lake.

From the Babcock junction, the sandy Fletcher Creek trail ascends steadily through a moderate forest cover, staying just east of Fletcher Creek. After ¾ mile this route breaks out into the open and begins to rise more steeply via rocky switchbacks. From these zigzags one can see nearby in the north the outlet stream of Emeric Lake—though not the lake itself, which is behind a dome just to the right of the outlet's notch. If you wish to camp at Emeric Lake—and it's a fine place—leave the trail here, cross

Boothe Lake and Tuolumne Pass

Fletcher Creek at a safe spot, climb along the outlet creek's west side and then camp above the northwest shore of Emeric Lake. The next morning, circle the head of the lake and find a trail at the base of the low granite ridge at the northeast corner of the lake. Follow this trail ½ mile northeast to a scissors junction in Fletcher Creek valley.

If you choose not to camp at Emeric Lake, continue up the trail into a long meadow guarded in the west by a highly polished knoll and presided over in the east by huge Vogelsang Peak. When you come to the scissors junction, take the left-hand fork up the valley and follow this rocky-dusty trail through the forest fringe of the long meadow that straddles Fletcher Creek. This trail climbs farther from the meadow and passes northwest of a bald prominence that sits in the center of the upper valley of Fletcher and Emeric creeks, separating the two. After topping

a minor summit, the trail descends slightly and then winds almost level past several lovely ponds that are interconnected in early season. Then, immediately beyond an abandoned section of old trail, there is a lakelet 100 yards in diameter that would offer good swimming in some years. Just beyond it, the old trail veers sharply right, and our rutted meadow trail, going left, traverses northeast to a little swale with another possible swimming pond before reaching an overlook and nearby campsite above Boothe Lake. Our trail contours along meadowy slopes just east of and above the lake, passing a junction with a rutted use trail down to the lake. About ¼ mile farther we pass a reunion of this trail and then in an equal distance climb gently up to Tuolumne Pass. Here is the junction with the trail to Vogelsang, from where we retrace our steps north back to Tuolumne Meadows.

Hike 57   Tuolumne Meadows-Vogelsang-Lyell Canyon Semiloop

Distance: 20.5 miles (33.0 km) semiloop

Grade: 5D, moderate 2-day hike

Trailhead: Same as the Hike 45 trailhead. **F3.**

Introduction: This is a popular weekend hike because you can reach the Vogelsang area in only a morning's walk. This gives you a whole afternoon to explore its half-dozen nearby lakes or more distant Emeric Lake. The second day's walk is mostly downhill, and unlike the first day's ascent, is mostly open, giving the hiker many interesting, diverse views.

Description: Follow **Hike 56** 7.1 miles up to Tuolumne Pass. From it you can hike southwest to nearby Boothe Lake or 3.7 miles to Emeric Lake, or you can traverse south 0.8 mile to Vogelsang High Sierra Camp. At the camp you can branch off to explore Vogelsang, Upper Fletcher, Townsley and Hanging Basket lakes plus the alpine lake one mile above Townsley Lake. A good exercise in fairly easy cross-country hiking is to go to Ireland Lake from Upper Fletcher Lake. First follow its inlet creek up to Townsley Lake, then climb northeast from

The Sierra crest from Mt. Dana to Mt. Conness, seen from the Evelyn Lake bench

it to a large, broad plateau. Strike east across this, then climb up to a long ridge north of Peak 11440+, a high point on the Cathedral Range. From this ridge the descent southeast to Ireland Lake is obvious.

Our trail, however, leaves Upper Fletcher Lake, climbs steadily up to an indeterminable drainage divide, eases its gradient and passes through a flat-floored gully whose walls contain large, blocky feldspar crystals so typical of Cathedral Peak granodiorite. Beyond the gully a far-ranging view opens before us and on a large flat below us lies spreading, shallow, wind-swept Evelyn Lake, to whose outlet we now descend. Hikers who would like to try a slightly adventurous alternative to the Lyell Canyon trail as a route back to Tuolumne Meadows can leave the trail at this outlet and stroll down the west slope of this creek's canyon. You will pass through a beautiful, large, secluded meadow and walk beside delightful sections of the unnamed stream. Eventually, you will find, on the west side of the stream, a cliff which gradually diminishes in height. When the height has diminished to about ten feet, find a place to scramble up the cliff and then walk a few hundred feet west to find the well-worn Rafferty Creek trail.

Leaving desolate Evelyn Lake and its population of Belding ground squirrels, we stroll east, then climb through an open forest of stunted whitebark pines before dropping to a smaller, unnamed lake. Though higher than

Evelyn Lake, it has some whitebark pines nearby, providing protection from the wind for those who would camp here. About a ½-mile climb northeast from this shallow lake takes us up to a low point on a long north-south crest. We have now left the Cathedral Peak pluton (a large, granitic body) behind and tread upon another pluton—one that lacks the conspicuous feldspar crystals.

Descending from this view-packed crest and its brushy whitebark pines, we follow a trail segment that contorts down slab after bedrock slab, soon bringing us to a junction with the 1½-mile-long Ireland Lake trail. Lying beneath both granitic and metamorphic peaks, this large alpine lake is unsuited for camping unless you've brought along a tent to protect you from the wind.

Starting east from the trail junction, we soon descend gently south for ½ mile, then angle northeast to make a long 2-mile descent that usually stays within earshot of Ireland Creek. Starting first along this creek's tributary, we are in a dense forest of lodgepole and whitebark pines, but the latter give way before we reach the flat floor of Lyell Canyon. This descent could be more enjoyable if the trail were not so steep. On the floor of Lyell Canyon our trail ends at **Hike 58**, which has many trailside campsites in this part of the canyon. The walk back to Tuolumne Meadows through this nearly level canyon is very easy—good therapy for the shocked knees incurred on the descent we've just completed.

Hike 58   Tuolumne Meadows to Silver Lake via John Muir Trail

Distance: 26.2 miles (42.2 km) one way

Grade: 5D, moderate 3-day hike

Trailhead: Same as the Hike 45 trailhead. If you are starting at Silver Lake, go 60 yards west

on the spur road that is opposite the entrance to the Silver Lake Campground. This entrance is on the June Lake Loop road (Mono County Road 158). From Highway 395, northbound drivers reach this spot by driving on the loop road (past June Lake) for 8.5 miles while southbound drivers reach it by driving (past Grant Lake) 7.1 miles. **F3, G4.**

Introduction: This section of the John Muir Trail is described in its easiest direction—southbound—to the Park's border, then out to the first trailhead, although most hikers go no farther than upper Lyell Canyon. If you plan to hike Yosemite's *entire* section of the John Muir Trail (JMT), then you'll want to start from Silver Lake, which is easier than starting from Yosemite Valley. You could start at Agnew Meadows or Reds Meadow, but the road to them is restricted and, being deeply buried by winter snow, is one of the last roads to open in the Yosemite region. Doing the whole walk from Silver Lake to Yosemite Valley, you cover 50.9 miles (81.9 km). Following this hike's description in reverse, you can get to eastern Tuolumne Meadows, then you walk west past the base of Lembert Dome to the iron-stained Soda Springs. From them walk south across the western meadows, cross Highway 120, then in a few minutes traverse west to the start of **Hike 51**, which guides you to Yosemite Valley.

Potter Point reflected in Lyell Fork

Description: Follow **Hike 56** 1⅔ miles to the Rafferty Creek trail junction. Here you branch left and cross two branches of Rafferty Creek. The first ford may be difficult in early season. East of the creek the trail traverses alternating wet-meadow and forest sections—with some of the worst mosquito clouds to be found aywhere—then veers southward, climbing between two resistant granite outcrops. The silent walker may come upon grazing deer in the meadows and an occasional marmot that has ventured from the rocky outcrops. Fields of wildflowers color the grasslands from early to late season, but the best time of the year for seeing this color is usually in July. From the more open parts of the trail, one has excellent views of the Kuna Crest as it slopes up to the southeast, and the river itself has delighted generations of mountain photographers. In the meadows of Lyell Canyon you can see Ragged Peak and its crest, to the northwest.

About 4.4 miles past the last junction, our nearly level route passes a trail branching southwest to Evelyn Lake and Vogelsang High Sierra Camp (**Hike 57**), with many campsites around the junction. Look for bear-proof cables. Beyond, the trail fords multibranched Ireland Creek, passes below Potter Point, and ascends gently for three miles to the fair campsites at Lyell Base Camp, just beyond cascading Kuna

Creek. This camp, surrounded on three sides by steep canyon walls, marks the end of the meadowed sections of Lyell Canyon, and is the traditional first-night stopping place for those touring the Muir Trail south from Tuolumne Meadows.

From Lyell Base Camp the lodgepole-shaded trail ascends the steep southern terminal wall of Lyell Canyon, leaving an understory of sagebrush behind before reaching a granite bench. On it we pass a few campsites just before the confluence of the Maclure Creek tributary of the Lyell Fork. Then our route crosses the bridge to the east side and switchbacks up to some very used campsites among clumps of whitebark pines just before recrossing the fork at the north edge of a subalpine meadow. The rocky underfooting beyond the crossing takes us up past the foot of superb alpine meadows, from where views of the glaciers on the north faces of Mt. Maclure and Mt. Lyell are superlative. Hikers who wish to obtain a more intimate view or to ascend to these ice fields via the lake-dotted basin at their feet should take the ducked route that leaves our trail where we turn east and recross the infant Lyell Fork at the north end of a boulder-dotted pond.

From this ford our trail winds steeply up rocky going and eventually veers southeast up a long, straight fracture to Donohue Pass

From near Donohue Pass: Amelia Earhart Peak, Lyell Canyon and Kuna Crest

(11056') at the crest of the Sierra and on the border of Yosemite Park. Just before and just after the pass—not at it—one has great views of the Sierra crest, the Cathedral Range to the northwest and the Ritter Range to the southeast. At the broad pass we leave Yosemite National Park and enter Ansel Adams Wilderness. On a sometimes obscure trail we descend northeast away from a prominent peak and go past blocks and over slabs before turning east for a wet slog across the tundra-and-stone floor of an alpine basin. West of this basin is a conspicuous saddle, which westbound early-season hikers too often mistake for Donohue Pass. When the JMT is largely snowbound, these hikers will have to remember to hike southwest up toward the prominent peak until the real Donohue Pass becomes obvious.

Beyond the alpine basin, whitebark pines rapidly increase in size and numbers as we drop farther. Generally heading southeast, the JMT winds excessively in an oft-futile attempt to avoid the boulders and bogs of our near-timberline environment. Three miles from Donohue Pass we arrive at the Marie Lakes' outlet creek, which is best crossed at an obvious jump-across spot slightly downstream. Immediately beyond the creek we meet a trail that climbs southwest up to the lower, large alpine lake, and then we parallel these lakes' outlet ⅓ mile down-canyon to a low ridge. On it we get our last good views of—east to west—Banner Peak, Mt. Ritter and Mt. Davis, then we descend via short, steep switchbacks to a junction with the Rush Creek trail. This junction is in the Rush Creek Forks area, which sprouts a lot of small camps, virtually all of them illegal since they are within one hundred feet of a creek or trail. A seasonal ranger, sometimes camped two hundred yards southeast of the junction, may enforce the rules. Although you have left Yose-

mite, you have not left its black bears, for they have spilled beyond the Park's boundaries in search of backpacker camps. If you camp here, expect to have these night-time visitors.

Among lodgepoles we leave the John Muir Trail to follow the Rush Creek trail 9½ miles down to Silver Lake. Immediately we ford two of the creek's many forks, then descend ⅔ mile to a small campsite on the west shore of Waugh Lake. Our trail hugs this lake, then in about 10 minutes we pass our second lodgepole-shaded, lakeshore campsite. After an easy mile hike beyond it, some of the distance being past sagebrush, we leave the lake, switchback down below the base of its dam and immediately meet a trail that climbs to Weber and Sullivan lakes.

Paralleling Rush Creek, we continue down-canyon—now on a lodgepole-lined, closed service road of the Southern California Edison Company—and in a few minutes reach a large campsite. Another campsite is passed just where our road leaves Rush Creek to climb through a 30-foot-high, glacier-polished granite gap. Beyond it we hike down toward Rush Creek, curve northeast and in ¼ mile reach a short spur trail that goes south to a large creekside campsite. On our road we quickly meet the junction with a trail to Agnew Pass. At this junction we turn left, climb north past a pond and a closer, larger one, Billy Lake, and in ¼ mile top a low notch in a ridge that is composed of metavolcanic rocks. A short, steep descent east follows, then a gentle one north. The road quickly descends to the west shore of Gem Lake, but before it does so, we leave it and traverse north ¼ mile on trail to Crest Creek. Here, among an abundance of small-lodgepole-shaded campsites, we meet the Alger Lake trail. By following **Hike 60** in reverse you can take this extremely scenic trail back into Yosemite National Park and then descend Highway 120

4.6 miles to the Dog Lake trail, on which you quickly drop to your trailhead parking lot. This high-altitude loop is 41.4 miles (66.6 km) long and is for those who want to escape the crowds at the expense of some strenuous climbing.

In late season we can rock-hop Crest Creek, but normally one must cross it on a log. Aspens—brilliant in early fall—join ranks with lodgepoles in shading a creekside campsite. Farther east aspens give way to sagebrush, junipers and Jeffrey pines and even to an occasional whitebark pine. Our trail generally stays above Gem Lake's steep shoreline, then climbs to one ridge before descending and climbing to a second one, this one above the lake's dam. This ridge and the bedrock north and south of it are composed mostly of Paleozoic-age sediments that have been metamorphosed, usually to hornfels. These ancient rocks are roughly 100 times older than the dark andesite flows we see above Gem Lake's forested south slopes. These thick, horizontal flows originated along a fault when the Sierra crest began to form about three million years ago as the land east of the fault began to drop.

We leave Gem Lake behind and, for a spell, Ansel Adams Wilderness, as we descend to the Agnew Lake dam. On this descent, mountain mahogany dominates our dry, south-facing slopes, in contrast to the forested, north-facing ones just below Agnew Pass. In the dam's vicinity you're likely to see giant blazing stars, whose oversized yellow flowers will be blooming for late-season hikers.

Beyond the dam, switchbacks lead us north down alongside a tramway, which we cross twice, and then we descend slopes toward Silver Lake. At first these slopes have mountain mahogany, juniper and even pinyon pine, but then, not far beyond a small waterfall, they are gradually replaced with waist-high vegetation. Draining west into Silver Lake is Reversed Creek, which has an interesting history. Glaciers originating near the Sierra crest descended to the large canyon we're in, then split into two lobes, each lobe going on one side of Reversed Peak. Each glacial lobe built up a considerable terminal moraine at its snout, and when these lobes finally retreated, a lake formed behind each moraine. Before the waters backing up behind the June Lake moraine were able to breach it, they overflowed southwest into the Grant Lake drainage, and today these waters continue to flow in that direction—directly opposite that of the glacier's flow—as *Reversed Creek*. It is also reversed in the sense that it is the only creek on the eastern Sierra margin that flows toward the range's crest rather than away from it.

Near Silver Lake's west corner our trail almost touches the June Lakes Loop road, which has very limited parking here, then our path arcs behind Silver Lake Resort and fords several branches of Alger Creek. It finally traverses behind Silver Lake Trailer Court to quickly end at a trailhead parking area amid sagebrush, mule ears, rabbit brush and bitterbrush.

Hike 59   Dana Meadows to Mono Pass

Distance: 8.0 miles (12.9 km) round trip

Grade: 2C, moderate half-day hike

Trailhead: Mono Pass trailhead, which is 5.6 miles east of the Tuolumne Meadows Campground, or 1.4 miles south of Tioga Pass. **F3.**

Introduction: This day hike to a historic pass on the Sierra crest is great for alpine scenery, for the views improve constantly and culminate at the pass, from where one can gaze down the great gash of Bloody Canyon to the vast, high desert east of the Sierra.

Description: Starting under a dense canopy of lodgepole pines, we leave the Dana Fork parking lot, descending on a wide, well-worn trail—once a dirt road. In a meadow ¼ mile from the trailhead, a trail branches from our road and

it parallels the road's east side for a few hundred yards before rejoining it. You can take either route. Lodgepoles ceaselessly attempt to invade this and other High Sierra meadows, but wet years raise the water table and this may directly or indirectly kill them. These young trees' needles are also susceptible to brown-felt fungus and to icy winter winds.

About ½ mile from the trailhead we cross Dana Meadows creek and Dana Fork just above their confluence. Immediately before these two crossings is an old trail that once led to Tuolumne Meadows but now quickly aborts. Beyond these two crossings our trail climbs to the crest of a low moraine, crosses two more, and then near Parker Pass Creek comes to the roofless remains of a pioneer log cabin.

A lakelet straddles Mono Pass, backdropped by the Kuna Crest and Mammoth Peak

Sagebrush intermingles with lodgepoles as we pass creekside meadows that in early morning hours often have browsing deer in them. A little more than two miles from our trailhead we come to a junction, and from it a trail climbs 1.9 miles gently up along Parker Pass Creek to shallow, meadow-bordered Spillway Lake (camping prohibited). This and other lakes of the Mono Pass-Tioga Pass area have California gulls as frequent visitors, these birds nesting on islands in large, alkaline Mono Lake (**Hike 61**). From Spillway Lake you could hike cross-country east up to alpine Parker Pass, then head back on a trail to the Mono Pass area.

Our trail up to the Spillway Lake trail junction has been easy, but now it climbs nearly 700 feet, passing the ruins of a second pioneer cabin, on the right, just ¼ mile before the Parker Pass trail junction. From that junction, near a large whitebark pine, **Hike 60** describes that trail all the way to Gem Lake. After ¼ mile of nearly level hiking our trail passes a lakelet situated between two ponds. From the east shore of the lakelet a trail starts south toward five old cabins but dies out in 300 yards. From that point, however, the cabins just south above you are easily reached. These cabins, constructed from local whitebark pines, once housed workers on the nearby Golden Crown and Ella Bloss gold mines, both now defunct. If you visit these cabins, you'll get a good view north of Mt. Gibbs' south shoulder. Note the difference between its lower slopes and steeper higher ones. Whitebark pines are able to grow on the lower slopes, but not on the unstable upper ones. You'll also note that the upper slopes have patterned ground, which indicates slope movement. In Yosemite's alpine areas, mass movement takes place only on slopes of metamorphic rocks, not those of granite, because ice wedging breaks metamorphic bedrock into many small, unstable rocks, whereas it heaps granite into large, relatively immobile blocks.

Just east of the cabins' spur trail we encounter Summit Lake, straddling breezy Mono Pass.

The lake appears to lie immediately east of the pass—the Park's boundary—but careful scouting among the lake's west-end willows will reveal that the lake does indeed have a west-flowing outlet as well as a more obvious east-flowing one. Nesting beneath the willows are white-crowned sparrows, which are usually seen with Brewer's blackbirds. The blackbirds nest at lower elevations during the spring but usually migrate up to these heights by the time the Mono trail is snow-free. Our hike has followed only a small portion of the Mono trail, which is an old Indian trail that started near Cascade Creek, high above westernmost Yosemite Valley. This trail started like today's eastbound El Capitan trail, but continued northeast along Bluejay Creek to Yosemite Creek, then up to Porcupine Flat, from where it took a route similar to that of the later Old Tioga Road. From Mono Pass the Mono trail continued down Bloody Canyon, which may have been named for the reddish colored bedrock of metamorphosed sediments, but more likely was named for the treachery of this canyon. In 1864 William Brewer and Charles Hoffmann—two younger members of Josiah Whitney's State Geological Survey—descended Bloody Canyon. Brewer later said of it:

> You would all pronounce it utterly inaccessible to horses, yet pack trains come down, but the bones of several horses or mules and the stench of another told that all had not passed safely. The trail comes down three thousand feet in less than four miles, over rocks and loose stones, in narrow canyons and along precipices. It was a bold man who first took a horse up there. The horses were so cut by sharp rocks that they named it "Bloody Canyon," and it has held the name—and it is appropriate—part of the way the rocks are literally sprinkled with blood from the animals.

Today this trail is still a steep descent over rocks and loose stones, but it is considerably safer. Upper Sardine Lake, only ¾ mile distant by this trail, is worth the effort, but beyond it a big drop to cold, deep Lower Sardine Lake makes for an exhausting return hike.

Hike 60   Dana Meadows to Silver Lake via Parker Pass

Distance: 20.0 miles (32.1 km) one way

Grade: 5D, moderate 2-day hike

Trailhead: Same as the Hike 59 trailhead. If you're starting from Silver Lake, consult the Hike 58 trailhead information. **F3.**

Introduction: Knowledgeable backpackers prefer this route to the popular, nearby section of the John Muir Trail (Hike 58). Being mostly along metamorphic terrain, this route is certainly more colorful, and by staying high—often at or above timberline—it has a wild aspect about it. At these elevations dark glasses and sunscreen are a must. This route is no place to be caught in a lightning storm or a snowstorm, so only weather-wise backpackers should attempt it. However, the 10.5 miles to Parker Pass and back make a fine high-altitude day hike for anyone in good health.

Description: Follow **Hike 59** 3½ miles up to a junction just ½ mile short of broad, deep Mono Pass. From a large whitebark pine near the junction, strike south-southwest 300 yards across a meadow, following ducks that guide you to a resumption of your tread. Continuing in the same direction, we climb up to the crest of a broad moraine that here and there has rusty exposures of Triassic-period metavolcanics (metamorphosed volcanic rocks). On this ascent you pass a nearby whitebark snag which in the proper lighting can be very photogenic. Most whitebark pines around here, however, are reduced to shrub height, so you get largely unobstructed views that include shallow Spillway Lake, lying at the base of the Kuna Crest. Note how the upper slopes of this granitic crest differ not only in color but in shape and texture from the lower metamorphic slopes. Up at timberline, we see the deep cleft of Parker Pass more than a mile before we attain it. Stunted whitebarks and yellow-blossomed bush cinquefoils yield to mats of alpine willow—a favorite summer haunt of white-crowned sparrows—then these bushes yield to sedges and finally, at the broad, signed pass, to coarse gravel. A low, broad moraine south of us hides barren Parker Pass Lake and it also provides a suitable habitat for marmots. Briefly during midsummer, a marmot's sole food source may be Sierra wallflowers and Brewer's lupines. The first species can turn the moraine's slopes bright yellow and mask the presence of the equally prevalent lupine. Other plant species appear both before and after these two, and all provide the marmot with a diverse selection, which he readily consumes before going into hibernation in October.

From Parker Pass, day hikers can wander northeast up to a crest that leads to the top of windswept Mt. Lewis. However, don't attempt this technically easy but thin-air climb if the weather looks threatening. At Parker Pass backpackers enter Ansel Adams Wilderness and leave all vestiges of the granitic Yosemite landscape behind. Descending on Paleozoic-era metasediments, they first cross an outlet creek from two nearby ponds, recross it at a third, and then traverse southeast toward a series of ominous looking switchbacks that climb the northwest slope of Parker Peak. About ¾ mile beyond the pass we cross a seasonally churning tributary that gets its vigor from a permanent

A marmot surveys its domain in an alpine fell-field near Parker Pass

Even without all its signs, Parker Pass couldn't be mistaken for anything else

snowfield lodged high on the slopes between Kuna and Koip peaks. Just past this tributary the deep canyon cleft between Mt. Lewis and Parker Peak begins to open, and through it we see the Mono Craters and the distant White Mountains. The latter were part of the Sierra Nevada until about 4 million years ago, when they were first isolated as today's basin lands began to sink.

One-half mile closer to trail's end, we reach an alpine tarn and from it can gaze straight down the enormous Parker Creek cleft. Parker Lake is almost hidden, but larger Grant Lake, with its giant lateral moraines, is easily seen. This stupendous view may divert one's interest from the seemingly ordinary tarn. This pond is, however, very un-Sierran, for near its outlet the shallow rocky bottom is patterned with a network of polygon stone rings. Repeated freezing and melting of ice over hundreds of years have separated the coarse rocks from the finer particles. If you step in the middle of one of these polygons—usually a hexagon—you'll sink into clay. This phenomenon is not seen at many High Sierra ponds because they typically exist in granitic terrain. This pond, however, is in metamorphic terrain, and at high elevations like here, metamorphic rock is shattered by ice wedging, which breaks it into many small, unstable blocks.

Beyond this tarn we are confronted with a ¼-mile net vertical climb to Koip Peak Pass. First we climb to our second glacier-fed Parker Creek tributary. Its glacier, like the first, became an inactive snowfield by the summer of 1977, if not earlier. Panting up to the first of many switchbacks, we take a breather, scan the ever-improving panorama and now see most of large, alkaline Mono Lake and the summits of Mts. Gibbs and Conness, the latter rising above Parker Pass. During July you may see the unmistakable sky pilot, a blue-petaled polemonium that thrives in the bleakest alpine environments. Around Yosemite you'll rarely find it growing below 11,000 feet. Sharing this harsh habitat are members of the *Draba* genus, which has a dozen hard-to-key species that exist

above timberline in the Sierra Nevada. You'll note that its yellow flowers are virtually identical to those of the Sierra wallflower, often seen west of Parker Pass, for both are mustards.

Finally, switchbacks yield to a gradually easing ascent southwest to shallow Koip Peak Pass, which at 12,280 feet is one of the Sierra's highest trail passes. Before early August, snowfields may cover parts of the trail to the pass, and they could present a problem since you have 600 feet of steep, potentially fatal slopes below you. On your ascent to the pass you may have noticed the smooth, gentle slopes of Parker Peak, Mt. Wood and even Mt. Lewis. These slopes, like our broad pass, are unglaciated and they give you an idea of what the near-crest Sierran topography was like before glaciers sunk their icy teeth into it. If you have the time, you might scramble up the loose, unsteep scree slopes to either Koip or Parker Peak.

Leaving the pass, we exchange views of Mts. Conness, Gibbs, Dana and Lewis for ones of the Alger Lakes, the June Lake ski area, volcanic Mammoth Mountain, distant Lake Crowley and the hazy central Sierra Nevada crest. While topographic constraints made a string of short switchbacks necessary for our ascent, they are lacking for our descent, which is a pleasant, occasionally switchbacking drop deep into the Alger Lakes basin. As the trail's gradient eases, we cross Alger Creek, and then, with a low, fresh-looking moraine on our right, parallel the creek for ¾ mile before crossing the multi-crested moraine and descending cross-country past cairns for ¼ mile to a point between the two fairly large Alger Lakes. Only 50 yards and a 2-foot drop separate the two timberline lakes, and on the bedrock landmass that separates them you can set up camp among its windblown whitebark pines. These will be the first partly sheltered sites you'll encounter on this hike, for no camping is allowed in Yosemite's Dana Fork drainage and all possible sites beyond Parker Pass are above timberline. Immediately beyond lower Alger Lake's outlet you'll also find a trailside campsite.

From the outlet we climb up our moraine's low crest, glancing back across the open terrain at the dramatic setting of this deeply glaciated, somber-toned rock basin, which has metasediments composing the northeast canyon wall and metavolcanics composing the southwest one. Now 6 miles from Parker Pass and 4 from Gem Lake, we follow the generally open moraine's crest south past a nearby lakelet, then descend steeply about 300 feet to a second one, along whose fragile shore one should not camp. Along this morainal route you'll probably note the flat-topped mass standing immediately east of Gem Pass. Like Koip Peak Pass it was untouched by glaciers, although they certainly cut deep into its flanks. This pre-glacial summit is a full 2,700 feet below unglaciated Parker Peak, and we can therefore surmise that just prior to the onset of glaciation, the Sierra Nevada already had substantial relief.

Despite the high altitude, our second lakelet provides an acceptable habitat for dozens of yellow-legged frogs. Large rocks forming small islands testify to the instability of a nearby cliff. Just 250 yards beyond this tarn, we enter our first stand of lodgepoles. Among its protective confines we immediately discover an improved campsite, on the left, which is certainly the place you'll want to camp if you have to wait out a lightning storm. Only a minute's walk toward Gem Lake, you'll come to a shallow pond—your camp's closest water source. Beyond this pond you climb for ½ mile to forested Gem Pass while Alger Creek, hundreds of feet below you, drops out of sight to your final goal, Silver Lake. Shortly before Gem Pass the trail forks. The left branch descends, only to climb again, but it may be the better of the two in early season, when the snow is piled deep. From 10,500-foot Gem Pass we have our first views of the famous Ritter Range, dominated by Mt. Ritter and Banner Peak. Now under a continual canopy of protective forest, we descend first through whitebark pines and then lodgepoles, cross Crest Creek after ¾ mile, and switchback down alongside it, reaching well-used campsites above Gem Lake after a 2-mile, 1,400-foot drop. Among these campsites you'll meet the Rush Creek trail, on which you hike almost 5 miles east to trail's end, near the Silver Lake Campground. This stretch is described in the last part of **Hike 58**.

Hike 61   Mt. Dana

Distance: 5.8 miles (9.3 km) round trip

Grade: 2D, strenuous half-day hike

Trailhead: On Highway 120 at Tioga Pass—the Park's east entrance. **F3.**

Introduction: Dark glasses and good health are both necessary for this climb to the second highest summit in Yosemite. Only Mt. Lyell exceeds it—by only 61 feet—but the Lyell summit requires mountaineering skills. Because Dana vies with Mt. Hoffmann as Yosemite's most accessible peak, it is very popular, and on weekends you may find dozens of persons walking up it. Its summit views are among the Sierra's best, but turn back if the weather looks threatening.

Description: The trail up Mt. Dana, like the one up Mt. Hoffmann (**Hike 27**), is one of use and not an officially maintained trail. Dana's trail, however, is not random, but rather was established by Dr. Carl Sharsmith—Yosemite's eminent botanist—who decades ago chose a route that would minimize damage to this area's fragile subalpine and alpine environment. From Tioga Pass the footpath starts due east, then winds southeast past the south shores of two ponds that are among two dozen that developed when the last major glacier retreated. Cirque glaciers originating on the Kuna Crest, about 6 miles south of us, coalesced to form a trunk glacier that mainly descended the Dana Fork to unite with the Lyell Fork glacier and create the Tuolumne glacier. Being strengthened by dozens of feeder glaciers, this mammoth glacier was able to descend tens of miles down-canyon, well into the realm of temperate climates. About 20,000 years ago, at the height of the Tioga glaciation, the Dana Fork branch was about 1000 feet thick where it overflowed *north* across Tioga Pass to join the Lee Vining glacier. This originated in the nearby Hall Natural Area, and together they descended to the base of the Sierra escarpment. However, by about 14,000 years ago it appears that the Lyell Fork glacier had retreated sufficiently so that now the Lee Vining glacier briefly overflowed *south* into the Tuolumne drainage.

About 200 yards beyond the second pond our path starts a moderate ascent, then ⅓ mile later it becomes a steep one and generally stays that way for almost 1500 vertical feet. About midway up this steep stretch you can rest in an *alp*—a miniature alpine pasture. The end of the steep section is noted by a 3-foot-high cairn atop a south-descending spur ridge. Here, well above timberline, the path ends, 1.1 miles from and still 1400 feet below the summit. Several paths of use—one more prominent than the others— head up the rubbly, ancient slopes to the windy summit. Most people climb east to a shallow saddle, at about 12,150' elevation and immediately east of a crest high point, then hike southeast up the ridge to the top. Early in the hike the views west are great, but the panorama continually expands with elevation, saturating the optic nerves with overpowering vistas. When you hike southeast up the ridge, your views take on another dimension, adding to your elation. However, take this crest ascent slowly, for the atmosphere is thin and in your euphoria you can easily overexert yourself. Being above the 12,000' elevation, July hikers can expect to see the sky pilot, which with its dense head of blue flowers, is the most conspicuous alpine wildflower in the Sierra Nevada.

At the summit your exhausting efforts are rewarded by a stupendous 360° panorama. The Sierra's east escarpment can be viewed as far as the Wheeler Crest, about 40 miles to the southeast. East of it extends a long north-south mountain chain, the White Mountains, which were a part of the Sierra Nevada before the land between them began to subside around 3-4 million years ago. At the north end of the White Mountains stand the pale, isolated twin summits of Montgomery and Boundary peaks, both over 13,000 feet high. Gambling is allowed on the Boundary Peak summit for it is ¼ mile in from the Nevada border. Below these twin summits rises Crater Mountain, the highest of Mono

Craters' many volcanic summits, and, like most of them, less than 10,000 years old.

The youthfulness of Mono Craters strongly contrasts with the ancient age of giant, orbicular Mono Lake, directly north of them. Lakes are generally short-lived features, but Ken Lajoie of the U.S. Geological Survey puts its age at one million years, and it may even be double that. The reason for this great age is that Mono Basin has existed as a subsiding basin for at least the last 2 million years, and it is still subsiding fast enough today to offset incoming sediments. In these 2 million years, almost 4000 feet of sediments have accumulated beneath the floor of today's lake. Granitic bedrock lies at the base of these sediments, and before 3 million years ago this bedrock stood about 10,000 feet higher—as part of the Sierra Nevada.

Ironically, this lake's longevity is threatened by humans—water-hungry Los Angeles residents in particular—who have diverted inflowing creeks, thereby causing the lake to drop 40 feet in historic times. This drop has increased the lake's alkalinity almost to a pH of 10 (feels like clothes-detergent water). In addition, when the lake reached a then-all-time low during the summer of 1977, a corridor emerged, linking 1000-year-old Negit Island to the Black Point shoreline. This island, a major nesting ground for thousands of California gulls and other birds, thus became accessible to predators. With diminishing nesting sites and increasing alkalinity, the populations of gulls and other migrant birds have unfortunately decreased.

During the Tahoe glaciation, which a number of glaciologists believe may have been at its height perhaps about 75,000 years ago, the Lee Vining glacier actually descended into Mono Lake. Back then the lake was at least 600 feet

Summit view of Dana Plateau and Mono Basin. Circle indicates plateau's Cape Royal. The plateau was once a lowland during preglacial, prefaulted times.

higher than it is today, and it likely overflowed the basin. Then, instead of being an alkaline desert lake, it was a fresh-water lake that likely had glacier-spalled icebergs floating in it! In all of North America, only two other large lakes are known to have had glaciers encroach upon them: Lake Tahoe and Lake Bonneville (now existing in dwarfed form as Utah's Great Salt Lake).

The glacier that once encroached upon Mono Lake also helped to deepen steep-walled Glacier Canyon, immediately below our summit. Today only the few-hundred-year-old Dana "glacier" (more snowfield than glacier) clings to the north face of our peak. Being only a two-hour hike up-canyon from Tioga Lake, it is frequented by mountaineers who practice their skills on it. practice their skills on it.

Another feature worth visiting is the broad, gently sloping Dana Plateau, with its rare snow willows, which like Peak 12568, 1½ miles southeast of us, is a relict of an old, unglaciated landscape. For that matter, Mt. Dana and Mt. Gibbs are left over from that landscape, as are many of this area's gentle-sloped peaks. By scanning the horizon you can see a number of them and then you can mentally reconstruct the pre-glacial eastern-Yosemite landscape, which, you'll note, had considerable relief. Mt. Dana, for example, stood more than 3000 feet above the Mammoth Mountain area, which in pre-glacial times was quite low, for that volcano hadn't yet erupted.

Continuing our counterclockwise scan west, we see deep-blue Saddlebag Lake and above it, the serrated Shepherd Crest. Next comes pointed North Peak, with its south-facing pre-glacial surface, then a true "Matterhorn," Mt. Conness. Beyond a sea of dark-green lodgepoles lies Tuolumne Meadows and its guardian, Lembert Dome, whose bald summit is barely visible. On the skyline above them stand Tuolumne Peak and Mt. Hoffmann, while south of these stands the craggy Cathedral Range. Examining it counterclockwise, you can identify blocky Cathedral Peak, north-pointing Unicorn Peak, clustered Echo Peaks and the nearby Cockscomb plus the fin-like Matthes Crest, extending south from it. A bit farther are sedate Johnson Peak, more profound Rafferty Peak and glacier-cut Tuolumne Pass. To the south-southwest stands the Park's highest peak, Mt. Lyell (13,114'), which also harbors the Park's

Members of an alpine-botany course at Dana Plateau's Cape Royal

largest glacier, today cleft in two by a northwest-dropping ridge. When members of the Whitney Survey first climbed our summit in 1863, they saw a Lyell glacier twice today's size, and it partly buried the ridge as well as extending north beyond it. Flanking Lyell is Mt. Maclure and its glacier, to the west, and pointed Rodgers Peak, to the southeast. Mt. Ritter and Banner Peak barely poke their summits above the temporarily stagnant Kuna Peak-Koip Peak glacier, to the south. Finally, Parker Peak and Mt. Wood stand above closer Mt. Gibbs, while Mt. Lewis—of intermediate distance—projects just east of them. Once part of a low continental borderland, all the red or dark metamorphic summits (including Mt. Dana's) are made of rocks with an extremely long history—see the first part of Chapter 4 (the area's early geologic history) for details.

Tall trees are dwarfed by the lower part of Middle Cathedral Rock's northeast face

Section 6

Trails of the Yosemite Valley Area

Introduction: Rightly called "The Incomparable Valley," Yosemite Valley is a magnet that attracts visitors from all over the world. As John Muir noted long ago, the Sierra Nevada has several "Yosemites," though none of them matches Yosemite Valley in grandeur. Hetch Hetchy, to the north, is the foremost example of such a Yosemite. Though some of these "Yosemites" rival or exceed Yosemite Valley in the depth of their canyons and the steepness of their walls, none has the prize-winning combination of its wide, spacious floor, its world-famous waterfalls, and its unforgettable monoliths—El Capitan and Half Dome.

This section is actually composed of four parts. Hikes 62-67 acquaint you with the views and natural history seen along the Valley floor. Hikes 68-70 guide you up to and along the Valley's north rim, while Hikes 71-76 guide you along its south rim. Finally, Hikes 77-81 direct you up a multi-stepped climb east from the Valley to thundering Vernal and Nevada falls, forested Little Yosemite Valley, intimidating Half Dome, and popular Merced Lake.

Supplies and Services: Yosemite Village is a small-scale urban center—and like one, it is all too crowded. Parking space is at a premium, so I recommend you reach it by taking a free shuttle bus or by walking or bicycling. At the "Village" is the Visitor Center and Museum plus a general store, eating establishments, medical clinic, post office and other services. The services are expected to undergo some changes in the 1990s; in particular, the gas station and vehicle-repair garage will be removed.

The only service you'll find lacking at the Village is lodging, which is available—along with meals—at Yosemite Lodge to the west, the Ahwahnee Hotel to the east, and Curry Village to the southeast. Due for closure some time in the '90s is the Curry Village's Housekeeping Camp, which currently has a laundromat next to its showers. Showers are also available at Camp Curry proper and at Yosemite Lodge. These two operations each have a swimming pool, a bike rental, and a post office. The prestigious Ahwahnee hotel formerly had tennis courts and a 9-hole golf course, but now only offers (besides elegant ambience) a guest-only swimming pool. At Glacier Point, high above the Valley's southeast end, you can buy snacks, film and a few other items. The same is true at the foot of the Glacier Point cliff—Happy Isles.

Wilderness Permits: Most of the hikes in this section are day hikes. For multiday hikes, get your permit at the Visitor Center.

Campgrounds: There are eight campgrounds in Yosemite Valley, including the Group Campground and the Backpackers and Sunnyside walk-in campgrounds (the first two are located next to each other). All but the two walk-in campgrounds have their sites reserved through MISTIX (see page 2). For south-rim trails, you should stay at Bridalveil Campground, south of the Valley, whose entrance is midway along the Glacier Point Road.

Hike 62   Valley Floor, West Loop

Distance: 6.9 miles (11.1 km) loop trip

Grade: 2B, easy half-day hike

Trailhead: Bridalveil Fall parking lot, 120 yards before the descending Wawona Road reaches a junction on the floor of Yosemite Valley. **C5.**

Introduction: This is the first of six Yosemite Valley floor hikes in this book, which are arranged from west to east. Because the Valley contains so much history, natural history and spectacular scenery, the hike descriptions are long even though the hikes are short. On this first loop hike you'll see Bridalveil Fall, the Cathedral Rocks and El Capitan all at close range.

Description: You could start this loop from Fern Spring, Bridalveil Meadow, Bridalveil Moraine, El Capitan Meadow or Devils Elbow, but we're starting from the Bridalveil Fall parking lot, since it has the most parking space. From the lot's east end you hike just two minutes on a paved trail to a junction, veer right and parallel a Bridalveil Creek tributary as you climb an equally short trail up to its end among boulders and bay trees. During May and June, when Bridalveil Fall is at its best, your trail's-end viewpoint will be drenched in spray, making photography from this vantage point nearly impossible. Early settlers named this fall for its filmy, veil-like aspect, which it has in summer after its flow has greatly diminished. However, their predecessors, the Miwok Indians, named it *Pohono,* the "fall of the puffing winds," for at low volume its water is pushed around by gusts of wind. Wind certainly blows at other falls, but it is most effective at Bridalveil, since this fall leaps clear into space—away from its dead-vertical cliff.

Of Yosemite's other falls, only Vernal Fall leaps free over a dead-vertical cliff, but its flow—the Merced River—is too strong to be greatly affected by the wind. The other major falls drop over cliffs that are less than vertical, and hence the falls partly glide down them.

Bridalveil's cliff owes its verticality to vertical joints along which the cliff's granite flakes off. Glaciers may have steepened this cliff, but even without glaciers it would have appeared impres-

Bridalveil Fall

sive when the first glacier entered Yosemite Valley, perhaps about 2 million years ago. Back then it is likely that Bridalveil Fall already existed, either as a true waterfall or as a series of smaller falls. Over millions of years Yosemite Valley has been widening principally through rockfalls, although glaciers certainly trimmed back and steepened Yosemite's cliffs to a degree. Along most of our easy hike, we'll be treading across sediments, deposited since the glaciers left, that are as much as 1000 feet deep. Ancient glaciers first cut deeply through Yosemite Valley before later, smaller ones filled up most of the excavation with sediments.

After descending back to the trail junction, we quickly encounter three branches of Bridalveil Creek, each churning along a course that cuts through old rockfall debris. Ignoring all spur trails, we keep to our wide trail—the old Wawona Road until 1933—almost to the Valley's eastbound road, then quickly angle right to climb up to the crest of Bridalveil Moraine. From it we get a good view of the loose west wall of Lower Cathedral Rock and also the overhanging west wall of Leaning Tower. Bridalveil Fall is now out of sight, for it lies hidden in the recess that may have developed through rockfalls since the last glacier scoured its massive wall. It's been widely believed by the public as well as by some prominent geologists that diminutive Bridalveil Moraine, left by the Tioga-age glacier about 14,000 years ago, dammed the Merced River to create mammoth (though mythical) Lake Yosemite. However, an even larger lake probably formed about 800,000 years ago, after the gargantuan, valley-deepening Sherwin-age glacier retreated from the Valley.

In post-glacial times, the Valley often may have been quite swampy due to temporary dams created by periodic rockfalls that originated on Lower Cathedral Rock's loose north wall, above us. Indeed, the first visitors found the Valley too swampy and mosquito-ridden, so in 1879 the large rockfall blocks clogging the nearby Merced River channel were blasted apart, which deepened the channel some 4½ feet and thereby lowered the Valley's water table. The river, rather than meandering widely and changeably across the Valley, became entrenched, and ponderosa pines and incense-cedars invaded at the expense of wet-meadow vegetation and black oaks. The blasting was also expected to reduce all flooding, but major floods occurred about every 15–20 years. One of the larger ones s the 1955 flood, which covered almost two ds of the Valley's floor.

Just past the moraine's crest we enter a gully lined with big-leaf maples, and here we have an excellent head-on view of mammoth El Capitan. Then, only yards away from the base of the forbidding north face of Lower Cathedral Rock, we can stretch our necks and look up at its large ledge, covered with gold-cup oaks, that almost cuts the face in two. While violet-green swallows perform aerial acrobatics high overhead, we continue east through a conifer forest, soon crossing a narrow, open talus field. At its base stands a second moraine, similar to Bridalveil Moraine, and like all the Valley's moraines it is *recessional*—that is, it was left where a glacier temporarily halted its retreat.

Walking among white firs, incense-cedars, ponderosa pines, Douglas-firs and black oaks, we continue on a generally view-impaired route to a brief climb almost to the base of overwhelming Middle Cathedral Rock, and here you'll find it worth your effort to scramble 50 yards up to the actual base. From it you'll see most of El Capitan plus Middle and Lower Brother, North Dome, Sentinel Rock and Taft Point. But greater than this panorama is a sense of communion one gets with nature just by touching the base of this rock's overpowering, 2,000-foot-high, monolithic face. It can be a humbling experience.

Beyond the massive northeast face and its two pinnacles, we gradually descend to a level area, from which you could walk northwest a bit to a turnout on the eastbound road. From that turnout you can plainly see the two Cathedral Spires. These spires, and the 500-foot-high buttress they stand on, resemble a two-towered Gothic cathedral—hence the name. Despite their apparent inaccessibility, both were first climbed way back in 1934, during the early days of Yosemite Valley rock climbing. Until the 1960s both were popular climbs, but today most climbers want much harder routes.

After about a ⅓-mile traverse across a forested flat, we arrive at a signed trail, veer left on it, and descend to a point on the eastbound road only 20 yards west of the Cathedral Picnic Area entrance. The few people who head north to the picnic area will be rewarded with two classic views, one of El Capitan and another of the Three Brothers. Our route, however, continues northwest almost to a bend in the Merced River, from which you are bound to see—at least on summer days—sunbathers basking on the long, sandy "beach" of the far shore. Since our route eventually goes over to that vicinity, hikers with swimsuits on can shortcut (from about July through October) across the chest-deep Merced to that sunny beach. Others follow the trail briefly west to the El Capitan Bridge. Here, by the eastern edge of El Capitan Meadow, the hiker gets a noteworthy view of the Cathedral Rocks, and one can see why the Miwok Indians visualized the lower monolith as a giant acorn. Across the meadow are some trees that in spring 1976 were subjected to prescribed burning. Such intentional burning began in 1971, when the Park Service decided that fires were necessary in order to return Yosemite Valley's vegetation to its former character—a more-open, mixed stand of oaks and conifers. The many years of fire suppression had seen the growth of a dense, view-obstructing conifer forest.

From the El Capitan Bridge you walk north either along the road or its adjacent riverbank trail to a sharp bend. By continuing east about 250 yards you can reach the extremely popular Devils Elbow Picnic Area. Not only does it have the finest "beach" in the Valley, but it also has a splendid mid-river rock that is perfect for diving. The rock's obstruction of the Merced's channel forces the river to flow more swiftly past it, and the water scours the channel and makes it deep enough for safe diving. This rock, which has been here a long time, came from a rockfall high on El Capitan's massive face.

At the river bend we cross the main road and start west along an old paved road that in ⅓ mile comes to a small hollow from whose north end a *de facto* trail climbs to the nose of El Capitan. For the visitor new to Yosemite Valley, the size of El Capitan, like the Cathedral Rocks and other Valley landmarks, is too large to really comprehend, and many visitors who first try to estimate its size swear it is only 1000 or so feet high. If you take the *de facto* trail up the left side of El Cap's nose, you'll probably see rock climbers, who hundreds of feet up the 3000-foot-high wall are reduced to antlike stature. The left (southwest) base of El Cap has about three dozen relatively short routes that go nowhere near the top, and climbers are usually found in this area almost any day. If you've ever wondered how it is possible to climb "unclimbable" cliffs, walk up the trail and see for yourself. The trailside vegetation of Mariposa manzanita and gold-cup oaks, growing on talus deposits, is ideal for California ground squirrels and other animals, who in turn make suitable prey for rattlesnakes. You probably won't see these snakes, but they nevertheless exist, as do loose boulders, so for safety's sake don't bring any children.

Beyond this vicinity our road rolls gently west to a junction with a trail (on which **Hike 21** descends), but we stick to our closed road and quickly reach the main road at the west end of El Capitan Meadow. By building a parking strip along this road's meadowy stretch, the Park Service eliminated the parking jams that used to result in the '60s and early '70s when visitors parked their cars in the road as they searched for climbers—just specks—ascending one or more of the major routes up El Capitan. Today one can park and leisurely set up a telescope without impairing traffic. During mid-summer, sensible climbers stay off El Capitan's multiday routes, for then the rock's temperature often exceeds 100°F, requiring many gallons of extra water.

After Yosemite became a national park in 1890 El Capitan Meadow became the Valley's first free public campground and Bridalveil

Two climbers near base of El Capitan

Meadow soon became the second, though its use was mostly by US Army troops sent to patrol the Park. Three other campgrounds—all in meadows—were soon operating, in contrast to the forested ones we have today. Back then, horse pasturage was a prime concern—hence the need for meadow sites. In 1906, however, all five were closed, because sanitation—or lack thereof—had become a problem.

Leaving the meadow's edge you walk briefly west along the paved road and cross two usually dry branches of Ribbon Creek. (In pioneer days it was known as Virgin Tears Creek—a name in harmony with Bridalveil Creek, across the Valley floor). In ¼ mile we come to a dirt road, and by walking just a few paces up it we reach a little-used westbound trail. After walking about five minutes west on it we cross a low recessional moraine, then drop almost to the paved road's edge. Here a turnout provides drivers and us with an unobstructed view of Bridalveil Fall. From this turnout, you might note that the Merced River's south-bank, water-laid deposits contrast with the angular north-bank rockfall deposits. We are now at the foot of deposits derived from an unstable band of highly fractured cliffs called the Rockslides. Continual rockfalls from the Rockslides eventually led to the closing of the Old Big Oak Flat Road and its replacement with today's tunneled road in June 1940. Under the pleasant shade of ponderosa pines and incense-cedars we continue west, passing some cabin-size rockfall blocks immediately before skirting the north end of the Bridalweil Meadow recessional moraine. We don't find a terminal moraine, since the Tioga-age glacier likely ended lower down, in the Merced Gorge, where it was buried by rockfalls and/or removed by floods.

Soon we enter a swampy area with cattails and at its west end cross trickling Black Spring. Here, pioneers got an oak-and-conifer-framed view of Bridalveil Fall and the Cathedral Rocks, but due to the Park's old fire-suppression policy, incense-cedars and other conifers invaded the area, totally obstructing the view. Past the spring our trail more or less parallels the westbound road, shortly arriving at the back side of the Valley View scenic turnout. The view from the riverside turnout is one of the Valley's most famous, and it is a shame that the one-way road system prevents visitors from seeing this awe-inspiring view until they are ready to leave the Valley. Here we see El Capitan, Bridalveil Fall and the Cathedral Rocks magnificently standing high above the stately conifers that line Bridalveil Meadow. Barely rising above the

trees are the distant landmarks of Clouds Rest, Half Dome and Sentinel Rock.

From the Valley View area we reach our trail's westernmost point at the Pohono Bridge, which is the current ending point of north-valley one-way traffic. From a stream-gaging station across the bridge our feet tread a riverside path past popular roadside Fern Spring, then past generally unknown trailside Moss Spring. Pacific dogwoods add springtime beauty to this forest as sunlight filters down to light up their translucent leaves and their large, petal-like, creamy-white bracts. Douglas-firs locally dominate the forest as we hike through it to Bridalveil Meadow, which is a shallow bowl that attracts enough ground water to generally prevent trees from invading it. From its edge we see a panorama from Ribbon Fall clockwise past El Capitan, the Cathedral Rocks and the Leaning Tower up to often-ignored points on the Valley's south rim. Avid map readers will identify Dewey, Crocker, Stanford and Old Inspiration points, all of them located along the Pohono Trail (**Hike 71**).

Now you walk northeast along the road's side, staying above seasonally boggy Bridalveil Meadow. By the meadow's edge, the trail resumes, and it goes north to a bend, where you cross the Bridalveil Meadow moraine. From here one can walk 40 yards north to a large rock by the Merced River's bank and see a plaque dedicated to Dr. Lafayette Bunnell, who was among the first-known party of white men—the "Mariposa Battalion"—to set foot in Yosemite Valley. Camping in the meadow on March 27, 1851, they held an evening campfire, at which Bunnell suggested the name "Yo-sem-i-ty," which he had incorrectly inferred was the name of the Indian tribe that inhabited this spectacular Valley. Nevertheless, the name stuck, and Bunnell in 1880 would write a very interesting account of the discovery of Yosemite Valley and other related adventures.

From the moraine we parallel the Merced River southeast almost to the paved one-way road, which you can take a ¼ mile east back to the Bridalveil Fall parking lot. Doing so in springtime avoids the possibility of getting your feet wet in the nearby fords of multibranched Bridalveil Creek. After the last ford the trail parallels the creek's northern branch east about 300 yards to the Valley's eastbound road. Here you can head southwest on it to the parking lot or walk northeast 200 yards to a resumption of the trail, on which you then head southeast toward Bridalveil Fall, perhaps revisiting it as you retrace your last steps back to the lot.

Hike 63   Valley Floor, Yosemite Lodge Loop

Distance: 7.0 miles (11.3 km) loop trip

Grade: 2A, easy half-day hike

Trailhead: Yosemite Falls parking lot, which is immediately west of the Yosemite Creek bridge and immediately north of the Yosemite Lodge complex. **D5.**

Introduction: Most of this loop is relatively quiet and lightly traveled. On it you'll get a classic view of the Three Brothers plus other less famous but equally dramatic views.

Description: Behind the restrooms at the west end of the Yosemite Falls parking lot you'll find a trail heading southwest. On it you almost touch the main road, then curve right to the base of Swan Slab, which is a low cliff that attracts many rock climbers. Before 1956, when the new lodge was opened, the main buildings of Yosemite Lodge were located here, while south of them hundreds of tent cabins lay scattered around the forest floor. During the 1960s the new lodge was shifting its orientation away from tent cabins to fairly luxurious motel units. Some people cried "profiteering," but in fact the vacationing public had changed: America had come to expect less spartan accommodations. Perhaps we can define an "old timer" as one who longs for the return of the lodge's primitive, woodsy tent cabins.

A little less than a ½ mile from the falls' lot we intersect the Yosemite Falls trail (**Hike 68**), then pass behind Sunnyside Campground. This was converted to a walk-in campground in 1976, the last of the Valley's *old* campgrounds to be converted to camp-only-in-designated-sites status. Before then, campers used to jam into this camp, transforming it into a noisy "tent city." In the late '60s this was true for all the campgrounds, and on 3-day weekends crowds of 50,000 or more would park their cars bumper to bumper, finding less peace and quiet here than in the noisy cities they had fled. Today all the Valley campgrounds are more pleasant, for they hold only a fraction of this number, but the crunch of the population explosion, coupled with increased mobility, is certainly felt daily by thousands of summer visitors who are forced to camp outside the Valley or even outside the Park. Back in the '60s Camp 4—the old Sunnyside Campground—was specifically designated for dogs and climbers—the two being nearly indistinguishable in the eyes of many. Climbers, as evidenced by the many brightly colored climbing ropes seen around the camp, still make up most of the camp's patronage.

Just west of Sunnyside Campground our trail once skirted along the Valley's paved, one-way road to a flat, gravel turnout. Today this is littered with debris from a March 1987 rockfall. If you look above the turnout you'll see a huge water-streaked wall, whose black streaks of moss mark the paths of the most persistent—though still ephemeral—streams of water. This wall has the Valley's best examples of glacier polish—in the form of small patches high on the wall and also near the base of Rixon's Pinnacle. Not a real pinnacle, this giant slab is recognized by gold-cup oaks growing on its summit as well as by one prominent specimen growing on a ledge halfway up it. Note also the large, curving band of granite—a dike—cutting across the face of the wall. The wall's rock, solidifying beneath the earth's surface about 90 million years ago, was fractured and injected with this dike material, which came from another, slightly younger molten mass of magma that was intruding it.

You get more views of these features after you cross the paved, one-way road and on a trail parallel it southwest. In about a minute you may see a trail, branching southeast. This unofficial path goes across the west edge of grassy Leidig Meadow to a sandy beach beside the Merced River, and then parallels it about ½ mile upstream to a long, sturdy bridge that spans this river. From the west edge of the meadow you can see a sandy beach on the opposite bank of the Merced River. This is only lightly visited by users of Sentinel Creek Picnic Area, reached from the Valley's eastbound, one-way road.

In Leidig Meadow you get one of the Valley's best views of North Dome, Royal Arches, Washington Column, Clouds Rest and Half Dome. Partly obscuring Half Dome is a large descending ridge on whose dry slopes the Four Mile Trail (**Hike 76**) zigzags down from Glacier Point. Leidig Meadow—the *original* Camp 4 site—is named for George F. Leidig, an early resident who ran a hotel (popular because of his wife's cooking!) near the base of Sentinel Rock. As late as 1924 dairy cattle grazed in this and other Valley meadows. Looking west from this meadow, you get a clear view of the Three Brothers, named for three sons of Chief Teneiya taken prisoner here in May 1851 by the Mariposa Battalion. The vertical east face of Middle Brother was the origin of the March 1987 rockfall that left most of the rocky debris you are about to cross.

Leidig Meadow view of North Dome, Royal Arches, Washington Column below Clouds Rest, and Half Dome

Returning to the main trail, we find that it is now confined to a narrow strip of vegetation between the busy, paved road above us and the quiet river at our feet. Along this part you'll see evidence of a huge March 1987 rockslide from high on the Three Brothers. Soon we leave the river's side and parallel the road at a short distance, hiking through a forest of ponderosa pine, incense-cedar and black oak. After a mile of pleasant walking along the main trail, part of it with fair views, we arrive at the east end of the riverside El Capitan Picnic Area. Our trail resumes at the area's west end, starting first as an abandoned road. In ⅓ mile we enter a meadow and have good views of many of the Valley's prominent features, particularly looming El Capitan, the angular Three Brothers and the domed Cathedral Rocks. Beyond the meadow the trail skirts along the road quickly into the popular, congested area known as Devils Elbow Picnic Area. You'll find outhouses about 100 yards north of the road. This area's popularity stems in part from the river's riviera-like sandy beach and an adjacent deep pool. Both are the Valley's best, though better, warmer pools can be found downstream outside the Park below El Portal. In addition to having a large rock that is ideal for sunbathing or diving, this pool sometimes has a rope tied high on a tree, providing people of all ages with a splashing entry into the pool.

From the picnic area our trail quickly curves south, hugging both road and river for ¼ mile to the El Capitan Bridge, which is one of the Valley's most scenic spots (see **Hike 62**). At the north side of the bridge's east end the trail resumes, heads east to a bank opposite the south end of the Devils Elbow beach, then angles southeast to the eastbound Valley road. Just 20 yards east of us lies the entrance to the Cathedral Picnic Area and on its road we walk north down to the riverbank for two famous and instructive views. Looking northeast we note the amazing similarity among the Three Brothers. They present a classic case of joint-controlled topography. Each is bounded on the east and south by near-vertical joint planes and on the west by an oblique-angle joint plane. These three planes govern the shape of each brother, and when a rockfall does occur, the rock breaks off parallel to one of these planes, thus maintaining the triangular shape. (An excellent display of the Three Brothers and their governing planes is seen in the Valley's museum.)

Looking northwest we see the massive south face of El Capitan and on the east part of it identify the dark-gray "North America map," which is a band of diorite in a sea of granite. About five dozen extremely difficult climbing routes have been pushed up El Capitan. Perhaps the most famous route is the "Nose," which goes from the monolith's foot up to its brow, and the most infamous one is the "Wall of the Early Morning Light," which ascends the blank wall just right of it. The former, first climbed *continuously* in 6½ days back in 1960, but was climbed in a grueling 17-hour ascent in the mid-

1970s. Later, faster ascents were done, and now to do it in one day is nothing special for first-rate climbers. The latter route, first climbed in 1970, took 26½ days—an unheard of time—and the ascent upset many climbers, angered Park officials and received national press coverage.

Leaving the willow-lined Merced, we return to our trail, cross the road, and walk 250 yards southeast to a junction with the Valley's southside trail. On it we start east and immediately cross a creek bed that is densely lined with young ponderosa pines. These pines probably sprouted after the usually dry creek became a swollen torrent during a flood in the 1950s when it, like other creeks, created fresh soil exposures that became ripe for seed germination. Looking upstream we see overhanging Taft Point, then get other views of it as we progress east. After ½ mile of shady, south-side walking, we come to a huge, trailside slab, on whose flat summit you'll find about 20 mortar holes used by the Indians to grind acorns to flour. Not a glacier-transported rock, this 1000-ton slab broke off a steep wall of the side canyon above us. After perhaps sliding down a layer of ice and snow, this slab came to rest at this spot centuries ago. As we continue on, Douglas firs and white firs mingle with the more dominant ponderosa pines, incense-cedars and black oaks. Gray squirrels scamper away from us today, and in earlier days they vied with Indians for acorns. However, they in fact

Mortar holes

benefited the Indians, for they buried many acorns and forgot about some, and these sprouted to produce the Indians' most cherished food source, the black oak.

Scattered views are obtained over the next mile from the big slab, and near its end we cross Sentinel Creek—barely a trickle on the first day of summer. After the summer solstice you're lucky if multistage Sentinel Fall, seen high above the creek, is even a gossamer mist. Voluminous only in flood stage, this fall is best seen in the warming days of late May, when runoff is about maximum and when winter's dormant seeds have awakened to dot the forest floor with a multitude of wildflowers.

After crossing the creek we come to an old spur road—the end of the Four Mile trail from Glacier Point (**Hike 76**). In this vicinity Leidig's Hotel, the westernmost of several pioneer hotels, once stood. Beyond here our trail soon draws close to the Valley's eastbound road, and where we see a large roadside parking area, about ¼ mile beyond the old spur road, we leave our trail, cross the busy Valley road, and enter a picnic area. Black's Hotel once stood in this area, together with Clark's cabin. Galen Clark was one of the Valley's first tourists, being one of about 30 visitors to see it in the summer of 1855. Later, discovering he had a serious respiratory condition, he returned to the mountains, perhaps to die, but Yosemite's environment acted like an elixir, restoring his health. He first established a small lodge at Wawona, then became Yosemite's first guardian, later saw it made into a National Park, and in 1910—during the Hetch Hetchy controversy—died at a ripe old age of 96.

Descending through the picnic area we reach a long, sturdy bridge that replaces an earlier suspension bridge across the Merced River. From it you have good views of Yosemite Falls, Royal Arches, Washington Column, North Dome, Clouds Rest, Sentinel Rock, the Cathedral Rocks and the Three Brothers. From the far end of the bridge, two *de facto* paths start west, the right one circling the perimeter of Leidig Meadow as it traces the river downstream. We take a broad, paved path north to a bend in the road on the grounds of Yosemite Lodge. Walk 100 feet along this bend to the path's resumption. It starts east, then curves northward, finally crossing the Valley's one-way road by the main entrance to the lodge's grounds. This spot is also the west entrance to the Yosemite Falls parking lot, your starting point.

Hike 64   Valley Floor, Yosemite Village Loop

Distance: 3.3 miles (5.4 km) loop trip
Grade: 1A, easy 2-hour hike
Trailhead: Same as the Hike 63 trailhead. **D5.**
Introduction: Famous views of Yosemite Falls, Half Dome and Royal Arches are seen along this short hike.

Description: While a steady stream of visitors make a short pilgrimage north to the base of Yosemite Falls, we walk southeast, bridge Yosemite Creek, then start east on a trail along the south side of the main road. Our trail quickly branches, and we angle right, away from the road to immediately cross a short spur road that heads south. Near its end a water well was drilled in the early 1970s, and it went 1000 feet down before hitting bedrock. Yosemite Valley is in reality a 4000-foot-deep canyon, for on the average its bedrock floor is buried under 1000 feet of sediments. Beneath the grounds of the Ahwahnee Hotel, one mile east of us, these sediments are 2000 feet thick.

Beyond the spur road our paved trail enters a beautiful, view-packed meadow, through which we start southeast but have the option to branch right, bridge the Merced River and head toward the Yosemite chapel. Ironically the chapel stands close to the site of the Valley's first murder, which occurred in May 1851 during the so-called "Indian Wars." Two braves tied to a tree were allowed to free themselves so they could be shot down. The villainous soldier who planned this foul deed succeeded in killing only one of the Indians, but unfortunately it was Chief Teneiya's favorite son, and this certainly increased the old chief's mistrust of the intentions of the Mariposa Battalion. However, in all fairness it must be stated that the battalion behaved with remarkable restraint in rounding up the chief's band, especially considering that some of its volunteers had suffered personal losses at the hands of the Indians.

By not branching right in the meadow, we end at a parking area with picnic tables, just north of Sentinel Bridge. Particularly during August, when Upper Yosemite Fall is only a wispy vestige of its springtime self, splashing children slowly raft down the river, adding a human element to the famous tree-framed view of stately Half Dome. By strategically locating their hotel in the area between this bridge and the chapel, Buck Beardsley and G. Hite in 1859 provided guests with the best of all possible views. Business, however, was poor, and in

Half Dome in winter, from Sentinel Bridge

1864 James Hutchings—one of the Valley's first tourists—bought the hotel. Hutchings earlier had begun to attract tourists to the Valley by exposing this great California wonder to them in his magazine, "Hutchings' Illustrated California Magazine," a monthly that existed from 1856 to 1860. As he closed his magazine, he replaced it with a book called *Scenes of Wonder and Curiosity in California,* a popular guide that had a long section on Yosemite. Hutchings also encouraged the development of our local Valley area, both through words and investments, and there gradually arose what is now referred to as the "Old Village," which contained, among 21 structures, the National Park Headquarters. Today the Yosemite chapel is the only significant structure remaining. Originally built between Black's and Leidig's hotels in 1879, it was later moved ½ mile northeast up the road to its present site and today it stands as the Valley's oldest building.

From the south end of Sentinel Bridge we walk east on a paved riverbank trail, then cross the adjacent road. Onward, we continue east beside

A black-oak shaded view of Royal Arches, Washington Column, Half Dome and Ahwahnee Meadow

the road, pass the bustling Housekeeping Camp, and soon arrive at a granite structure, the LeConte Memorial Lodge. A student of world-famous Louis Agassiz, Joseph LeConte was invited to become the first professor of geology at Berkeley's then-infant University of California. During the summer of 1870 he visited Yosemite Valley, met John Muir, and was profoundly impressed by both. As a pioneering geologist he would later trek through much of the High Sierra much as the Whitney Survey had done in the Civil War days. However, like Muir, LeConte was not interested in topographic mapping and potential mining sites but rather in the beauty and origin of this "range of light." Appropriately, LeConte died in one of his most loved sites, Yosemite Valley, in 1901. During 1902-03 the commemorative lodge was built, erected near the youthful Camp Curry. The camp, however, prospered and expanded, so in 1919 the lodge was dismantled and then rebuilt, stone by stone, at its present location. This site was selected by Yosemite's foremost photographer, Ansel Adams, who chose it for its clear view up the Valley. As you can see, tall incense-cedars and ponderosa pines obstruct most of the view today. This lodge was once the terminal point of the John Muir Trail,

but today it seasonally has children's programs, and the John Muir Trail (**Hikes 51** and **58**) ends at Happy Isles.

Leaving the LeConte Memorial and its trailside Indian mortar holes, we cross the road and follow a short path north along the east side of the Housekeeping Camp. In a few minutes we reach a sturdy bridge that links this camp to Lower Riverside Campground. Rafting has become a popular activity by children of all ages, and those wise in the sport know that by staying in the eddy currents generated by the bridge's pillars, they can float there almost indefinitely rather than being carried downstream. Heading toward Yosemite Falls, we turn our backs on views of Glacier Point, the sweeping Glacier Point Apron and Grizzly Peak as we follow a path downstream, passing riverside alders and willows. Along this short stretch we note man's attempt to control nature: large blocks to stabilize the riverbanks. All told, about 14,500 feet of bank have been lined! However, the Park Service has plans to remove some or all of the rip-rap revetment. Ponderosa pines, incense-cedars and black oaks provide shade until a small stretch of the Ahwahnee Meadow, just before the Valley's central road. In this small stretch our path crosses another one and heads straight toward Upper Yosemite Fall and, looking right, we have unobstructed views of North Dome, Royal Arches, Washington Column and Half Dome. Below these towering landmarks stands one of America's grandest hotels, the Ahwahnee. Opened to the public in 1927, this magnificent granite-and-timber architectural treasure replaced Kenneyville, which like the Old Village and Camp Curry was a site of active tourism. Before that there had been the nearby Harris Camp Grounds, established in 1878, in which, for a fee, you could camp. However, with the establishment of Yosemite National Park in 1890, free public campgrounds were opened and this privately run camp folded.

After we cross the Valley's central road, we walk north, shaded by large black oaks growing along the edge of Ahwahnee Meadow. In ¼ mile we reach the west end of the Church Bowl, which has a paved roadside path and a dirt one, just behind the first, which we'll ascend northwest into the gold-cup oaks. But first note that the Valley crossing we have just completed contains a sufficient diversity of plant species to allow selective feeding by all seven of the Valley's common summertime warblers. In the shady, moist confines immediately behind the LeConte memorial, you might find MacGillivray's warblers foraging among the thimbleberries and bracken ferns. Just north, in the ponderosa pines and incense-cedars, you might stretch your neck and see yellow-rumped and hermit warblers. The larger, more common yellow-rumped warbler hunts for insects in the outer foliage of the trees' lower and middle branches while the misnamed hermit warbler hunts among the upper branches. Along the Merced River you might observe yellow and Wilson's warblers, the former searching among the alders and cottonwoods, the latter searching lower down among the willows and adjacent shrubs. Along the northbound traverse of the edge of Ahwahnee Meadow, the Nashville warbler would be expected in the black oaks overhead, and, upon climbing into the gold-cup oaks above the Church Bowl, you'd expect to see the black-throated gray warbler. Thus you may see seven different warblers *all* hunting insects in Yosemite Valley, yet none is in direct competition with any other, for each has found its own niche. Competition is mainly among individuals of the same species.

Climbing from the Church Bowl up past the medical clinic, we quickly reach Indian Canyon

Creek. Its canyon was a principal Valley exit used by Indians heading up to the north rim, and early pioneers built a trail of sorts up it, then west to a Yosemite Falls overlook. In early season you may note one of the Valley's lesser-known falls, Lehamite Falls, which plunges down a branch of Indian Canyon. Lehamite is actually the name Chief Teneiya's people gave to Indian Canyon.

Beyond the canyon's creek and its huge rockfall boulders, we climb northwest to avoid a mosaic of Park buildings and residences of the "New Village," then contour west beneath sky-piercing Arrowhead Spire and the highly fractured Castle Cliffs. Approaching a spur trail down to the nearby government stables, we spy Lost Arrow—a giant pinnacle high on the wall of Upper Yosemite Fall. Heading west ¼ mile toward Lower Yosemite Fall, we pass the Park's family-residence tract and its associated elementary school, then come to a junction. From it you could take a trail down along Yosemite Creek to your trailhead, but then you'd miss this hike's best attraction, Yosemite Falls, whose base is just to the west. Along this ¼-mile stretch a sawmill once stood. It was located here because fast-flowing Yosemite Creek provided the water power necessary to turn the sawmill's large blade. John Muir built this sawmill for James Hutchings "to cut lumber for cottages . . . from the fallen pines which had been blown down in a violent wind-storm [winter of 1867-68] a year or two before my arrival." When not off on his treks Muir sometimes worked at this mill, for at it he could enjoy "the piney fragrance of the fresh-sawn boards and be in constant view of the grandest of all the falls." His love of wilderness had grown so great that he preferred to spend the night perched on a ledge above the Valley floor, lulled to sleep by a splashing lullaby from nearby Lower Yosemite Fall.

From the bridge of Lower Yosemite Fall early-summer visitors are treated to the thunderous roar of the fall, a sound that reverberates in the alcove cut in this rock. During this season the visitor is further treated to the fall's spray as well. By late August, however, the fall, like its upper counterpart, is usually reduced to a mist, and even this can be gone by the Labor Day weekend. Dry or not, the fall should not be examined at close range, for even if boulder-choked Yosemite Creek is bone-dry, its rocks are water polished to an icelike finish. You may see climbers ascending the near-vertical walls surrounding the fall, and ironically they are in a safer environment than you are if you clamber around on the creek's rocks. A rope will stop their fall; you, on the other hand, being unroped, can fracture a vertebra or crack your skull.

Our scenic bridge is occasionally swept away. It has been dislodged by winter's intense, flood-causing storms, which periodically occur, but it has also been dislodged by unseasonably warm springtime weather that causes rapid snowmelt. This in turn causes the huge snow cone at the base of the upper fall to swell with water and rapidly descend, avalanche-style, carrying the winter's rockfall debris with it as it plunges over the lower fall and slams into the bridge.

Before leaving the bridge, note how the lower fall has indirectly cut its alcove. Stream action has cut only a few feet into the granitic bedrock since glaciers last left the Valley, but in winter the fall's spray freezes in the surrounding rocks, expands, and pries loose lower slabs that in turn remove support from the upper ones—hence the rocky nature of Yosemite Creek's bed in this area. Walking back to your parking-lot trailhead, stop many times to get views of both falls. Long ago a swath of trees was logged just to provide these views.

Lower Yosemite Fall

Hike 65   Valley Floor, Camp Curry Loop

Distance: 2.8 miles (4.5 km) loop trip

Grade: 1A, easy 2-hour hike

Trailhead: Camp Curry parking lot, in eastern Yosemite Valley. **D5.**

Introduction: More like a stroll, this is about the easiest hike described in this guide. It is recommended for those who enjoy a leisurely pace, and want to take the time to commune with the squirrels, birds and wildflowers and to reflect on the Valley's natural and human history.

Description: Back in the 1860s, long before a car entered Yosemite Valley, the Camp Curry parking lot was an apple orchard, and rows of these fruit trees are still seen in the area today. This orchard stands at the south end of Stoneman Meadow, whose grasses were nightly trampled by summer spectators watching the Firefall being pushed off Glacier Point—until the show was ended in January 1968. That meadow got its name from Governor George Stoneman, who was the State's chief executive when a large, state-financed hotel, the Stone-

Gossamer Staircase Falls, above Camp Curry

man House, was completed in 1887. The stillborn child of a political scandal, this pretentious but shoddy hotel began to fall apart almost as soon as it was finished, and fortunately it burned to the ground in 1896, thus ridding the Valley of one of its true eyesores. Today, Camp Curry's west-end shuttle-bus stop occupies the approximate site of that hotel. Three years after the fire, Camp Curry made a very modest start, and as a company it eventually outgrew all its competitors to become the Park's largest concessioner.

From the southeast corner of Curry's lot we follow a paved path east past employees' tent cabins, then curve southeast and meet a short spur road that branches right to a nearby gravel pit. Years ago this pit used to be the site of the Camp Curry garbage dump, but it attracted so many bears that it was closed. Today bears together with raccoons and coyotes nightly roam through the campgrounds in search of food. During the day Steller's jays and gray squirrels are the chief scavengers. Just beyond the gravel pit—which may become the horse stables' new site—you can make a five-minute climb south up a talus slope to the base of a broad, curving buttress known as the Glacier Point Apron, which is a very popular climbing area. Until the 1980s most of its routes were quite difficult. However, with the advent of "sticky-soled" shoes, climbers found they could waltz up virtually any route. Hence new routes proliferated and now over 100 exist.

From the spur road, our trail parallels the camp's road southeast to a nearby junction with a limited-access shuttle-bus road. About a

Glacier Point Apron

minute's walk beyond it, we reach a trail branching right. Since this is a quieter route, we take it. It starts south, then rolls southeast, staying about 100–150 yards from the unseen shuttle-bus road, and in ⅓ mile intersects a southbound stock trail that links the Valley stables to the John Muir Trail. Beyond this intersection we head east on planks across a boggy area, and although mosquitoes may be bothersome in late spring and early summer, the bog does produce some nice wildflowers then. At a huge, lone boulder by the bog's east side, our trail angles southeast to several buildings in the Happy Isles area.

You'll probably see dozens if not hundreds of visitors in this area, and here you'll find an informative nature center, a curio shop and restrooms. Spend some time at the nature center, and also visit the two Happy Isles, each surrounded by the splashing, joyously singing Merced River.

Immediately below the lower isle you'll see a gaging station by the east end of a wide bridge. Records show that late in the summer, just before autumn rains, the river's discharge can fall to less than 5 cubic feet per second, while during a rampaging flood it can rise almost to a staggering 10,000 cubic feet per second! Most of the river's sediment is transported during times of high water, and since the Merced River's volume is considerably greater than that of Tenaya and Yosemite creeks, it brings a disproportionately large amount of sediment into the Valley. Overall, the historic rate of sediment transport is quite insignificant, being—according to the author's calculations— about 2500 tons per year for the Merced River and 330 tons for all the Valley's remaining creeks that lie east of Lower Cathedral Rock (that is, within the Valley proper). Yosemite Valley is buried in sediments, its surface generally standing about 1000 feet above the bedrock floor at the base of the sediments. The volume of these sediments is tremendous—so large that if all these sediments had been deposited at the current average historic rate, 2830 tons per year, a full 3 million years of sedimentation would have been required to fill the Valley to its present level. Glaciers, however, were directly and indirectly responsible for depositing most of these sediments during about the last 800,000 years.

Departing north from Happy Isles, you have a choice of three pleasant routes: the Merced's west-bank trail, its east-bank trail, and the road's east-side trail. The east-side trail begins about 100 yards north of the gaging station, where it branches right, away from the east-bank trail. On the east-side trail you pass some cabin-size, moss-and-lichen-covered rockfall blocks, and then, where the trail climbs to cross the Medial Moraine, you descend across the road to the west-bending river. Both riverbank trails are relaxing strolls along the azalea-lined river, but perhaps the east-bank trail is more interesting since it traverses the base of the controversial, west-trending Medial Moraine. François Matthes, who produced a monumental report on Yosemite glaciation in 1930, concluded that this moraine was probably left at the lower end of a glacier extending down Tenaya Canyon. Eliot Blackwelder, his contemporary, disagreed, saying it was a medial moraine, that is, one left between two glaciers, which in this case would be glaciers from Tenaya and from the upper Merced Canyon. I believe this west-trending ridge is a *moraine left by the retreating Merced Canyon glacier*. The evidence lies in the Stanislaus River drainage. Its Clark Fork glacier

received much of its ice from an eastern, over-flowing glacier just as the Tenaya Canyon glacier was fed by the overflow of the Tuolumne River glacier. The Clark Fork glacier retreated before the adjacent Middle Fork glacier did, due to reduced overflow about 14,000 years ago. In like manner, the Tenaya Canyon glacier would have retreated prematurely as the waning Tuolumne glacier cut off its source of ice.

Skirting the south base of this moraine, the east-bank trail goes northwest almost to the Valley stables. Here, at the moraine's end, we turn left and immediately cross Clarks Bridge, named for Galen Clark, the Park's first guardian. From its west side those who took the Merced's west-bank trail now join us for a brief walk past the entrances to the Upper and Lower Pines campgrounds. Beyond them we meet a south-heading shuttle-bus road, but we turn right and walk west along a roadside trail to Stoneman Meadow and our parking lot trailhead.

Hike 66   Valley Floor, Mirror Meadow Loop

Distance: 3.6 miles (5.9 km) loop trip

Grade: 1A, easy 2-hour hike

Trailhead: Drive through the Pines camp-grounds to a parking lot by a shuttle-bus stop just across Clarks Bridge. Here are the Yosemite Stables, but in the future they may be relocated to the former Camp Curry dump site. **D5.**

Introduction: Although Mirror Lake essentially diminished to a wide creek by 1988, its environs still attract countless hikers and bicyclists. Since the lake is no longer accessible by shuttle bus, the setting now is quieter.

Description: The low ridge you see just behind the shuttle-bus stop is the Valley's controversial "Medial Moraine," a glacial moraine whose origin is examined near the end of **Hike 65**. A trail goes east along each side of the moraine, the south-side trail being more scenic since it also goes along the Merced River. It is also quieter, for there aren't any trailside bicyclists. On this south-side trail we walk east along the base of the smooth moraine, leave the riverside trail, cross a paved bike path from Happy Isles, then continue east about 40 yards up to a north-south trail. Starting north on it we immediately top the moraine's crest, then descend northwest toward a road junction. The shuttle-bus route takes the road west, back toward our starting point, while

bicyclists bound for Indian Cave or Mirror Meadow take the road north. Still on our trail, we meander north, skirting around an area of large rockfall boulders that testify to the instability of Half Dome's west flank. Beyond the boulders we come to a trail intersection next to Tenaya Bridge. To cut your trip in half you could continue north from the bridge on a short trail to the Indian Caves area, or to cut it even more, you could parallel the south bank of Tenaya Creek west back to the Yosemite stables. However, the described route turns right, starts east, and then parallels Tenaya Creek northeast up to a footbridge across that creek.

We cross the footbridge, climb briefly to the paved bicyclists' road, and head up it past a yearly diminishing pond, which in the past lay just below the outlet of Mirror Lake. (By this pond is the start of a southwest-heading foot path, which is an alternate route back.) When you reach the road's end at what was once a parking area for autos and then a turnaround area for shuttle busses, you'll see that Mirror Lake exists no more. The lake used to dry up by late September, and at that time in past years the Park Service would excavate the lake, some-times removing thousands of tons of sand and gravel. This material was later spread on snow-

Mirror Lake as it appeared in 1976

covered winter roads to make them more driv-
able. It was an efficient system. Environmentalists, however, thought otherwise, so the
procedure was stopped, and after 1971 Mirror
Lake began to silt up. Today, sand (and many
Park employees) are transported to the Valley,
expending wasteful amounts of fuel that add
unnecessary carbon dioxide to an already over-
laden atmosphere.

There will be many disheartened tourists to
Mirror Meadow, but perhaps, as with the
Firefall (see the start of **Hike 65**), the public was
led to expect the unnatural to be natural. Mirror
Lake was not a deep, reflective gem when it was
discovered, but rather was a shallow, rockfall-
dammed pond. However, with the addition of a
manmade dam about 1890, the lake assumed its
reflective qualities, which were then maintained from 1914 to 1971 by yearly excavation.

Today visitors must console themselves with
Mirror Meadow, which by the late '80s was more
of a gravely lake bottom than a grassy meadow.
However, by the turn of the century vegetation
could cover all of the meadow—unless the lake's
manmade dam is removed. This would lower the

water table and allow trees to invade the
meadow, ultimately obscuring all views.

Without the fortuitous rockfall, Mirror Lake
would not have been created and hence would
not be missed. Another nearby feature, remem-
bered perhaps only by historians, is also gone:
Iron Spring. Located by Tenaya Creek just 500
yards down the road from Mirror Lake's
satellite pond, the spring was the focal point of
Camp 10, whose popularity exceeded available
resources. Consequently, the camp was closed
in 1916 and the spring was gradually forgotten.
At some time between the government's mapping of the Valley in 1958 and the author's
mapping of it in 1976—perhaps during the 1964
flood—Tenaya Creek changed its course, over-
running and obliterating this mineral-water
spring.

To resume our loop hike, we look for a trail
that starts near the back end of the former
parking area. (Since this is a horse path and is
heavily used, you might want to take the previously mentioned foot path for a fresher-
smelling route.) Starting south on the horse path,
we see, high above, North Dome and Half
Dome. Next, our trail passes myriad oversize
boulders that came from the vertical east wall of
Washington Column. Soon our trail switchbacks briefly down to the paved road, then it
goes 100 yards west to a trail departing south
toward nearby Tenaya Bridge. Our trail continues west another 100 yards to enter the
Indian Caves area. In the past this area was a
favorite with its several caves located among
dozens of house-size boulders. However, apparently there were too many climbing accidents
and too much liability for the Park, so in the
early '90s the area officially ceased to exist.
Still, in this area, inspect a large, low slab that
lies along the trail's north side. On its flat top are
mortar holes made by the Yosemite Indians and
used by them to pulverize acorns.

Continuing west you have a choice: either
stay on the trail or take the paved bike path, just
south of the caves. The two diverge, and then,
near the northeast corner of the Group Camp
(old Camp 9), they come together. On this
stretch you pass under the forbidding south face
of Washington Column and you may think you
hear faint voices coming from high up on it. You
actually might, for there are several popular
crack systems on it that rock climbers ascend to
the top. Where the trail and the bike path come
together, we can look up a deep cleft—eroded
along a vertical fracture—which separates

Washington Column's east face

Washington Column from that giant lithic rainbow, Royal Arches.

After 150 yards of westward traverse our two parallel paths cross a very low moraine, which François Matthes, an eminent geologist, speculated might be the northern part of the Medial Moraine. The low moraine has both glacier-transported boulders and rockfall boulders, the latter coming from Royal Arches. Note that all the rocks are *entirely* covered with crustose lichens, a growth process that takes centuries. On the basis of their age, together with age estimates of the tall surrounding ponderosa pines and incense-cedars, we can see that a major rockfall has not occurred here for hundreds of years. Perhaps the source of the last major rockfall was the greatly thinned skyline

arch, which is just a fraction of its former self. The large skyline arch just west of Royal Arches proper could fall any day, but then it might stand for millennia.

About a two-minute walk past the low moraine we come to a trail junction, where, by cutting south through the Group Camp, one can save ⅓ mile. However, by continuing west for a few minutes along the bike path (the trail goes to the Ahwahnee Hotel), we reach the Sugarpine Bridge, named for a huge sugar pine growing by the northeast corner of the bridge. Like a royal arch, this stately giant could fall any day. From the bridge we take a trail first southeast up the Merced River, then briefly northeast up Tenaya Creek. Where we meet the southbound shortcut trail we take it, immediately bridge Tenaya Creek and walk southeast past the back side of North Pines Campground to the bus stop.

Under the old system of campground nomenclature Upper, North and Lower Pines campgrounds used to be, respectively, Camps 11, 12 and 14. Camp 13 never existed, for superstitious reasons. The camps' names were changed when they were modified to a fixed-site system. This system limited the number of vehicles per campground and greatly reduced the number of campers, who previously used to pack the camps till they overflowed. This dramatic campsite reduction resulted in a reduction in Valley sewage, from over one million gallons per day sent down to the Bridalveil Moraine sewage plant, to well below that number. In May 1976 this plant was replaced by a new sewage plant opened in El Portal, thus removing one more undesirable, manmade feature from the Valley.

The campgrounds now seem about as perfect as one could realistically desire; however, there has developed recently, so to speak, a crucial *underlying* problem: root rot. In prehistoric times the Valley's vegetation was in part dynamically governed by periodic fires. After fire-suppression policies were introduced the Valley's oak woodlands were invaded by conifers, resulting in the campground cover we see today. This conifer concentration, lacking periodic burns, invited attack by a root-rot fungus, *Fomes annosus*. The aging conifers are bound to fall, but the fungal invasion hastens their doom, and some Park officials are worried about the risk of camping in these forest groves. The lesson to be learned: man's changes in Nature, even when well-intentioned, often lead to unwanted or unforeseen results.

Hike 67   Valley Floor, Tenaya Canyon Loop

Distance: 6.6 miles (10.6 km) loop trip
Grade: 2A, easy half-day hike
Trailhead: Same as the **Hike 66** trailhead. **D5.**
Introduction: In addition to visiting the site of former Mirror Lake, you get ever-changing views of Half Dome and other features of deep, glaciated Tenaya Canyon.
Description: First follow Hike 66 to the end of the paved bike path—a turnaround area—which is above the site of Mirror Lake. Before continuing onward, you'll want to descend a few steps to what was once Mirror Lake's most famous viewpoint. Visitors who have seen beautiful photographs of Mt. Watkins reflected in the lake's calm morning waters are due for a rude surprise. As elaborated in **Hike 66,** Mirror Lake, originally formed behind a rockfall and then artificially raised by a manmade dam, is now just a broad stream and an adjacent meadow.

Now from the former parking area you take a broad trail that quickly comes to the northwest arm of the former lake. About 100 yards beyond it, where the trail bends right, you may see a cliff with polish imparted by a glacier before it retreated up the canyon about 14,500 years ago. Unfortunately a 1986 rockfall obliterated a short trail up to this polish. In contrast to this glacier, the upper Merced Canyon glacier, which flowed through Little Yosemite Valley, lingered at the east end of Yosemite Valley for perhaps a few hundred years before it retreated up its canyon.

Our trail leads us up-canyon under a shady forest cover, and soon we approach Tenaya Creek—a good picnic spot. Beyond it our trail rolls northeast toward the south spur of Mt. Watkins, which is occasionally seen through the forest canopy. About 1.1 miles from the trailhead we come to a junction to which a Tuolumne Meadows trail, with its nine dozen switchbacks, descends from Snow Creek. At most you'll want to *ascend* only the first dozen switchbacks, an effort sufficient to get you above the dense gold-cup oaks and present you with a view of Half Dome and much of Tenaya Canyon. From your vantage point in early summer, when the creek's flow is brisk, you ought to be able to see Tenaya Creek falls, at about your elevation and about ½ mile up-

canyon. From the junction our canyon-floor trail again approaches the creek, and in ⅓ mile bridges it. From this point one could take an optional use trail that heads about 0.3 mile up along the south bank to the creek's falls, whose brim is a worthy goal for safety-minded hikers.

Our return hike starts along the south side of Tenaya Creek, and it provides as pleasant a route as did our easy ascent route. About 1¼ miles from the creek's bridge we reach the east edge of Mirror Meadow, then soon stroll past its dam, an artificial feature built around 1890 to add depth to the lake and to increase its photographic attributes. Just below the dam we descend to a pond that is rapidly diminishing. In years past, it was one of the favorite swimming holes to be found in the Valley. Beyond the pond we branch from the trail to Happy Isles, cross a footbridge and briefly walk up the paved bike path. Follow the second half of **Hike 66** ("To resume our loop hike . . ."), which first goes down a horse path to the Indian Caves area before returning to your starting point.

Glacier polish on cliff above Mirror Meadow

Hike 68   Yosemite Falls

Distance: 6.6 miles (10.6 km) round trip

Grade: 2D, strenuous half-day hike

Trailhead: Park in the westernmost part of the Yosemite Lodge parking lot close to the gas station that is on the north side of the main road. **D5.**

Introduction: Most Park visitors walk to the base of Lower Yosemite Fall. This popular trail gets you to the other end—the brink of Upper Yosemite Fall. Like other early trails of Yosemite Valley, the Yosemite Falls trail was privately built and then was operated as a toll trail. From 1873 to 1877 John Conway labored intermittently to produce a route to the Upper Fall's brink—a route to replace the defunct Indian path that once climbed Indian Canyon. After reaching the fall's brink he extended the trail up to airy Eagle Peak.

Description: From the gas station, pick any route up along the east edge of Sunnyside Campground and then continue upslope a minute or so to the north-side Valley floor trail (**Hike 63**). By walking west on it for a minute or so, you should reach the start of the Yosemite Falls trail. We leave conifers behind as we start up nearly four dozen switchbacks. Characteristic of old trails, each switchback leg is short. Beneath shady gold-cup oaks, which dominate talus slopes like the one we're on, our so-far viewless ascent finally reaches a dry wash that provides us with framed views of Leidig Meadow and the Valley's central features.

With more than one fourth of the elevation gain below us, we pass more oaks and an occasional bay tree as we now switchback east to a panoramic viewpoint, Columbia Rock, which is a worthy goal in itself. At its safety railing we can study the Valley's geometry from Half Dome and the Quarter Domes west to the Cathedral Spires. Looking down on the Valley floor you might observe some old, abandoned meanders of the Merced River. A few gravelly switchbacks climb from the viewpoint, and then the trail traverses northeast, drops slightly, passes an enormous Douglas-fir, and bends north for a sudden dramatic view of Upper Yosemite Fall. Hiking toward it you can see that some of its spray is caught behind the top of a large, notched flake, and this water then flows from the notch as a minor fall. West of Upper Yosemite Fall's lower section is a large white

scar, over 200 feet high, from which a 1,000-ton rock slab fell, after being struck by lightning in June 1976. In clear weather in November 1980, there was another major rockfall, which left a conspicuous scar on the cliffs west of and above the trail. Three hikers were killed. Another rockfall occurred nearby in July 1985. Other trails climbing out of the Valley have also experienced rockfalls—the Valley's walls aren't as eternal as they may appear.

Our climb up the long, steep trough ends among white firs and Jeffrey pines, about 135 switchbacks above the Valley floor. Here, in a gully beside a seasonal creeklet, our trail turns right while the Eagle Peak trail, **Hike 69**,

Sentinel Rock, from Yosemite Falls trail

continues ahead. Our trail makes a brief climb east out of the gully and reaches a broad crest with several overused campsites. Their heavy use puts a strain on this area's vegetation, and it is best not to camp here. Along the crest we follow a trail south almost to the Valley's rim; then at a juniper we veer east, descend steps almost to Yosemite Creek and finally descend more steps to a fenced-in viewpoint. If you're acrophobic you should not attempt the last part of this descent, for it is possible, though unlikely, that you could slip on loose gravel and tumble over the brink. Beside the lip of Upper Yosemite Fall we see and hear it plunge all the way down its 1430-foot drop to the rocks below. Just beyond the fall is a large roof—one that indicates the size of a slab that broke loose from this cliff in the not too distant past. On the skyline beyond the roof stands the pride of the Clark Range, finlike Mt. Clark.

After returning to the crest campsites you can descend east to a bridge over Yosemite Creek and obtain water. However, be careful! Every year one or more persons, wading in the creek's icy water, slip on the glass-smooth creek bottom and are swiftly carried over the fall's brink. From the creek's bridge you could continue eastward ¾ mile up a trail to Yosemite Point, a highly scenic goal.

A large roof by brink of upper fall

Hike 69   Eagle Peak

Distance: 12.4 miles (20.0 km) round trip

Grade: 3E, strenuous day hike

Trailhead: Same as the Hike 68 trailhead. **D5.**

Introduction: Strategically located Eagle Peak, highest of the Three Brothers, provides commanding views both up and down Yosemite Valley. The hike to it also provides exciting vews, including some close-range ones of Upper Yosemite Fall.

Description: Follow **Hike 68** up to the Upper Yosemite Fall fenced-in viewpoint, then return to the trail junction in the gully west of the fall. Here at the junction you're bound to see chartreuse-colored staghorn lichens growing on the white firs and Jeffrey pines. They thrive on the firs but do poorly on the sappy pines. However, lichens, being capable of photo-synthesis, do not require nourishment from a host to thrive. Indeed, most of Yosemite's lichens grow on bare rock, and their organic

secretions may be the first agents to initiate chemical decomposition of the rock. Lichens, which in the past were incorrectly classified as plants, are composed of a fungus and an alga. In a symbiotic relationship the fungus provides structure and protection from the elements while the photosynthetic alga produces nourishment for both.

We now commence a shady trek north, climbing out of our gully, descending into a second and climbing out of a third to a trail junction. These gullies plus the one north of the junction are all in line and they probably owe their existence to relatively easy erosion along a straight, major fracture in the granitic bedrock. Leaving the Yosemite Creek environs, whose northbound trail is described in **Hike 21**, we climb more than 300 feet, at first steeply, before levelling off in a bouldery area—part of a terminal moraine. This moraine marks the southernmost extent of a glacier that descended from the west slopes of

Mt. Hoffmann during late Pleistocene time. Now we turn south, generally leaving Jeffrey pines and white firs for lodgepole pines and red firs as we climb to Eagle Peak Meadows, whose north edge is blocked by an older moraine. It is this moraine that diverts Eagle Peak Creek northeast, and it also dams up the meadow's ground water, thereby keeping conifers out of it.

Beyond the sometimes boggy meadow we cross the headwaters of Eagle Peak Creek and in

Summit View east toward Half Dome

a few minutes reach a hillside junction. From it an old trail climbs and drops along a 1¾-mile course to the El Capitan spur trail. To reach the summit of that monolith, it is easier to start from Tamarack Campground (**Hike 31**). From the junction we branch left for a moderate ⅔-mile ascent to the diminutive summit of Eagle Peak. Like El Capitan, this summit has a register. From the weather-pitted, brushy summit we get far-ranging views that extend all the way to the Sierra crest along the Park's east boundary. Below us central Yosemite Valley spreads out like a map and if you've brought along a map of this Valley, you should be able to identify most of its major landmarks plus dozens of minor features.

At 3200 feet above the Valley floor we can appreciate the Valley's magnitude, which is a product of stream, glacial and mass-wasting processes. About two million years ago, when glaciers first entered the Valley, it was already about 3000 feet deep and was broader than the Sierra's other stream-cut canyons. Rockfalls and glaciers widened it further, and the earlier glaciers cut deep into the broad floor. During the Sherwin glaciation, which lasted from about 900,000 to 800,000 years ago, a giant glacier came to within 200 vertical feet of our summit, leaving it as a tiny north-rim island in a sea of ice. When this glacier retreated, it likely left the Valley with an enormous lake that eventually was filled in with sediments brought by later glaciers. Beneath spacious Leidig Meadow, directly below you, there are sediments that are about 1000 feet thick, while up-valley, across from Royal Arches, they are an impressive 2000 feet thick—the maximum depth of that 8½-mile-long Lake Yosemite. After the Valley's latest glaciation, there was no such lake.

Hike 70   North Rim Traverse

Distance: 19.2 miles (30.9 km) one way

Grade: 4E, strenuous day hike

Trailhead: Same as the Hike 68 trailhead. **D5.**

Introduction: Since good campsites are off-route, do this as a day hike. Only those in good condition should attempt it for it has a total elevation gain of about *6300 feet*. This may seem too strenuous to be a day hike, but it represents a typical daily effort I expended while researching for this book. Turn back if you're exhausted when you reach Yosemite Point.

Description: As in **Hike 68** climb to the Upper Yosemite Fall viewpoint, then backtrack to the main trail and then descend briefly east to the sturdy Yosemite Creek bridge. Here, bilingual signs warn us of the very real danger of waders being swept off their feet for a one-way trip over Upper Yosemite Fall. From the bridge our climb to Yosemite Point first goes north, then east up short switchbacks on brushy slopes, and finally south to the rim of Yosemite Valley. Here at Yosemite Point the view is even more spectacular than that from the Yosemite Fall

Lost Arrow spire

viewpoint. The dramatic panorama extends from Clouds Rest south past Half Dome and Glacier Point, then west to the Cathedral Rocks. Near us a massive shaft of rock, Lost Arrow, rises almost to the Valley's rim and beyond it we can see most of the switchbacking Yosemite Falls trail. A better view of Lost Arrow would certainly be desirable but to obtain it you have to get dangerously close to this spire. Don't attempt it.

Leaving Yosemite Point we start up a crest and in a few minutes pass a quartz vein, the source of crystals you may have noticed on the slope just before you reached the point. About 120 yards farther we encounter pitted boulders, which are glacial erratics left by a Sherwin-age glacier about 800,000 years ago. Just higher on the crest we pass a low, pitted knob of glaciated but very weathered bedrock, then climb moderately for 300 feet before crossing a forest-clad crest. With no more major climbing between here and North Dome we breathe an exhausted sigh of relief and start a shady, gentle descent north. White firs and Jeffrey pines dominate the terrain, though by a trailside knoll you'll see at least one mature sugar pine, which is recognized by its large cones growing at the end of the tree's long branches. At about 7300 feet elevation these trees are close to the upper extent of their elevation range. Beyond the knoll we dip into a shallow bowl, pass three more trailside knolls and make a ⅓-mile descent through a red-fir-shaded gully. Indian Canyon Creek heralds the end of our descent and provides a well-deserved drink. An Indian trail once descended Indian Canyon, hence the name, and careful hikers can still find their way down to the Yosemite Medical Clinic at the foot of the canyon. Careless hikers will find themselves in it. With minor but time-consuming obstacles in it, this canyon is definitely *not* a shortcut to the Valley floor.

Beyond a low ridge east of the Indian Canyon Creek ford we encounter Lehamite Creek, which lies a minute's walk past a trail junction. From it a trail climbs 1.6 miles up to a saddle, then 1.8 miles beyond to Highway 120. We'll climb to that saddle after first visiting North Dome. Beyond generally flowing Lehamite Creek, which *no one* should try to descend, we climb over a slightly higher ridge, then drop to seasonal Royal Arch Creek, shaded by white firs, Jeffrey pines and sugar pines. These give way to brush, particularly huckleberry oak, as we climb to lower Indian Ridge. Ascending it, we quickly encounter a spur trail that drops south to the summit of North Dome. This summit and its views are described in the last part of **Hike 33**, a route which you now follow in reverse up Indian Ridge to the aforementioned saddle. If you don't take the side trip up to delicate Indian Ridge arch, you'll cut a ½ mile off the length of your hike. From the saddle a shady trail lined with red firs and silver pines descends east to cascades along Porcupine Creek and then, in the realm of white firs, descends south to a junction near a bridge across Snow Creek. From it you follow the last part of **Hike 35** down to the floor of Tenaya Canyon—a spectacular descent—then walk southwest 1.1 miles, following the first part of **Hike 67** in reverse to trail's end above Mirror Meadow. Since you're bound to be tired, take the shortest route—the 1.2-mile-long paved bike path—down to the shuttle-bus stop just east of Clarks Bridge.

Hike 71   Wawona Tunnel to Dewey Point

Distance: 10.9 miles (17.5 km) round trip

Grade: 3D, moderate day hike

Trailhead: Discovery View, at the east end of Wawona Tunnel, on the Wawona Road 1.5 miles west of the Bridalveil Fall parking lot entrance. **C5.**

Introduction: Five viewpoints are visited: Inspiration, Old Inspiration, Stanford, Crocker and Dewey. The first two, however, are somewhat blocked by vegetation. By hiking only to Stanford Point, you cut about 2½ miles and 900 feet of climbing from your hike. The creeks found along this route typically dry up by early summer so make sure you bring enough water.

Description: Our signed trail starts at the west end of the south-side parking lot and makes a switchbacking, generally viewless 500-foot ascent for 0.6 mile up to an intersection of the old Wawona Road. Constructed in 1875, this old stage route got a lot of use before it was closed with the opening of the newer Wawona Road in 1933. Today it provides a quiet descent 1.6 miles down to the newer road, meeting it just ⅓ mile above the entrance to the Bridalveil Fall parking lot.

Beyond the intersection our oak-and-conifer shade stays with us all the way up another 500-foot ascent, keeping us cool but also hiding most of the scenery. At Inspiration Point we meet a bend in the old Wawona Road, a point where early travelers got their first commanding view of El Capitan, Bridalveil Fall and the Cathedral Rocks. Today the passage of time has taken its toll, and youthful incense-cedars, black oaks and ponderosa pines obstruct the view.

With most of our climb still ahead of us, we push onward, winding up 1200 vertical feet of the Pohono Trail before arriving at springtime-active Artist Creek. Sugar pines and white firs now replace the lower conifer species, though Douglas-firs make sporadic appearances all the way to Stanford Point. Now at an elevation with cool rather than warm afternoon temperatures, we make a steep 300-foot climb to signed Old Inspiration Point, whose view is in part blocked by a large sugar pine.

Red firs now add shade to the forest canopy as we briefly ascend before dropping to a welcome spring and nearby Meadow Brook. If any water remains along this trail through mid-summer, it will be found here. Beyond the creek and its large grove of alders we head north and soon descend to our first significant viewpoint, at the

end of a short spur trail—Stanford Point. From it we see the gaping chasm of western Yosemite Valley and we identify easily its prominent landmarks: Leaning Tower, Bridalveil Fall, the Cathedral Rocks, El Capitan and, seasonally, Ribbon Fall. Excited by this stunning panorama we climb ½ mile farther, reaching Crocker Point after more than 400 feet of elevation gain. Crocker Point, standing at the brink of an overhanging cliff, provides a heart-pounding view similar to the last one, though better. Now most of the Valley's famed landmarks stand boldly before us and we look over all the Cathedral Rocks to see the Three Brothers. To the left of Clouds Rest we see twin-towered Cathedral Peak and broad-topped Mt. Hoffmann, with distant Mt. Conness between them, marking the Sierra crest along the Park's northeast boundary.

After the Crocker Point revelation, can we expect anything better? You'll have to judge for yourself after continuing ⅔ mile to Dewey Point. Now closer to the Cathedral Rocks, your perspective is different and you look straight down the massive face that supports Leaning Tower. Also intriguing is the back side of Middle Cathedral Rock, whose iron-rich, rust-stained surface stands out among the rest of the Valley's gray, somber colors. Finally you see the Cathedral Spires head-on so they appear as one. After scanning the Valley and the horizon, leave the point and descend the way you came. About 300 yards west of this point your trail passes an area of flattened white firs. A powerful gust of wind, blowing from the northeast perhaps in early 1976, dislodged these firs from their deep, gravelly soils.

Precipitous Crocker Point

Hike 72   Bridalveil Campground to Dewey Point

Distance: 10.0 miles (16.1 km) round trip

Grade: 3C, moderate half-day hike

Trailhead: From a signed junction along the Wawona Road, drive 7.6 miles up the Glacier Point Road to the Bridalveil Creek Campground spur road. Turn right and drive 0.5 mile to the campground's entrance. **C5-D5.**

Introduction: This is the easier of two routes to scenic Dewey Point and it requires less than half the climbing effort of the previous hike, but then it doesn't visit Stanford and Crocker points.

Description: At the entrance to Bridalveil Campground a closed road departs southwest away from the camp's Loop A. On it we soon cross a creek that drains Westfall Meadows, then immediately meet a trail. Heading south, this undesirable trail passes through these meadows, then makes a brush-choked descent to an old logging area—a 1920s "battleground" between environmentalists and the Yosemite Lumber Company. The environmentalists won, but the scars remain.

We take a trail north, which climbs gently over weathered terrain to the Glacier Point Road. By starting here—¼ mile west of the campground's spur road—you could knock 1¾ miles off your total distance. From the road our lodgepole-shaded route gently descends almost to the north tip of largely hidden Peregoy Meadow before topping a low divide. Next we drop moderately and reach the south edge of sedge-filled McGurk Meadow, in which we cross its creek. At times,

the meadow may have an abundance of wildflowers such as shooting star, paintbrush, cinquefoil and corn lily. Looking east from the meadow, we see the low, unglaciated summits of the Ostrander Rocks, whose west slopes supported a small glacier that joined the Bridalveil Creek glacier. Our entire route down to the Pohono Trail was glaciated about 900–800,000 years ago, a time so remote that weathering has removed most of the glacial evidence.

At the meadow's north end we first re-enter a lodgepole forest, soon crest a shallow, viewless saddle, and then descend at a reasonable gradient to a low-crest trail fork. The fork right quickly joins the Pohono Trail and drops to Bridalveil Creek. We fork left, quickly joining that trail, and start west on it. Nearing a broad, low divide, we traverse a dry, gravelly slope dotted with streptanthus, pussy paws and mat lupine.

The forest cover now becomes dominated by firs—both red and white— and on the damp shady floor beneath them you may find wintergreen, snow plant and spotted coralroot, the last two living off soil fungi. Two Bridalveil Creek tributaries are crossed, then a smaller third one before we start up a fourth that drains a curving gully. On the gully's upper slopes Jeffrey pine, huckleberry oak and greenleaf manzanita replace the fir cover and in a few minutes we reach highly scenic Dewey Point, described at the end of **Hike 71.** If you can get someone to meet you at the Wawona Tunnel, then descend to it along this highly scenic portion of the Pohono Trail.

Hike 73   The Fissures at Taft Point

Distance: 2.6 miles (4.1 km) round trip

Grade: 1A, easy 2-hour hike

Trailhead: From a signed junction along the Wawona Road, drive 13.2 miles up the Glacier Point Road to a scenic turn out, on your left, which is 2.3 miles before the Glacier Point parking-lot entrance. **D5.**

Introduction: The views from Taft Point rival those from Glacier Point. However, since Taft Point is reached by trail, it is sparsely visited compared to Glacer Point. Generaly lacking protective railings, Taft Point and the Fissures are potentially dangerous, so don't bring along children unless you can really keep them under strict control.

Description: From the road-cut parking lot we descend about 50 yards to a trail, turn left, and start southwest on it. After about 150 yards of easy descent we pass a trailside outcrop that is almost entirely composed of glistening whitish-gray quartz. It also has small amounts of pink potassium feldspar. Lacking the surrounding bedrock's dark minerals, which are more prone to weathering, this outcrop is eroding more slowly than the adjacent landscape, so it protrudes. In a minute we come to seasonal, murmuring Sentinel Creek whose limited drainage area keeps Sentinel Fall downstream from being one of Yosemite Valley's prime attractions. After boulder-hopping the creek we follow an undulating trail west past pines, firs and brush to a crest junction with the Pohono Trail. Just north of it you'll notice some large, weathered boulders. Not left by glaciers, these boulders weathered in place and will continue to "grow" as the surrounding bedrock is stripped away.

From the junction we descend to a seeping creeklet that drains through a small field of corn lilies. In this and two other nearby damp areas you may also find bracken fern, lupine, paintbrush, mountain bluebell, mountain monkey flower, arrowhead senecio, Richardson's geranium, green gentian and alpine lily. The last two, like corn lily, can grow to head height. Descending toward the Fissures, we cross drier slopes that are generally covered with brush. Here you may find two wildflowers belonging to the same wildflower tribe: the single-stemmed senecio and the cordilleran arnica. The first has alternate leaves, the second has opposite ones. Two other yellow wildflowers seen are the sulphur flower, a buckwheat, and the Sierra wallflower, a mustard. Soon you arrive at the Fissures—five vertical, parallel fractures that cut through overhanging Profile Cliff, beneath your feet. Because the Fissures area is unglaciated, it is well weathered, and a careless step could result in an easy slip on the loose gravel— dangerous in this area.

Overhanging, exposed Taft Point

One of the five Fissures

Beyond the Fissures we walk up to a small railing at the brink of a conspicuous point and get an acrophobia-inducing view of overhanging Profile Cliff, beneath us. For the best views of Yosemite Valley and the High Sierra walk west to *exposed* Taft Point, from where you see the Cathedral spires and rocks, El Capitan, the Three Brothers, Yosemite Falls and Sentinel Rock. Broad Mt. Hoffmann stands on the skyline just east of Indian Canyon and east of that peak stands distant Mt. Conness, on the Sierra crest. Taft Point was named to commemorate President William Howard Taft's October 1909 visit to Yosemite Valley. On it he met John Muir, who hoped to convince the President to prevent construction of a dam in Hetch Hetchy. The President, tiring of Muir's arguments, jokingly suggested that Yosemite Valley also be dammed. Muir, not seeing the humor, was offended. To his credit, Taft did oppose the dam, but it was built later. From Taft Point the Pohono Trail is described westward in **Hike 75.**

Hike 74   Sentinel Dome

Distance: 2.4 miles (3.9 km) round trip

Grade: 1B, moderate 2-hour hike

Trailhead: Same as Hike 73 trailhead. **D5.**

Introduction: Sentinel Dome is one of the most-climbed domes in the Park, and it was noted for its famous gnarled Jeffrey pine growing on its summit. Lembert Dome and Pothole Dome, both in the Tuolumne Meadows area, may be climbed more often, but neither is a true dome but rather each is a *roche moutonnée*—an unsymmetrical glacier-formed feature.

Description: From the road-cut parking lot we descend about 50 yards, turn right and make a curving, generally ascending traverse ¾ mile north almost to the south base of Sentinel Dome. Here we meet and briefly hike north on a road, then come to a fork, where we veer left, and in 30 yards, at another fork, we veer left again. In a few minutes we arrive at the dome's north end, where we meet a path from Glacier Point. We now climb southwest up a bedrock route to the summit. Though a real trail up to it doesn't exist you should have no problems getting there.

At an elevation of 8122 feet, Sentinel Dome is the second highest viewpoint above Yosemite Valley. Only Half Dome—a strenuous hike—is higher. Seen from the summit, El Capitan, Yosemite Falls and Half Dome stand out as the three most prominent Valley landmarks. West of Half Dome are two bald features, North and Basket domes. On the skyline above North Dome stands blocky Mt. Hoffmann, the Park's geographic center, while to the east, above Mt. crest of the Clark Range. Until the early 1980s, most summit visitors photographed its wind-swept Jeffrey pine. Sadly, the tree was repeatedly vandalized and, although the road to the dome's base was closed to reduce abuse, the tree died. While up here you might ponder a botanical question: This summit is an ideal habitat for western junipers—why are they absent?

Before leaving the summit, check out the surrounding area. Typical of unglaciated, low-angle granitic bedrock, this surface has slowly developed weathering pits. It is possible that the dome's summit was barely overridden by a very ancient glacier but no glacial evidence is found above the base of the dome. During the time of that maximum glaciation about 900–800,000 years ago, Half Dome, across the Valley, protruded only 600 feet above the giant glacier.

Sentinel Dome's lone Jeffrey pine, as it appeared in 1976

Hike 75   South Rim Traverse

Distance: 13.5 miles (21.7 km) one way

Grade: 3D, moderate day hike

Trailhead: From a signed junction along the Wawona Road, drive 15.5 miles up the Glacier Point to its end. **D5.**

Introduction: This hike, the Pohono Trail, takes you past several excellent viewpoints, each showing a different part of Yosemite Valley in a unique perspective. After early June carry enough water (usually one quart) to last until midpoint, Bridalveil Creek, which is the hike's only permanent source of water.

Description: From the extreme east end of the Glacier Point parking lot, we start up a trail that in a minute forks. **Hike 87** branches left but we branch right and under white-fir cover cross the Glacier Point Road in another minute. From it we immediately branch right again since the path ahead climbs to a ranger's residence. Our still-climbing trail curves west up to a switchback, then south to a road. This we cross and continue up the relentless grade to a north-descending crest which we cross before climbing briefly south to a gully. In it, almost a mile from Glacier Point, we are faced with a choice. Our route, the Pohono Trail, goes west to the brink of Sentinel Fall—usually dry by midsummer—while the alternate route, which starts north before climbing south, goes to scenic Sentinel Dome. Should you take the dome route, you can return to the Pohono Trail or you can take a more level route that adds ⅔ mile to your total distance. From that dome you follow **Hike 74** in reverse, then the first half of **Hike 73**, which takes you back to the Pohono Trail.

Our main route, the Pohono Trail, leaves the gully, traverses southwest across a lower face of Sentinel Dome, then drops to a gravelly gully with north-side boulders. These were left here by a Sherwin-age glacier that once filled Yosemite Valley up to this level about 900–800,000 years ago. Such glacial evidence stays with us along our short, sometimes steep descent to Sentinel Creek. Paralleling its bank we can walk 90 yards out to a point where we get our first good Valley views since Glacier Point. Those hiking before mid-June will also see upper Sentinel Fall splashing down a chute immediately west of the point.

Beyond the sometimes stagnant creek we climb past lodgepole pines and white firs, then, before a crest junction, past Jeffrey pines and red firs. At the junction we rejoin the alternate route and, as in the second half of **Hike 73**, descend a trail to the Fissures and Taft Point. Be careful when exploring this scenic though precipitous area. From the westernmost fissure the Pohono Trail descends south, then contours west to a low ridge. By following the ridge about 250 yards out to its end you'll reach an unnamed viewpoint that gives you a view down upon the Cathedral Rocks, lined up in a row. Descending from the low ridge, the shady Pohono Trail drops 700 feet to a bridge over Bridalveil Creek, on whose south bank is the hike's only possible campsite, nestled under lodgepole pines.

From the creek, which is our hike's approximate midpoint, we climb west to two junctions with a lateral trail. This lateral climbs 2 miles south to the Glacier Point Road, then a short mile beyond it to Bridalveil Campground. This lateral trail constitutes the first half of **Hike 72** (described in the northern direction), and turning to the second half of that hike's description, we let it guide us over to Dewey Point. West from that point we follow **Hike 71**, described in the reverse direction, down to Discovery View, at the east end of Wawona Tunnel.

Hike 76   Glacier Point to Yosemite Valley
via Four Mile Trail

Distance: 4.5 miles (7.2 km) one way

Grade: 1A, easy 2-hour hike

Trailhead: Same as Hike 75 trailhead. **D5.**

Introduction: This trail provides a very scenic, enjoyable descent to Yosemite Valley—a descent that will acquaint you with the Valley's main features. This descent also gives you a feel for the Valley's 3000-foot depth.

Description: Before building the Yosemite Falls trail (**Hike 68**) John Conway first worked on this trail, completing it in 1872. Originally about 4 miles long, it was rebuilt and lengthened in 1929 but the trail's name stuck. Our trail starts at the north side of a snack shop, which together with a curio shop and restrooms replaced the grand Glacier Point Hotel. This three-story hotel, together with the adjacent historic Mountain House—built in 1878—burned to the ground in August 1969. Descending west from today's small structures, we enter a cool bowl whose shady white firs and sugar pines usually harbor snow patches well into June. Contouring northwest, we eventually emerge from forest shade and, looking east, can see Glacier Point's two overhanging rocks capping a vertical wall. Soon we curve west, veer in and out of a cool gully, then reach a descending ridge. On it we generally leave behind views of Royal Arches, Washington Column and North Dome for those of Yosemite Falls, the Three Brothers, El Capitan and, foremost, Sentinel Rock, which provides a good gauge to mark our downward progress.

Chinquapin, greenleaf manzanita and huckleberry oak dominate the first dozen switchback legs, thereby giving us unobstructed panoramas, though making the hike a hot one for anyone ascending from the Valley floor on a summer afternoon. However, as we duck east into a gully, shady conifers appear, though they somewhat censor our views. If you had been on this trail on some early morning through the 1970s until June 1990, when hang gliders were banned, you could have seen pilots land in meadows below you—taking sky trails from Glacier Point to the Valley floor.

About midway down the series of switchbacks, gold-cup oaks begin to compete with white firs and Douglas-firs, and our view is obstructed even more. After descending two thirds of the vertical distance to the Valley floor, our switchbacks temporarily end. A long steady descent now ensues, mostly past gold-cup oaks, though black oaks and incense-cedars also appear. After ¼ mile we cross a creeklet that usually flows until early July and near its seasonally lush vegetation we get an excellent view down at Leidig Meadow.

Our steady descent again enters oak cover and we skirt below the base of imposing Sentinel Rock without hardly seeing it. At last a final group of switchbacks carry us down to an abandoned parking loop, closed in about 1975, and we proceed north, intersecting the Valley floor's southside trail, **Hike 63**, halfway to our end point, the eastbound road.

By today's climbing standards, the north face of Sentinel Rock is a relatively easy climb

Hike 77   Vernal Fall Bridge

Distance: 1.6 miles (2.6 km) round trip

Grade: 1A, moderate 2-hour hike

Trailhead: Happy Isles shuttle-bus stop in eastern Yosemite Valley. **D5.**

Introduction: Of all the Park's hikes this one—along a broad, paved path—is one of the most popular. If you have time for only one short (but steep) hike, this is the one to take.

Description: From the shuttle-bus stop you head south across a shady flat to the Happy Isles area, which has the informative Happy Isles Nature Center. By a curio shop you cross a bridge, and at its east end reach a gaging station. Its records show that in late summer the river's discharge can fall to less than 5 cubic feet per second, while during a major flood it can approach a staggering 10,000 cubic feet per second. From this station the famous John Muir Trail heads about 210 miles southward to the summit of Mt. Whitney.

Bay trees, Douglas-firs and gold-cup oaks dominate the forest canopy as we start up the John Muir Trail. In a few minutes we meet a trail on our right that descends to upper Happy Isle. In a few more yards we reach a small cistern with questionable spring water. Beyond it the climb south steepens, and before bending east we get a glance back at Upper Yosemite Fall, partly blocked by the nearby Glacier Point Apron. This smooth, curved apron contrasts with the generally angular nature of Yosemite topography. Scanning the canyon wall south of

the apron you'll see a series of oblique-angle cliffs—all of them remarkably similar in orientation since they've fractured along the same series of joint planes. At the canyon's end Illilouette Fall plunges 370 feet over a vertical, joint-controlled cliff. Just east of the fall is a large scar which marks the site of a major rock-fall that broke loose during the winter of 1968–69.

Climbing east we head up a severely glaciated canyon, one that in times past was buried by as much as 3500 feet of glacier ice. Hiking beneath the unstable, highly fractured south wall of Sierra Point, we cross a talus slope—an accumulation of rockfall boulders. The May 1980 Mammoth Lakes earthquake set up three rockfalls here, which later occurred in conjunction with heavy rains in February 1986. Among the boulders are drab California ground squirrels. Don't let these abundant squirrels or the fluffy-tailed gray squirrels beg a meal from you. Feeding them now would only create more starvation next winter, after you've gone.

Entering forest shade once more, we first struggle up the steep trail before making a quick drop to our destination, the Vernal Fall bridge. From it we see Vernal Fall—a broad wall of water—plunge 320 feet over a vertical cliff before cascading toward us. Looming above the fall are two glacier-trimmed masses, Mt. Broderick (left) and Liberty Cap (right). Just beyond our bridge you'll find restrooms and an emergency telephone. **Hike 78** continues the description up-canyon.

Hike 78   Vernal-Nevada Falls Loop

Distance: 5.9 miles (9.5 km) semiloop trip

Grade: 2D, strenuous half-day hike

Trailhead: Happy Isles shuttle-bus stop in eastern Yosemite Valley. **D5.**

Introduction: Mile for mile, this very popular hike may be the most scenic one in the Park. The first part of this loop goes up the famous (or infamous) Mist trail—a steep, strenuous trail that sprays you with Vernal Fall's mist. Take a poncho or other rain gear or, if it is a warm day, strip down to swimwear, for you can dry out on the sun-drenched rocks above the fall. For the best photos start after 10 a.m.

Description: The previous hike tells you what to see along your hike up to the Vernal Fall

bridge. About 200 yards beyond the bridge we come to the start of our loop. Here the Mist trail continues upriver while the John Muir Trail starts a switchbacking ascent to the right. This is the route taken by mules and horses. We'll go up the Mist trail and down the John Muir Trail. You can, of course, go up or down either, but by starting the loop up the Mist trail, you stand less chance of an accident. Hikers are more apt to slip or twist an ankle descending than ascending, and the Mist trail route to Nevada Fall has ample opportunity for such a mishap. Descending from Nevada Fall, you negotiate a series of short, tight switchbacks, walking on smooth, sometimes loose rocks—your first danger. Your second is the descent of the slippery, spray-drenched Mist trail, and, if you speed down to avoid a drenching, you invite disaster. If you don't want to get wet, stick to the Muir Trail.

In swim suit or rain gear we start up the Mist trail and soon, rounding a bend, receive our first spray. If you're climbing this trail on a sunny day, you're almost certain to see one, if not two, rainbows come alive in the fall's spray. The spray increases as we advance toward the fall, but we get a brief respite behind a large boulder. Beyond it we complete our 300-odd steps, most of them wet, which guide us up through a verdant, spray-drenched garden. It would certainly be the ideal place to study moss, ferns and wildflowers were it not for the deluge that allows these plants to thrive here in the first place. We struggle up the last few dozen steps under the shelter of trees, then, reaching an alcove beneath an ominous overhang, scurry left up a last set of stairs. These, protected by a railing, guide us to the top of a vertical cliff. Pausing here we can study our route, the nearby fall, and the river gorge. Our railing ends just upriver from the brink of Vernal Fall. It is there for a reason. Every year several people are swept over the Park's falls because they ignore warnings. Sunbathers, trying to reach the far side of Emerald Pool, which lies just above the brink, usually underestimate the danger of the river's slippery rocks and the danger of its treacherous current. Don't be taken in.

Plunging into the upper end of chilly Emerald Pool is churning Silver Apron. Late in the summer when the Merced's flow is noticeably down, one is tempted to glide down this watery chute into Emerald Pool. This too is hazardous, for one can easily crash on some boulders just

Vernal Fall, from trail up to Clark Point

beyond the end of this silvery chute. Rivers are not to be taken lightly.

You'll see a bridge spanning the narrow gorge that confines the Silver Apron, and this structure is our immediate goal. The trail can be vague in our area for so many paths have been trampled through it, but our route leaves the river near the east end of Emerald Pool, climbs briefly south, then angles east to a nearby junction. From it a view-packed trail climbs almost ½ mile to Clark Point, where it meets the John Muir Trail. We, however, stay low and curve left over to the bridge spanning the Silver Apron. Beyond it we have a short, moderate climb up to a broad bench which was once the site of La Casa Nevada. Opened in 1870 it was managed by Albert Snow until 1891, when a fire burned the main structure to the ground. Today one can find outhouses in this area.

Spurred onward by the sight and sound of plummeting Nevada Fall, we climb eastward, soon commencing a series of more than two dozen compact switchbacks. As we ascend them, Nevada Fall slips out of view, but we can still see towering Liberty Cap. Our climb ends at the top of a joint-controlled gully through which the Merced River *may* have flowed in earlier times or *may* flow in future times. A large glacier can rearrange a river's course. Here, on brushy slopes, we once again meet the John Muir Trail, which from here makes a short climb into Little Yosemite Valley. You have to ascend this trail a full mile (**Hike 79**) before you will find any legal campsites. Our route is day-use only.

From this junction hikers descending from Tuolumne Meadows, Clouds Rest, Half Dome and Merced Lake join us as we head southwest toward nearby Nevada Fall. Along this stretch you may notice knobby boulders—rich in feldspar crystals—that strongly contrast with the bedrock they lie on. These boulders are *erratics*—that is, rocks left by retreating glaciers which were here perhaps as recently as 13,500 years ago. Nearing the Merced River you may also notice patches of bedrock that have been polished, striated and gouged by a former glacier.

Just a few yards before the Nevada Fall bridge you can strike northwest on a short, easily missed spur trail down to a viewpoint beside the fall's brink. This viewpoint's railing is seen from the fall's bridge, thereby giving you an idea where the trail ends. Don't go straying along the cliff's edge and, as mentioned earlier, respect the river—it too often sweeps people over the fall. Standing near the tumultuous brink of the Merced River, you can look across its glaciated canyon to distant Glacier Point. Vernal Fall, which lies just beyond Emerald Pool, plunges over a vertical wall that is perpendicular to the one that Nevada Fall plunges over. This part of the Merced River canyon is bounded by major

Liberty Cap and Nevada Fall

fracture planes, or joint planes, which account for the canyon's angular landscape.

From the Nevada Fall bridge we strike southwest, immediately passing more glacier polish and erratic boulders as well as an outhouse, off in the trees. Our short, gentle climb ends at a junction just beyond a seeping spring, where we meet the Glacier Point-Panorama trail. Folks descending from Glacier Point (**Hike 87**) join us here for a descent to Happy Isles along the John Muir Trail. This Muir Trail segment starts with a high traverse that provides an ever-changing panorama of domelike Liberty Cap and broad-topped Mt. Broderick. As we progress west, Half Dome comes into prominence, its hulking mass vying for our attention. Eventually we descend to Clark Point, where we meet a scenic lateral trail that switchbacks down to Emerald Pool. If you enjoyed the Mist trail you can visit it again by first descending this lateral, but remember to be careful while descending the Mist trail.

Backpackers and those wishing to keep dry continue down the John Muir Trail, which curves south into a gully, switchbacks down to the base of spreading Panorama Cliff, then switchbacks down a talus slope. Largely shaded by gold-cup oaks and Douglas-firs, it reaches a junction with a horse trail—no hikers allowed— that descends to the Valley's stables. We continue a brief minute more to a junction with the Mist trail, turn left and quickly arrive at the Vernal Fall bridge. From it Happy Isles is a brief 15-minute descent.

Hike 79   Little Yosemite Valley

Distance: 7.9 miles (12.7 km) semiloop trip

Grade: 2D, easy 2-day hike

Trailhead: Happy Isles shuttle-bus stop in eastern Yosemite Valley. **D5.**

Introduction: Many a backpacker has spent his first night in the "wilderness" in Little Yosemite Valley. Indeed, more backpackers camp in it than in any other Yosemite backcountry area. Perhaps too, more bears visit it than any other backcountry area. During the summer a friendly ranger is usually around who'll provide you with a lot of good advice on backpacking techniques and wilderness courtesy.

Description: Follow **Hike 78** up the Mist trail or John Muir Trail to a junction just northeast of the brink of Nevada Fall. From this brushy

junction we climb up a gully that is generally overgrown with huckleberry oak. From its top we quickly descend into forest cover and reach a fairly large "swimming hole" on the Merced River. Though chilly, it is far enough above the river's rapids to provide a *short*, refreshing dip. A longer stay would make you numb. Beneath lodgepole and Jeffrey pines, white firs and incense-cedars we continue northeast along the river's azalea-lined bank, then quickly encounter a trail fork. The left fork climbs and then descends the low east ridge of Liberty Cap. It is a "shortcut" to the Half Dome trail, but the amount of climbing it requires offsets the little distance you'll save on it. We keep right on the main trail, and go a short half mile to another junction, from where the John Muir Trail/Half

Dome trail branches north while the Merced Lake trail continues east. Just east of this junction you're likely to find a summer ranger who can give you advice on where to camp, how to bear-bag your food, where to find the outhouse, and what sights to see. Many hikers on their way to Half Dome (**Hike 80**) or Merced Lake (**Hike 81**) spend their first night here. You might note that the Half Dome trail starts north alongside a low crest—a glacial moraine.

Some nearby landmarks—all off trail—make interesting side trips: Liberty Cap, Mt. Broderick, Lost Lake and the Diving Board. After starting on the "shortcut" trail you can head west up the east ridge of Liberty Cap and

Liberty Cap's long east rib

quite safely reach its summit. Mt. Broderick is another matter. You have to know how to use a map and how to climb. Some hikers may also want to bring a rope. Its summit, however, provides better views than does Liberty Cap's, particularly of Nevada Fall. Both are *roches moutonnées*—they are dome-like resistant features that were sculpted by glaciers. Each of the probably dozen or more glaciers that advanced down-canyon planed down these monoliths' back sides but quarried back into their front sides, leaving each very un-symmetrical.

Don't get lost looking for Lost Lake—a swamp at the east base of Mt. Broderick. Trapped between moraines left by a glacier receding up-canyon perhaps only 13,500 years ago, this "lake" has been slowly filling with sediments, most of them being end products of organic decomposition. Lost Lake will appeal to the naturalist but probably not to anyone else. Beyond Lost Lake one can climb to the steep-faced Diving Board. Good mountaineering sense and cross-country ability are prerequisites for this brushy ascent. In the author's opinion the Diving Board provides you with the best of all possible views of Half Dome's giant, intimidating northwest face. Before trying any of these side trips, first check out with a ranger at the Park's Visitor Center or with one stationed in Little Yosemite Valley.

Hike 80   Half Dome

Distance: 16.4 miles (26.4 km) round trip
Grade: 4E, strenuous day hike
Trailhead: Happy Isles shuttle-bus stop in eastern Yosemite Valley. **D5.**
Introduction: If I were allowed to make only *one* day hike in the Park, I would unquestionably choose this hike—the one that introduced me to Yosemite and fired my desire to "climb every mountain." Half Dome is certainly not for acrophobics, and if you are not in excellent condition, you'll want to spend a night in Little Yosemite Valley on your way up. This grandest of the Valley's summits, rising as a monolith toward the heavens, acts as a giant lightning rod, and you should not ascend it in threatening weather.

Description: Half Dome "is a crest of granite rising to the height of 4,737 feet above the Valley, perfectly inaccessible, being probably

the only one of all the prominent points about the Yosemite which never has been and never will be trodden by human foot." So wrote Josiah D. Whitney—California's first prominent geologist—in his 1870 *Yosemite Guide-Book.* Just five years later the impossible was accomplished, when George Anderson labored for weeks drilling a row of holes up to the "inaccessible" summit, reached on the 12th of October, 1875. Today, hundreds if not thousands of visitors reach the summit every year, climbing a frightening cable stairway that lies close to the original ascent route.

During midsummer, thunderstorms are common, though they usually don't expel their lightning bolts until midafternoon. Therefore, you should plan to reach the summit and leave it by early afternoon. Depending on your hiking ability, you should plan to start from Happy Isles at 6 or 7 a.m. if you intend to do this as a day hike, or by 9 a.m. if you're starting from Little Yosemite Valley. Follow **Hike 77** up to the Vernal Fall bridge, then the first part of **Hike 78** up to the junction just beyond Nevada Fall; or stay on the Muir Trail from the bridge, following the last part of **Hike 78** in reverse. As in **Hike 79** climb east to the west end of Little Yosemite Valley, meet a trail fork, and take either path. Where they rejoin you begin a steady, unrelenting climb to the base of the dome's cables. After 1⅓ miles of forested ascent you leave the John Muir Trail, which climbs east to Tuolumne Meadows, and you continue up the Half Dome trail.

After 0.6 mile of ascent we meet a spur trail that goes about 280 yards east to a spring. If you're not stocked up with water, you'll want to get it here—your last opportunity. Hikers have camped along this spur trail, but camping space is so limited that you had best not expect to find any. If you must camp nearby, eat your dinner in this area (no fires please!), fill your water bottles, then spend the night on the broad saddle about ⅛ mile above the spur-trail junction.

The trail bends west before reaching that saddle, and it then climbs through a forest of red firs and Jeffrey pines instead of white firs and incense-cedars. On this section Half Dome's northeast face comes into view and, topping a crest, we get a fine view of Clouds Rest and its satellites, the Quarter Domes. Here you'll likely find a use trail that thoughtless hikers have taken back toward Little Yosemite Valley. It has become obvious enough that some hikers descending from the summit have followed it by mistake. Please try to avoid it when you descend.

A crest traverse reveals more views, including Tenaya Canyon, Mt. Watkins, Mt. Hoffmann and much of the upper Merced River basin. This traverse ends all too soon at the base of Half Dome's shoulder, where a sign warns us of the potential lightning hazard. Some hikers, seeing that thunderstorms are still miles away, ignore the sign and continue onward. Too often they end up a statistic. Even when thunderstorms are miles away, static electricity can build up on the summit. Out of a clear blue sky a charge can bolt down the cable, throwing your arms off it—or worse. If your hair starts standing on end, beat a hasty retreat!

Almost two dozen short switchbacks guide us up the view-packed ridge of the dome's shoulder and, near the top, a cable lends additional aid. A real danger on this section is loose gravel, which could prove fatal to a careless hiker. Topping the shoulder we are confronted with the famous

Half Dome's cable route

intimidating Half Dome cables and are likely to mutter, "You gotta be kidding." (The cables are put up in mid-May and removed in early October in a normal year.) The ascent starts out gently enough, but it too quickly steepens almost to a 45° angle. On this stretch, first-timers often slow to a snail's pace, clenching both cables with sweaty hands. Looking down, they can see that you *don't* want to fall.

The rarefied air certainly hinders our progress as we struggle upward, but an easing gradient gives new incentive and soon we are scrambling up to the broad summit area. About the size of 17 football fields, it provides quite an area to explore. With caution most hikers proceed to the dome's high point (8842'), located at the north end, from where they can view the dome's overhanging northwest point. A few stout-hearted souls actually peer over the lip of this overhanging point for a super-frightening view down the dome's 2000-foot face. To non-climbers it is hard to imagine that anyone could climb such a face, yet it has been ascended thousands of times by various routes. Please don't throw rocks—there may be climbers below.

From the broad summit of this granodiorite monolith you have a 360° panorama. You can look down Yosemite Valley to the bald brow of

El Capitan and up Tenaya Canyon past Clouds Rest to Cathedral Peak, the Sierra crest and Mt. Hoffmann. Mt. Starr King—a dome that rises only 250 feet above us—dominates the Illilouette Creek basin to the south, while the Clark Range cuts the sky to the southeast. Looking due east across the summit of Moraine Dome, one sees Mt. Florence, whose broad form hides Mt. Lyell, behind it.

Sharing our summit views are two very dissimilar vertebrates: the golden-mantled ground squirrel and the rare Mt. Lyell salamander. One of these squirrels, begging for food, may have followed you up the cables, staying close enough to you to avoid becoming the prey of a sharp-eyed hawk or eagle. The salamander, being a lungless kind, must stay in cool, moist crevices during the day in order to keep its skin moist and breathable. Hunting during the summer evenings and nights, it searches for insects or spiders, nourishing itself in preparation for a long, cold winter. No one knows how long these salamanders have resided here. Perhaps they were here during a glacial episode when glaciers flowing down Tenaya and Merced canyons left the top of Half Dome as an island above a sea of ice. During the maximum glaciation, glaciers came to within 600 feet of the summit. During that time, about 900–800,000 years ago, glaciers completed their deepening of Yosemite Valley, which today is partly filled with sediments, and in the deepest point they filled it to a depth of about 6000 feet. Such a thickness would have exerted a pressure of about 170 tons per square foot on the Valley floor.

Hiker at brink of Half Dome's summit

Hike 81   Merced Lake

Distance: 27.4 miles (44.1 km) semiloop trip

Grade: 5E, moderate 3-day hike

Trailhead: Happy Isles shuttle-bus stop in eastern Yosemite Valley. **D5.**

Introduction: Best done in three days with overnight stops at Little Yosemite Valley and Merced Lake, this hike is often done in two by energetic weekend hikers. Its route—up a fantastic river canyon—is hard to beat anywhere in the Sierra Nevada.

Description: If you are wearing a backpack, you should climb to the top of Nevada Fall by the John Muir Trail, not by the Mist trail. **Hike 77** describes the route to the Vernal Fall bridge; then you follow the last part of **Hike 78** in

reverse up the obvious route to Nevada Fall. The last 1¼ miles along this section are very scenic, with views of Half Dome, Mt. Broderick, Liberty Cap, Nevada Fall and the Merced River canyon. Beyond the Nevada Fall bridge we soon meet the end of the Mist trail—the short, wet, strenuous alternate route—then climb up and over into Little Yosemite Valley, described in **Hike 79.** In its western part we leave the John Muir Trail, which veers north, then embark on a shady two-mile stroll, following the Merced Lake trail through the broad, flat valley. The valley's floor has been largely buried by glacial sediments, which like beach sand make us work even though the trail is level. At times our sandy trail widens to 30 feet—evidence of past hikers' attempts to circumvent this linear sand trap. Progressing east through Little Yosemite Valley, we stay closer to the base of glacier-polished Moraine Dome than to the Merced River, and along this stretch you can branch off to riverside campsites that are far more peaceful than those near the John Muir Trail junction, which tends to be a "Grand Central Station." The valley's east end is graced by the presence of a beautiful pool—the receptacle of a Merced River cascade. Leaving the camps near the picturesque area, we climb past the cascade and glance back to see the east face of exfoliating Moraine Dome, made vulnerable to rockfall by extensive glacial steepening. Sweeping across this face is a long arch which marks the breakoff line of one or more previous rockfalls. Large accumulations of talus testify to this cliff's instability.

Our brief cascade climb heads toward the 1900-foot-high Bunnell Point cliff, which is exfoliating at such a prodigious rate that it, in stark contrast to the shiny dome opposite it, has virtually no remaining trace of glacial evidence. Rounding the base of the Sugar Loaf, a glacier-smoothed dome, we enter Lost Valley, where no fires are allowed. Careless campers have started fires both up- and down-canyon, and the Park

Service would like to prevent the forest on this verdant island, bounded by sublime cliffs, from going up in smoke. At the valley's end we switchback up past Bunnell Cascade, which with the magnificent canyon scenery can easily distract us from the real danger of this exposed section of trail. Don't let the scenery carry you away. Although the scenery may overpower *us,* past glaciers did not overpower this part of the canyon. Overtop it they did, at times flowing over as well as around Bunnell Point, yet their massive thicknesses, exerting over 100 tons per square foot, failed to significantly widen this canyon from a **V** to a **U** shape. However, just beyond this **V** gorge, glaciers did widen it a bit and in this miniature valley we bridge the Merced River for a minute's walk to a low, pounding cascade.

Our up-canyon walk, which has been amazingly easy since Nevada Fall, soon reaches a series of more than a dozen switchbacks that carry us up 400 feet above the river—a route necessitated by another **V**-shaped gorge. Our climb reaches its zenith amid a spring-fed profuse wildflower garden, bordered by aspens, which in midsummer supports a colorful array of floral species. Alpine lily, monkshood and arrowhead butterweed grow

Merced Lake and a view east up Lewis Creek and Merced River canyons

chest-high, as if to divert our attention away from the dozen or so smaller though equally beautiful wildflowers.

Beyond this glade we soon come out onto a highly polished bedrock surface. Here we can glance west and see Clouds Rest—a long ridge—standing high on the horizon. Now we descend back into tree cover and amid the white boles of quaking aspens brush through a forest carpet of bracken ferns and cross several creeklets before emerging on a bedrock bench above the river's inner gorge. From it we can study the features of a broad, hulking granitic mass opposite us whose south face is bounded by an immense arch. A "hairline" crack along its east side indicates that a major rockfall is imminent and that this arch, which is already usurping an east-face arch, will grow even larger. Traversing our bench, we soon come to a bend in the river and at it bridge the Merced just above the brink of its cascades. Strolling east, we reach the west end of spacious Echo Valley—the charred site of an unnecessary holocaust—and proceed to a junction at its north edge.

Here, near an Echo Creek campsite, is the start of an alternate route you might consider taking back to Little Yosemite Valley. When our up-canyon route was built in 1931, the old, high trail to Merced Lake fell into disuse, for it is almost a mile longer and climbs 750 feet more. It also has less water, fewer campsites and fewer views. On the plus side, it does provide access to the rewarding summit of Moraine Dome. This alternate route climbs about 450 feet, passing a moraine about midway to a junction with the Echo Creek trail (**Hike 52**). It then branches west for a shorter climb to a broad granitic surface. Across bedrock it winds briefly down to a stagnant lakelet. Beyond it you get an incredible view—one that justifies the effort—of the glaciated slabs and walls that bound the Merced River canyon.

Leaving the broad surface, that high trail makes a brushy ascent up to an ephemeral creek, crosses it and on gentle bedrock slopes goes through a bouldery moraine. This topographic feature, which you can trace west, is only one of many lateral moraines left high on the river canyon's north wall. The tremendous views soon disappear. One then begins a mile of exhilarating walking through a forest of Jeffrey pines, lodgepoles and white firs which shade patch after patch of vivid-green bracken ferns.

Still in forest one climbs slightly, cutting across the crests of two lateral moraines just before a junction with the John Muir Trail. About 150 yards up this trail, beyond yet another moraine crest, you'll find the south end of the Forsyth trail, and a two-minute walk along it will get you to a good Sunrise Creek campsite. Our alternate return route from the high-trail junction coincides with the John Muir Trail, following the last part of **Hike 51** down to Little Yosemite Valley.

But with Merced Lake our first goal, we immediately bridge Echo Creek, strike southeast through burned-but-boggy Echo Valley, and climb east past the Merced River's largely unseen pools to Merced Lake's west shore. Don't camp here, but rather continue past the north shore to Merced Lake High Sierra Camp and the adjacent riverside campground, about 9¼ miles beyond the John Muir Trail junction in Little Yosemite Valley. You can count on seeing bears here, so store your food in a bearproof food box or with the High Sierra Camp. The lake, being a large one at a moderate elevation, supports three species of trout: brook, brown and rainbow.

François Matthes, after completing his monumental work on Yosemite Valley, later wrote about Merced Lake and its river canyon. He noted that "wherever the joint structure of the granite in the Sierra Nevada permitted glaciers to quarry out blocks on a large scale, the canyons were profoundly modified by glaciation; but wherever the granite was massive, so that glaciers could only grind, the changes effected were relatively small." So true. Where joints abounded in the right combination, the river canyon widened, as one sees in Little Yosemite Valley, Lost Valley, Echo Valley and the valley that holds 80-foot-deep Merced Lake. Matthes noted that Merced Lake and Washburn Lake (about 3 miles up-canyon) have advancing deltas and that both will eventually be filled in. Much of these deltas was probably deposited during the waning stage of the last glacier, which retreated up the canyon about 13,500 years ago. Since that time very little sediment has entered these lakes, and we can expect each to survive at least 100,000 years. Unfortunately, both will be eradicated sooner, perhaps in the next few thousand years, by an advancing glacier, which, as in past cycles, will later retreat, only to initiate the sedimentation process once again. We are viewing just a fleeting moment of a multi-million-year glacial history.

Merced Peak, from switchback at 8480 feet in Merced Peak Fork canyon (Hike 89)

Section 7

Trails south and east of the Glacier Point Road

Introduction: This section, like Section 2, is one of contrasts, ranging from 3250 feet (991 m) at the bottom of the Alder Creek trail, outside the Park, up to 11,180 feet (3407 m) at Red Peak Pass. All of the Park's plant communities are found within this altitudinal range. Along Hikes 82, 83 and 92, few hikers will be met, but at Ostrander and Royal Arch lakes, Hikes 84 and 86/91 respectively, camping space may be at a premium. This section is unique in that it has a network of trails through a grove of giant sequoias (Hike 93); no such trail system exists at the Park's two other groves. Although thousands of persons visit this section's Mariposa Grove each week during the summer, the vast majority take the tram. The few who explore the grove on foot are richly rewarded.

Supplies and Services: Wawona is the "urban" center for this area, having a large, historic hotel, a store, a gas station and other amenities. In addition to a golf course, the hotel has a pool, but the natural pools on the South Fork Merced River are more enjoyable and get more use. Some of these are located just up from the river's covered bridge, but more are located beside stretched-out Wawona Campground.

Just north of the river, the Chilnualna Road branches east from the highway—the Wawona Road—and it takes you past the History Center and its stables (with rides available) to North Wawona, a private in-Park settlement with additional food and lodging.

North of the Wawona area you'll reach the start of the Glacier Point Road at a signed junction. At this road's end at Glacier Point you can buy snacks, film and a few other items.

Food, lodging, gas and most supplies are also available in Fish Camp, a small Highway 41 settlement just 2 miles south of the Park's south entrance station. Oakhurst, 13½ miles south of this settlement, has virtually everything.

Wilderness Permits: Get these at the Wawona District Office, which is at the end of a short road that branches right from the Chilnualna Road immediately past the Pioneer Yosemite History Center.

Campgrounds: For Hikes 83-89, stay at Bridalveil Campground, whose entrance is found midway along the Glacier Point Road. For Hikes 82 and 90-93, stay at Wawona Campground, about one mile north of the Wawona Hotel. Both are very crowded. An alternate camp to Wawona Campground is the Summerdale Campground, about ½ mile north of the settlement of Fish Camp.

Hike 82   Alder Creek Trail to Bishop Creek

Distance: 6.3 miles (10.2 km) round trip

Grade: 2C, moderate half-day hike

Trailhead: On the Wawona Road 3.9 miles north of the Wawona Campground entrance and 280 yards west of the Alder Creek crossing; also 7.4 miles south of the Glacier Point Road junction. **C6.**

Introduction: Your descent to Bishop Creek can be one of the Sierra's most pleasant springtime hikes, though by early summer the creeks run dry and temperatures soar. Most of this trail's length is across rolling topography carpeted with mountain misery; nowhere else in the Park will you see such a spread of this low, lightly scented shrub. Despite its sticky nature, it is a favorite food of deer. Another bush to look for is the large Mariposa manzanita, easily recognized by its smooth, red bark and its gray-green leaves. The quiet forest shading these bushes is a classic ponderosa-pine forest, though incense-cedars and black oaks prevail here and there, and occasionally a multitrunked Digger pine will be seen. In late May or early June you're likely to see many wildflowers blooming, including Indian pink, Indian hemp, soap plant, milkweed, miners lettuce, small larkspur, cinquefoil and others. Birds-foot, wood and bracken ferns add spice to the carpeted forest floor, and at Bishop Creek alders, azaleas and creek dogwoods provide an interesting contrast. Most of these plants, shrubs and trees were used by the local Indians either for food, drink or medicine or for basketry, bows or shelter.

Description: From the road's bend near a cut through weathered granite, our trail drops below the Wawona Road and parallels it northwest. The trail quickly widens along an abandoned road, which it momentarily leaves. After about ½ mile of traversing, it begins a long drop to the South Fork Merced River. About 1.2 miles from our trailhead, we leave the Park and in the Sierra National Forest descend 0.8 mile to a springtime creek. In a short ¼ mile beyond it we climb to a low ridge, on which you'll find about a half dozen Indian mortar holes, perhaps covered with black-oak leaves, just a few yards west of the trail. From the ridge we have a steady descent, one that winds in and out of gullies as it drops about 550 feet to the banks of Bishop Creek. From there you could continue down to the South Fork Merced River, which involves a total drop of almost 800 feet along a dry, steep 1.4-mile course. However, the steepness, heat, and springtime ticks for many people make the descent not worth it.

Mountain misery carpets the floor of a ponderosa-pine/Mariposa-manzanita woodland

Hike 83   Bridalveil Campground-Wawona Loop

Distance: 30.3 miles (48.7 km) semiloop trip

Grade: 6E, moderate 3-day hike

Trailhead: Bridalveil Campground (see Hike 72 trailhead). Park at the campground's *far* end. D5.

Introduction: Sparkling lakes, deep canyons and alpine crests are not found along this hike—but then, neither are the backpacking crowds. This is a hike for those who love quiet forest trails.

Description: Gaining only about 200 feet in the first 3⅓ miles, our hike certainly starts out as one of the Park's easiest backpack trails. Although white firs and red firs are occasionally seen, they are greatly overwhelmed by a superabundance of lodgepole pines along this creekside stretch. After about 1.6 miles of it—on a ridge above nearby Bridalveil Creek—we join a trail that comes 1.7 miles from the Glacier Point Road (the **Hike 84** trailhead). A 1987 forest fire caused moderate damage in this vicinity. Leaving fire scars, we briefly keep above the creek, then curve over to an ample camp along the creek's tributary. Like others we'll meet, this camp can have lots of mosquitoes before late July. A two-minute walk upstream from the camp ends at the tributary's ford, and on the east bank we meet our second junction. The lightly used trail to the left climbs a short mile east to the Ostrander Lake trail (**Hike 84**).

Turning right, we head south and climb gently for a mile to the tributary's upper basin. In it our climb becomes a moderate one and then a steep one as we struggle up to a nearby crest that separates the unglaciated Alder Creek drainage from that of the long-ago-glaciated Bridalveil Creek drainage. Jeffrey pines yield to red firs as we traverse slopes over to a junction near a saddle. The trail we'll be returning on climbs to here from Deer Camp, down to the west. Starting southeast, we quickly cross the broad saddle, enter the partly glaciated Chilnualna Creek drainage, and begin a rolling, gentle, 1¼ mile-descent that goes through several small meadows—all with abundant corn lilies. A few minutes before we reach the next junction, our trail touches the east edge of long Turner Meadows, and here you can make a fair camp.

At the junction we veer right, hop Turner Meadows creek, then start an unnecessary 300-foot climb up to a ridge instead of around it. On

this moderate, shady ascent one has a crest view of gentle-but-glaciated Buena Vista Peak, to the east. We then make a long, 3800-foot drop to the Wawona area. On it western white pines yield to their close cousins, the sugar pines, while farther down red firs yield to the closely related white firs. As this vegetative transition is taking place the sharp-eyed hiker may notice a shrubby black oak, which at about 7540 feet elevation is near the top of its altitudinal range. Only on Smith Peak (**Hike 17**) can you find a specimen a couple of hundred feet higher. This oak is just past a secondary crest, and from it we plunge down to a creeklet—lined with ferns, azaleas and willows—then make an equally long drop to its larger counterpart. From its verdant banks we have an easy ½-mile descent to a junction just above Chilnualna Creek. Here, near the confluence of this creek and its southbound tributary, you can find a suitable spot to spend your first night. You may want to first investigate Chilnualna Fall, just downstream, but be extremely careful if you do, for the rock can be treacherously slippery and there are no safety railings to keep you from being swept over the fall.

After a possibly memorable sunset and a good night's sleep, descend the trail 4.0 scenic miles to its end, following the description of **Hike 90** in reverse. Then, gradually descending west, walk 1⅓ miles along a road that goes through North Wawona—a private-land area within the Park. In this settlement you can get supplies, meals and lodging. Our next trail, the Alder Creek trail, begins about ⅓ mile beyond the settlement's school, and this trailhead is just north of the Wawona District Office, which is a source of information and wilderness permits. Before resuming your loop hike, make a side trip to the nearby Pioneer Yosemite History Center, which you enter just west of a junction with the district office's spur road. At the center, which is highlighted by a covered bridge across the South Fork Merced River, you'll learn a great deal about pioneer homes, culture and technology in this area. By walking 200-300 yards upstream from the covered bridge you'll discover some small pools in the river that are among the warmest "swimming holes" found anywhere in the Park.

The signed Alder Creek trail begins about 75 yards east of a west-heading service road. Starting north, the trail quickly turns west to make a ⅓-mile-long, diagonal climb across gullies up to a junction with a short spur trail that descends to the end of the service road. At our low elevation temperatures often soar into the 80s by early afternoon and water may be absent until we reach Alder Creek, about 6 miles from the trailhead. At the end of a 2¾-mile-long, generally viewless ascent we reach a mile-high junction, from which a steep trail descends ¾ mile to the heavily traveled Wawona Road.

Starting east, we begin a 2¾-mile rolling traverse in and out of gullies and around or over low ridges to a view of 100-foot-high Alder Creek fall below. Along the last mile or so of this section you may see railroad ties, which are the few tangible relics of a dark period in the Park's history. From the early days of World War I through the 1920s, the Yosemite Lumber Company laid railroad tracks in and around western Yosemite to log out some of the Sierra's finest stands of sugar pines. Ironically, some of this timber—more than 6 million board feet—was cut to use in the construction of Hetch Hetchy's O'Shaughnessy Dam, completed in 1923. More than ½ *billion* board feet were cut before 1930, when John D. Rockefeller, Jr. and the US Government split the cost of buying up the logging company's interests.

Beyond the fall our abandoned-railroad route approaches lushly lined Alder Creek, parallels it north gently upstream for 1¼ miles, then crosses it to reach a nearby junction. Here or elsewhere along Alder Creek you can make your second

night's camp. From the junction a trail climbs north 1⅓ miles to an old logging road, on which you could walk ½ mile east to the trail's resumption, which climbs a little over 3 miles to the Bridalveil Campground entrance. The thick brush—the result of logging—makes this route undesirable, but it is shorter than the recommended route and it is a real eye-opener to just how much logging was done in this area (considerably *more* was done in the Crane Flat-Mather area).

The recommended route angles right at the Alder Creek junction, immediately refords the broad creek, and then climbs east for 1¾ miles, paralleling a murmuring tributary. This white-fir-shaded stretch ends at Deer Camp, a desolate roadend flat along the south fringe of the logging area. You can camp here, though you won't find it esthetic. From the camp our trail continues east and, typical of old trails, it winds and switchbacks all too steeply up most of a 1100-foot ascent. Midway up it, views expand, providing us with an overview of the Alder Creek basin. After about 1¼ miles of climbing, we top a crest, then momentarily descend to a trickling creeklet. Should you want to camp in this vicinity, camp at the nearby crest top, where mosquitoes are much fewer. Leaving the creeklet we climb around a meadow—rich in sedges, willows and corn lilies—then make a final short push southeast up to a junction near a saddle. From it we retrace our first day's steps 4.9 miles back to the trailhead.

Hike 84   Ostrander Lake

Distance: 12.7 miles (20.5 km) round trip

Grade: 3C, easy 2-day hike

Trailhead: From a signed junction on the Wawona Road drive 8.9 miles up the Glacier Point Road to a turnoff, on your right. This parking area is 1.3 miles past the Bridalveil Campground spur road. **D5.**

Introduction: Ostrander Lake, being the closest lake to the Glacier Point Road, is the object of many summertime weekend backpackers. It is also popular in winter and spring with cross-country skiers.

Description: The first half of our hike is easy—a gentle ascent through a forest that is interspersed with an assortment of meadows. We start along a former jeep road, and soon

encounter the first of several areas of lodgepole forest badly burned in a 1987 fire. Just ⅓ mile from the trailhead we cross a sluggish creek, then amble an easy mile to a ridge junction, passing two more burned areas en route. From the ridge, a short lateral quickly drops to Bridalveil Creek—a potentially difficult June crossing—then climbs equally quickly to the Bridalveil Creek trail (**Hike 83**).

From the junction our jeep road contours southeast past unseen Lost Bear Meadow, leaves the burned lands, and after a mile makes a short ascent east up along a trickling creek to its crossing. Just past the ford our road curves west to a nearby junction with a second lateral to the Bridalveil Creek trail. Though we are now about halfway to Ostrander Lake, we've climbed very little, and from this junction we face 1,500 feet of

Ostrander Lake, nestled in a cirque at the west end of Horse Ridge

vertical gain. Our steepening road climbs east through a mixed forest, then climbs more gently south across an open slab that provides the first views of verdant Bridalveil Creek basin. Views gradually disappear as we curve southeast into a Jeffrey-pine stand, then climb east through a shady white-fir forest. These firs are largely supplanted by red firs by the time we top a saddle that bisects Horizon Ridge. Climbing southeast up the ridge, our road passes through a generally open stretch decked with lupines, sulphur flowers and, surprisingly, sagebrush. Four hundred feet above our first saddle, the road switchbacks at a second one, then curves up to a third. From it our road makes a momentary descent southeast before bending to start a short, final ascent south. Near this bend we get far-ranging views across the Illilouette Creek basin. We can see the tops of Royal Arches and Washington Column and, above and east of them, North, Basket and Half domes. Behind Half Dome stands the Park's geographic center, broad-topped Mt. Hoffmann. Lording over the Illilouette Creek basin is Mt. Starr King and its entourage of subsidary domes. To the northeast the jagged crest of the Clark Range cuts the sky.

Beyond our short, final ascent south we drop in several minutes to Ostrander Hut—a ski hut used in spring by the Yosemite Association. By contacting this association—or better yet, join-

Ostrander Hut, built atop a moraine

ing it—you can get information about its Ostrander Lake cross-country ski trips, which follow our road's obvious painted markers to the lake. Some trips explore the winter ecology of this region up to the crest of Horse Ridge, which stands above our 25-acre, trout-populated lake. Late in the Ice Age, glaciers originated on the north slopes of Horse Ridge and extended down below Ostrander Lake for about 1½ miles. Much earlier, about 900–800,000 years ago, all but the Horizon Ridge part of our route was glaciated. This was so long ago that most hikers don't recognize the well-weathered glacial evidence. At the lake, camping is good along its west shore.

Hike 85   Ostrander Lake-Mono Meadow Loop

Distance: 19.6 miles (31.6 km) loop trip

Grade: 4D, moderate 2-day hike

Trailhead: From a signed junction on the Wawona Road, drive 10.1 miles up Glacier Point Road to a forested saddle with a parking area, on your right. **D5.**

Introduction: Like the previous hike, this one is a good one for weekends. Being a loop trip it can be walked in either direction. It is described counterclockwise because the 2¼-mile cross-country stretch is easier to hike and follow in that direction.

Description: Park at the Mono Meadow trailhead, then walk west down the Glacier Point Road for 1.2 miles to the **Hike 84** trailhead. From it follow that hike 6⅓ miles up to the north shore of Ostrander Lake. You can spend the night either here or at the Hart Lakes, about 1½ miles to the east.

To begin your cross-country route to those lakes, start from the northeast shore of Ostrander Lake and go southeast on a ducked routed that diagonals upslope. If you're on course, you should approach the north shore of a pond after about ¼ mile of hiking. After reaching this check point, you now strike east for an easier ¼-mile ascent to the north shore of a shallow lakelet—not a desirable camping area. Beyond the lakelet's east end you soon curve northeast and climb 200 vertical feet up to a ridge, which you ascend southeast for about 200 yards. Then you make a ⅓-mile traverse, having distant views across the Illilouette Creek basin, to a view of the Hart Lakes. A gully descends southeast to the larger Hart Lake, but it is choked with brush. We stay just north of the

gully, but chinquapin bushes do cause some problem on our ducked route down to this larger lake. Rimmed with lodgepoles, Labrador tea and red heather, it harbors mosquitoes through late July, but has pleasant camping after that. A tent solves the problem before then. In the early morning you may find the lake's placid surface occasionally broken by leaping rainbow trout.

Leave the larger Hart Lake at its northeast corner and go northeast about 250 yards to the east side of a low summit, then begin a moderate descent north toward soon-sighted Edson Lake. Midway between the Hart Lakes and this lake you'll reach open granite slabs across which you can diagonal northeast to a moraine, and the Buena Vista trail. This trail runs along the moraine's crest for more than 300 yards before making a noticeable drop west from it. On this trail you follow the first part of **Hike 86** in the reverse direction, first descending almost 7 miles to an intersection with the Mono Meadow trail, then ascending it 3 miles southwest to the Mono Meadow trailhead.

Largest Hart Lake and Horse Ridge

Half Dome and Mt. Starr King, from slabs above Edson Lake

Hike 86   Mono Meadow to Buena Vista and Royal Arch Lakes

Distance: 30.4 miles (48.9 km) round trip

Grade: 6E, easy 4-day hike

Trailhead: Same as the Hike 85 trailhead. **D5.**

Introduction: The subalpine lakes nestled around Buena Vista Peak can be reached from North Wawona—**Hike 91**—or from three trailheads along the Glacier Point Road. This hike starts from one of these trailheads and visits five of the peak's lakes. Although this route is slightly longer than Hike 91, it requires 20 percent less climbing effort. Also see **Hike 94** for a little-used route to these lakes.

Description: At our trailhead, shaded by magnificent red firs, ancient glaciers once prowled, just barely overtopping today's forested pass but deeply burying most of the Bridalveil and Illilouette basins. During the last two major advances, glaciers made little headway in the Bridalveil basin, but in the Illilouette basin, rimmed by a higher crest, they descended half way to Yosemite Valley.

Our trail begins with a steady, moderate descent north, followed by an easing gradient east to lodgepole-fringed Mono Meadow. Until mid-July you may face 200 yards of muddy freshets and meadow bogs, soaking your boots before you reach the narrow meadow's east edge. During this period, desperate hikers try to circumvent the mire, and several paths may spring up to confuse you. The real trail crosses the meadow on a 120° bearing, and it becomes obvious once you're within the forest's edge.

Beyond the meadow our Mono Meadow trail crosses a low divide, then makes a generally viewless, easy descent to a major tributary of Illilouette Creek. Here, 1½ miles from your trailhead, is your first possible campsite. We ford the tributary at the brink of some rapids, and in early season this ford could be a dangerous one. Then, cross upstream so that if you do happen to slip, you won't be carried down the rapids. From the tributary we have a short though unnecessary climb, with 200 feet of elevation gain. The climb does have some merit, for at the crest and on our descent east from it we're rewarded with views of North, Basket and Half domes, Clouds Rest and Mt. Starr King. After a descent through a fir forest we emerge on an open slope and descend straight toward Mt. Starr King, the highest of the Illilouette Creek domes. Immediately after the view disappears,

we reach a junction with the Buena Vista trail, which links Glacier Point with the Buena Vista Peak lakes. Turning right, we go 40 yards up-canyon to a second junction, from where our Mono Meadow trail goes 300 yards to a usually wet ford (for hikers) of broad Illilouette Creek. Near this ford you'll find campsites—heavily visited by hikers and bears—along both banks. Bears have downed steel cables strung here so if you camp here, be prepared for a potential problem. If you can find a deep crack in bedrock just downstream from the camps, then stick your food in it. If the crack is thin enough or deep enough bears won't be able to get the food. **Hike 89**, descending Illilouette Creek from Merced Pass, traverses through this camping area, then follows the Buena Vista trail northwest toward Glacier Point.

From our camping-area junction we now climb southeast up the Buena Vista trail. Unfortunately, the next several miles of scenery have been marred from the effects of major forest fires. In 1¼ miles we come to a creeklet with a fair camp on its west bank. Our trail's gradient gradually eases, then we cross a broad divide and in ¼ mile angle sharply left to descend along the edge of a sloping meadow. Beyond it we enter an aspen grove that hides a step-across creek. Just a few minutes' walk east of it we cross a slightly larger creek, then make a gentle ascent southeast across sandy soils to steep slopes above Buena Vista Creek.

Camping is poor along the west bank, but good—and isolated—above the east bank. Fallen lodgepoles or other snags may provide access across the bouldery creek to these sites. Fallen trees are common here because the soil is very loose, being derived from bouldery glacial sediments. Late in the Ice Age, glaciers advanced about 1-1½ miles beyond this area and dropped an enormous load of sediment here. A lot of outwash (stream-transported glacial sediments) can be found downstream, for example, at the bear-prone campsites by the Illilouette Creek ford.

Soon our trail leaves Buena Vista Creek, curves southwest and climbs moderately in that direction for 1½ miles to a ford, between two meadows, of diminutive Edson Lake creek. From a poor campsite, the trail ascends along a moraine crest, then in 1 mile leaves it to angle southeast up to a higher crest. Where our trail makes a sudden angle left, you can leave it and contour ⅓ mile west over to a campsite at isolated Edson Lake. Our trail follows the higher moraine crest southwest for more than 300 yards, finally leaves the burned area, then makes a ¼-mile, view-packed descent to Hart Lakes creek. Where the trail leaves the crest, you can continue cross-country southwest along this crest, soon diagonal up slabs, then climb south up to the Hart Lakes. This is the reverse of the last described part of **Hike 85**.

From brush-lined Hart Lakes creek we make a short contour over to a second creek, this one having a small campsite on its east bank. This creek is incorrectly labeled "Buena Vista Creek" on the USGS map. After ½ mile of moderate ascent we cross the real Buena Vista Creek, which bends northeast, then continue south up a slightly shorter ascent to a recrossing of that creek. Immediately beyond we cross its western tributary, then follow this stream south briefly up to two ponds, from which we switchback up a cirque wall with ice-shattered blocks to a crest junction. **Hike 91**, ascending from North Wawona, now joins our route for a loop around the lakes of Buena Vista Peak. The first lake we encounter, about ⅓ mile southeast from the junction, is rather bleak Buena Vista Lake, containing both rainbow and brook trout. Nestled on a broad bench at the base of the cool north slope of Buena Vista Peak, this lake is the highest and coldest one we'll see. It does, however, have two good camps, though you might avoid them if a thunderstorm is approaching. Then, it is better to camp at a lower elevation.

Starting at the lake's outlet, we ascend short switchbacks up to a broad pass. From the viewless pass you can climb ¾ mile up a gentle ridge to Buena Vista Peak for an unrestricted panorama of the Park's southern area. From the pass we descend 2 easy, winding trail miles to everyone's favorite lake on this loop, Royal Arch Lake, which lies below a broad arch. This lake, like Buena Vista Lake, has populations of rainbow and brook trout. Just past the outlet, near the lake's southwest corner, you'll find an excellent campsite—one probably occupied by another hiker who hopes to watch the rays of the setting sun dance upon the multihued arch. For more solitude you can head cross-country ¾ mile west to less attractive Minnow Lake, in which you'll find brook trout.

Leaving Royal Arch Lake we parallel its outlet creek for a ½ mile, then angle south across

Clouds building over bleak Buena Vista Lake

slabs to a trail junction. From here **Hike 94**, heading northwest from Chiquito Pass and Buck Camp (a ranger station), climbs ¾ mile to Royal Arch Lake. We descend west toward Johnson Lake, reaching good campsites along its northwest shore in just ¾ mile—with hordes of mosquitoes in early season. Before glaciers cut through the low ridge just south of Johnson and Crescent lakes, both lakes drained west into Chilnualna Creek.

We don't see large Crescent Lake, but on meeting its inlet creek, about ⅓ mile beyond a meadowy divide, one can walk 150 yards downstream, passing a fair camp before reaching the lake's shallow, trout-filled waters. You might visit the lake's south end, or camp near it, for from the outlet you get a revealing view of the 2800-foot-deep South Fork Merced River canyon.

Beyond Crescent Lake's inlet creek our trail quickly turns north, passes a small creekside meadow, then climbs more than 150 feet to a second broad divide. From it we descend into the truncated headwaters of a Chilnualna Creek tributary. Our moderate-to-steep gradient ends when we approach easy-to-miss Grouse Lake. Two use trails descend about 100 yards to a fair campsite on the north shore of this shallow, reedy lakelet. It is well named, for it lies in the heart of grouse country, typified by the dusky bird's favorite trees: lodgepole pines and red firs. In one study, more than 1500 lodgepole-needle tips were found in the crop of one bird!

Lodgepoles and red firs monopolize the slopes along our 2-mile descent from this lake down to a hillside junction. Here, hikers completing **Hike 91** head west down-canyon to their trailhead. Hikers on the second day of that hike join us for a short northwest stretch, first up over a nearby divide, then down more than 400 feet to Chilnualna Creek. Just above its north bank is a good, medium-sized campsite, and just beyond that is another trail junction. From it **Hike 91** trekkers climb east while we traverse northwest. During midsummer, our gently ascending traverse is brightened by the orange sunbursts of alpine lilies, growing chest-high along the wetter parts of our trail. As we near Turner Meadows we encounter a trail junction from which **Hike 83** departs southwest down to the Wawona area.

We now backtrack along the first part of that hike, first ascending past and through a series of "Turner Meadows," then topping a forest pass

Grouse Lake

to quickly meet a trail down to Deer Camp. Spurning it, we keep right, traverse to a crest and descend to a tributary of Bridalveil Creek. Before reaching that creek, however, we meet a junction, turn left and then cross the tributary. Along the tributary we momentarily pass a moderate-sized camp and in a ½ mile reach another junction. The main trail continues 1.6 miles northwest to Bridalveil Campground, but we veer right, drop to nearby Bridalveil Creek, ford it, and make an equally short climb up to the Ostrander Lake trail—a closed jeep road. In 1½ miles our northbound hike ends at the Glacier Point Road, on which we climb gently east for a half hour back to our trailhead.

Royal Arch Lake is well-named

Hike 87 Glacier Point to Yosemite Valley via Nevada and Vernal Falls

Distance: 9.1 miles (14.6 km) one way

Grade: 2C, moderate day hike

Trailhead: Same as the Hike 75 trailhead. **D5.**

Introduction: Of all the trails one could take down to the floor of Yosemite Valley, this one is the most scenic. Either take a bus up to Glacier Point or have a friend drop you there and meet you at Camp Curry, down in the Valley.

Description: From the early 1870s until January 1968, a large pile of embers was pushed off Glacier Point at evening darkness to create the renowned Firefall—a glowing "waterfall." Quite a spectacle. Then from the early 1970s until June 1990, people in the chilly early morning hours would take running leaps from the point out into space. This hang gliding was also quite a spectacle.

Keeping to *terra firma* our trail is certainly a less euphoric one, though probably a safer route to the Valley floor. Our trail starts on the highly scenic crest beside the east end of the Glacier Point parking lot and climbs to a fork. The Pohono Trail, **Hike 75**, veers right, but we veer left, climbing a bit more before starting a

moderate descent. A switchback leg helps ease the grade, then we descend, usually without views, through a predominantly red-fir forest. A 1987 fire blackened most of the forest from the trailhead to just beyond the upcoming Buena Vista trail junction, but most of the trees survived. Between charred trunks, great views occasionally appear of Half Dome, Mt. Broderick, Liberty Cap, Nevada Fall and Mt. Starr King. After 1⅔ miles and an 800-foot drop, our Glacier Point-Panorama trail meets the Buena Vista trail. In 2.2 miles this heads up-canyon to Illilouette Creek, then heads up along it to intersect the Mono Meadow Trail (**Hike 86**).

Our trail branches left and switchbacks down to a spur trail that goes down a few yards to a railing. Here, atop an overhanging cliff, we get an unobstructed view of 370-foot-high Illilouette Fall, which splashes down over a low point on the rim of massive, joint-controlled Panorama Cliff. Behind it Half Dome rises boldly toward the heavens while above Illilouette Creek Mt. Starr King rises even higher.

In ¼ mile our trail descends to a wide bridge upstream from one that was washed out in the

Glacier Point view: Tenaya Canyon, Half Dome, and Mt. Lyell above Little Yosemite Valley

1950s. Just a few hundred yards upstream from our bridge are two small moraines that are convex up-canyon, not down-canyon, as is usual. The reason is that the glacier that left these moraines did not descend Illilouette Creek. Rather it *ascended* the creek, for a huge Merced Canyon glacier, overtopping part of Panorama Cliff, spilled over into this part of Illilouette Creek, damning it behind a wall of ice. During colder times at least one glacier, existing about 900–800,000 years ago, did descend

Illilouette Fall

Illilouette Creek all the way to the larger trunk glacier, and together they overwhelmed Glacier Point, burying it beneath at least 500 feet of ice.

From the bridge and its dangerously slippery slabs, we face a major climb up along the rim of Panorama Cliff. First we pass above the brink of Illilouette Fall, noting the joint-controlled cliffs—all in a line—west of it. Then we gently ascend northeast along the brushy rim. Our ascending trail quickly veers away from the rim to switchback up a gully, then returns to it at Panorama Point. Here, at the upper end of a monstrous rockfall that broke loose during the winter of 1968-69, we have a scenic view that is surpassed by another one about ⅓ mile up the trail. From it you have a panorama extending from Upper Yosemite Fall east past Royal Arches, Washington Column and North Dome to Half Dome.

Our forested, moderate climb ends after 200 more feet of elevation gain, and then we descend gently to the rim for some more views, contour east, and absorb even more views, dominated by Half Dome, Mt. Broderick, Liberty Cap, Clouds Rest and Nevada Fall. Our contour ends at a junction with the Mono Meadow trail, which climbs southwest over a low ridge before descending to Illilouette Creek. At this junction, as at numerous points along our rim traverse, we see Douglas-firs, which at an elevation of 6600 feet seem to be out of place in our white-fir forest. They are usually found at much lower elevations.

Beyond the junction a major, mile-long descent ensues, dropping us via many switchbacks through a generally viewless forest to a trail fork, from where each branch descends but a few yards to the John Muir Trail. To complete your hike, descend west along this scenic, view-packed trail, but not until you've first walked over to the brink of roaring Nevada Fall. The descent along the John Muir Trail is described in the last part of **Hike 78**.

Alternately, you could descend the Mist trail, a shorter route, which begins a few hundred yards northeast of Nevada Fall. Being shorter, it is also steeper, and is potentially dangerous for those who try to descend it too rapidly. This wet route is described in the opposite direction in the first part of **Hike 78**. From the reunion of the John Muir and the Mist trails, you walk but a minute to the Vernal Fall bridge, then follow **Hike 77** in reverse down to the Happy Isles shuttle-bus stop. From it you can ride or walk west to Camp Curry, the Valley's east hub of activity.

Hike 88

Glacier Point to Merced and Washburn Lakes

Distance: 53.2 miles (85.5 km) semiloop trip
Grade: 7G, moderate 6-day hike
Trailhead: Same as the Hike 75 trailhead. **D5.**
Introduction: Along this route you'll make a thorough examination of the Merced River above Yosemite Valley. The length of this route gives you an appreciation for the magnitude of its past glaciers, at least one having extended as far down-canyon as the El Portal area by the Park's west border.

Description: As in **Hike 87** you make a scenic excursion 5.4 miles to the John Muir Trail. Some backpackers making this loop prefer to start from Happy Isles, and though their hike to our junction is 2.3 miles shorter, it involves 1000 more feet of climbing—something to consider with a full pack on your back. In a few minutes from where we hit the Muir Trail, we reach Nevada Fall, then in an equally short time reach the upper end of the Mist trail. From there we follow **Hike 81** to campsites near the east shore of Merced Lake, a long though relatively easy 16.0 miles from our Glacier Point trailhead. If you are traveling to this lake in one day, you'll traverse the entire circuit in four days. Most hikers, however, should plan on six, spending their nights in Little Yosemite Valley, at Washburn Lake, along the High trail, at Merced Lake and again in Little Yosemite Valley.

Our trail description takes up where **Hike 81** leaves off—in the area of the Merced Lake High Sierra Camp. Leaving it, we climb around a low trans-canyon rib, down which the Merced River shoots to a campside pool. Beyond the rib we have a level ¾-mile stroll past lodgepoles and aspens to a junction beside the Merced Lake Ranger Station. Descending to it is the Lewis Creek trail, named for the multibranched creek we bridged just before this junction. We'll be starting a 23.9-mile loop from this junction and will complete it along the last part of the Lewis Creek trail, which can also be followed up to Vogelsang High Sierra Camp and Tuolumne Meadows (**Hike 56**). Don't hike this loop in the reverse direction, for though it involves the same amount of climbing, the climbing comes in larger steps. The described route has a much more gradual ascent.

Starting southeast from the junction we skirt along the edge of a broad, flat canyon floor

A giant arch on a dome, one mile southwest of Echo Valley

which, like the next 7½ miles, is dominated by lodgepoles. The ½-mile width of the canyon floor leads one to expect its sediments to extend more than 200 feet down to bedrock. No one has asked why we don't see a "Merced Lake" here; the valley is certainly large enough to hold one, and it has the necessary bedrock dam—the trans-canyon rib we rounded—to pool up such a lake. Perhaps the answer lies in the valley's position, which is at the junction of three glaciated canyons: the Clark Range canyon from the south, the Merced River canyon from the southeast, and the Fletcher Creek canyon from the northeast. The author suggests that as the glaciers in these canyons retreated to oblivion about 13,500 years ago, they dropped their prodigious sediments in the basin, filling in the lake.

About ¾ mile from our junction, we rejoin the Merced River at a point where a bedrock dam cuts across it, forming pools both above and below it. Just upstream we see another bedrock dam and then see a large, smooth slab on the canyon's southwest wall which, like other similar sites, in the past has borne avalanches. As our trail's gradient changes from level to a gentle ascent, junipers, Jeffrey pines and white firs become prominent. Mule ears, found in abundance on volcanic soils, merely dot the slopes here, and at a large tributary, aspens radiate their own charm. Immediately beyond this tributary the Merced River cascades through a small gorge, and beside it you'll find ochre-stained slabs—the art work of soda springs. Climbing onward, we note a progression toward dryness as expressed in a sequence from bracken fern to chinquapin to huckleberry oak and ultimately to sagebrush. Next, a river cascade enchants us, followed by a long, tempting pool, which lies just below a rocky moraine. Then we pass an even larger pool, beside a trail blasted in bedrock, immediately before reaching bedrock-dammed Washburn Lake.

Washburn Lake's popularity with backpackers is verified by the presence of an outhouse above the north shore. In the lake's cold waters—at least 86 feet deep—brook and rainbow trout await the skillful angler. Most of the lake's campsites are along the lake's south end, where incoming sediments are slowly filling the lake. Here you'll notice a plant succession away from the shore. Sterile, newly deposited sand covers the shore, but a few feet back, sedges take hold. Farther back, willows start to shade them out and these in turn are shaded out by lodgepoles and aspens. Until late July, mosquitoes can plague campers here, and before then the rocky north-end campsites are more desirable.

Beyond the lake, whose basin was buried under at least 1800 feet of glacier ice late in the Pleistocene epoch, we hike up-canyon, soon noting a cleft in our canyon's west wall—the result of erosion along a large, straight fracture. Momentarily our trail approaches the Merced River, where we spy a good campsite 150 yards below a very photogenic fall. Continuing southeast, we leave most backpackers for an excursion into the upper reaches of the Merced River. In ½ mile our trail bends east, and beyond a tumultuous cascade it gradually levels off, curves south, and passes a packer campsite about 40 yards before bridging the Merced River near its confluence with the Lyell Fork.

More cascades are passed as we make an effort south up the Merced Peak Fork canyon, whose east wall has one exposure of very massive dikes. Beyond this view we soon bridge

Calm, early morning waters of Washburn Lake; Peak 11370 in distance

the fork beside another packer camp, then switchback eastward across open slopes. Along this ascent we see the two summits of Mt. Florence, above the Lyell Fork canyon to the north-northeast, and the two summits of Merced Peak, above a cross-country route to the south-southwest. Once in the Triple Peak Fork canyon, about 4 miles beyond Washburn Lake, our trail first climbs for ½ mile. It then makes a very gentle 2¼-mile climb across glaciated slabs and through a thinning lodgepole forest to a riverside junction. From here **Hike 89** climbs to Red Peak Pass and **Hike 98** descends from the pass to our junction. The area of our riverside junction is a scenic one to camp in, but if you're making this hike in six days, you should plan to camp higher up.

Look for a log hereabouts to cross the wide tributary of Triple Peak Fork; then, back on the trail, head southeast to a quick ford of the fork. From the ford our trail makes a gentle ascent south, paralleling the unseen fork for ½ mile to the start of a switchbacking climb northeast. Here is the place to leave the trail for an easy ½ - mile cross-country jaunt up to seldom-visited Turner Lake. At 9540 feet elevation, it is the only nearby lake you'll find where campfires are legal. All the others we'll approach lie above the 9600-foot contour—stoves only. The 550-foot climb northeast is generally a viewless one, due to the lodgepoles and hemlocks, though you may get an occasional view north of the Mt. Florence ridge and of the Matthes Crest, in the distance west of it. Our climb ends on a small flat below

the west spur of unseen Isberg Peak. From here, beside a tall cairn, **Hike 98** continues up to Post Peak Pass. For a campsite, you may want to follow that route for ⅓ mile, then traverse ¼ mile east to a farily large, unnamed lake, whose northwest shore is bordered with protective lodgepole pines.

Our hike, however, proceeds north from the cairn along the High trail, quickly reaching a step-across creek that, if followed upstream for an easy ¾ mile, leads to a timberline lake. Following **T** blazes north, we descend to a shallow, glaciated trough, then climb up to three ephemeral creeklets. From the creeklets you could hike ⅓ mile cross-country up to a small subalpine lake. Our ascent yields to a contour, then to a descent to a trickling creeklet, from which we climb to a low nearby saddle and then descend once again to another creeklet. A lake lies on a bench about ¼ mile east of it, but the climb to it is quite steep. In about ¼ mile our high-altitude traverse, shaded by lodgepoles and hemlocks, crosses Foerster Creek, then about ¾ mile farther, after you briefly ascend the second of two gently descending ridges, you can leave the trail for a ¼-mile contour east to a lovely little lake. This ducked cross-country route begins about 30 yards before the trail makes a short, steep descent into a gully. Rather than camp on the fragile shoreline vegetation—something one should never do—camp just west of the lake among tufts of sedge ("grass").

Beyond the gully our trail undulates to a forested crest. From this crest we can look back

Foerster Creek Lake near sunset

Fletcher Creek and Hike 56 run along the east (right) side of Babcock dome

and see the twin summits of rusty, metavolcanic Isberg Peak and the pointed summit of gray, granitic Post Peak. We can also identify slightly rusty Triple Divide Peak. West of it stands dark-gray, metamorphic Merced Peak, then the vari-colored other peaks of the Clark Range. In the distant northwest rise Clouds Rest and Mt. Hoffmann, while east of them stands the Parks highest massif—the Mt. Lyell complex.

Leaving the bouldery crest, we descend into the deep, glaciated Lyell Fork canyon via dozens of short switchbacks—one with an excellent viewpoint—then eventually reach the seasonally powerful Lyell Fork, bordered by mountain hemlocks. This is the northernmost locality in which you'll want to set up your third night's camp. No camping space is found at the ford, so either follow the tumbling stream a couple of hundred yards downstream or about ⅓-⅔ mile upstream. If you want to head upstream, leave the trail about 200 yards beyond the Lyell Fork, where it starts a traverse northwest. The trail here can be hard to follow for a short distance, so look for ducks and blazes.

Soon starting a westward climb, we pass by four large junipers, which add contrast to our typically pine-hemlock landscape. Beyond a conspicuous notch we get a revealing panorama of the Clark Range and the expansive bench, below it, which borders the rim of the deep Merced River gorge. This "gorge within a canyon" topography has previously been interpreted as the result of two distinct uplifts in the Sierra Nevada. However, the canyon below us lies *parallel* to the Sierra crest, and therefore its river's gradient should not have been in-

creased by any uplift. The gorge is an example of stepped topography enhanced by glaciation.

After the view we re-enter forest and cross a small Mt. Florence creek at the base of its splashing waterfall. From it we climb past joint-controlled slabs, ascending almost 500 feet over a mile's course to a bouldery summit. Along the ascent to this forested summit, we come to a viewpoint that provides the trail's best panorama of the upper Merced River canyon, from Peak 11210 (about one mile east of us) and Foerster Peak (about 1½ miles south of it) south to Triple Divide Peak and then north along the entire Clark Range. The trail, which has climbed unnecessarily, now descends ½ mile to a second Mt. Florence tributary, with camping potential, then climbs an equal distance to a slope below unseen Cony Crags, which we saw from points south of the Lyell Fork.

With no more major climbing to come until after Nevada Fall, we can enjoy the trail's course, which ducks down into a shallow-but-glaciated side canyon, with a creekside campsite, then beyond it switchbacks more than 30 times down to a junction in Lewis Creek canyon. Here we join **Hike 56** for a considerable descent to the Merced Lake Ranger Station—at the end of our loop. Midway along this descent we pass a junction with the Fletcher Creek trail—the return route of **Hike 56**. From the ranger station we backtrack to Merced Lake and Echo Valley, then, as in **Hike 81**, decide which of two routes to take to Little Yosemite Valley. Beyond this valley and Nevada Fall we soon retrace the steps of **Hike 87** back to our trailhead at Glacier Point.

Hike 89

Glacier Point to Merced, Washburn and Ottoway Lakes

Distance: 48.6 miles (78.2 km) loop trip

Grade: 6F, moderate 5-day hike

Trailhead: Same as the Hike 75 trailhead. **D5.**

Introduction: The Park's trails exceed 11,000 feet in only three places: Donohue Pass (11,056-Hike 58), Parker Pass (11,100-Hike 60) and Red Peak Pass (11,180-Hikes 89 and 98). This hike reaches the highest—Red Peak Pass—by ascending the spectacular Merced River canyon. From the pass, which cleaves the multihued Clark Range, our route follows the subdued Illilouette Creek canyon—a very relaxing stretch—back to the trailhead.

Description: The first 23.8 miles are the same as the first part of **Hike 88**. In that hike you start from Glacier Point, spend your first night in Little Yosemite Valley, hike past Merced Lake and spend your second night at Washburn Lake. Hiking up-canyon on your third day, you should reach a junction in upper Triple Peak Fork canyon at or before noon. Here **Hike 88** and **98** branch east to immediately cross the fork.

Our trail angles west, begins a moderate ascent, and in a few minutes climbs steeply up a short, straight gully. Above it the trail climbs moderately for about a 250-foot elevation gain, then rolls southwest across granitic benches. These, like the gully, are angular, and they were formed as a result of glaciers excavating along the many joints, or fractures, in the granitic landscape. The smooth, generalized contour lines of the Merced Peak area often mislead the hiker, for between the lines lie many small ups and downs.

With more than half of our multiday hike behind us, we soon begin a switchbacking course northwest up to a granitic crest—quartz monzonite in composition—that divides the

A feldspar dike arcs toward slabs stained by soda springs, below Washburn Lake

Triple Peak Fork from the Merced Peak Fork. Although the crest does support lodgepoles, mountain hemlocks and whitebark pines, the forest cover is thin enough for us to see many of the peaks that rim the upper Merced River basin. From the crest, we have a moderate though reasonably short descent to the two-branched Merced Peak Fork. You could camp in this vicinity or else hike cross-country ⅔ mile gently downstream to a shallow lake.

The trail to a second crest—one that separates the Merced Peak and Red Peak forks—has interesting nearby features and pleasant tree-filtered views to distract us from the effort of the climb. We reach the second crest at a broad saddle that conveniently holds a scenic lakelet, which makes a good place for an extended stop. Having a fair number of conifers, its surrounding slopes provide your last wind-shielded camp-sites this side of Red Peak Pass. Rather than climb toward that pass, our trail first makes an unnecessary descent north from the lakelet, then

Red Peak Pass panorama: Rodgers Peak, Electra Peak, Foerster Peak and Harriet Lake bench

turns southwest to climb. Here, at the start of the climb, you could descend cross-country northwest to Red Devil Lake. About ½ mile distant, its lengthy, intricately winding shoreline provides the best near-timberline campsites.

Our trail, which until now has been across granitic terrain, enters a metamorphic one as it climbs to a broad bench. On it we pass two sizable, windswept ponds, neither one having desirable camping. In midsummer, low wildflowers abound on this bench, attracting many pollinating insects that in turn may end up as food for resident yellow-legged frogs or altitude-transcending Brewer's blackbirds.

Leaving the bench, we climb northwest past the last holdout of whitebark pines, then switchback southwest up a bleak alpine ridge. On it we have unobstructed views of the greater part of the upper Merced River basin. Tufts of sedge cluster around almost every available crack, and occasional wildflowers catch our eye as we struggle in a thin atmosphere up past tiny tarns toward a ragged, notched crest. Our trail, which soon becomes a series of short, steep switchbacks, heads for Red Peak Pass, which may be snowbound well into summer. When the switchbacks are not under snow, their rocky nature can easily turn your ankle if you take a careless step.

Along your ascent to Red Peak Pass you might notice a small glacial moraine—a remnant of the Little Ice Age—lying at the edge of the Red Peak cirque. It may look like a collection of boulders that slid down Red Peak, but its large blocks are gray, not red, as they would be if they came from the peak. Rusty talus boulders, derived from the peak, do rest atop the moraine, whose gray blocks came from the south.

At Red Peak Pass you have views as far as Matterhorn Peak, along the Park's north rim. Closer, Mt. Lyell crowns the upper Merced River basin and is flanked on the northwest by Mt. Maclure and on the southeast by Rodgers Peak. Twin-peaked Mt. Florence breaks the horizon west of this trio while east of all of them the dark, sawtooth Ritter Range pokes above the Park's eastern crest boundary. Below the peaks lies a broad upland surface that is cleft by the 2000-foot-deep Merced River canyon. Turning south, we have a tunneled, almost lifeless view of dark-gray Merced Peak, its western outliers, and rockbound Upper Ottoway Lake.

By late summer 1977, after two dry years, the Merced Peak snowfield had completely disappeared. When John Muir first saw it in the autumn of 1871, it was an active snowfield— that is, a small glacier. Muir was not the first to see a Sierra glacier, but he was the first to recognize one. On July 2, 1863, William Brewer and Charles Hoffmann—both members of the Whitney Survey of California—climbed the Lyell Glacier and almost reached the summit of Mt. Lyell. However, several feet of fresh snow covered the glacier and perhaps because of that they saw few crevasses. In his journal Brewer wrote:

> A great glacier once formed far back in the mountains and passed down the valley (Lyell Canyon), polishing and grooving the rocks for more than a thousand feet up on each side, rounding the granite hills into domes. It must have been as grand in its day as any that are now in Switzerland. But the climate has changed, and it has entirely passed away. There is now no glacier in this state—the climate conditions do not exist under which any could be formed.

In *The Mountains of California* John Muir disagrees. Muir was familiar with the characteristics of a glacier, as is revealed in the following passage of his 1871 discovery of the Merced Peak glacier:

> I observed a series of small terminal moraines ranged along the south wall of the amphitheater, corresponding in size and form with the shadows cast by the highest portions. The meaning of this correspondence between moraines and shadows

Panorama, cont'd.: Harriet Lake bench, Banner Peak, Mt. Ritter, Long Mtn. and Minarets

By early fall, Merced Peak's "glacier" can all but disappear; view from Red Peak Pass

was afterward made plain. Tracing the stream back to the last of its chain of lakelets (the one above Upper Ottoway Lake), I noticed a deposit of fine gray mud worn from a grindstone, and I at once suspected its glacial origin, for the stream that was carrying it came gurgling out of the base of a raw moraine that seemed in process of formation. Not a plant or weather-stain was visible on its rough unsettled surface. It is from 60 to over 100 feet high and plunges forward at an angle of 38°. Cautiously picking my way, I gained the top of the moraine and was delighted to see a small but well-characterized glacier swooping down from the gloomy precipices of Black Mountain (Merced Peak) in a finely graduated curve to the moraine on which I stood. The compact ice appeared on all the lower portions of the glacier, though gray with dirt and stones embedded in it. Farther up the ice disappeared beneath coarse granulated snow. The surface of the glacier was further characterized by dirt bands and the outcropping edges of the blue veins, showing the laminated structure of the ice. The uppermost crevasse, or "bergschrund," where the *névé* was attached to the mountain, was from 12 to 14 feet wide, and was bridged in a few places by the remains of snow avalanches. Creeping along the edge of the schrund, holding on with benumbed fingers, I discovered clear sections where the bedded structure was beautifully revealed. The surface snow, though sprinkled with stones shot down from the cliffs, was in some places almost pure, gradually becoming crystalline and changing to whitish porous ice of different shades of color, and this again changing at a depth of 20 or 30 feet to blue ice, some of the ribbon-like bands of which were nearly pure, and blended with the paler bands in the most gradual and delicate manner imaginable. . .

After this discovery I made excursions over all the High Sierra, pushing my explorations sum-

mer after summer, and discovered that what at first sight in the distance looked like extensive snowfields, were in great part glaciers, busily at work completing the sculpture of the summit-peaks so grandly blocked out by their giant predecessors.

On August 21 (1872) I set a series of stakes in the Maclure Glacier, near Mount Lyell, and found its rate of motion to be little more than an inch a day in the middle, showing a great contrast to the Muir Glacier in Alaska, which, near the front, flows at a rate of from five to ten feet in twenty-four hours.

Thus Muir can be credited with the first discovery of Sierra glaciers.

From Red Peak Pass our descent to Lower Ottoway Lake—the ideal place to spend your third night—is a two-stage descent, each with more than two dozen switchbacks. Our initial descent may appear to be lifeless—only cold granitic rocks and gravel—but closer inspection reveals the presence of alpine sedges and wildflowers. These are present in sufficient quantity to permit pikas to thrive up to the very pass itself. A high, nasal voice often gives away the presence of these diminutive, short-eared members of the rabbit family. They are preyed on by the short-tailed weasel, a small voracious predator that dons a white coat in the winter.

Our first descent stage ends just above a pond and adjacent Upper Ottoway Lake. Neither of these cold, shimmering jewels has suitable camping, but you can make an interesting side trip over to them and then east up into the deep cirque that once held Muir's glacier. Today only its moraines exist, which show the size of the once-living snowfield.

Our second stage begins with a moderate descent west followed by the usual short switchbacks. On this descent many wildflowers are seen, including paintbrush, penstemon, monkey flower, little elephant's head, coyote mint, columbine, phlox, leptodactylon, cinquefoil, yarrow, senecio, aster and daisy. Sagebrush, heather and dwarf whitebark pines appear before we reach the eastern arm of Lower Ottoway Lake. A slab above its northeast shore makes a good sunbathing area after a quick dip in its cold waters. Nonswimmers can dangle lines for a tasty rainbow-trout meal. You'll find the best camps under lodgepole and whitebark pines above the lake's northwest shore. The lake makes an ideal base camp for exploring the Merced Peak environs.

From the west shore we parallel Ottoway Creek west, log-cross it after ⅔ mile, then ramble southwest up and down a glaciated landscape for 1¾ miles, crossing Illilouette Creek before reaching a junction with the Illiouette Creek trail. From it you can start south up along the east bank of a creek, cross it after a minute's walk, and reach very good campsites along the west shore of Upper Merced Pass Lake. Bears may visit this lake (and Lower Ottoway Lake), but here there are enough deep, bear-proof cracks to hid your food in. (Before you drop your food sack in a deep crack be sure you'll be able to retrieve it.)

Hike 98 descends north from Merced Pass to our trail junction and then it climbs northeast up to Red Peak Pass. Our hike, however, descends northwest along the Illilouette Creek trail, passing unseen Lower Merced Pass Lake. To avoid mosquitoes at this relatively warm, shallow lake with a water-choked, spongy shore, camp on the granitic ridge west of the lake.

Below this nearby lake, our trail crosses several creeklets and in places can be hard to follow. Look for blazes on the lodgepoles. About 1¾ miles below the last trail junction, we cross to the east bank of Illilouette Creek, which we then parallel for 3¾ miles. You can find several places to camp along the creek's east bank, or if you cross to the west bank, even better ones.

Where the canyon's late-Pleistocene moraines force Illilouette Creek west over toward Buena Vista Creek, we continue northwest, cross the crests of five low moraines, and drop to a tributary of the Clark Fork. Steep banks prevent creekside camping, so we traverse over to nearby Clark Fork, which has several good campsites above its south bank. These sites, about 7 miles from your trailhead, are a good choice for your fourth night on the trail.

From the camps we log-cross the Clark Fork, and engage an easy 1¼-mile traverse through a pleasant Jeffrey-pine/white-fir forest to a junction. Before reaching it, however, we pass some nearby boulders—one the size of a house—that fell from a dome north of here hundreds of years ago. Near these boulders we see some evidence of 1970s and '80s forest fires that scar much of the landscape in the Illilouette Creek basin.

From the junction you can reach your trailhead at Glacier Point by two ways. Keeping right, you can make a high traverse to the Glacier Point-Panorama trail, then reverse the first part of your first day's hike. This alternate route adds about 600 feet of climbing and a little more than 2 miles to your total hiking effort, but is worth it to those who enjoyed the spectacular Panorama Cliff traverse.

Our hike's regular route branches left at the junction, immediately crosses a spring-fed creeklet, then starts down the partly burned slopes. Our moderate ridge descent ends on a

Swimmers sunbathing on a flat slab at Lower Ottoway Lake

Lower Merced Pass Lake is fairly scenic

Dome 7730, along the alternate route about one mile west of Mt. Starr King, displays a human face under proper lighting

gravelly, open slope above Illilouette Creek. From here the Mono Meadow trail climbs north 2⅓ miles back up to the trail we had earlier branched away from, while a use trail heads briefly ahead (west) toward some good, near-creek campsites. Our route turns south, descends the glacial outwash sediments to adjacent Illilouette Creek, and on its sandy, fly-infested north bank we find more camps. A tent comes in handy here as long as a bear doesn't rip it apart. Hang your food on a bear cable if there is one available.

After a usually wet creek crossing, we reach this busy area's most popular camps, above the creek's south bank. Beyond them we hike a minute to a junction with the Buena Vista trail (**Hike 86**) and a few yards farther reach a junction with the westbound Mono Meadows trail (also **Hike 86**). The westbound trail climbs 3.0 miles up to the Glacier Point Road. Our route, the northbound Buena Vista trail, descends along Illilouette Creek, climbs up to the Glacier Point-Panorama trail, and then ascends it for a total of 3.8 miles to our trailhead at Glacier Point. Because camping is prohibited within 4 trail miles of Glacier Point, you can't camp along this entire stretch even though several spots are tempting. Use them only for rest stops.

Hike 90   Chilnualna Fall

Distance: 8.1 miles (13.0 km) round trip

Grade: 2D, moderate day hike

Trailhead: At the end of the Chilnualna Road. The Chilnaulna Road starts immediately north of the bridge across the South Fork Merced River, near Wawona. On it you drive past the Pioneer Yosemite History Center and a nearby fork right to the Park's district office. In a few hundred yards you'll reach the signed Alder Creek Trail, ½ mile along your road. Then, in 1⅓ miles, at the east end of North Wawona, the Chilnualna Road ends above its namesake, Chilnualna Creek. Another road, branching left from Chilnualna Road at "The Redwoods," parallels our road to this end point, the start of the foot trail. If you are taking horses you should start at another trailhead. Branch left on this higher road and follow it ¼ mile to an intersection with a paved road. Turn left and drive ⅓ mile up to its second switchback. From it a horse trail climbs 280 yards east to the end of the foot trail. Park at this switchback or at the road's end, about 150 yards farther. **C6.**

Introduction: Although glaciers may have descended Chilnualna Creek, they were probably few in number and played a minimal role in carving the lower Chilnualna Creek canyon. Hence, Chilnualna Fall, like Feather Fall in the extreme northwestern Sierra Nevada, is largely the product of stream processes. It gives the hiker an idea of what some of the Yosemite Valley falls may have looked like before glaciation.

Description: Our foot trail starts within earshot of dashing Chilnualna Creek and climbs steeply almost to the creek's 25-foot high fall that splashes into a tempting pool. From this point our trail, overshadowed by a low, vertical cliff, climbs even more steeply than before, soon reaching a junction with the horse trail. Continuing upward from it, we leave gold-cup oaks as we cross a manzanita-decked ridge, then enter a forest of ponderosa pines and incense-cedars. On this ascent a few breaks in the vegetation allow us to survey the Wawona area to the south, Wawona Point to the southeast and Wawona Dome to the east. In early summer we hear Chilnualna Creek cascading down its steep, multistepped channel. Climbing east we reach the creek in a few minutes, then briefly follow it up-canyon. Where the trail bends away from the creek, make sure you have enough

water to last until the campsites above Chilnualna Fall, almost 3 miles farther. In mid and late summer the ascent can be hot and dry.

On a moderately graded trail we now climb more than a dozen switchbacks of various lengths up into a cooler forest before making a fairly open traverse southeast toward Chilnualna Fall. On it we see the entire length of the fall, which churns for hundreds of feet down a deep, confining chute. Our trail comes to within a few yards of the fall's brink, but due to loose gravel and a lack of protective railing, you should not venture any closer to it.

Not far above Chilnualna Fall is an upper fall, a 60-foot-high cascade that is quite impressive in early season. To get around this fall and its small gorge, our trail switchbacks north, then curves south above the lip of the gorge. Views extending over the forested Wawona area are left behind as we reach a trail junction. Just below this junction and also below the main trail east of it, you'll find several good campsites. From the junction **Hike 91** follows the trail climbing northeast up Chilnualna Creek, while **Hike 83** follows the trail descending south from Turner Meadows.

While *cautiously* investigating the Chilnualna Fall area, you might look for a small natural bridge below and just downstream from the trail junction. The stream was deeply undercutting a granite slab while at the same time its boulders were drilling a pothole through the slab. Eventually the slab was drilled completely through, and the creekside rim of the pothole stands today as a small bridge.

A small, boulder-drilled natural bridge

Hike 91

North Wawona to Royal Arch, Buena Vista and Chilnualna Lakes

Distance: 28.3 miles (45.6 km) semiloop trip

Grade: 5E, easy 4-day hike

Trailhead: Same as the Hike 90 trailhead. **C6.**

Introduction: Glaciers originating on the slopes of Buena Vista Peak descended north, south and west, then retreated to leave about a dozen small-to-medium lakes. This hike visits seven of these plus dashing Chilnualna Fall—one of the Park's highest falls outside Yosemite Valley.

Description: Hike 90 guides you up through a changing forest to campsites—a possible first night's stop—in an area around a trail junction and a south-flowing tributary of Chilnualna Creek. From that tributary our trail makes a short, steep ascent northeast, then traverses southeast. Soon reaching Chilnualna Creek, you'll find additional campsites along both its banks.

After crossing to the southeast bank, we head upstream toward a cabin site and then veer away from it and the creek to make a short, moderate ascent to a low gap. Past it we enter a damp meadow—an early-season mosquito haven— then climb for a mile, paralleling the usually unseen creek at a distance before we intersect its tributary, Grouse Lake creek. Usually a jump-across creek, it can be a 20-foot wide, slippery-slab ford in late spring. Now just above 7000 feet, we feel the effects of a higher elevation as well as see them—as expressed in the

predominance of stately red firs and occasional lodgepole pines. Before reaching a junction after a ¾-mile ascent, we also note our first trailside western white pines.

At the junction we join **Hike 86** for a short northwest stretch, first up over a nearby divide, then down more than 400 feet to Chilnaulna Creek. Just above its north bank is a good, medium-size campsite, and just beyond that is another trail junction. Here we turn right while **Hike 86** continues ahead, bound for Turner Meadows and the Glacier Point Road.

Eastbound, we make a moderate ¼ mile ascent, followed by a gentler one that goes 1¼ miles along the lodgepole-shaded bank of Chilnualna Creek. After a ¼ mile walk along this gentler stretch, you'll find an acceptable campsite. At the end of the stretch we cross the seasonal creek that drains the middle and northern Chilnualna Lakes. We go a few yards along the larger creek that drains the southern and eastern Chilnualna Lakes, then leave it to cross a close-by bouldery ridge that is a recessional moraine left by a Tioga-age glacier about 13,500 years ago. At its maximum, about 20,000 years ago, this glacier calved icy blocks over the brink of Chilnualna Fall, as did the earlier, Tahoe-age glacier, which was at its maximum about 75,000 years ago.

Young glacial evidence in the form of moraines, erratics and polish is often seen along the remaining 1⅔-mile, shady climb to waist-

Johnson Lake

deep southern Chilnualna Lake. Being so shallow, it is one of the warmest lakes of this hiking circuit to cool off in. The best of the Chilnualna Lakes is also the least visited: the southern lake, at the base of Buena Vista Peak's western shoulder, about ½ mile east-southeast of our western lake. A more-visited lake is the middle one, which is easier to reach. From the far end of our lake, head ¼ mile up its inlet creek to a small pond, then walk due north over a low ridge to the nearby middle lake. From it one can easily regain the trail by continuing north.

Leaving our western lake and its fair west-shore campsite, we climb over a low, bouldery morainal ridge, skirt a small meadow, and cross the middle lake's ephemeral creek. Past it we curve clockwise over to the northern lake's outlet creek, parallel it upward, and then, just ¼ mile before the lake, cross over to the north bank. Upon reaching the shallow, narrow lake we find a good campsite among red firs and western white pines. If weather is threatening, camp here rather than east at an exposed pass.

At that 9040-foot-high pass, about a ¾ mile winding ascent from the northern lake, we meet the Buena Vista trail. Now we follow most of the second half of **Hike 86** as it goes past Buena Vista, Royal Arch, Johnson, Crescent and Grouse lakes. You may want to visit all of them, and you should plan to spend at least a day in this scenic glacier-lake area. A little more than 2 miles west of Grouse Lake you'll leave **Hike 86** where you first met it, and descend the way you came—past Chilnualna Fall.

Hike 92   Wawona to Mariposa Grove

Distance: 13.0 miles (20.9 km) round trip

Grade: 3D, moderate day hike

Trailhead: Several. Park at Wawona Hotel, at the store north of the hotel, or at the Pioneer Yosemite History Center. **C6.**

Introduction: Though most visitors drive to the Mariposa Grove, one can also walk to it. This hike describes the forested pathway to the Mariposa Grove of Big Trees, or Wawona, as the Indians used to call them.

Description: Regardless of where you start in the Wawona area, you shouldn't have much trouble finding the trailhead. A north-south road cuts across a low crest along the east side of the Wawona structures, and just north of the actual crest, the Two Hour Ride Trail climbs east from the road.

On this dusty horse trail we quickly pass an old, abandoned canal, climb to the crest, and in a short mile from the trailhead reach a crest fork. To the left, a broad horse path—an old road—descends to a summer camp. From it the broad horse path climbs southeast back up to a junction with our trail. This junction is reached after a second short mile of dusty trail hiking, most of it right along the forested crest. Views of large Wawona meadow, below and southwest of us, are generally poor or nonexistent. The alluvial valley that holds this meadow is exceptionally large and flat for its elevation.

From the saddle where the broad horse path rejoins our trail, we turn south, briefly descend to a point a stone's throw from the noisy, paved Wawona Road, and parallel it an equally brief distance east to a junction. Here the Two Hour Ride Trail leaves us, crossing the nearby highway to return to the Wawona area. Now on a less used route, we climb east up a steepening ridge before veering south on our 1⅔-mile ascent to a usually flowing creek.

Our trail maintains its moderate gradient as it climbs south above the headwalls of two eroding, enlarging bowls. Then in ½ mile it begins to switchback up to a broad-crest junction with a ridge trail. If you intend to follow **Hike 93,** you'll end it at this junction, then descend the way you came back to Wawona. The combined length of Hikes 92 and 93 is 17.5 miles (28.2 km)—a strenuous 4D day hike.

Now merged, Hikes 92 and 93 follow a rolling, wandering trail a long ½ mile southeast to a junction, from which you could continue your traverse an equal distance to the tunneled California Tree and the enormous Grizzly Giant. Rather, we turn right and on a switchbacking trail descend an equal distance to the upper (northeast) end of the Mariposa Grove parking lot. After walking through it you'll reach the end of Hike 92—an information kiosk—from which **Hike 93** begins. Along it you'll thoroughly explore the giant sequoias and their interesting natural history.

Hike 93   Mariposa Grove of Big Trees

Distance: 6.9 miles (11.0) km) loop trip; other, shorter loops possible

Grade: 2C, moderate half-day hike

Map: On page 201

Trailhead: At the Park's south entrance station turn right and drive east 2.1 miles up to the Big Trees parking lot. On some days this can easily fill by mid-morning, so consider taking a free (summer only) shuttle bus up from Wawona. **D6** on book's topographic map.

Introduction: The giant sequoia, or big tree, with its "grand domed head seems to be poised about as lightly as a cloud, giving no impression of seeking to rise higher. Only when it is young does it show like other conifers a heavenward yearning, sharply aspiring with a long quick-growing top. . . . No other California conifer produces nearly so many seeds, except, perhaps, the other sequoia, the redwood of the Coast Mountains. Millions are ripened annually by a single tree, and in a fruitful year the product of one of the northern groves would be enough to plant all the mountain ranges in the world." So wrote John Muir in his 1912 guidebook, *The Yosemite,* which is as much an account of his interesting Yosemite wanderings as it is a guide to the Park. Muir made many observations of the giant sequoias and although a few of them were inaccurate, most were perceived with remarkable insight. In the preceding quote Muir paints a picture of a grand forest monarch with the potential capability of expanding its domain worldwide. With the aid of modern man sequoias *have* been planted worldwide, and they grow particularly well in Europe. Why then, one may ask, do we find these fecund giants in such limited distribution today? This question, and many others, will be answered as you walk through the Mariposa Grove on this hike.

Description: Near the southwest end of the parking lot is an information kiosk in which visitors can get introduced to the Mariposa Grove while waiting to take the tram. The tram ride gives you an instructive, guided tour of the grove's salient features and, where it stops, you can get off, explore the immediate area, then get on the next tram. However, by hiking from the kiosk rather than riding a tram from it, one gets a more intimate (and with this guide, a more informative) experience with the giant sequoia and the associated plants and animals that share this shady habitat.

Our path, signed the MARIPOSA GROVE FOOT TRAILS, starts eastward up along a quiet, azalea-lined creeklet that drains the shady slopes. Judging from this environment, one would conclude that sequoias are shade-loving trees. However, extensive research done in the 1960s and early '70s under the leadership of Richard Hartesveldt (and continued under Thomas Harvey after his untimely death) showed that the very opposite is true. (Their research and others is brilliantly written for naturalists and general public alike in *The Giant Sequoia of the Sierra Nevada,* published by the National Park Service—see "Recommended Reading and Source Books.") Hartesveldt and Harvey discovered that abundant sunlight is important in every stage of the tree's development. In our introductory quote, Muir noted the youthful giant's "quick-growing top," which then gave way to an expanding "grand domed head." The tree, growing at 1-2 feet per year, is in a race to the sky with competing conifers. Only when it reaches the 200-foot mark—after about 150 years—is it more or less assured of extreme longevity.

The giant's race toward the sun begins at the very start—with the seeds. Muir observed that each sequoia produces an incredible number of seeds. He overstated its fecundity, but a mature giant sequoia can nevertheless produce 300-400,000 seeds in a year and more than a *half billion* if it lives to a ripe old age. Why then doesn't a grove of sequoias "plant all the mountain ranges in the world?" Hartesveldt and Harvey answer: "The giant sequoia is a classic example of reproductive fragility." They say that of paramount importance is the tree's access to sufficient soil moisture during the growing season. This is especially true for the seed and seedling.

For the seed to begin its journey toward the sun, three elements are important, if not absolutely essential. They are the chickaree (Douglas squirrel), *Phymatodes nitidus* (a small cerambycid, or long-antennaed, beetle) and fire. Cones can stay green and unopened on a giant sequoia for 20 years or more. Staying green this long can be a disadvantage, for in 4-5 years foliose lichens may appear, grow over the cone and eventually prevent seed dispersal. However, activities by the chickaree and the beetle hasten the cone's drying and/or increase seed dispersal.

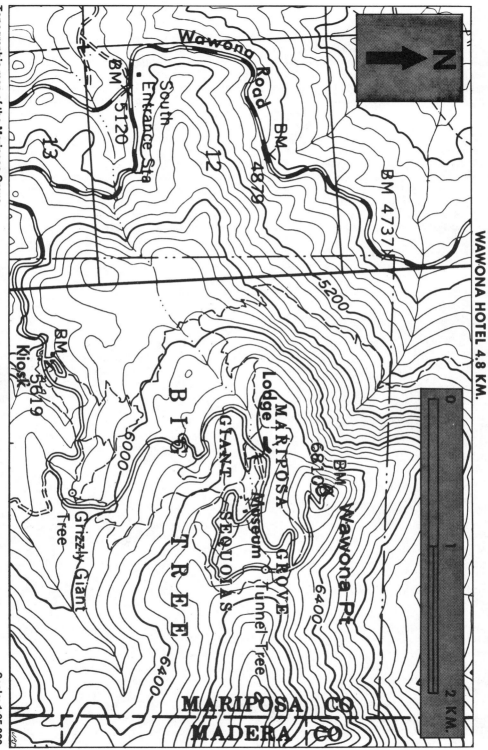

Topographic map of the Mariposa Grove.

Scale: 1:25,000.

WAWONA HOTEL 4.8 KM.

N

0   1   2 KM.

The chickaree feeds on the *seeds* of many conifers, and in our sequoia community the seeds likely to be eaten are those of the sugar pine, white fir, ponderosa pine and incense-cedar. But, as Hartesveldt and Harvey point out, chickarees do not feed on the tiny sequoia seeds. Rather they feed on the scales of the cones—ones generally 2-5 years old—much as you would scrape the flesh off an artichoke leaf. Seeds may drop to the ground in this feeding process, or the partly eaten cone may turn brown, open, and disperse its seeds. Finally, the squirrel may cut off the cones, which, after falling to the ground, turn brown and release their seeds. Some squirrels have a compulsion to cut down cones in far greater numbers than they can ever feed upon. One was observed to cut 12,000 cones in one day—about one every 4 seconds. Since the average mature sequoia has about 11,000 cones, it could in theory be stripped clean in one day! Prolific sequoias will have up to 40,000 cones on them at one time.

A sequoia cone, ¾ life size

The cerambycid beetle lays eggs on the cone, which then give rise to tunneling larvae. The tunnels bored by the larvae obstruct the cone's vascular system, leading to the browning of the cone and subsequent seed release. The beetle prefers cones 4 years old or older, and hence it does not directly compete with the chickaree. The beetle or its ancestors may have been performing a similar role as long as sequoias have existed, which may be for 150 million years. Modern squirrels developed much later, during the Miocene epoch, and may have been associated with the sequoia line for only the last 20 million years. The sequoia community, like any plant community, evolves through time, and the 150+ species of insects that depend in part on the giant sequoia have also changed over time, evolving in response to the tree's change, to changes in other communal plants and animals, and to changes in the physical environment.

Fire, the last element important to sequoia continuation prepares the ground for seed germination. Without fire-suppression policies the Mariposa Grove would have a ground fire every 8-20 years. Generally, such fires consume only ground litter, brush and the smaller trees. If the fire is large, it will also burn mature conifers *other than* giant sequoias, which are generally resistant to *total* consumption by fire. Before the Park's fire-suppression policy, which lasted until the early 1970s, fire kept white firs to a minimum. These trees greatly increased their numbers in the Mariposa Grove, making it considerably shadier than it was before human intervention. This shade hinders sequoia regeneration. A major fire will destroy white firs and other conifers, thereby increasing light on the forest floor.

A ground fire does several beneficial things. Perhaps foremost, it burns the litter and duff, leaving a soft, friable (easily crumbled) mineral soil. This resulting soil has temporary voids, destroyed in time, in which a sequoia seed may land. Were the seed larger, it wouldn't fit into one of these voids. As you can readily imagine, an enormous number of seeds must be produced in order for some of them to end up in these protective voids. Outside a void, a seed comes to a quick end, for it cannot survive the high temperatures found at the soil's surface.

The fire, which has provided the protective pockets, also kills harmful fungi and rids the area of potentially lethal, shade-producing competitors. Furthermore, a fire increases both the soil's wetability and its soil-moisture retention. These changes are important, for a germinating sequoia seedling's roots, having no hairs, need all the moisture they can get. Growing from its void, optimally about ¼ inch below the soil's surface, the struggling seedling now faces a hot summer sun above and diminishing water supply below. If it is one of the fortunate few that survives their first three summers, it may stand a fighting chance of becoming an adult, for by then its root has grown down about 14 inches. This is the approximate crucial level above which the soil is likely to dry completely in response to the rays of the hot summer sun. Once past this crucial stage, the sequoia now a sapling, grows 1-2 feet per year, racing with competing conifers toward the sun. Should a neighboring tree overshadow it, it is doomed to a premature death.

Pondering over the tremendous odds a sequoia seed has to overcome—more than a million to one—we continue on our walk away from the grove's information kiosk. Our shady trail gives rise to a short path that crosses our trailside, azalea-lined creeklet to reach the adjacent tram road. We take a second path, about 250 yards from the start of our trail, and walk a few paces over to the Fallen Monarch, a huge, downed sequoia lying beside the road. This giant fell before Galen Clark's exploration of the Mariposa Grove in 1857. Just how long it has lain "in state" is anybody's guess. Through radiocarbon-dating techniques scientists have shown that a sequoia such as the Fallen Monarch can resist decay for 20 centuries or more. Unlike its thin, outer sapwood, the tree's heartwood—by far the great bulk of the tree—is *almost* immune to fire, insect and fungal attack.

Visitors are dwarfed by the Grizzly Giant

Since our short path to the Fallen Monarch ends near the tree's roots, you might take a look at them. Note how shallow they are. Even the largest sequoias rarely send their massive roots more than three feet down, and then these roots, extending laterally, approach the surface, coming to within a foot or less of it. These shallow roots are the sequoia's "Achilles' heel," for though the mature tree is usually immune to almost any kind of attack, it is likely—especially in old age—to be toppled during a violent windstorm. As we've already noted, much of the spreading crown of the mature giant sequoia rises above the tops of other trees, subjecting it to these winds and extreme snow loads.

Near the uphill end of the Fallen Monarch, the Pillars of Heaven Nature Trail begins from the tram road's south side and climbs northeast before uniting with our main route—an old road. Along the nature trail you'll see that fire can damage a sequoia, though one rarely destroys it. Since debris piles up on *any* tree's upslope side, that is the side that is likely to burn with the greatest intensity in a ground fire. One fire may hardly damage a sequoia's bark, which is fire-resistant because it is soft and fibrous and contains very little pitch. A dozen or more fires, however, can do extensive damage, as we'll see along our hike.

From the north end of the nature trail our main trail, an old stage road, climbs about 200 yards to a crossing of the paved tram road. Here, near the Bachelor and the Three Graces, our path forks, and we go right (east) up to the Grizzly Giant. Like the Leaning Tower of Pisa, this 2500-year-old giant—declining about 17° from the vertical—seems ready to fall any second and one wonders how such a top-heavy, shallow-rooted specimen could have survived as long as it has. A giant it is, ranking fifth largest

among the sequoias, and having enough timber to build 20 homes. Fortunately, sequoia wood is very brittle and when a giant was felled in days past by lumbermen, it usually broke into thousands of small useless pieces. Hence the sequoia, in contrast with its western cousin, the coast redwood, was not economical to log.

Heading north from the east end of the enclosure circling the Grizzly Giant, we reach the California Tree, also enclosed, in 50 yards. This sequoia, like the famous Wawona Tunnel Tree, had a deep burn in its lower trunk, which was then cut away to make a tunnel. The famous tunnel tree, located about 750 feet higher on slopes northeast of us, often would not become snow-free until early summer. Before then, the early stage drivers would at times take their springtime tourists through the lower California Tree, which conveniently had a *Wawona* sign tacked to it to further convince the tourists they had seen and passed through the real specimen.

Immediately beyond the California Tree we meet an east-west trail. By heading ¼ mile west on it you'll reach a junction with a spur trail that descends to the Bachelor and the Three Graces. By contouring another ¼ mile west, you'll reach a junction from where the trail from Wawona (**Hike 92**) descends south to the parking lot and kiosk. We'll return along that descent.

First, however, we still face the great bulk of our climbing as our trail immediately turns north and climbs 200 yards to a crossing of the tram road. From that road we climb almost one mile and 500 vertical feet up forested slopes to a trail junction just below the road's upper-loop section. Along this moderate-to-steep ascent, white firs dominate over incense-cedars, which in turn dominate over ponderosa pines and sugar pines. Had fire suppression never been imposed we would expect to see less of the first species and more of the last.

The fire-scarred Clothespin Tree

From our junction one could ascend the Upper Loop trail as it climbs counterclockwise, paralleling the road's loop over to the Wawona Tunnel Tree. Rather, we turn left and descend a few yards northwest, meeting a trail that climbs ½ mile up from the tram road. Instead of making our 500-foot trail ascent, you could hike ⅔ mile up the tram road to a hairpin turn, then take the ½-mile trail up to our Upper Loop trail. This slightly longer alternate route has one advantage: you see the Clothespin Tree, which stands near the hairpin turn. Fire has burned away part of its lower heartwood, forming a 60-foot-high cleft that splits the tree in two like an old-fashioned clothespin.

Trees of its stature have been overestimated with regard to weight. Mature sequoias, once thought to gross 1000 tons are in reality only about 200. Even the largest sequoia—the General Sherman in Sequoia National Park—weighs only about 450 tons, dry weight, and the Grizzly Giant weighs about 300. The reason for the tree's "light" weight is the low density of its wood; it weighs only 18 pounds per cubic foot, about ⅓ that of an oak. The giant sequoia, with its lightweight, brittle wood *needs* its garguantuan, wide-diameter bulk to support its mushrooming, windswept crown.

From the upper junction with the alternate route, our main trail traverses about 110 yards north to a junction with an east-west trail. Westward this trail descends a few hundred yards to the tram road, crosses it, then quickly ends at the trail we'll eventually descend on. From our junction beside the tip of a large, fallen giant, we proceed east up-trail through a spacious forest with mature sequoias to the Mariposa Grove Museum. A few yards before it another eastbound trail, on our left, merges with ours. To the west this trail forks, one branch quickly ending at our eastbound trail, while the other branch crosses a creeklet and the tram road, then goes past the closed Big Trees Lodge before ending at our eventual descent route.

Be sure to visit the museum. In it you will find information and displays on the giant sequoia, its related plants and animals, and on the area's history. On the museum's exterior is a hole drilled by a white-headed woodpecker, one of several dozen bird species that inhabit the

The Mariposa Grove Museum, situated in a Brobdingnagian forest

sequoia community. By making the entrance hole small, the parents effectively prevent predators from reaching the young inside. Please don't enlarge the hole.

You can take any of four routes from the museum up to the Wawona Tunnel Tree. On the tram road you can either go north, passing Pluto's Chimney—a dead-but-standing sequoia (a rare sight)—or you can go south, passing the Columbia Tree, which at almost 290 feet is the grove's tallest. The most direct route is a trail that climbs ⅓ mile northeast up to the Tunnel Tree. Finally, the route the author prefers starts south along the tram road, then after a few yards—just before the Columbia Tree—leaves it and heads southeast back up to the road. Along this trail stretch you'll pass the Stable Tree, a giant that fell in the *summer* of 1934. Most sequoias fall during the long, stormy winter. Note how much of the bark and sapwood still remain on it. The heartwood, which makes up the bulk of the tree, may stay unchanged for centuries.

View straight up the Telescope Tree

Where the preferred route crosses the tram road you'll see the amazing Telescope Tree, which has been hollowed out by fire. Inside it you can look straight up to the heavens. Despite its great internal loss, this tree is still very much alive for its vital fluids—as in all trees—are conducted in the sapwood, immediately beneath the bark. The heartwood is just dead sapwood whose main function is support. The Telescope Tree, with its hollow interior, is a good candidate for blowdown.

From the back side of the tree our trail climbs 35 yards to the Upper Loop trail, which we then follow ⅓ mile counterclockwise over to the Wawona Tunnel Tree. During the late winter or

spring of 1969 this 2200-year-old giant fell, after bearing 88 years of tourist traffic. Orginally fire-scarred like other giants, it was tunneled through in 1881 to provide stagecoach riders with a thrill of a lifetime—riding *through* a tree. In later days tourists would wait up to an hour or more to drive through it, each driver slowly passing through it while a friend or relative recorded the event on film. This giant tree may have fallen of its own accord, from a strong windstorm, from the 1-2 tons of accumulated snow in its crown, from the adverse effects of tunneling, from weakening roots, or perhaps a combination of these.

After examining this downed giant, continue north on the Upper Loop trail or the tram road to a nearby crest saddle. Just 40 yards east of it is the Galen Clark Tree, a fine specimen named for the man who first publicized this grove and later became its guardian. The Upper Loop trail crosses the saddle at a road junction, and before we descend along it we first angle right and follow the crest road ¼ mile up to Wawona Point. No giant sequoias are found along this road, probably because of insufficient ground water. At the point we see the large, partly man-made meadow at Wawona, to the northwest, and the long, curving cliff of Wawona Dome, breaking a sea of green, to the north.

After returning to the crest saddle, we descend west along the Upper Loop trail. About ⅔ mile from the saddle our trail gives rise to a wide path that departs south down to the close-by Big Trees Lodge. Near this path junction we see the first giant sequoia since the Galen Clark Tree, and will see more farther down. In a few minutes we come to a second junction, and here the Upper Loop trail branches left to quickly cross the tram road. We curve right and drop about 470 feet along a moderate, short-mile descent to a junction with **Hike 92**, climbing 5.0 miles up from the east end of the Wawona complex. As in that hike we follow a rambling trail a long ½ mile southeast to a junction, turn right, and make a shady, moderate descent back to the parking lot and its information kiosk—our starting point.

To get away from hordes of people at the Mariposa Grove and at the Tuolumne Grove, north of Crane Flat, visit the Merced Grove, which has about a dozen mature specimens. From Crane Flat drive 3.7 miles west on Highway 120 to the trailhead, then hike down a closed road (fork left at a junction). The round trip is about 3½ to 4 miles, depending where you decide to turn back.

Clouds building over largest of the Staniford Lakes

Section 8

Trails of Yosemite's Southeastern Backcountry

Introduction: This section explores the back ways into southeastern Yosemite. As roads in the Sierra National Forest are steadily being upgraded—particularly Road 5S07—more and more hikers are discovering—and returning to—this scenic area. The Chain Lakes and the lakes of the southwest part of Ansel Adams Wilderness already rival many of the Park's better-known lakes in popularity. Much of the landscape is lodgepole-pine forest, but around Fernandez, Post Peak and Isberg passes, the vegetation shifts to a sub-alpine nature. Truly alpine Red Peak Pass, standing at 11,180 feet (3407 m) elevation, is the highest *trail* point in the entire Park. Two of this section's natural attractions are not found anywhere else in the other sections: a broad, scenic sub-alpine plateau and an unbelievable mottled-granite landscape—both seen along Hikes 98 and 100.

Supplies and Services: Oakhurst, at the crossroads of Highways 41 and 49, has just about everything you'll need for a backcountry hike. Closer to the trailheads is a settlement at the south end of Beasore Road, just above the north shore of Bass Lake. Here you'll find a substantial market, coffee shop and a gas station. After driving 13.5 miles north up Beasore Road 434 (also signed 5S07), you'll reach Jones Store, with a few but very pertinent food items. Also selling food plus other assorted items is the Minarets Pack Station, currently located on Road 5S88 (see the third major trailhead description in Hike 97). This large pack station, located near Miller Meadow, serves the western part of Ansel Adams Wilderness and the southeastern part of Yosemite National Park.

Wilderness Permits: Get one at the Oakhurst Ranger Station, on Highway 41 at the northeast end of town if you are going to backpack in from the Chiquito Pass trailhead (Hikes 94–96). For the other, eastern trailheads, get a permit at the North Fork Ranger Station, inconveniently located in the town of North Fork about 5 miles south of Bass Lake. You can't get permits at Upper Chiquito Ranger Station, which is at the lower end of Upper Chiquito Campground, or at Clover Meadow Ranger Station, which is at the entrance to Clover Meadow Campground. Both are infrequently manned.

Campgrounds: If you are driving up late at night, you might want to stop at Chilkoot Campground, 4 miles up Beasore Road. Otherwise, use Upper Chiquito Campground for Hikes 94-96. Its three entrances branch left from Road 5S07 about one mile beyond a junction with Road 5S04, opposite Globe Rock. For Hikes 97-98 use Bowler Group Camp if you are in a group or else use Clover Meadow Campground. Both are mentioned in Hike 97's trailhead information. For Hikes 99-100 use Granite Creek Campground, mentioned in Hike 99's trailhead information.

Hike 94   Royal Arch Lake via Chiquito Pass

Distance: 19.6 miles (31.5 km) round trip
Grade: 4E, moderate 2-day hike

Trailhead: From the Highway 49 junction in Oakhurst, drive north on Highway 41 3.5 miles up to a junction with Road 222. Follow this east 3.5 miles to a fork, veer left and continue east 2.4 miles on Malum Ridge Road 274 to a junction with *north*-climbing Beasore Road 434. This junction is about 80 yards past a junction with south-dropping Beasore Road. Our paved Beasore Road climbs north 4.0 miles to Chilkoot Campground then soon becomes signed Road 5S07. It reaches an intersection at Cold Springs Summit after 7.4 miles of climbing beyond the campground. Road 6S10 heads west from this intersection, winding 5.5 miles over to a junction near Kelty Meadow, where it meets the alternate-trailhead route. From Cold Springs Summit our well-signed major logging road, Road 5S07, winds 8.6 miles, going past Beasore Meadows, Jones Store, Muglers Meadows and Long Meadow before coming to a junction with Road 5S04, opposite Globe Rock. Turn left and drive up the road 2.4 miles to a signed trailhead—28.2 miles from Highway 41—atop a small, flat ridge area. *Trail mileages for Hikes 94-96 are based from this trailhead.* From it a trail climbs 2.9 miles to Chiquito Pass. **E6.**

A lesser known route gets you to a trail that *drops* to Chiquito Pass in only 0.8 mile—a 2.1-mile saving each way. This higher, later-opening alternate route is a mile shorter to drive than the one just described but, being on narrower roads, takes a little more time to drive. Starting from the Highway 49 junction in Oakhurst, you drive north on Highway 41 3.5 miles up to Road 222, then continue 0.6 mile past it to a right turn onto Gooseberry Flats Road 632. The pavement on this road soon ends and it becomes Sky Ranch Road 6S10. After climbing 11.4 miles from Highway 41, Road 6S10 meets a junction and then winds 5.5 miles over to the regular route at Cold Springs Summit. You veer left at the junction, driving 1.7 miles north to a junction with Road 6S07, on the left, which descends 8.2 miles west to Highway 41 at the southern fringe of the town of Fish Camp. This rocky road has one potentially bad creek ford and is not recommended for automobiles.

Our road curves right and immediately passes the entrance to Fresno Dome Campground. Just 1.5 miles past our junction with Road 6S07 a

Globe Rock

road branches left toward the Star Lakes area. Beyond this junction you could get lost. At *most* junctions our road is the wider, obvious one. (Because new logging spurs are continually being built, this guide will mention only the important junctions.) Our road divides after 3.1 miles past the Star Lakes junction, and we curve left and wind 0.9 mile up to another misleading junction. Here we keep right, on the level, rather than climb left. We then drive 4.5 miles to a major junction. If you're on the correct road you should cross two saddles, pass Lost Lake (on your right) and a trail to Grizzly Lake (on your left). A rockslide area along this 4.5-mile stretch sometimes releases boulders that temporarily block the road—the only real gamble with this route.

From the major junction with a wide logging road branching left, our wide road traverses 2.7 miles, veers right around a descending ridge and in 0.5 mile reaches a spur road branching left. Follow this road 0.4 mile to a turnaround at its end, 26.7 miles from Highway 41. From here a short trail descends to Chiquito Pass. In early season you may not be able to drive it all the way. The main road goes 0.4 mile to an unofficial camping area, with tables and spring, then 0.6 mile to a turnaround. **E6.**

Introduction: The shortest way in to Royal Arch Lake is along this route from Chiquito

Pass—only 7.6 miles from the alternate trailhead. Perhaps because the hiker has to first drive about an hour along dirt roads, this route is spurned in favor of routes from North Wawona (**Hike 91**) or from the Glacier Point Road (**Hike 86**). Each approach to Royal Arch Lake and other lakes around Buena Vista Peak has its own merits.

Description: On a flat area atop a granitic ridge, our well-signed Chiquito Lake trail traverses northwest away from curving Road 5S04. Jeffrey pines largely dominate the broken forest cover, and often grazing beneath them are cattle. These will be with us on and off until we leave Sierra National Forest at Chiquito Pass. About ⅓ mile from our trailhead we cross a short-lived creeklet then climb moderately an equal distance to a trail junction. Before the 1970s the trail we see climbing to us was the first part of a once longer route in to Chiquito Lake. Today the trail is abandoned, its right of way being usurped by down-canyon logging operations and by our trailhead Road 5S04.

Progressing northwest from the junction, we are first blessed with another easy traverse that takes us past another creeklet and over to the bank of Chiquito Creek. Now our climbing begins in earnest as we gain about 500 feet over a short-mile ascent up a large, dusty lateral moraine. Hikers descending this occasionally steep Chiquito Lake trail sometimes take shortcuts, resulting in confusing paths, but these always quickly rejoin the main trail, should you be led astray. Fortunately our unrelenting ascent is usually shaded by red firs and by western white, Jeffrey and lodgepole pines.

Our climb is essentially over when the moraine gives way to a small bedrock knoll. After traversing for a few minutes beyond it, we drop to ford seasonally wide Chiquito Creek. Once across it we crest the top of a low terminal moraine and arrive at a spacious campsite—one of several—along the south shore of disappointing Chiquito Lake. Were Chiquito Lake not dammed, it would be little more than a waist-deep swamp. Even with the dam it is little better, its tainted waters attracting both cows and mosquitoes. Should you for some reason decide to camp beneath lodgepoles by this sedge-lined lake, bring a tent and boil the water.

Just beyond, at the lake's southwest corner, a now-abandoned trail began its climb to Chiquito Pass, but we take a newer path 250 yards west to a junction with the "lesser known route." Those taking it join us for a ⅓-mile walk north

over to Chiquito Pass, where we leave the grazing cows and their muddy shoreline environment behind. Around the broad pass you may see former, abandoned trails that could lead you astray on your return trip.

Note that Chiquito Pass, signed 8039 feet in elevation, sits atop a long, multicrested moraine. Glaciers of the Tioga glaciation left this moraine when they retreated from this area about 14,000 years ago. Except for its ridgecrests and mountaintops, the entire South Fork Merced River basin, north of us, lay under a sea of ice during this period. This enormous ice field failed to overflow at Chiquito Pass but rather it just rubbed edges with a much smaller glacier that flowed west from Red Top and ended just below the south shore campsites of Chiquito Lake. During the preceding glaciation, the Tahoe, the two had merged into one and descended 1⅔ miles down Chiquito Creek. Our 500-foot ascent was up its eastern lateral moraine. This glacial period was cold and wet enough to create a glacierette on the north slopes of Quartz Mountain, near our alternate trailhead.

During the earlier Sherwin glaciation, which existed from about 900,000 to 800,000 years ago, the sea of ice was amazingly large. Then, a mantle of ice covered virtually all the landscape from Cold Springs Summit and Chiquito Ridge east to the Sierra crest. François Matthes, who died in 1948 before completing his study of this San Joaquin Basin ice field, described it as "by far the largest system of confluent glaciers in the Sierra Nevada, measuring more than 50 miles in length along the crest of the range, and 30 to 35 miles in breadth. Of the 1,760 square miles comprised in the San Joaquin Basin, almost 1,100 square miles were covered by glaciers. . . . The length of the San Joaquin glacier system, measured from the head of the South Fork branch to the terminus of the trunk glacier, was nearly 60 miles." At the start of your trailhead road, Road 5S04, you may have seen amazingly round Globe Rock perched on a pedestal. It is a glacier-transported boulder that was perhaps carried to its resting point during the Sherwin glaciation. It did not fortuitously land on a pedestal but, rather, the pedestal developed, protected from erosion by the overlying erratic as the bedrock surrounding it was gradually stripped away over countless millennia.

Just within the fence—and Yosemite National Park—at Chiquito Pass, the trail

Evening comes to Royal Arch Lake

splits. **Hikes 95** and **96** go right, northeast, along the moraine, while we go left and descend northwest away from this bouldery, multicrested feature. Our descent into a red-fir/lodgepole-pine forest momentarily abates at wide Spotted Lakes creek, which in early season is crossed on large boulders. Leaving its banks of alders, willows and wildflowers, we now continue on a lesser gradient, our trail curving west to cross the South Fork Merced River at Gravelly Ford. A medium-size camp exists on each bank, and to get from one to the other you'll probably have to wade unless a large log is handy.

After leaving the gravelly banks, we climb up a low, dry, sagebrush-clothed slope, then curve down to the west end of rightly named Swamp Lake. Beyond it is a wet meadow, which like the lakelet sires hordes of mosquitoes that last well into August. This is unfortunate, for in July and early August it has also one of the better assemblages of tall, water-loving wildflowers. Leaving the wet flat for better-drained, less-mosquitoed slopes, we climb northwest 1 mile up a gradually steepening trail. The gradient becomes an exhausting one just before we top a gravelly, boulder-strewn moraine ridge. From it we plummet down to diminutive Givens Creek, only to climb again. After an easy ⅓ mile of climbing we meet a little used though perfectly good trail that goes 3½ miles east to a junction with the Chain Lakes-Moraine Meadow trail. After 2¾ miles east along this trail you'll find a short spur trail that descends a few hundred yards to a cold, bubbly, rust-stained soda spring similar to the ones in Tuolumne Meadows.

Starting west, we go but 60 yards before a sometimes faint trail branches right. Staying out of sight, it parallels our conspicuous trail ¼ mile before it climbs northwest an equal distance to a main trail. On that trail one can hike northeast 1.6 miles to a junction with the Givens Lake trail. **Hike 96** returns along this route from Givens Lake.

From the junction with the sometimes faint trail we climb 0.6 mile west to the above mentioned main trail, first crossing a glacier-polished ridge before meeting the junction atop a second ridge. Leaving this ridge, we descend southwest through a red-fir-dominated forest interspersed with sunlit, grassy openings. Lodgepoles and Jeffrey pines increase in number westward, and then we climb northwest to the meadowy environment of Buck Creek. Just west of it and south of the main trail stands Buck Camp Ranger Station—the summer "headquarters" for patrols through the South Fork Merced River basin. Its network of trails, though well signed, can confuse unprepared novice backpackers, for prominent landmarks are absent.

A mile-long slog, first along and through wet, sloping meadows, confronts us beyond Buck Camp. We end this moderate-to-steep 720-foot climb in a fairly deep ridge cleft where views are blocked by red firs and western white pines. An equally steep trail segment, descending almost ½ mile west, ends at the Buena Vista Peak loop trail. Here we turn right and make an easy ascent ¾ mile up to an excellent campsite at the southwest corner of dramatic Royal Arch Lake. As in Hikes 86 and 91 you could make a circuit of the Buena Vista Peak lakes. The last part of **Hike 86** describes this loop from Buena Vista Lake south past Royal Arch, Johnson, Crescent and Grouse lakes, while the last part of **Hike 91** describes the rest of this loop past the Chilnualna Lakes.

Hike 95   Chain Lakes

Distance: 16.5 miles (26.6 km) round trip

Grade: 3D, easy 2-day hike

Trailhead: Same as the Hike 94 trailhead. **E6.**

Introduction: Reached in three hours from the standard trailhead and only two from the alternate one, these lakes receive considerable backpacking pressure. Only the long road to each trailhead prevents them from being overrun. The charm of middle Chain Lake draws the crowd while the shore of upper Chain Lake provides a base camp for peakbagging mountaineers.

Description: The route up to the Yosemite National Park boundary at Chiquito Pass is described in **Hike 94.** Leaving it, we head northeast and pass a stagnant pond trapped between the crests of two bouldery, bushy moraines. The one on our left stays with us for a full ½ mile before we cross it and make a slight descent to a flat-floored forest. In early summer, several creeks and creeklets are flowing, and then the flat-floored traverse can be a muddy one that hikers hurry along to evade a marauding horde of mosquitoes so typical of this shady, damp environment.

The last creek crossing is the widest, and beyond it we have a mile-long ascent up to a small, moraine-dammed meadow. From it one could contour east cross-country over to a creek draining Spotted Lakes. However, these lakes are best reached by starting from the end of a jeep road that traverses the southwest slopes of Red Top. From this road, which ends 4.4 miles beyond the Chiquito Pass trailhead, you have only a 1½-mile cross-country hike to these trout-inhabited lakes. Furthermore, from the end of an east branch of this jeep road you can reach the summit of Red Top in less than a mile's ridgecrest hike. This rusty peak, largely composed of ancient, metamorphosed rocks, contrasts with our trailside landscape. So far our hike has been along the same kind of "granite" found in Hike 94—quartz monzonite. However, at our destination, the Chain Lakes, the "granite" will be granodiorite—a slightly darker plutonic rock.

From the moraine-dammed meadow we climb a short ½ mile up to a low point on a glacier-polished ridge, cross it, and make a rolling, short-mile traverse northeast to a trail junction on the north bank of boulder-choked

Gale Peak reflected in Middle Chain Lake's tranquil water

Chain Lakes creek. From it, **Hike 96** follows the creek downstream. We turn right, upstream, and hike east on a moderate-to-steep trail up to shallow, lower Chain Lake, at about 8950 feet elevation. This fairly warm lake is too shallow for swimming, but is heavily fished. Its trout may periodically die, though it can be repopulated from the middle lake's trout. Camps here are inferior to those by the deeper middle lake.

From the outlet of the morained-dammed lower lake, our maintained trail climbs over a low ridge and drops to a *de facto* north-shore foot trail at the lake's far end. Next, we make a short, fairly steep ascent up along a creek to picturesque, island-dotted middle Chain Lake. The warm bedrock islands are easily reached, particularly from the excellent oversized camp along the lake's southwest shore. To reach that camp—a favorite with boy scouts—cross the lake's *two* outlet creeks and then follow a primitive path along the west shore. In case the scouts have beaten you to a rainbow-trout dinner, you can console yourself with a pleasant

swim in the 20-foot-deep lake, which warms to the mid-60s in early August. This is a classic subalpine lake, rimmed with lodgepole pines, western white pines and mountain hemlocks understoried with Labrador tea, red heather, western blueberry and dwarf bilberry. The last two plants, both huckleberries, produce edible berries in late summer, after the crowds have left, and then the birds, bears and golden-mantled ground squirrels have a feast.

Beyond the middle lake the trail is less traveled. It steeply climbs to the bouldery crest of a moraine, winds over to a stagnant pond, and drops south to a photogenic lakelet. Near this lakelet our trail twice divides and reunites, then briefly climbs to deep upper Chain Lake. Cold, windswept and rock-rimmed, it offers marginal camping but it is a good staging area for experienced mountaineers planning to climb slopes up to Gale Peak and the Park's southeast boundary crest. Anglers may have a better chance up here than down at heavily fished middle Chain Lake.

Hike 96   South Fork Merced River Loop

Distance: 23.4 miles (37.7 km) semiloop trip
Grade: 5E, easy 3-day hike
Trailhead: Same as the Hike 94 trailhead. E6.
Introduction: While many backpackers follow the beaten path to the Chain Lakes, to Breeze Lake, or to the Buena Vista Peak lakes, far fewer take the faint path to Givens Lake, which is visited along this hike. Givens Lake, lying on a bench below Moraine Mountain, has the most incredible moraine assemblage to be found at any of the Park's lakes. For those interested in glacial geology, these moraines alone make the hike worthwhile.

Description: Follow the first part of **Hike 94** up to Chiquito Pass (or down to it, if you take the alternate route), then follow **Hike 95** up to middle Chain Lake—7.4 miles (12.5 km) by the longer, regular route. On the second day backtrack to the junction mentioned in Hike 95 and make a moderate-to-steep descent along Chain Lakes creek. In ⅓ mile the trail veers north to a nearby junction with a lateral trail heading west to the Chiquito Pass-Buck Camp trail (**Hike 94**). This westbound lateral descends ¾ mile to a signed spur trail, which you can descend a few hundred yards to a cold,

bubbly, rust-stained soda spring that is similar to the ones in Tuolumne Meadows. Beyond the spur trail the lateral trail drops and climbs across ground moraines and bedrock slabs, terminating in 2¾ miles.

Rather than take this alternate route to Givens Lake (as briefly described in **Hike 94**), we continue north on a winding, rolling path, first passing a couple of stagnant ponds. From bedrock benches and slabs we see forested Moraine Mountain, a broad mass to the northwest. Nearing the South Fork Merced River, we note that the landscape becomes gentler—almost flat—and the lodgepoles, being ideally suited to it, completely exclude red firs and western white pines from the forest's cover.

Above the south bank of the South Fork you'll find a medium-size camp that is good when the mosquitoes aren't biting. Once you ford the broad South Fork, you'll find a similar camp—used by equestrians—90 yards downstream. From the bank we head north through Moraine Meadow, which is more of a forest than a meadow. In 200 yards we come to an east-west trail and now join followers of **Hike 98** for a 1½-mile traverse west. After walking ½ mile along

Givens Lake, sitting on bedrock, dammed by an impervious moraine

it, we pass through a bedrock gap, then soon swing northwest down into a small though impressive gully with straight, vertical walls. About ⅓ mile further we cross a small creek that descends from slopes below Merced Pass, then in a like distance we climb southwest to a junction, passing a crescentic pond midway. From here, those following **Hike 98** depart north, bound for Merced Pass.

Among red firs, western white pines and lodgepole pines we start southwest, drop into a gully, curve into a larger one and then climb more than 300 feet to a forested, boulder-strewn pass. If you want to climb Moraine Mountain, above us, this is the starting point for the shortest cross-country ascent to its summit. Lacking views, it is a worthy excursion only for confirmed earth scientists.

From the pass we descend past a wet meadow—rich in corn lilies—then continue to gradually drop as we cut across slopes down to a lower saddle. Here you'll see a faint, ducked path—our route—climbing northwest up a broad ridge from us. One-quarter mile up it we reach a wet meadow in which one could lose the tread. It heads at a 250° bearing across the meadow, turns north, and in a ¼ mile stretch, crosses three prominent lateral moraines before ending at the northeast shore of Givens Lake. What makes these moraines prominent is not their height (which isn't great) but rather the way they stand out so sharply above the bedrock bench they lie upon. The innermost moraine curves around Givens Lake, enclosing its

bedrock basin with an amazingly leakproof earthfill dam.

You'll find the best campsite near the blunt peninsula at the lake's south end. Spend your second night at this shallow, relatively warm lake, perhaps getting in a good swim and catching one or more rainbow trout before the sunlight fades on Moraine Mountain.

The next morning retrace your steps back to the signed saddle and then make a mile-long, 600-foot descent southwest through a red-fir forest to the lodgepole-lined Givens Meadow creek. After crossing it—on large, upstream boulders in early season—we curve west and soon parallel the creek's south bank for a brief spell. Leaving the south bank of the creek, we swing southwest on a short ascent to a wide gap. On it our trail passes *through* a tiny, seasonal pond that lies due west of a minor summit.

About 250 yards past this low summit, we reach the first of two paths that leave our wider trail just before a shallow saddle by an exfoliating cliff. We take the first path, which soon merges with the second; then we descend in a short, fairly steep ½ mile to a junction with an east-west trail. West, it climbs 0.6 mile to a junction with the main trail we recently left. East, we go 60 yards to a signed junction. You could continue east, taking this lateral trail over to the Chain Lakes-Moraine Meadow trail for a second visit to middle Chain Lake. This hike, however, reverses the first part of **Hike 94** for a 3.1 mile walk southeast to Chiquito Pass. From that pass retrace your steps to the trailhead.

Hike 97   Lillian Lake Loop

Distance: 12.6 miles (20.2 km) semiloop; side trips extra

Grade: 3D, easy 3-day hike

Trailhead: Follow the Hike 94 trailhead description 20.0 miles up Road 5S07 to the junction with Road 5S04, opposite Globe Rock. Continue along Road 5S07—an obvious route—7.5 miles to a junction with the Norris Creek road. This junction is 0.4 mile past the Bowler Group Camp entrance and 100 yards *before* a crossing of Ethelfreda Creek. Your first of three major trailheads is found at a parking area above Norris Creek, 1.9 miles up the Norris Creek road. Be aware that there may be a rough creekbed crossing about ½ mile before the parking area. This trailhead provides the shortest mileage for any hike along the Lillian Lake Loop. It is also the start of a trail to Norris and Jackass lakes, the latter being worthy goals. The route to these lakes is not described, since when I mapped the routes to them back in 1977, they lay outside Minarets Wilderness. They were incorporated in 1984, when the wilderness was greatly expanded and its name was changed to Ansel Adams Wilderness. **F6.**

The second major trailhead—*the one from which the trail mileages of Hikes 97 and 98 are based*—is at the end of Road 5S05. This forks left only 100 yards *after* Road 5S07 crosses Ethelfreda Creek, and then it climbs 2.3 miles to the trailhead and its large turnaround/parking area. Logging operations have added spurs to this road, but you should not have any problem finding the trailhead. By starting at it you hike 0.6 mile farther in each direction than you would from the first trailhead. **F6.**

The third major trailhead is in the Clover Meadow area. On Road 5S07 drive east from the Road 5S05 fork, passing Road 5S88, which branches south 0.4 mile to Minarets Pack Station and then meets the Minarets Road. This road branches south 52 miles to North Fork—definitely the long way to any of our trailheads. Continue on Road 5S07 1¾ miles up to a junction at the Clover Meadow Ranger Station, which is at mile 31.5 along Road 5S07. Turn left here and drive 0.3 mile along Road 4S59 to the Clover Meadow Campground entrance. Midway along this road the signed Fernandez Trail starts from its south (left) side. You can also locate this trail at the far end of the campground. This trail climbs 1.4 miles west to the north side of the parking area at the second major trailhead. **F6.**

Introduction: You could hike this entire circuit in one day without overexerting yourself. However, it is so scenic that three days are recommended—sufficient time to visit Lady, Chittenden, Staniford and Rainbow lakes. Visiting all four of these desirable lakes lengthens your hike to 21.1 miles (33.9 km) and changes its classification to a 5E, moderate 3-day hike.

Description: From our trailhead at the end of Road 5S05, you could head west into Ansel Adams Wilderness on any of three trails. We'll enter it on the lake-blessed Lillian Loop trail and return on the Fernandez trail. The third trail begins on a crest that is reached from our trailhead by hiking ¼ mile north along the closed section of Road 5S05. This trail is described in the eastward direction in the last part of **Hike 100.**

Starting west up the signed Fernandez trail, we pass through a typical mid-elevation Sierra forest: white fir, Jeffrey pine, lodgepole pine and scrubby huckleberry oak. After ⅓ mile of gentle ascent across morainal slopes, we reach the lower end of a small meadow and meet a junction at its west side. From it a trail meanders almost a mile to the vicinity of the first trailhead before climbing up to Norris and Jackass lakes. Beyond the junction our trail's gradient becomes a moderate one, and red firs quickly begin to replace white firs. The forest temporarily yields to brush—huckleberry oak, chinquapin, green manzanita and snow bush—as we struggle up short, steep switchbacks below a small, exfoliating "dome." Now entering Ansel Adams Wilderness, we have a steady ¼-mile pull up to a near-crest junction with a steep, mile-long trail from the first major trailhead. If you come up this short, exhausting route, remember this junction, for it can be easy to miss as you later descend the Fernandez trail.

We continue a moderate ascent up the Fernandez trail for only a few more minutes, then reach a crest junction. If you are following **Hike 98** and are in a hurry, you can keep right, staying on the Fernandez trail. Although this lakeless route bypasses the best part of Hike 97, it will save you 2.4 miles in your ascent to Fernandez Creek.

Heading west toward peaks and lakes, we veer left and start up the Lillian Loop trail. This

Dark, metamorphic Madera Peak stands above granite-rimmed Lady Lake

trail's first 2 miles are generally easy. Conifers shade our way first past a waist-deep pond, on our right, then later past two wet, moraine-dammed meadows—both mosquito havens. Then the trail climbs to a bedrock notch in a granitic crest. On the crest we arc around a stagnant pond, then make a short descent to a junction just above Madera Creek. If you plan to camp at very popular Vandeburg Lake, you could leave the trail here and descend southwest to find some campsites along its east shore.

From the junction the right branch—for horses—descends north to Madera Creek, then circles counterclockwise ⅓ mile to rejoin the left branch above the lake's west shore. We take the left branch, curving above good-to-excellent campsites along the lake's north shore. From them, steep, granitic Peak 9852, on Madera Peak's northeast ridge, is reflected in the lake's placid early-morning waters.

Where the two trail branches reunite, we start a 250-yard climb up bedrock to a trail junction at the edge of a lodgepole flat. Here a spur trail takes off south and climbs gently to moderately up to a large campsite on the north shore of granite-rimmed Lady Lake. On the east-shore moraine that juts into the lake, you'll find an even better campsite, though not quite as large. This lake's irregular form, speckled with several boulder islands, makes it a particularly attractive lake to camp at or to visit, especially

since it is backdropped by hulking, metamorphic Madera Peak. Like all the lakes you might visit along this hike, Lady Lake is stocked with trout. Because it is shallow, it is a good lake for swimming from late July through mid-August.

Beyond the Lady Lake trail junction our Lillian Loop trail crosses the lodgepole flat, then climbs a couple of hundred feet up fairly open granitic slabs. On them you can stop and absorb the skyline panorama from the Minarets south to the Mt. Goddard area in Kings Canyon National Park. During the period of maximum glaciation virtually all of this panorama except for high crests and mountain peaks was under ice.

Descending northwest from a ridge on a moderate-to-steep gradient, we reach, in ¼ mile, an easily missed, unsigned junction. Here, close to a Staniford lake creek, one can start a mile-long climb up to cliffbound Chittenden Lake. (If you miss this junction, then you probably wouldn't be able to follow the obscure, ducked trail to that lake anyway.) Where the ducked trail curves from northwest to southwest at the lower end of a small, wet meadow, you could follow an equally obscure trail ¼ mile northwest up to extremely shallow Shirley Lake—best left to the cows.

The last slabby trail section to Chittenden Lake is so steep that cows and horses rarely visit it. Chittenden may be the most beautiful of all the lakes in this part of Ansel Adams Wilderness—though Lady and Rainbow lakes offer competition. Although Chittenden's water is usually in the low 60s, the lake's three bedrock islands will certainly tempt swimmers. If there are more than two backpackers in your group, don't plan to camp at this fairly deep lake, for flat space is really at a premium.

Back in the Staniford Lakes basin you go north on the Lillian Loop trail only about 200 yards past the unsigned Chittenden Lake trail junction before you see a Staniford lake. A waist-deep, grass-lined lakelet, this water body, like Shirley Lake, is best left to the cows. After a similar distance you'll come to a trailside pond atop a broad granitic crest. In this vicinity you can leave the trail, and on your third optional excursion descend southeast briefly cross country on low-angle slabs to the largest of the Staniford Lakes. This is certainly the best lake to swim in, and if any sizable lake along this route will warm up to the low 70s in early August, it will be this one. The great bulk of the lake is less than 5 feet deep, its only deep spot being at a diving area along the west shore.

More ponds are seen along the northbound Lillian Loop trail before it dips into a usually dry gully. It then diagonals up along a ridge with many glacier-polished slabs. We soon cross the ridge, then quickly descend to Lillian Lake's outlet creek, which drains southeast into Shirley Creek. A short walk upstream ends at the lake's low dam and an adjacent, lodgepole-shaded area that once comprised the largest campsite in this part of the wilderness. Now, camping is prohibited within 400 feet of the northeast shore; be inventive and try elsewhere. Being the largest and deepest lake we'll see along this hike, Lillian Lake is also the coldest—not good for swimming. However, its large population of trout does attract many anglers.

With our basic hike now half over, we leave the lake's outlet and descend a mile east past lodgepoles, hemlocks, western white pines and red firs down to a two-branched creek with easy fords. The Lillian Loop trail ends in ¼ mile, after a short, stiff climb over a gravelly knoll. Here, at a junction on a fairly open slope, we rejoin the Fernandez trail. **Hike 98** describes this trail from this point upward.

Your fourth optional side trip ascends this trail 1 mile northwest up to a junction, from which the Rainbow Lake trail first wanders ¾ mile southwest and then ¾ mile northwest to that prized lake. This trail unfortunately becomes vague on bedrock slabs where it bends from southwest to northwest, and unsuspecting hikers often continue southwest down toward Lillian Lake, 400 feet below, before realizing their mistake. The correct route ends at a large, former camp 50 yards above Rainbow Lake. Today, camping is prohibited within ¼ mile of the lakeshore. One can cross this multilobed lake by swimming from island to island.

Youths relaxing and fishing at the largest of the Staniford Lakes

View southwest toward Sing Peak, from Lillian Lake's outlet

Island-blessed Rainbow Lake

From the Lillian Loop-Fernandez trails junction we descend ⅓ mile east to a linear gully, follow it a bit, then drift over to the crest of a moraine. After its end we soon engage a few short switchbacks near some junipers, and here get a good view of much of our basin's landscape.

Below the switchbacks, the Fernandez trail descends ½ mile to a trail junction. If you were to follow the trail north 70 yards to a crest saddle, you would see that it forks into the Post Creek trail (left) and the Timber Creek trail (right). The Post Creek trail ends after a 1.9-mile climb to a packer camp on the West Fork of Granite Creek. The Timber Creek trail eventually climbs up to the Joe Crane Lake trail (**Hike 99**).

From the junction, the Fernandez trail descends briefly past lodgepoles and junipers to a gravelly flat along the north bank of Madera Creek. This spacious flat is well suited for camping, and from it you can inspect the dark plug of olivine basalt, above you, which was once part of the throat of a cinder cone. On our flat, two trail spurs quickly join to head east and cross wide Madera Creek about 250 yards below the Fernandez trail ford. **Hike 100** exits along this route. You too could follow it 2.9 miles to the old abandoned Strawberry Mine Road, then pound along its bed ¼ mile south to the trailhead.

However, our hike adheres to the Fernandez trail, which climbs a full 400 feet higher than the alternate route. Our ridge ascent ends after contouring southeast to a wilderness-boundary junction with the start of the Lillian Loop trail. From it we have a scenic, pleasant descent as we retrace our first day's steps back to the trailhead.

Hike 98   Southeast Park Loop

Distance: 48.0 (77.3 km) semiloop trip
Grade: 6F, moderate 6-day hike
Trailhead: Same as the Hike 97 trailhead. **F6.**
Introduction: Along this double-loop hike you cross four major divides and sample lakes in the Granite Creek, South Fork Merced River, Illilouette Creek and Merced River basins. On one divide you cross Red Peak Pass, at 11,180 feet, the highest pass in Yosemite National Park.

Description: On your first hiking day follow **Hike 97** either to the large Staniford lake or ⅔ mile farther to Lillian Lake. Then, on the second day, head east to the Fernandez trail junction mentioned in that hike. From that point we make a mile-long, winding climb northwest up granite slabs through an open forest to a meadowside trail junction immediately beyond a low gap. From here a trail, described in **Hike 97**, climbs 1½ miles up to rewarding Rainbow Lake. We, however, keep to the Fernandez trail, climbing ½ mile north to a broad crest, then traversing ¾ mile northwest to a junction. Early on this traverse we recognize the Park boundary's two named summits, broad Triple Divide Peak and narrow Post Peak. At the junction, above the south bank of Fernandez Creek, a trail branches right, eventually climbing to Post Peak Pass. We'll descend on that trail, which is described in **Hike 100.**

Keeping to the Fernandez trail, we immediately pass a good campsite, on our left, jump across Fernandez Creek, and above its north bank meet a connecting trail that briefly descends to a meadow and the Post Peak Pass trail. More campsites are found near this meadow.

Our Fernandez trail climbs west and after ½ mile it switchbacks high above Fernandez Creek

to give us down-canyon views. These disappear as we curve right into a bowl and meet a trail that makes an exhausting ¼-mile climb to Rutherford Lake. If you make this side trip, you'll find the best camps along the east shore, about 200 yards beyond the south-end dam. Another dam is at the lake's northeast bay.

Beyond the Rutherford Lake trail we face a two-stage ascent to Fernandez Pass. Short switchbacks elevate us 200 feet to a broad, shallow gap, from which we descend into a large, granite-lined bowl. After crossing its cow-infested subalpine meadow, we begin our second stage—far more taxing—which climbs by more than two dozen switchbacks 450 feet almost up to an unnamed crest saddle. From the saddle, which is well dressed with whitebark pines and mountain hemlocks, the view west is surprisingly unimpressive. However, from our trail the view east is quite impressive, ranging over much of the Granite Creek basin and extending to the Ritter Range and the central Sierra Nevada crest. From the saddle we traverse south ¼ mile across generally open slopes, heading toward a fin on the boundary ridge just yards before dropping to 10,175-foot-high Fernandez Pass.

The pass is named for Sergeant Joseph Fernandez, who with Lieutenant Harry Benson and others explored, mapped and patrolled the Yosemite backcountry in the 1890s. They also planted trout, starting a practice that continued without serious question until the 1970s, when biologists began to study the ecological effect of fish in the high country. At the pass, decked with ragged hemlocks, lodgepoles and whitebark pines, your views are far more restrictive than from the saddle you recently left. You'll note

From Fernandez pass (l. to r.): Post Peak, Banner Peak, Mt. Ritter, Minarets and Iron Mountain

that an old trail drops northeast down a gully to the granite-lined bowl. Though still used by many hikers, this trail was abandoned years ago because of its steepness and the long-lasting snowfield that lingered in much of the gully. Unlike our overly engineered ascent to the pass, our descent is steep, dropping 600 feet along an old trail to a junction. Along this descent we see Breeze Lake, where we'll spend our second night.

From the junction we follow a winding path toward this lake. Midway to it, however, the path dies out along the west shore of a reflective pond. You continue upward, soon entering a straight, joint-controlled gully that takes you to deep, rockbound Breeze Lake. Being larger than average and also lying in a cirque at the foot of a high ridge, the lake lives up to its name. A few small campsites will be found along the lake's north and west shores.

On your third morning, return to the main trail and start west down the canyon. Midway to a chest-deep lake and its shallower neighbor, we pass some giant mountain hemlocks and mature lodgepoles—both among the best to be seen in the Park. During the afternoon the deeper lake can provide a refreshing swim, and its shore makes a good spot for a trail break. From these small lakes our descent along morainal ground quickly steepens, then we cross the lakes' creek for an easing descent to the wildflowered banks of the South Fork Merced River. Once on its north bank—sometimes reached by a wet ford— we walk a viewless mile along a rolling trail to a junction in Moraine Meadow. By walking south 200 yards through the lodgepole-invaded meadow, you can reach the South Fork, which has a medium-size camp above its south bank and a similar one 90 yards downstream on its north bank.

Hike 96 joins our route at the Moraine Meadow junction, and continuing west on our trail, we pass through a bedrock gap after ½ mile, then soon swing northwest down into a small though impressive gully with straight, vertical walls. About ⅓ mile farther we cross a small creek, then in a like distance climb southwest to a junction, passing a crescentic pond midway. Here, those following **Hike 96** turn left, bound for Givens Lake.

We turn right and contour north ½ mile to the wildflowered creek we earlier crossed, crossing it twice more. A short, steep climb then ensues, bringing us up to a small meadow, at whose head we cross our now-trickling creek. With the pass now more or less in sight, we climb easily over to our final creek crossing—hardly worth noting— then make a final, short push up to signed 9295-foot Merced Pass. Lodgepoles and western white pines totally preclude any view, so, after catching our breath, we descend ¾ mile to a creek that drains Upper Merced Pass Lake. Just before this creek you can traverse east across slabs to the nearby lake, which is blessed with very good campsites.

Above the northeast bank of the lake's outlet creek, we come to a junction from which Hike 89 descends northwest down Illilouette Creek canyon. We now follow part of **Hike 89** in reverse, climbing about 2.6 miles up to the northwest shore of Lower Ottoway Lake, to spend our third night. On day four, we continue backtracking along Hike 89, climbing 2.1 miles breathlessly up to Red Peak Pass before making a generally descending, 6.6-mile trek to a trail junction beside a tributary of the Triple Peak Fork of the Merced River.

After spending our fourth night somewhere in this vicinity, we bridge the tributary as in **Hike 88**, using a downstream log, if available.

Lower Ottoway Lake and Merced Peak

Approaching Post Peak Pass, you have a view back at a broad, open expanse

On a trail we then make a rapid ford of the Triple Peak Fork. From this easy ford our trail makes a gentle ascent south, paralleling the unseen tributary for ½ mile to the start of a switchbacking climb northeast. This 550-foot climb is generally a viewless one, due to lodgepoles and hemlocks, though you can get an occasional view north of the Mt. Florence ridge and of the Matthes Crest, in the distance west of it. Our climb ends on a small flat below the west spur of unseen Isberg Peak. Here, 1⅔ miles from the Triple Peak Fork, we leave **Hike 88** and head south from a tall cairn. In ⅓ mile we enter a broad, open expanse—an awesome landscape of a sort not seen anywhere else along Yosemite's trails. From the northwest edge of this expanse you could traverse ¼ mile east to a fairly large, windswept lake with a sandy beach along its north shore. Protective lodgepole pines shelter a campsite near it.

On our open trail we see a pond lying immediately west of the unseen lake, then soon enter a struggling grove of lodgepoles growing on rocky ground. Venturing beyond this grove is unwise in threatening weather, for we won't find any more protective cover until we cross Post Peak Pass and descend *below* Porphyry Lake.

From the grove our trail gradually curves left, and looking back, we have a startling view: we seem to be at land's end, with the world dropping off beyond our broad, alpine surface. Starting to climb, we can scan an entire stretch of crest from Isberg Peak clockwise to Triple Divide Peak. After a moderate ascent for a 200-foot gain, we arrive at a meadowy junction to which **Hike 100**, from visible Isberg Pass, descends. Now we follow that hike, first ⅓ mile generally east up to a crest saddle, then south along the crest to Post Peak Pass. Hike 100 descends past Porphry Lake and you should spend your last trail night well below it, perhaps at Post Creek or Fernandez Creek. The next day, hike out to your trailhead via the Fernandez trail, as described in the last part of **Hike 97**.

Hike 99   Cora and Joe Crane Lakes

Distance: 18.6 miles (29.9 km) round trip
Grade: 4D, moderate 2-day hike

Trailhead: As in the description of the route to the third Hike 97 trailhead, drive 31.5 miles up Road 5S07 to the Clover Meadow Ranger Station. Continue 0.5 mile along the main road to a junction, from where the rocky, narrow Granite Creek road winds 1.0 mile to a parking area, in Granite Creek Campground, just before multibranched Granite Creek. Cross it *at your own risk* since there is no towing service available. The signed Isberg trail begins from your road only a few yards east of Granite Creek and its creekside Road 4S57 junction. If you don't want to get your feet wet, start south on a road to lower Granite Creek Campground, reaching a horse bridge in about 120 yards. Cross it over to Road 4S57. Walking north, you'll still have to contend with the East Fork of Granite Creek, which is smaller than the multibranched West Fork. **F6.**

In some years the Granite Creek road may be snowbound or impassable through early July. Then park your car near the Clover Meadow Ranger Station, walk 230 yards up Road 5S07, then start on the Mammoth trail, which is mentioned near the end of this hike. **F6.**

Introduction: Granite Creek Campground, our trailhead, was designed with horseback riders in mind. Because our trailhead is one of the most remote in the Sierra Nevada—a 1½-hour drive from the nearest settlement, Bass Lake—there are relatively few hikers. Beyond Cora Lakes, a favorite with packers, you'll have most of the glaciated, subalpine scenery to yourself. If your time is limited to 1 or 2 days, then middle Cora Lake is a worthy goal in itself. It is a 9.2-mile (14.8 km) round trip.

Description: Because old yellow license plates are nailed high on trailside tree trunks, our Isberg trail is easily followed even where there are still abundant snow patches. The trail starts across a lodgepole flat, then climbs to a slightly higher one along which we approach bouldery East Fork Granite Creek. The creek's large boulders, like our flat's gravels, are glacier-derived. That is, they were deposited here by a retreating glacier. During the maximum glaciation—the Sherwin, which lasted from about

900–800,000 years ago—almost the entire Granite Creek basin (both forks) lay under ice. Only the metavolcanic summit of Timber Knob, high above the Cora Lakes, rose above the sea of ice, which extended continuously to Mt. Goddard, in northern Kings Canyon National Park, about 42 miles southeast of us.

After paralleling the East Fork for a few minutes, we begin to climb through a predominantly fir forest and soon enter a poorly defined side canyon. In it we cross, then recross its diminutive creek, whose bed has oversize boulders, deposited by a glacial stream, not by the current creek. Near its head the canyon becomes a well-defined gully, which we ascend to a forested divide separating a 7842-foot-high knoll from the south end of the Post Peak-Timber Knob crest. From the divide we circle clockwise, passing many firs and a few aspens before climbing high on the wall of a deep box canyon. Just before some deep, parallel furrows—one confining the cascading East Fork—we see pyramidal Squaw Dome, 6 miles to the south, and also broad, gentle Kaiser Ridge, on the far, hazy horizon behind it.

At the brink of one furrow we enter Ansel Adams Wilderness, spot a medium-size creek-side campsite, and hike up a shallow, forested canyon. After a 1⅓-mile ascent, we come to another medium-size campsite, this one beside a junction with the Stevenson trail. That trail immediately crosses the East Fork, then gives rise to other trails that radiate across the upper San Joaquin Basin. These routes are favorites

Yosemite boundary crest, from meadow by East Fork Granite Creek

Post Peak above timberline Joe Crane Lake

with horsemen, including the route to Devils Postpile and Reds Meadow.

Our Isberg trail curves left for a brief upstream hike, and is joined by two faint trails just before crossing the broad East Fork. The first, a horse trail, comes 2 miles from a road in a logging area above Strawberry Tungsten Mine. This route is not open to the public. The second trail, starting a few yards before the ford, heads about 200 yards upstream before dying out. A usually plentiful supply of mosquitoes tends to discourage camping by this bank.

After making the typically wet ford of the East Fork, you go but 35 yards east to a bend. A less-used, ¼-mile lateral trail continues straight ahead over to the Stevenson trail. If you start across it, you're likely to see an established packer camp not far south from it. The broader Isberg trail angles north from this lateral and soon makes a short, steep climb that fortunately yields to a gentle ¾-mile ascent through a verdant, rich forest growing on deep, morainal soils. Our ascent ends just after we cross Cora Creek and arrive at the southeast corner of middle Cora Lake. Camps once dotted the lake's east shore, but now camping is prohibited within 400 feet of this shore. Good sites are along the north shore. Though the lake's water may be unfit to drink untreated, its shallow, trout-stocked water is excellent for swimming.

Beyond middle Cora Lake we make a short, dusty climb to the top of a low volcanic ridge. An even shorter descent brings us to a junction with the east-starting Chetwood trail. If you are hiking only to middle Cora Lake, but would like an alternate route back, you can take this easy trail 2¼ miles over to the Stevenson trail, then go ½ mile southwest down that trail to the East Fork and the Isberg trail. The total distance of this semiloop hike is 11.1 miles (17.9 km).

Although we now leave most horseback riders and backpackers behind, we meet many of this canyon's cattle population, which can make us forget we are in a wilderness. Our 2.4-mile hike northwest to the Joe Crane Lake trail is an amazingly easy one. At first our trail hugs the base of a volcanic plateau, keeping just above wet meadows. After 1.1 miles we pass the meadow-bordered site of Knoblock Cabin—no longer standing—which is just past our first view of Isberg and Post peaks. Sometimes you may see a coyote in this meadow looking for ground squirrels as much as for a sick calf. You can camp by the meadow's end, above most of the cow pollution. Here we cross the signed East Fork Granite Creek and find better camping along its west bank. Joe Crane Creek is also signed, encountered after a mile of fairly easy ascent. A few minutes beyond, we reach the Joe Crane Lake trail. **Hike 100** continues the description of the Isberg trail up-canyon.

Mountain hemlocks temporarily dominate our shady, well-graded climb of 300 feet up the Joe Crane Lake trail. Then, in more open terrain, the trail contours south before bending southwest gently up to a slab at the base of a descending ridge. Here you'll see a trail branching left down to nearby Joe Crane Creek—the Timber Creek trail. From it our trail climbs more than 500 feet to the lake. Above the east shore of Joe Crane Lake is a lodgepole-shaded packer site, complete with table. A smaller camp lies on the lake's southwest shore. Certainly the packer camp is more desirable, for from it you can watch the sun's first rays light up Post Peak, a scene that is exquisitely reflected in the lake's tranquil waters. Whether you come here for the view, the peace, the trout, or a swim (temperature in the low to mid 60s), you're almost certain to be pleased.

Hike 100   Granite Creek Forks Loop

Distance: 28.4 miles (45.7 km) loop trip
Grade: 5E, moderate 3-day hike
Trailhead: Same as the Hike 99 trailhead. **F6.**
Introduction: Those wanting to make a longer, more scenic loop than Hike 99 should try this loop. It crosses three alpine passes, entering Yosemite National Park for just under a mile between the first two. It then descends to the Porphyry Lake environs, which geologists and nongeologists alike will admit is one of the strangest landscapes to be found in the entire Sierra Nevada.

Description: As in **Hike 99**, climb 4.6 miles up the Isberg trail to middle Cora Lake, then continue on an easy ascent 3.1 miles to the Joe Crane Lake trail junction. Keeping to the Isberg trail, we leave Hike 99 as we make an easy up-canyon climb ⅔ mile to a ford of East Fork Granite Creek. Now a multistage climb to Isberg Pass begins. Here, short, steep switchbacks up at around 9000 feet can tire hikers. If you stop and rest, you might look to the west and try to determine the rate of recovery of a lodgepole grove that in the '70s was mowed down by a snow avalanche from the west. The gradient abates after more than 300 feet of precious altitude gain, and after a relaxing ¼-mile creekside ascent we reach a junction with a trail to McClure Lake. This trail immediately fords the creek, skirts the south shore of Sadler Lake, and climbs ½ mile to that cold, deep lake. A massive cliff encircles most of McClure Lake, but its esthetic appeal is offset by a dam on the lake's outlet. Furthermore, the tightly rimmed lake has no flat space for adequate camping.

Better camping is found at Sadler Lake, which the Isberg trail reaches in less than 200 yards beyond the McClure Lake trail junction. Our trail curves to the lake's north shore, the site of a large, former camp. Today, camping is prohibited within 400 feet of this shore. Try smaller camps, such as the one near the inlet on the lake's west shore. These are the last good ones until Post Creek. Sadler Lake, though fairly large, is extremely shallow—barely chest-deep.

From the north shore of Sadler Lake our trail starts its second steep ascent, making feeble efforts to switchback up the slopes. As before, after 300 feet of ascent, the gradient eases and at a sharp bend left, a sign points toward alpine McGee Lake, unseen on a broad bench ½ mile northeast of us. We climb southwest, reaching a ridge that dams shallow, bedrock-lined lower Isberg Lake. On the short descent to the north shore of this lake you'll probably note some giant erratics, looking as fresh as on the day a glacier dropped them. You could camp among lodgepoles north of the lake, but the sites are definitely inferior to those at Sadler Lake.

Donning our dark glasses, we climb south up the lake's inlet creek, leave it, and pass a large mountain hemlock before reaching the McClure Lake Vista, on a barren, granitic ridge. From it you see the deep lake lying at the base of a forbidding cliff. A moderate climb, made difficult by thinning air, takes us ¼ mile west up to truly alpine, 10,090-foot-high upper Isberg Lake. Our trail keeps its distance from the lake's west shore in order to avoid its fragile alpine turf. The trail then does a remarkable thing: it zigzags more than two dozen times, climbing—you

Sadler Lake and the Yosemite National Park crest boundary

guessed it—more than 300 feet northwest *away* from Isberg Pass. From the top of this climb you have nearly a half-mile traverse over to 10,520-foot Isberg Pass.

An old trail used to climb from upper Isberg Lake directly southwest up to the pass, much as did an old trail up to Fernandez Pass (**Hike 98**). The old Isberg trail, however, was not painfully steep, nor was it in a snowbound gully. And, being entirely across solid bedrock, it posed no danger to either hiker or environment. The author recommends that you leave the lower switchbacks and head cross country directly up the old route to the pass. But if you are on horseback, then by all means keep to the switchbacking trail.

Leaving signed Isberg Pass and its prostrate whitebark pines, we enter Yosemite National Park and actually climb a bit, going from ledge to ledge, before dropping ½ mile on an irregular course to a trail junction. Near the trail junction, you can scan most of the upper Merced River basin, rimmed by a spectacular alpine crest. The Clark Range borders the basin to the west, the Cathedral Range to the north and the Park boundary crest to the east. With map and compass you can identify many peaks, including Mt. Hoffmann and Tuolumne Peak on the distant skyline about 18 miles northwest of us.

From the junction **Hike 98** joins our route as we climb ⅓ mile up to an unnamed saddle—at 10,620 feet—on the boundary crest. As at Isberg Pass, we now have a view of the Ritter Range, but also one of upper Ward Lake, below us, and much of the enormous San Joaquin Basin. Staying at or near the crest, we traverse south for ½ mile, getting high from the spectacular views as well as from the rarefied air. At last we climb almost to the top of Post Peak's northern satellite, then drop to desolate, 10,750-foot Post Peak Pass. Despite its height, its orientation prevents us from having the far-ranging views found along the crest traverse.

Our trail descends from Post Peak Pass via short, very steep switchbacks that force us to constantly brake. Be careful on this descent, for there are many loose boulders and this is no place for an injury. After dropping more than 550 feet, we skirt across bedrock benches above the east shore of tiny Porphyry Lake. The lake—a home for yellow-leg frogs—is a suitable place to rest your aching knees. Camp space, however, is nonexistent.

This area looks like it came down with a very bad case of measles. And not just the lake shore. The "outbreak" spreads across hundreds of

acres, dotting the landscape with countless thousands of dark, tightly-packed, beachball-size spheres. Nowhere else in the Sierra will you find such a landscape. Dallas Peck, the USGS geologist who mapped the *Merced Peak* quadrangle, has an explanation for this phenomenon. The "beachballs" are quartz-diorite inclusions in a matrix of rock known as the "granite porphyry of Post Peak." The lighter-colored granite porphyry, which has quartz and feldspar crystals in a fine-grained ground mass, intruded a mass of quartz diorite about 98-100 million years ago. The intrusive process broke the quartz diorite into thousands of angular blocks, and the molten granite, before solidifying, began to melt the blocks, the way water melts ice cubes sitting in it. Because the molten-granite pluton intruded the solid quartz-diorite pluton at a relatively shallow depth, the granite cooled faster than usual. Had the intrusion taken place at the usual, greater depth, the quartz diorite might have been greatly or completely melted, and a typical granitic landscape would have developed.

The "beachballs" stay with us for at least ⅓ mile south of Porphyry Lake, and we leave them only after our moderately descending trail crosses a gully and takes on a gentler gradient. Now in cow pastures once again, we make a 1½-mile traverse south through wet meadows before entering a lodgepole forest. In it we soon start down the snout of a giant lateral moraine, briefly angle east, then descend ¾ mile southwest to Post Creek. Crossing to the west bank of Post Creek, you'll find an adequate campsite. It would be rated "good" were it not for the abundance of mosquitoes. A tent is highly desirable here.

"Beachball" landscape near Porphyry Lake

The route climbs southwest from the Post Creek camp, cutting through a low divide after ¼ mile, then descending toward a reedy lake. On the short descent to it you'll see some more exposures of intruded quartz-diorite. Our trail skirts along the southeast shore of the small lake, though at its outlet a second trail briefly descends the north bank, only to climb back up the south bank. This trail is taken when the first is flooded. From the lake's southwest end you can continue a few yards in that direction and make camp—away from most of the mosquitoes—on a low divide. Leaving this gap, the trail drops southwest ¼ mile, crossing a creekbed immediately before a junction with the Slab Lakes trail. This primitive trail— essentially cross country along its last ¾ mile— climbs 2⅓ miles to the two timberline lakes. They can serve as a staging area for a strenuous but safe ascent up Triple Divide Peak.

Fifty yards west of the trail junction we cross the main Slab Lakes creek—one of three parallel washes—then momentarily enter a small, cow-grazed meadow. Camps can be found among lodgepoles near the confluence of Slab Lakes creek and Fernandez Creek, as well as up Fernandez Creek. At the meadow's southwest end we meet Fernandez Creek, with a trail ascending each bank. We cross the creek and climb 250 yards up to a junction with the Fernandez trail. On this trail we hike 1¼ miles southeast over to a junction with the Rainbow Lake trail, then continue for another mile down to a junction with the Lillian Loop trail. This 2¼-mile stretch is described in the first paragraph of **Hike 98**.

From our junction you can take a highly scenic, lake-blessed alternate route by following the first half of **Hike 97**, described in the opposite direction, along the Lillian Loop trail. You'll end at the Fernandez trail parking area, from which you follow an alternate route, described below.

The shorter, regular route, however, leaves the Lillian Loop trail junction and descends the Fernandez trail, as in the second half of **Hike 97**, for 1.8 miles down to a gravelly flat along the north bank of Madera Creek. Here you branch left, leave the Fernandez trail, and cross the creek about 250 yards below the Fernandez trail ford.

Leaving the east bank, our trail switchbacks steeply up to a nearby gap that rewards us with a crest panorama from Madera Peak past Sing, Gale, Triple Divide and Post peaks to Timber Knob. Now, on the remaining 2¾ miles of trail, our route is mostly downhill or an easy traverse. A few more views are had before we leave a crest and wind in and out of gullies and strike across forested slopes. Our unsigned, narrow trail ends on the old, abandoned Strawberry Mine Road. From this point just 10 yards south of a crest, we can follow the road in either direction.

The alternate route—almost a mile longer— heads south on the road ¼ mile over to the Fernandez trail trailhead and parking area. If you've decided to extend your hike by taking the Lillian Loop trail, you'll end here. From the north side of the parking area you descend 1.4 miles, passing either through or just above Clover Meadow Campground minutes before reaching the Clover Meadow Ranger Station. From it you follow the main road 230 yards northeast to the start of the Mammoth trail—a pleasant, mile-long route that takes you to lower Granite Creek Campground. A ⅔-mile walk north up its road gets you to the Granite Creek Campground road and your nearby car. About 120 yards before this junction, a sturdy horse bridge crosses Granite Creek. Beneath it you can clean up in chilly, potholed pools. However, watch your step on the adjacent slippery, smooth rock.

The shorter, regular route immediately crosses the crest, rounds a gully, then descends northeast to a junction with a creekside road. Northwest, it is Road 4S02, on private property; southwest, it is Road 5S05. In times of high water you might want to climb ⅓ mile southeast up Road 5S05 to its junction with the broad, new Strawberry Mine Road and follow it an equal distance northeast down to a bridge and the adjacent jeep road. The shorter way, however, is to ford West Fork Granite Creek, climb up to the new Strawberry Mine Road and descend east along it to the jeep road, branching left just 50 yards before the bridge. This rarely used road along the creek takes you to the back side of Granite Creek Campground. About 200 yards before you come to the start of the Isberg trail, you'll see where the creek has cut a small gorge through some bedrock. There, you'll find a refreshing, though chilly, swimming hole.

Chapter 4

Evolution of the Yosemite Landscape

In his first book, *The Mountains of California,* published in 1894, John Muir recollects his first view of the Sierra Nevada back in 1868:

> When I first enjoyed this superb view, one glowing April day, from the summit of the Pacheco Pass, the Central Valley, but little trampled or plowed as yet, was one furred, rich sheet of golden compositae, and the luminous wall of the mountains shone in all its glory. Then it seemed to me the Sierra should be called not the Nevada, or Snowy Range, but the Range of Light. And after ten years spent in the heart of it, rejoicing and wondering, bathing in its glorious floods of light, seeing the sunbursts of morning among the icy peaks, the noonday radiance on the trees and rocks and snow, the flush of the alpenglow, and a thousand dashing waterfalls with their marvelous abundance of irised spray, it still seems to me above all others the Range of Light, the most divinely beautiful of all the mountain-chains I have ever seen.

Although he doesn't explicitly say so, Muir could have added that the pastel colors of the High Sierra's granitic bedrock—generally light gray but almost creamy in places—make it more luminous than the dark, volcanic Cascade Range, the variegated, geologically complex Rocky Mountains or the metamorphic, heavily vegetated Appalachian Mountains. But the high country of Yosemite and the rest of the High Sierra would not be very luminous if the overlying rocks intruded by molten "granite" had not been eroded away, if the volcanic rocks blanketing the northern Sierra had buried the entire range, and if glaciers had not developed on numerous occasions to remove the soil and create vast tracts of granitic-bedrock landscape. Had its complex geologic history taken a different course, the Sierra Nevada might not have gotten its three national parks—Yosemite, Sequoia and Kings. All three were set aside also because of their groves of giant sequoias and because of their glaciated high country. Additionally, Yosemite National Park was set aside also because of its renowned Yosemite Valley, arguably the world's most spectacular, which owes its origin not to unique geologic processes but rather to a unique pattern of major, generally vertical fracture planes in its granitic rock. Today's masterpiece was long in the making, executed over hundreds of millions of years. How was it produced?

To Build a Range

Geologic events during the first 4 billion years of the earth's existence (Precambrian eons—see the Geologic Time Scale) have only a slight relevance to the geologic history of the Sierra Nevada. Basically, over this unimaginably long time, several incipient continents first formed and then grew sporadically as a multitude of crustal blocks periodically collided with the continents. This growth process typically involved an *island arc*—a curving chain of island volcanoes such as today's Japanese Islands. Such arcs rode passively atop an oceanic *lithospheric plate* that was diving beneath the edge of a continent, which lay atop

Left: **Half Dome and Clouds Rest, although granitic, are very different landforms**

GEOLOGIC TIME SCALE

Era	Period	Epoch	Began (years ago)	Duration (years)
Cenozoic	Quaternary	Holocene	10,000	10,000
		Pleistocene	1,640,000	1,630,000
	Neogene	Pliocene	5,200,000	3,560,000
		Miocene	23,300,000	18,100,000
	Paleogene	Oligocene	34,000,000	10,700,000
		Eocene	56,500,000	22,500,000
		Paleocene	65,000,000	8,500,000
Mesozoic	Cretaceous	*Nine*	145,600,000	80,600,000
	Jurassic	*epochs*	208,000,000	62,400,000
	Triassic	*recognized*	245,000,000	37,000,000
Paleozoic	Permian		290,000,000	45,000,000
	Carboniferous	*27*	362,500,000	72,500,000
	Devonian	*epochs*	408,500,000	46,000,000
	Silurian		439,000,000	30,500,000
	Ordovician	*recognized*	510,000,000	71,000,000
	Cambrian		570,000,000	60,000,000

Precambrian eons   4,560,000,000   3,990,000,000

(Three eons with eight eras, the earliest beginning with the earth's formation about 4.560 billion years ago, and the latest ending with the start of the Phanerozoic eon 570 million years ago.)

Source: GTS 89 Definitive Time Scale (shortened and amended)

another plate. (A lithospheric plate is composed of a layer of crust atop a layer of the uppermost part of the earth's mantle. Both layers move more or less together as the plate drifts atop a more "fluid" mantle layer, the *asthenosphere.*)

Each time a chain of island volcanoes atop a plate reached the edge of a continent, it was too buoyant to sink with the diving plate, and instead was thrust against the edge of the continent. If a sufficiently large crustal block was involved, then large-scale compressional forces caused the rocks of both the block and the continent to deform through extensive faulting and folding. This deformation chemically and mineralogically changed the rocks, converting sedimentary rocks to metasedimentary ones and volcanic rocks to metavolcanic ones. Such a deformation event, which can last millions of years, is known as an *orogeny*, a term coined from the Greek word *oros*, which means mountain, since compression typically leads to the formation of mountain ranges.

However, it is one matter to thrust a block against the edge of a continent and another matter to keep it from breaking away. The block and the continent have to be joined together, and this is accomplished through "pluton stitching." This occurs as a lithospheric plate dives beneath another one, eventually reaching such high pressures and temperatures about 60 miles down that it undergoes partial melting. The fraction that melts is called *magma*, and because it is relatively buoyant, it works its way up through the upper mantle and into the crust of the overlying continental plate. Magma usually solidifies there—in the brittle, upper crust typically at depths of 3 to 5 miles—to form a body of rock, a *pluton*, which in the Sierra Nevada is typically of granitic composition. The magma rises into the lower parts of both the accreted block and the continental edge, solidifying as an assemblage of plutons—a *batholith*—which "stitches" the two units together. But if some magma gets too close to the surface before solidifying, it can create a volcanic eruption. Thus where one plate dives beneath another, a volcanic range typically forms above a batholith. The Sierra Nevada's batholith is composite, that is, one with a complex space-time history of pluton emplacement.

The Antler and Sonoma Orogenies

The Antler orogeny was centered in time at the Devonian-Carboniferous boundary (see the Geologic Time Scale), and it was the first orogeny to affect the Sierra Nevada's "lands." Back then, our area's rocks were deep-sea sediments of the ancient Pacific Ocean. A passively riding island arc was thrust into our area to lodge against western North America. This caused extensive deformation and metamorphism through east-directed thrusting of continental-border rocks onto central Nevada, where a mountain range formed. In this orogeny the Sierra's early Paleozoic marine sediments were metamorphosed and today their non-eroded remnants constitute the oldest rocks in the Yosemite area. Exposures of these early Paleozoic metasediments are seen along Highway 140, stretching a few miles west from El Portal. (Farther west, about 1½ miles before the highway bridges South Fork Merced River, there had long been a signed geological exhibit that identified "the area's oldest rocks". However, these are now known to be metasediments of Triassic age.) Remnants of early Paleozoic metasediments are also found east of the Park. The most accessible of these is in Lee Vining Canyon where the steeply descending Tioga Road eases off near the floor of the canyon and curves left around an imposing cliff, which is composed mostly of these ancient metasediments.

North America proper grew slightly westward thanks to the Antler orogeny, so that the continental edge now lay in central Nevada. A relatively quiet geologic period of about 100 million years ensued before another island arc impacted western North America. In the Yosemite area remnants of the late Paleozoic marine sediments (subsequently metamorphosed) that were deposited during this quiet time lie in a south-southeast-oriented belt that includes the Saddlebag Lake and Tioga Crest area and a zone from Dana Meadows past Mono Pass and Mt. Lewis to beyond Parker Peak.

The impact of this second volcanic island arc generated the Sonoma orogeny, which was centered in age around the Permian-Triassic boundary. As before, eastward thrusting generated by this orogeny caused the development of a mountain range that lay just west of the previous mountain range, and North America grew once more as a complex unit of rocks became permanently attached to it. Over Sierran lands, the island arc evolved into a continental-edge range that shed some of its volcanic detritus eastward into a marine basin that lay in present-day western Nevada. Remnants of the range's volcanic rocks (subsequently metamorphosed) are best expressed in a belt outside the Park which runs southeast past Flatiron Ridge to Twin Lakes and then south-southeast through the Green Creek and Virginia Lakes basins. A smaller remnant to the south holds the Alger Lakes.

If magma had been reaching the surface to erupt as lava or other volcanic products, then in all probability it was also cooling at depth to form plutons. The earliest surviving plutons in the Sierra Nevada are located in its southern part. They are about 240 million years old and appear to have formed as the Sonoma orogeny was waning. The earliest farther north, in the Yosemite area, are about 210 million years old—middle Triassic—and are found east of the crest.

After the Sonoma orogeny, the Farallon plate—an ancient oceanic plate underlying much of the Pacific Ocean—gradually changed its angle of attack against the North American plate, becoming increasingly less perpendicular. This caused *subduction,* or diving, to wane while *left-lateral* faulting waxed, the fault zone being preserved today in the Sierra's foothills. (In left-lateral faulting, the land on one side of the fault moves during an earthquake to the left with respect to an observer on the other side. It makes no difference which side of the fault the observer is on.)

During this period when left-lateral faulting was prominent, from about late Triassic through early Jurassic, both plutonism and volcanism were ongoing, although not necessarily at all times. Most of that ancient volcanic landscape has been eroded away, but many of the plutons, which had solidified from magma at a depth a few miles below the earth's surface, still remain. The bulk of these solidified between 210 and 155 million years ago—mostly Jurassic age—and today flank the core of the Sierra Nevada. That core is composed of Cretaceous-age plutons, emplaced mostly between 115 and 88 million years ago, during the middle Cretaceous. All told, 43 plutonic bodies have been identified in the area shown on this book's map.

The Nevadan Orogeny

In the middle Jurassic the angle of attack of the Farallon plate became increasingly more nearly perpendicular to the North American plate. Lands which had been transported hundreds of miles south along the west side of the left-lateral fault were now thrust more or less perpendicular against the Sierra Nevada. The Nevadan orogeny had begun. Named after the Sierra Nevada, where its record is best preserved, this orogeny sutured the range onto western North America. Like earlier orogenies, this one metamorphosed all of the area's previously existing sedimentary, volcanic and metamorphic rocks. One should also bear in mind that rising magma metamorphosed adjacent rocks, adding to the complexity of their history. Because less than 5% of today's landscape is metamorphic, these rocks are only locally significant for the Yosemite visitor.

During the orogeny's maximum, from about 163 to 152 million years ago, and then in its waning stages for many millions of years later through the early Cretaceous, the Sierra Nevada may have stood as a small part of a major range—a cordillera—that ran along the western edge of both North America and South America. As the orogeny waned, subduction became increasingly oblique, but in a right-lateral sense. Now, unaccreted lands lying west of the Sierra Nevada began to migrate northward. During the mid-Cretaceous, a right-lateral fault also developed in what is the eastern part of today's range. Over perhaps a few million years the bulk of the Sierra Nevada migrated northward at least 250 miles, rifting metamorphic rocks near the Park's

northernmost point from their eastern counterparts, which now lie in the western Mojave Desert.

During the Cretaceous, Yosemite lands lay near the Tropic of Cancer in what is today the western Atlantic Ocean. Dinosaurs ruled the land in a hot, humid climate. Still, the peaks may have been high enough, as in today's equatorial Andes, to support alpine and subalpine vegetation. (In the two earlier orogenies, high elevations may have been produced, but conifers were primitive and flowering plants had not yet evolved.)

The Range of Light

The bulk of today's Sierra Nevada batholith is composed of plutons of middle Cretaceous age, although the time span ranges from as old as 240 to as young as 80 million years in age. The chemistry of a pluton is controlled by the initial composition of the subducting crust (the source of the magma), and by the kind and amount of material that the rising magma incorporates as it intrudes through the upper mantle and its overlying crust. By the time the magma finally solidifies to form a pluton, its composition has become relatively enriched in elements that combine to form light-colored crystals of quartz, potassium feldspar and plagioclase feldspar and dark-colored crystals of biotite and hornblende. Because the light-colored crystals dominate, the color of the rock is also light, and the rock's composition is usually granite or granodiorite. Other minerals—usually dark—may be present, but not in significant quantities except in the dense, dark-gray intrusive rock, *gabbro,* which is uncommon in the Park. *Diorite,* which is less dense, is medium-to-dark gray and is locally abundant.

IGNEOUS ROCKS

generally increasing oxides of silicon, sodium and potassium	Volcanic Rocks		Plutonic Rocks	*generally increasing oxides of magnesium, iron and calcium; also, increasing melting point and increasing density*
	rhyolite	approximately equals	granite	
	rhyodacite	approximately equals	quartz monzonite	
	latite	approximately equals	monzonite	
	dacite	approximately equals	granodiorite	
	andesite	approximately equals		
			diorite	
	basaltic andesite	approximately equals		
	basalt	approximately equals	gabbro	

Note in the Igneous Rocks table that plutonic rocks such as granite and gabbro have volcanic equivalents. (*Igneous* rocks are ones formed from a melt.) If a magma is dioritic, it will produce an andesitic eruption. The volcanic rock andesite received its name from the Andes, a range having an abundance of this rock. However, most of the magma in the Sierra Nevada varied from granodiorite to granite, and therefore most of the volcanic products erupted at the surface varied from dacite to rhyolite.

A rock's composition can influence the development of a landscape. For example, if Yosemite Valley had been carved in diorite instead of granodiorite and granite, it likely wouldn't be part of a national park today (and the Sierra Nevada wouldn't be "the Range of Light"). Diorite does not form massive cliffs, and the best testimony of this lies in western Yosemite Valley. Here you'll see the Rockslides, which is a veneer of dioritic talus that fell from mundane, upper cliffs to cover minor, lower ones. Diorite, you see, fractures into many small pieces and decomposes much more readily than does the more-massive granite. The difference between dioritic and granitic landscapes is impressive. Note, for example, El Capitan, the towering, vertical-faced granite monolith conveniently located just east of the Rockslides to provide a ready comparison.

For the Sierra Nevada to become "the Range of Light," its plutons of light-colored granitic rocks first had to be exposed. This was accomplished through the erosion of the overlying rocks, which took 20 million years or more.

El Capitan is a towering, steep-sided monolith largely because of its granitic composition and its joint-free nature other than bounding master vertical joints. Glaciers had only a minor effect on its size and shape.

The Long Erosion

Through most of the Mesozoic era, the diving Farallon plate, which had come into existence before the Sonoma orogeny, steadily diminished in size. During mostly the mid-Cretaceous, from about 125 to about 88 million years ago, the locus of magma generation from this plate slowly migrated eastward across the ancestral Sierra Nevada, perhaps in response to a shallowing angle of the diving Farallon plate. Then, about 80 million years ago, the Farallon broke into three smaller plates. One plate, the remnant Farallon, shifted its angle of convergence with North America from oblique with a right-lateral component to head-on. Furthermore, it greatly increased its velocity and shallowed its angle of diving. The result of these changes is that the locus of magma generation shifted far east of the Sierra Nevada, creating the Laramide orogeny, a mountain-building episode in the Rocky Mountain area.

In the Sierra Nevada, magma generation stopped, as did volcanic eruptions. The range now began a protracted period of erosion. First the volcanic landscape was eroded away, exposing the older, underlying metamorphic rocks and perhaps some Triassic-age gabbroic and dioritic plutons. In time, this several-mile-thick layer was also eroded away, exposing the tops of some granitic plutons by about 60 million years ago. By about 50 million years ago, the Sierran landscape had become quite granitic in character, although it differed from today's in that it was covered with tropical or nearly tropical vegetation. Mountain rivers transported granitic detritus westward toward an inland sea, whose swampy edge lay around the trace of today's Highway 99. The rivers' gradients decreased almost to zero as they

approached this sea, and as their flow slowed, they dropped their heavier sediments. Some of these proved to be rich in gold, which had weathered out of metamorphic rocks in the western Sierra. Most of today's towns and hamlets beyond the Park's western boundary were originally gold-mining districts: Columbia, Sonora, Jamestown, Chinese Camp, Groveland, Hardin Flat, Oakhurst and Coarsegold. In addition, placer gold was also extracted along the Highway 140 stretch of the Merced River and at Hite Cove along the river's South Fork.

For about 20 million years after the granitic rocks were first exposed, the Sierra Nevada continued to be eroded away. The Yosemite area, which once may have possessed some lofty volcanoes, was now reduced to a gently rolling landscape with a maximum elevation of perhaps 5,000 feet where today's crest now stands. In this area, the highest summits stood about 1,000 feet above the valleys. The Tuolumne Meadows area might have been at about 2,000 feet, and so also Half Dome, which stood perhaps 1,500 feet above the floor of Yosemite Valley.

It is important to realize that the Sierra Nevada was broader back then, during the Eocene epoch. Today's crest did not exist back then, rather, the range's landscape continued to climb gently eastward up into westernmost Nevada. Back then, much of western Nevada was a mountainous highland perhaps akin to today's Tibetan Plateau, only lower, such as the 11,500–15,500-foot-high Altiplano that holds Lake Titicaca along the Peru-Bolivia boundary. It could have been 10,000 feet high or considerably higher, judging from Eocene-age subalpine conifers whose fossil remains were preserved in one of its high-elevation basins.

About 38 million years ago and then at the Eocene-Oligocene boundary 34 million years ago, there were two major cooling events during which populations of subalpine species could have temporarily spread downslope, though they likely did not reach today's Yosemite lands.

Early Volcanism and Initial Uplift

Also during the Eocene epoch, another major change would ultimately affect the Yosemite landscape. At our latitude the Laramide orogeny, mentioned earlier, came to an end about 40 million years ago as the Farallon plate slowed and steepened its dive. As the plate's descending edge retreated westward, a wave of volcanism followed behind it, sweeping west-

ward from the Rockies across the Great Basin and into the Sierra Nevada. The first known eruption there occurred in the Yuba River drainage, northeast of Sacramento, about 38 million years ago, burying its gold-laden gravels. Eruptions, which were few and far between, may have been minor in Yosemite.

It was during this early period of volcanism that the present *central* Sierran landscape may have experienced its first uplift, albeit a minor one. Here I'd like to emphasize the importance of distinguishing between the uplift of a *rock unit*, such as a lava flow or a granitic pluton, and the uplift of a *landscape*, such as Tuolumne Meadows. The uplift of a landscape is equal to the uplift of the bedrock *minus the lowering due to surface erosion*. Far too often in the past, geologists equated uplift of a rock unit with uplift of the adjacent landscape. Determining the rate and amount of uplift of the Sierra's landscape on the basis of a few uplifted, dateable rock units is nearly impossible, and exact figures found in the geologic literature may be quite erroneous.

Later Volcanism, Faulting and Crest Formation

During the Miocene epoch, a more profound period of volcanism affected the Yosemite area. What is today Mono Basin was a high land some 15 million years ago, when volcanism first appeared. The wave of volcanism moved westward, and from about 10 and 6 million years ago, the Park's northern lands were buried under layers of lava flows and volcanic mud flows that were andesitic in composition. The only significant remnants in the Park today are found on and about Rancheria Mountain, just north of the Tuolumne River. South of the river, whose course was diverted slightly southward by such flows, the Park's landscape—indeed, the rest of the Sierra Nevada—escaped major volcanism.

Minor volcanism occurred during the Pliocene epoch near the Park's south and southeastern lands. One remnant within the Park lies just south of Merced Pass, while another extends from the southern edge of the Mariposa Grove of giant sequoias southwest almost to Fish Camp. Most of the remnants, however, are in the San Joaquin River drainage outside the Park, and they are about 3 to 3½ million years old.

In the Great Basin, faulting went hand in hand with volcanism. As the wave of volcanism advanced westward, so too did a wave of faulting. Back in the early Miocene, by about 20

Small remnant of the Miocene-age Mehrten Formation found at trail junction above and north of Pate Valley, near Rancheria Mountain

million years ago, most of Nevada's high lands had begun to collapse in response to this faulting. By about 10 million years ago, the faulting had reached the easternmost part of the Sierra Nevada batholith—today's White Mountains—and it was accompanied by extensive volcanism. That no volcanic flows poured westward across what is now Sequoia and Kings Canyon National parks indicates that an ancestral Owens Valley already existed, albeit a high-elevation, shallow one. By late Miocene, about 6 million years ago, this valley may have begun down-faulting, and the modern Owens Valley was born. By mid-Pliocene, between 4 and 3 million years ago, major faulting commenced in both the Owens Valley and the Mono Basin. The lands sank and the modern Sierran crest came into being. At about 3.2 million years ago, a series of basalt flows, emanating along the newly formed crest, dammed the upper drainage of the San Joaquin River, which caused the river to pool up and then overflow south down through the relatively new Owens Valley and then east to Searles Lake to ultimately end in Death Valley.

The Sierra's Crest, Uplift and Sequoia Migration

The seeds of some plants are transported long distances either by the wind or in the digestive systems of migrating birds. Such is not the case for the Sierra's conifers. Populations of these trees slowly migrated southwest across western North America toward the Sierra Nevada in response to changes in both climate and topography. As I mentioned earlier, sub-alpine conifers thrived during the Eocene epoch in western Nevada's high lands.

The migration of giant sequoias deserves closer scrutiny. We know that by about 7 million years ago giant sequoias had advanced at least

as far west as the Mt. Reba area (above today's Highway 4, north of the Park). This was before Mt. Reba was a mountain. Earlier, I mentioned that the central Sierra's first uplift may have begun about 25 million years ago. The rate of uplift may have gradually increased over time, but major uplift did not begin until 6—or possibly 5—million years ago, that is, roughly the same time that Owens Valley began to form (this is likely no mere coincidence).

Was the Sierra Nevada relatively low 7 million years ago, before the start of this major uplift? The most comprehensive report on uplift, a 1981 U.S. Geological Survey Professional Paper by N. King Huber, indicates—if one extrapolates the meager data—that it was about 5500 feet lower. If one also extrapolates his data for the Mt. Reba area, then 7 million years ago it would have been about 4000 feet lower, having an elevation of about 4500 feet.

However, one must consider the climate back then. By about 8 million years ago, the Tibetan Plateau and adjacent Himalaya range had essentially attained their present elevations, and the worldwide climate had become "modern," having monsoons in Asia and a cold ocean current along California. So some 7 million years ago, when sequoias were in the Mt. Reba area (and possibly farther west), San Francisco would have been foggy and the summers, because of the cold current and the Pacific high that generated it, would have been dry. However, the climate back then was about 10 to 15 degrees warmer. So for sequoias to survive the hot, dry summers, they had to be about 3000 to 4000 feet higher, where temperatures were cooler. Therefore it would appear that even before "major" uplift began, the Sierra Nevada must have been quite high. And by about 3 million years ago, when the Mono Basin was subsiding and starting to become warmer and more arid, the range must have been high enough to have allowed subalpine conifers to grow on high summits just west of the Sierran crest.

Onset of Glaciation and the Origin of the Sequoia Groves

Starting about 6 million years ago, a cold wave gripped the world. Ice off Antarctica seems to have extended several hundred miles beyond today's limits, and a million years elapsed before the ice receded to today's limits. One can speculate that glaciers first arose in the Yosemite area about this time. Also, subalpine conifers such as foxtail, limber and whitebark pines—the first two found today only in the southern High Sierra—now migrated west beyond what would become the Sierra's crest.

The glaciers back then would have been small, perhaps no larger than those on Mts. Lyell, Dana and Conness during historic time. Although Lyell Canyon and other west-slope canyons existed back then, they were shallower, and as a rule they were generally V-shaped in cross section, not U-shaped. There were some notable exceptions. Despite extensive glaciation during the last 2 million years, the Grand Canyon of the Tuolumne River has remained narrow and Tenaya Canyon has maintained its V-shape. In contrast, Yosemite Valley was already somewhat U-shaped before extensive glaciation began. Finally, the Sierra's trunk canyons that have hanging tributary canyons today generally had such canyons at the advent of major glaciation, although they weren't hanging as much.

The world entered the Ice Age about 2½ million years ago, and since then there have

been about four dozen glacial-interglacial cycles. (We are currently in an interglacial phase.) Sediments in basins on both the east and west sides of the Sierra Nevada indicate that major glaciation of its lands began about 2 million years ago.

How did all these glacial advances affect giant sequoias? If you were to look at a map that shows both the distribution of today's 70+ giant-sequoia groves, which thrive at middle elevations, and the maximum extent of glaciation, you might conclude, as John Muir did in 1876, that these groves were once a continuous band of trees, and had been cut into isolated groves by glaciers. Such a tempting hypothesis, however, puts the cart before the horse. The first sequoias may have reached the Park's east boundary by 10 million years ago. (To the south, in what is today Sequoia and Kings Canyon National parks, they must have also crossed the future crest by this time, if not several million years earlier.) By 3 million years ago, when the Sierran crest had begun to form and populations east of it were facing extinction, the Tuolumne, Merced and San Joaquin river canyons were all deep and steep-sided, though possessing gentle uplands as the landscape does today.

One must bear in mind that the giant sequoia is not a canyon-bottom dweller, nor does it thrive well on the steep slopes of a deep canyon, and so the migrating populations were greatly restricted in the routes open to them, which largely accounts for their spotty distribution today. While migrating across the Sierran landscape over perhaps the last 10 million years the trees stayed high. In our area one population kept to the gently sloped highland between the rims of Yosemite Valley and the Grand Canyon of the Tuolumne River. It migrated southwest as the Sierra rose and the climate cooled, following a path not much different from today's Highway 120. At the onset of major glaciation some 2 million years ago, the population may have been near the rolling topography above El Capitan, which back then stood almost as high above the Valley's floor as it does today. Possibly, the population could have been closer to today's groves. During each of the four-dozen cold-warm climatic cycles of the Ice Age, the population descended to warmer climes, and like others in the Sierra, eventually was split into its current groves. These are the Tuolumne Grove and the Merced Grove, both near Crane Flat. It is important to note that at no time in the migration of this population was it ever overridden by glaciers.

Possible routes of giant sequoias

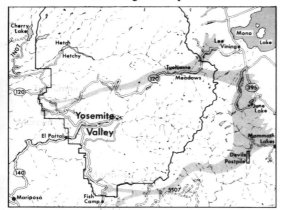

In the Yosemite area it is unlikely that a group of sequoias ever descended or traversed a major river canyon, and therefore sequoias of the Mariposa Grove and the Nelder Grove 5 miles south of it in all likelihood arrived at their destinations by a different route. They probably came through the Agnew Pass-Mammoth Mountain corridor. Neither the pass, the mountain, nor the volcanic flows between them existed back at the time they migrated through this zone, about 10 million years ago. From the corridor, they gradually migrated south, staying above the west slopes of the Middle Fork San Joaquin River canyon. By 7 million years ago, when the Calaveras population was around today's Mt. Reba, the topography along the Park's southeast border was high enough to allow these trees to migrate to within a few miles of their present locations. By the start of major glaciation, they had safely arrived at lands that would remain unglaciated. As with the Tuolumne and Merced groves, the Mariposa and Nelder groves were probably reduced to their present size during the last 2 million years.

A Glaciated Landscape

As I mentioned above, the world entered the Ice Age about 2½ million years ago, and since then there have been about four dozen glacial-interglacial cycles. At this time the Yosemite landscape was already quite spectacular. Its major canyons were about ¾ths of their present depths. Most peaks, however, were not very rugged, even though they had attained altitudes that were only about 1000 to 2000 feet lower than they are now. Back then today's knife-edge Cathedral Range, which extends from Cathedral Peak southeast to Mt. Lyell, may have looked very much like the gently rolling Buena Vista Crest, in the Park's southern quarter. This crest, averaging about 9700 feet in elevation, has received only minor glaciation compared to the Park's east and north quarters, and the development of *cirques*—bowl-shaped canyon heads—is minimal there. From 2½ to 2 million years ago about a dozen glaciers came and went, probably leaving the Cathedral Range looking like the Buena Vista Crest. It would have had small glacier-carved cirques with relatively unchanged canyons descending to the deeper trunk canyons.

Along the Park's east border the Sierra crest was still quite new, and the young east-slope canyons were shallow. Virtually all the ragged peaks in or adjacent to Yosemite National Park were more subdued back then and could be climbed without a rope, except perhaps for Half Dome and Mt. Starr King, which are two giant domes whose upper slopes have changed little during the Park's entire glacial history.

Most of the Park's peaks and canyons began to change dramatically about 2 million years ago, when major glaciation commenced. Glaciers repeatedly gnawed back into the flanks of peaks, especially on their north and northeast sides. There, glaciers were more protected from the sun's radiation, and hence glaciation was more severe. Not only did glaciers grow larger, but during slightly warmer times when glaciers on the south and west sides entirely disappeared, small ones remained in the cirques of the north and northeast sides, such as the ones existing in historic time on Mts. Lyell, Dana and Conness. Glacial backcutting was so extreme that some peaks, such as Matterhorn, Conness, Lyell, Rodgers, Electra and Clark, are mere pointed vestiges of their former selves.

Glaciers at high elevations created rugged peaks and crests. As a rule they also significantly deepened and broadened the Park's canyons as they descended to fairly low elevations. The Sierra's presumably longest glacier flowed 60 miles down the Tuolumne River canyon, its snout descending to an elevation of about 2000 feet at a locality about 15 miles downstream from Hetch Hetchy's O'Shaughnessy Dam. The largest known Merced River glacier, which flowed through Yosemite Valley, was a mere 37 miles long, but it descended to about 1800 feet, terminating over a mile below El Portal. The Merced's South Fork glacier, lacking a high source area other than Merced and Triple Divide peaks, was rather anemic, descending about 20 miles to the Wawona area, about 4000 feet in elevation.

Outside the Park the San Joaquin River drainage produced the Sierra's broadest glacier field, which extended from Yosemite's boundary southeast to Mt. Goddard and Muir Pass, in the northern part of Kings Canyon National Park. Despite its tremendous size, its snout descended only to 2500 feet elevation, though its length rivaled that of the Tuolumne glacier. From the Park's northeast boundary, a glacier from the slopes of Tower Peak flowed north 32 miles down the West Walker River, terminating at the south end of fault-formed Antelope Valley. The maximum extents of other glaciers in and around Yosemite are shown in this chapter's accompanying map. As you can see, in the Park all but the highest peaks and ridges and the western lands were submerged beneath ice. In deep canyons such as the Tuolumne River canyon the glaciers were about 4000 feet thick (locally up to 5800 feet thick in eastern Yosemite Valley), while atop the bordering uplands it was much shallower, typically about 1000 feet or less.

During this maximum glaciation—the Sherwin, which lasted from about 900,000 to 800,000 years ago—the High Sierra was completely covered with ice, save for its highest crests. At middle elevations, however, the ice was channeled down in the deep canyons—although the glaciers overrode the canyon rims in many places within the Park and over most of the San Joaquin drainage, outside the Park. Where the glaciers overrode rims and spread thinly across benches, such as in the Cottonwood Creek drainage south of and above Hetch Hetchy Reservoir, scouring was minimal. This is because a glacier's velocity is in part dictated by its thickness. One glacier twice as thick as another will have 16 times the velocity. Also, a glacier's velocity is proportional to the slope of its surface. Therefore, on flat benches above canyons, the velocity is feeble. The high-velocity, highly eroding glaciers are in deep canyons.

In the Yosemite Valley area during the Sherwin glaciation, Half Dome was a 600-foot-high bedrock island poking above an ice pack that may have been as deep as 5800 feet. Sentinel Dome was nearly overridden by ice, and almost all the highlands east of El Capitan, including North and Basket domes, lay beneath slowly moving ice. The Valley's south rim was less glaciated, since glaciers from the south had their origins along the north slopes of the low Horse Ridge-Buena Vista Crest and along the sunny west slopes of the higher Clark Range. A forest undoubtedly existed on the unglaciated highland between Bridalveil Creek and Sentinel Dome, but because temperatures back then may have been about 10 to 15 degrees cooler than those of today, the forest may have been more akin to present forests that are found 3000 feet higher than today's south-rim forest.

Controversial Views on the Origin of Yosemite Valley

On June 30, 1864, President Abraham Lincoln signed a bill that deeded Yosemite Valley and the Mariposa Grove of Big Trees to the State of California "for public use, resort and recreation." Earlier in this chapter I examined the migration of the giant sequoias and in Hike

93 dwelt at some length on the life history and ecology of these magnificent giants. Now I would like to dwell on the formation of Yosemite Valley. For a century, through the 1980s, it was called a classic glaciated valley, and it has been described and illustrated as such in countless geology and physical-geography textbooks, in guidebooks, in nature books and in coffee-table books. Glaciated it is; a prime example of a glaciated landscape it definitely is not. How did the Valley originate and why is it unique? One would think that these questions would have been resolved years ago, but instead the Valley's origin has been steeped in controversy.

The first visitors to the Valley in the 1850s and early '60s had their views on how it had formed. However, the first scientific view was proposed by Josiah D. Whitney, who was the first director of California's State Geological Survey. A reconnaissance of the state was made from 1860 through 1964 by the "Whitney Survey," which in fact was basically led by William H. Brewer. Whitney had briefly joined the team for a visit to the Valley in 1863, and later theorized about its origin in his *Geology of California,* volume 1 (1865):

> Most of the great cañons and valleys of California have resulted from denudation [basically, erosion by streams]. . . .
>
> It may, however, be stated, that it appears to us probable that this mighty chasm has been roughly hewn into its present form by the same kind of forces which have raised the crest of the Sierra and moulded the surface of the mountains into something like their present shape. The domes, and such masses as that of Mount Broderick, we conceive to have been formed by the process of upheaval itself, for we can discover nothing about them which looks like the result of ordinary denudation. The Half Dome seems, beyond a doubt, to have been split asunder in the middle, the lost half having gone down in what may truly be said to have been "the wreck of matter and the crush of worlds." It has been objected to this view, by some of the corps, that the bottom of the valley, in places where an engulfment must, according to this theory, have taken place, seems to be of solid granite. . . . But, again, this grand cataclysm may have taken place at a time when the granitic mass was still in a semi-plastic condition, although, perhaps, quite consolidated at the surface and for some distance down.
>
> In the course of the explorations of Messrs. [Clarence] King and [James] Gardner, they obtained ample evidence of the former existence of a glacier in the Yosemite Valley, and the cañons of all the streams entering it are also beautifully polished and grooved by

glacial action. It does not appear, however, that the mass of ice ever filled the Yosemite to the upper edge of the cliffs; but Mr. King thinks it must have been at least a thousand feet thick. He also traced out four ridges in the valley which he considers to be, without a doubt, ancient moraines.

[*Moraines* are coarse, unsorted sediments transported by glaciers. A *lateral* moraine is a linear deposit left along the side of a glacier. A *terminal* moraine is one left at the glacier's farthest down-canyon point. A *recessional* moraine is left at the snout of a retreating glacier where it temporarily halts its retreat. Both terminal and recessional moraines are end moraines, as opposed to lateral moraines. Finally a medial moraine is a special case of lateral moraine, formed where two converging glaciers merge together. Moraines are discussed in the last part of this chapter and are mentioned in the One Hundred Hikes where they are encountered en route.]

Whitney's subsidence theory neatly "explained" the angularity and verticality of Yosemite's walls as well as the very small amount of talus found at the base of these walls. However, Clarence King was not convinced by Whitney's theory and proposed that glaciation helped to shape the Valley. In 1866 an acquaintance of his and of Brewer, William P. Blake, later a professor at the University of Arizona, visited the Valley and a year later, in an obscure French journal, expounded an origin that involved both stream and glacial erosion. Whitney, who was very contentious, attacked him—and also King—in his 1868 *Yosemite Guidebook*:

A more absurd theory was never advanced than that by which it was sought to ascribe to glaciers the sawing out of these vertical walls and the foundering of the domes. Nothing more unlike the real work of ice, as exhibited in the Alps, could be found. Besides, there is no reason to suppose, or at least no proof, that glaciers have ever occupied the Valley or any portion of it, . . . so that this theory, based on entire ignorance of the whole subject, may be dropped without wasting any more time on it.

Thus in three years Whitney denied all the glacial evidence that he had described in his massive 1865 book because it threatened his theory. It is interesting to note that in his 1868 guidebook he mentions a glacial moraine above Hetch Hetchy Valley—a second "Yosemite"—which indicated this valley was once buried by a half-mile-thick glacier.

It is also interesting to note that Whitney, Brewer, King and Blake all studied science at Yale University. A fellow who did not, and who was equally as contentious as Whitney and soon to become his adversary, was John Muir, who would later found the Sierra Club, in 1892, two years after Yosemite became a national park.

Muir first visited Yosemite Valley briefly in 1868, then the following year spent the summer rambling, supposedly herding sheep, but in reality exploring the Yosemite high country, discovering abundant evidence of past glaciers and then telling everyone who would listen that Yosemite Valley owed its existence to glacial excavation. Whitney, feeling attacked again, countered in the next edition of his guidebook, calling Muir "a mere sheepherder, an ignoramus," not acknowledging his University of Wisconsin education.

In 1871 Muir was the first person to discover a living glacier, that is, a permanent snowfield with *flowing* ice. This was the Merced Peak glacier, and his recounting of its discovery is given in Hike 89. How did glaciers transform the Sierra's landscape? Muir would much later give this poetic account in his first book, *The Mountains of California*:

Careful study of the phenomena presented goes to show that the pre-glacial condition of the range was comparatively simple: one vast wave of stone in which a thousand mountains, domes, cañons, ridges, etc., lay concealed. And in the development of these Nature chose for a tool not the earthquake or lightning to rend and split asunder, not the stormy torrent or eroding rain, but the tender snow-flowers noiselessly falling through unnumbered centuries, the offspring of the sun and sea. . . .

Contemplating the works of these flowers of the sky, one may easily fancy them endowed with life: messengers sent down to work in the mountain mines on errands of divine love. Silently flying through the darkened air, swirling, glinting, to their appointed places, they seem to have taken counsel together, saying, "Come, we are feeble; let us help one another. We are many, and together we will be strong. Marching in close, deep ranks, let us roll away the stones from these mountain sepulchers, and set the landscapes free. Let us uncover these clustered domes. Here let us carve a lake basin; there, a Yosemite Valley; here, a channel for a river with fluted steps and brows for the plunge of songful cataracts. Yonder let us spread broad sheets of soil, that man and beast may be fed; and here pile trains of boulders for pines and giant Sequoias. Here make ground for a meadow; there, for a garden and grove, making it smooth and fine for small daisies and violets and beds of healthy bryanthus, spicing it well with crystals, garnet feldspar, and zircon."

Unfortunately, just as Whitney denied any glacial evidence in Yosemite Valley and therefore lost credibility, Muir, without any tangible evidence, overstated the power and extent of glaciers. In his guidebook, *The Yosemite,* published in 1912, just two years before he died, he emphatically stated:

All California has been glaciated, the low plains and valleys as well as the mountains. [Emphasis mine.]

He had reached this conclusion through the influence of his University of Wisconsin geology professor, Ezra Carr, who in turn had been influenced by *his* geology professor, Luis Agassiz. Agassiz originally had believed that glaciers originated at the north pole and then advanced more or less uniformly southward to mid-latitudes, covering all the lands. He substantially changed his views by 1847, and by 1863, when Muir left the university and Whitney visited Yosemite Valley, a basically modern view of glaciation had taken hold among most American geologists. It is ironic that Muir held steadfast to Agassiz' early erroneous views, since Agassiz was the Yale professor who had so influenced the members of the Whitney Survey!

In 1871 Muir accompanied Joseph LeConte in a traverse across the Yosemite landscape. LeConte, a geology professor at Berkeley's University of California, agreed with Muir that glaciers had played a role in excavating Yosemite, but like Prof. Blake before him, ascribed much of the excavation to streams.

In 1889 Prof. Israel Russell of the University of Michigan had completed his classic *Quaternary History of the Mono Valley, California.* He had been impressed by the magnitude of the moraines left by the Sierra's east-side glaciers and by the lack of similar-size moraines in Yosemite Valley. Therefore, he agreed with Whitney's theory, but he was the last researcher to do so. Other geologists that followed either concluded that the Valley was largely stream-carved, based on its similarities to known stream-carved canyons, or concluded that it was largely glacier-carved, based on the presence of tributary valleys presumably left hanging after a major glacier flowing through Yosemite Valley greatly deepened it.

During the summers of 1905 and '06, a young, Amsterdam-born, U.S. Geological Survey topographer, fairly fresh out of the Massachusetts Institute of Technology, surveyed the Valley and produced a map of it that would remain unsurpassed in accuracy until the 1990s. This was François Matthes (pronounced "Mat'-tees"), who during the winter of 1905 had studied under Harvard University's Prof. William Morris Davis, the most prolific American geomorphologist of his day. Matthes immediately embraced his views of landscape evolution, much as Muir had unfortunately embraced Agassiz' early glacial views. In time he became increasingly interested in geomorphology and less in topography. In 1900 he first wrote about glaciation, and between 1910 and 1913 he wrote four articles in the Sierra Club Bulletin on various aspects of the Yosemite landscape. In 1912 he wrote a 47-page *Sketch of Yosemite National Park and an account of the origin of the Yosemite and Hetch Hetchy valleys.*

Given Matthes' predilection toward glacial processes and his familiarity with the Yosemite landscape, it is not surprising that the Sierra Club requested the U.S. Geological Survey to have Matthes—an admirer of John Muir, who was still living—resolve once and for all how Yosemite Valley had been created. Perhaps he would vindicate Muir. Matthes began this task in 1913 and, being an uncompromising perfectionist, undertook several years of painstaking field research, leaving virtually "no stone unturned." When his comprehensive report, *U.S. Geological Survey Professional Paper 160,* was finally published in 1930, it became an immediate hit. One cannot fail to be impressed with the amount of work that went into it. In 1932 it received a rave review from Prof. Kirk Bryan, which began:

Occasionally in the history of science there appears a work so excellent, so comprehensive, that it becomes immediately a classic. Such a newborn classic is the long-awaited "professional paper" by Matthes on the Yosemite Valley.

I can find no evidence that Prof. Bryan ever did glacial research or ever did any kind of field work in the Sierra Nevada. He did, however, have one qualification: he was a colleague of Prof. William Morris Davis. And it was Davis' ideas on landscape evolution that Matthes had used to transform his extensive field notes into a convincingly logical picture of Yosemite Valley's geomorphic evolution. Unfortunately, Davis' pertinent ideas had been largely cast aside by most of the world's earth scientists a few years *before* Matthes published his work. No matter. It had officially been declared a classic, "the Bible truth," and therefore was above question.

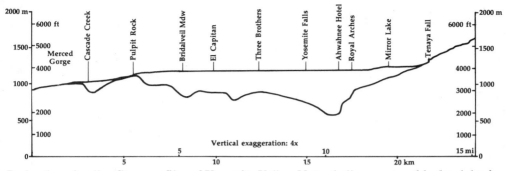

Bedrock and valley-floor profiles of Yosemite Valley. Note shallow west-end bedrock basin, two deeper, more-central basins and very deep east-end basin.

Because Yosemite personnel have interpreted Yosemite Valley according to Matthes for more than six decades, it is worth noting some of what he said. First, he once and for all refuted Whitney's view of a fault-formed valley. He also showed that Muir had greatly overstated the extent of glaciers and the power of their excavation, though he reserved kind words for Muir.

Matthes had two basic assumptions, based on Davis' ideas. First, there were three major pulses of uplift, each causing an inner canyon to be rapidly incised in the existing canyon and leaving the tributary canyons hanging. To reconstruct the Merced River's gradient before the first uplift, he extrapolated the stream gradient of each hanging tributary out to a point above the Merced River. Unfortunately, the only topographic map available in his day was so inaccurate that the gradient he reconstructed from three tributary canyons was only about 40% of the gradient one derives by using modern maps. Furthermore, one of his three points was hypothetical, since the map's topographer had drawn in a nonexistent tributary stream! There are problems with the two other uplifts, the most serious one being that the last uplift was the greatest and it cut the deepest inner canyon. However, he put this uplift at the start of the Ice Age, allowing absolutely *no time* for the canyon to be cut between uplift and glacial erosion.

Matthes' second basic assumption was that all stream canyons are V-shaped in cross-section, and all glaciated canyons are U-shaped. (Although I hadn't realized it at the time I wrote the first edition of this guidebook, during the 1960s Prof. Clyde Wahrhaftig of the University of California at Berkeley—and also of the U.S. Geological Survey—had refuted Matthes' two assumptions.

Matthes demonstrated that at the onset of glaciation, which back then was believed to be a convenient one million years ago, Yosemite Valley was already a deep canyon. Using his first basic assumption, he determined that opposite El Capitan the Valley was about 2400 feet deep, while opposite Glacier Point it was 2000 feet deep. Matthes found unmistakable evidence for two periods of glaciation and possibly for a third. He estimated that when the last of the glaciers had left Yosemite Valley—about 20,000 years ago by his reckoning—they had deepened the valley by 1500 feet at its east end, below Half Dome, while at Bridalveil Meadow— believed by Matthes and virtually everyone else to have been the farthest that the last (Tioga-age) glacier got—they had deepened it by only 500 feet. Matthes believed that overall the earlier streams and later glaciers had excavated roughly equal amounts of rock to create the Valley. He believed that all the glaciers scraped along the bedrock floor of the Valley. Thus when the last glacier left, most of the Valley's supposedly flat bedrock floor became flooded by Lake Yosemite, a huge lake about 5½ miles long and up to 300 feet deep.

As later evidence would reveal, there is a lot more to Yosemite Valley than meets the eye. In 1935 and '37 seismic surveys were undertaken to determine the depth and configuration of the bedrock floor beneath Yosemite Valley. The results showed that this granitic floor was very irregular—definitely not flat-floored (see the figure "Bedrock and valley-floor profiles of Yosemite Valley"). Furthermore, there were several basins, the easternmost one being the deepest, its floor now lying about 2000 feet below the Valley surface in the vicinity of the Ahwahnee Hotel. Matthes had proposed only 300 feet—the maximum depth of his Lake

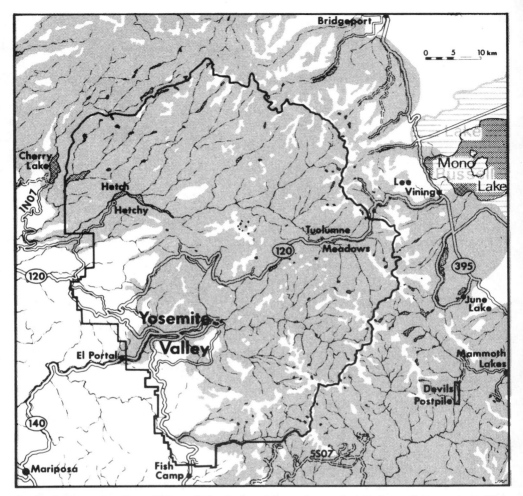

Author's reconstruction of Yosemite's glaciers (shown in gray) at their maximum extent. Note the size of Mono Lake's predecessor, Lake Russell.

Yosemite—and he refused to believe the seismic research.

The seismic evidence (which was later substantiated in the 1970s by drilling to bedrock) indicates that Yosemite's glaciers had been more powerful than Matthes had realized. They were and they weren't. First of all, they were because they had cut a basin out of bedrock to a depth that was a minimum of 2000 feet below the Valley's pre-glacial level. But then, just 4 miles upstream, in Tenaya Canyon, the cross section between Mt. Watkins and Clouds Rest is unmistakably **V**-shaped, so it would appear that glaciers there had barely altered the canyon.

An Unsolved Problem Solved

In the previous editions of this guidebook I posed an unsolved problem: when did the last glacier leave the Valley? Earlier in this edition, under the section "A Glaciated Landscape," I mentioned that the largest known glaciers occurred during the Sherwin glaciation, which lasted from about 900,000 to 800,000 years ago. The Sherwin-age glacier probably was the last one to scour away at the bedrock floor of Yosemite Valley, and when it retreated, dropping sediments along the way, it left a Lake Yosemite

Lake Yosemite, as envisioned by Matthes

how Matthes' post-Tioga Lake Yosemite could have been filled up by sediments in such a short time when much smaller lakes, such as Merced, Washburn, Tenaya and myriad tarns had only been filled with typically 10 to 20 feet of sediments. Fortunately, I had available to me hydrologic and sedimentary data for the Merced River that allowed me to calculate the Merced River's average annual sedimentary budget through the Valley—about 2830 tons per year. At that rate, the amount of time required to fill in the lake by stream processes alone, without the aid of glaciers or rockfalls, would have been almost 600,000 years. But there also must have been a wedge of sediments deposited atop the lake's sediments, since the Valley floor is about 40 feet higher at the east end than at the moraine just west of El Capitan Meadow, the site of the lake's west end. To fill in this wedge would take at least 300,000 years. So, the total time needed to fill Lake Yosemite would have been about 900,000 years, assuming that every bit of sediment entering the Valley was trapped within it. This may be a good assumption for a river entering a large lake, but not for a sloping river meandering across sediments. Rather, during most or all of post-Tioga time, the amount of sediments being transported out of the Valley has essentially equaled the amount being brought in.

When I discovered this, I still firmly believed that the rest of Matthes' work was perfect. To salvage Matthes' lake, I had proposed that the Tioga glacier (and perhaps even the Tenaya) only reached the eastern end of the Valley and there dumped prodigious amounts of sediments into it, filling the lake. However, an alternate interpretation, proposed by Malcom Clark of the U.S. Geological Survey, was that the Tioga-age glacier merely slid across the Valley's pre-existing sediments and left at best only a shallow lake. Later, evidence described by Clyde Wahrhaftig convinced me (after having verified it), that the Valley's westernmost moraine, just east of Bridalveil Meadow, indeed was deposited by a Tioga-age glacier. So, the unsolved problem was solved, the last glacier to advance through the Valley was of Tioga-age, and therefore a post-Tioga Lake Yosemite, depicted in so many books on Yosemite, never had existed.

In the 1980s, still trying to verify the correctness of the rest of Matthes' work, I proposed that the massive excavation of Yosemite Valley could be better explained if Tenaya Creek once was a large, powerful river that late in its history was beheaded much as the San Joaquin River

considerably larger than the one Matthes had proposed: 8½ miles long and up to 2000 feet deep. Since then there were about eight times when lesser glaciers grew large enough to enter, if not advance through, Yosemite Valley. Such glaciers, rather than scouring the bedrock floor, advanced across sediments left by previous glaciers and they added sediments during a retreat up-canyon. Of course, sediments were also added to the lake during interglacial times.

Of interest to us are two or three glaciations that left abundant evidence of their existence in the form of moraines. Two are the Tahoe, possibly being at its maximum about 75,000 years ago (although some have proposed a date about twice this), and the Tioga, reaching its maximum about 20,000 years ago. The Tioga perhaps began to recede by 16,000 years ago, certainly by 15,000 years ago, and it appears to have retreated up-canyon from Yosemite Valley by about 14,000 years ago. Nested between these two may have been another glaciation, the Tenaya, but this glaciation has also been interpreted as late Tahoe by some researchers and early Tioga by others.

While working on the first edition of this guidebook back in 1976 and '77, I had wondered had been. However, this interpretation required a modification of Matthes' model. N. King Huber, a colleague of Wahrhaftig's at the Survey, shot down this hypothesis, and I gave up trying to understand the Valley's evolution in terms of Matthes, whose views increasingly appeared unsalvagable. However, Pandora's box had been opened. The last part of my article on the Tenaya River (*Yosemite,* Summer 1987 issue) proved to be prophetic, although I did not realize it at the time:

> It will take years to quantify the Valley's geologic history, for if Matthes' major assumptions are wrong or questionable, geomorphologists are back to square one. Still, the challenge is surmountable, and I look forward to contributing to a new quantitative chronology of the Valley's geologic history.

In 1988 I returned to the University of California at Berkeley to work on a Ph.D., and spent the summers of 1990 and '91 doing field work to determine the extent of glaciers—and the pattern and timing of Tioga-age glacial retreat—in the Stanislaus River basin, just north of the Park. It was during this time that I finally realized how Yosemite Valley had evolved, this insight gained, ironically, by an almost incidental comment made by Huber in his critique of my Tenaya River hypothesis:

> Yosemite Valley, however, has not been completely filled with ice for at least 750,000 years, the minimum age of the Sherwin glaciation (probably equivalent to Matthes' El Portal glaciation). The major excavation of Yosemite Valley, including the bedrock basin beneath the valley floor, had to have been accomplished by that time. Since then, the upper reaches of Yosemite Valley cliffs have been shaped by spalling rather than by glacial scour.

If glaciers hadn't significantly broadened the Valley in the 800,000 years after the Sherwin glaciation, could they have widened it much in the first 1,200,000 years of glaciation? Although the Sherwin glacier was huge, most of the earlier glaciers likely were no larger than the Tahoe and Tioga glaciers, and possibly smaller. Additionally, I discovered evidence that the Tahoe and Tioga glaciers were significantly larger than anyone had realized. They not only advanced to El Capitan, but also continued west to the Merced Gorge. So, the glaciers had been larger than Matthes, Wahrhaftig and Huber (and originally I) thought, and yet they were *still* ineffective at significantly broadening the Valley. In late 1991 I started furiously writing up

my ideas, and in January 1992 officially switched my dissertation topic to the origin of Yosemite Valley.

The Uniqueness of Yosemite Valley

Why should the bedrock in the eastern part of Yosemite Valley be excavated to such a tremendous depth and then be filled with up to 2000 feet of sediments? Before answering that question, I'd like to emphasize that Yosemite Valley is *unique*. Too often it has been said that Yosemite is *the* classic example of a glaciated valley. Were this true, then all glaciated canyons should resemble it, having "Half Domes," "El Capitans" and a level floor underlain by deep layers of sediments. As I've noted, they don't. Yosemite Valley is unique because, as Matthes put it, the key to the secret of the Valley's origin lies in the pattern of variations—in size, spacing and orientation—of its joint planes ("joints" for short). Joints are often linear, usually parallel fractures in bedrock. Most of the Sierra Nevada is granitic and possesses joints, as do other types or rocks such as the massive sandstone, which in Utah's Zion National Park is cut by a rectangular grid of streams. But Yosemite Valley has a unique pattern of variations in its joint system. Actually, this pattern is only part of the solution; past researchers failed to find the other key—mentioned in the next section.

Without the presence of an overabundance of joints in the bedrock of the eastern floor of the Valley, near the confluence of Tenaya Creek and the Merced River, the deep excavation would never have occurred. The east end of the Valley would have been just like many other glaciated canyons having two major joining canyons—very little downcutting. Furthermore, Yosemite Valley has steep-sided walls—with over 1000 difficult climbing routes up them—because its walls are governed by the presence of vertical joints. Glaciers didn't make the walls vertical—their contribution was minor; the walls were already quite steep, due to vertical jointing, prior to glaciation.

In like manner, parts of Tenaya Canyon and of the Grand Canyon of the Tuolumne River may stay V-shaped almost indefinitely, for they lack this important control. I should note here that the *spacing* of joints is also important. If joints are closely spaced, the rock is more easily excavated—witness Indian Canyon and the Rockslides. In contrast, the hulking, vertical-

Angular shapes, rounded in time, abound in and around Yosemite Valley. The heavy lines depict master joints—large fractures in the granitic bedrock. These vertical joints are more susceptible to erosion than is unjointed rock, and deep valleys with steep-sided walls result. Not all joints are along vertical planes and neither are all Valley walls. Photo of Half Dome shows its joint-controlled front and back faces.

walled monolith of El Capitan is essentially joint-free, although at one time it had been bounded by several major, vertical joints and then had backwasted to its present state.

North of the Tuolumne River, Yosemite's backcountry is a fantastic landscape of joint-controlled, rectangularly oriented canyons. However, you probably wouldn't be aware of the rectangularity of this landscape unless you were to fly over it or examine 3-D aerial photos of it. A much easier way to visualize the effect of joints in controlling the development of a landscape is to drive up the Glacier Point Road and get a bird's-eye view of Yosemite Valley and environs. Your first stop should be at Washburn Point, from which you look directly across at Half Dome. Note that it is not really half of a dome, as its name implies, for it is rather symmetrical, the southeast face being almost as tall and as steep as the northwest face. The steepness of these two faces is in large part controlled by vertical, northeast-trending joints. These vertical joints were more closely spaced along the northwest face, and glaciers took advantage of this, cutting the face back by about 500 feet. However, contrary to what Whitney proclaimed in the 1860s, at no time in the dome's history did a northwest half of the dome fall into Tenaya Canyon.

Below and to the right of Half Dome you'll look down—from Washburn Point—on Mt. Broderick and Liberty Cap, both also bounded by vertical, northeast-trending joints. Glaciation has substantially enlarged the joint that separates the two monoliths.

The same joint that governs the southeast face of Liberty Cap also governs the cliff that Nevada Fall leaps over. Vernal Fall is also governed by a vertical joint, but it trends northwest, not northeast.

Before driving on to Glacier Point, look at Mt. Starr King, on the horizon east-southeast of you. It is rounded on all sides—a true dome, unlike most so-called domes. If it is so rounded, does that mean it is not controlled by joints? Not really. Mt. Starr King appeared on the Yosemite landscape about 50 million years ago, if not earlier. It was almost certainly bound by vertical, intersecting joint planes, and back in its early days it may have looked somewhat like Mt. Broderick, below you, looks today. Time and erosion, however, have taken their toll, eroding faster at the edges than at the faces, and even faster at the corners than at the edges (see the two following photos).

From Washburn Point continue down to the Glacier Point parking lot and walk to the brink of Glacier Point. The 1200-foot-dead-vertical cliff

Subsurface weathering of fractured bedrock creates miniature domes (left). These are similar to Yosemite's giant domes, such as Mt. Starr King (right), which become rounded while *above* the surface.

below you is governed by a major joint, but the curving Glacier Point Apron, below it, lacks major joints and has been very resistant to erosion. It's been planed down by glaciers perhaps a maximum of several hundred feet, not the 1800 feet proposed by Matthes.

From Glacier Point you can easily see how Half Dome got its name, for it certainly looks as if there had been a northwest half of the dome, which would have fallen into Tenaya Canyon. Looking up Tenaya Canyon, note that it is distinctly **V**-shaped in cross-section, not **U**-shaped, as a glaciated canyon is supposed to be. However, there are no major vertical joint planes in this canyon, so a "Yosemite Valley" never developed. Above the canyon stand North Dome and Basket Dome, both rounded like Mt. Starr King and both having a similar history. Both were covered by hundreds of feet of glacier ice during the Sherwin glaciation and possibly during earlier glaciations, in contrast to unglaciated Mt. Starr King, which at most had a Sherwin-age glacier lapping almost up to its base.

Yosemite Valley, a New Interpretation

Matthes had discovered one key to the secret of the Valley's origin—its unique joint pattern. However, there was another key that most geologists examining Yosemite must have been aware of, yet none used it to unlock Yosemite's secret. It is my basic assumption, and it is:

Jointed, fractured bedrock is more easily weathered and eroded than massive, joint-free bedrock.

Matthes was well aware of this, noting that massive, joint-free prominences such as El Capitan and Glacier Point Apron were highly resistant to glacial erosion, while highly fractured features were readily eroded. However, he felt that stream erosion occurred almost independently of bedrock jointing, as his series of pre- and post-glacial Valley cross sections illustrate. In his interpretation of the Valley's evolution, following Davis' ideas he believed it to have been initially **V**-shaped along its entire length and then transformed by glaciers to the multi-faceted landscape that exists today. For this to have happened, one has to hypothesize highly fractured Valley walls that were untouched by the stream at their base but were easily removed by ensuing glaciers. This view is similar to a more extreme view of Muir, quoted above.

Whereas a river obviously cannot erode a cliff above it, it can cut into its base. More important, as it deepens a canyon and steepens its sides, mass wasting—spalling, to use Huber's term—will occur in increasing amounts. And—this is the most important aspect of the second key—that mass wasting is dictated by the joint structure. One need only compare the highly fractured Rockslides with adjacent, joint-free El Capitan. Throughout time, both received similar amounts of glaciation, contrary to the widespread belief that the Tioga-age glacier barely got past El Capitan. This belief was based on the erroneous assumption that the moraine just east of Bridalveil Meadow was a *terminal* moraine.

It is important to know that the Tahoe and Tioga glaciers reached Merced Gorge. If they had advanced only to the vicinity of El Capitan or slightly beyond, then one could hypothesize that the reason the valley is so deep in its east end and shallow in its west end is that many glaciers reached its east end but few advanced beyond its west end (review the figure "Bedrock and valley-floor profiles of Yosemite Valley"). But as I stated earlier, the bedrock floor experienced its last scouring during the Sherwin glaciation, so later glaciers had no effect on the profile of the floor. One might ask, however, if the Tahoe- and Tioga-age glaciers advanced beyond Bridalveil Meadow and into the Merced Gorge, why then didn't they excavate the bedrock that now lies at the surface at Pulpit Rock and in the upper Merced Gorge (see the same figure mentioned above)? Indeed, why didn't the Sherwin-age glacier and previous large glaciers plane down these two stretches of bedrock?

The answer appears to be that these two stretches were joint-free and therefore were too resistant to be significantly eroded by even the strongest glaciers. This observation leads one to an important insight: if the glaciers had not significantly cut down these two stretches of bedrock then, just before the start of glaciation, this stretch of Merced River canyon must have been almost as deep as it is today, since neither the rim nor its floor has significantly changed. Furthermore, if unjointed bedrock is essentially uneroded, then highly jointed bedrock is severely eroded. Earlier, I mentioned this with respect to the deep, glacier-excavated basin in the eastern part of the Valley. What we can infer here is that, being highly jointed, this stretch of bedrock floor would have been readily eroded by the pre-glacial Merced River, and therefore, the river's gradient across it would have been quite flat. Indeed, that glaciers cut so deeply within Yosemite Valley suggests that most of its bedrock floor was fairly well jointed.

Knowing the above, one can reconstruct the approximate profile of the Merced River through the Valley at the advent of glaciation. The massive stretches of bedrock—sills—located at the upper part of the Merced Gorge, at Pulpit Rock and to a lesser extent near the Three Brothers, acted as local base levels for the river, and across them the river likely flowed as a series of rapids and/or small cascades (somewhat like it does through the Merced Gorge today). Behind the sills, the river flowed

smoothly across the fractured, easily eroded bedrock and had a nearly flat gradient. The flat stretches predominated, and overall from the Valley's east end west to Pulpit Rock, the river may have dropped only a few hundred feet along this length, about one third that proposed by Matthes. The river's profile resembled that of the unglaciated stretches of the Tuolumne River's South Fork and Middle Fork. Finally, Bridalveil Creek likely plunged down to the Merced as a fall and a series of cascades, just as today, in the unglaciated northwestern Sierra Nevada, Falls Creek leaps as Feather Falls and then tumbles down to the Feather River's Middle Fork.

The Valley's east end, like its west end, was almost as deep just before glaciation as it is today. From the east end, both the Merced River and Tenaya Creek had steep profiles with cascades and significant—though not renowned—falls. An excellent analog for the pre-glaciated stretch of the Merced River between Nevada Fall and Happy Isles is the upper stretch of the Carmel River, in California's central-coast Santa Lucia Range.

Can one reconstruct the width of Yosemite Valley just before it was glaciated? This is a more difficult task. If you consider only the ineffectiveness of glaciers at widening the Valley, then you are led to conclude that it was almost as wide back then as it is now. The conclusion is that the Merced River, in existence for some 50 million years, had plenty of time to meander in its low-gradient stretches, thereby creating a broad valley.

However, such an interpretation ignores mass wasting, which ranges from the prying loose of a single crystal to the catastrophic failing of a "Royal Arch." Most of the wasted debris ends up at the base of the Valley's walls and accumulates there to form talus slopes. Starting with Whitney, geologists marvelled at the minimal amount of talus lining the edges of the Valley's floor. Actually the talus is even less than what one might expect. Below the cliffs of the Rockslides, the talus slopes look huge, but in reality the talus is overall just a thin veneer burying most of the lower slopes. Nevertheless, when one calculates the amount of talus to have accumulated in the Valley since the Tioga-age glacier left it about 14,000 years ago—a thankless task—the amount is significant. At the current rate of talus production, the Valley could be filled to the rim in a few million years. From this information one could then conclude that Yosemite Valley has been almost entirely cut since significant Sierran uplift began near the end of the Miocene epoch.

As with the previous conclusion, this one has its problems. First, one is hard put to explain why the Merced River cut very little for some 45+ million years, cut some 3000 feet down in the next 3 million years, and then failed to cut down significantly in the last 2 million years, despite continued uplift and formidable glaciation. This also applies to the excavation of Tenaya Canyon. Second, giant sequoias migrated across the Park's western lands from the late Miocene through the Pliocene. If the landscape back then had been a gently rolling one, then there would have been no significant barriers to the sequoia's migration and today they should be quite widespread across the lands between the Tuolumne River and the South Fork Merced River. They are not.

Therefore, I conclude that the rate of mass wasting is much greater now than it was in earlier times, the increase likely brought about by the Valley's increasingly oversteepened slopes and by increasing seismic activity in the Mono Basin-Owens Valley trough. I envision Yosemite Valley just prior to glaciation as being nearly as deep as it is today, about half as wide, and quite steep, possessing some prominent, nearly vertical cliffs. The ensuing widening in the last 2 million years appears to be due more likely to mass wasting than to glaciation.

When the Tioga-age glacier retreated up through Yosemite Valley about 14,000 years ago, it did so at first sporadically, leaving several recessional moraines where its snout briefly stagnated between Bridalveil and El Capitan meadows. It then backwasted rapidly to the east end of the Valley, where a large moraine—parallel with the length of the Valley rather than perpendicular to it—was deposited. On some Valley maps, including the U.S. Geological Survey's 1990 Half Dome 7.5′ topographic quadrangle, it is identified as the Medial Moraine. This has indeed been interpreted as a medial moraine, although it is too large to be one. Matthes, on the other hand, concluded that it was a frontal moraine more likely left by the Tenaya Canyon glacier. He doesn't state whether the moraine was terminal or recessional, and it is important to know, since that can affect one's conclusions.

I'm quite convinced this west-trending ridge is a *recessional* moraine left by the retreating *Merced Canyon* glacier. The evidence for this lies, surprisingly, in the Stanislaus River drainage, north of the Park. Its Clark Fork glacier received much of its ice from an eastern, overflowing glacier just as the Tenaya Canyon glacier was fed by the overflow of the Tuolumne River glacier. The Clark Fork glacier retreated before the adjacent Middle Fork did, due to greatly reduced overflow about 14,000 years ago. In like manner, the Tenaya Canyon glacier would have retreated prematurely as the waning Tuolumne River glacier cut off its source of ice. This would account for the rapid retreat of the glacier through Yosemite Valley, since it was rapidly being deprived of a principal source of ice. The Merced Canyon glacier, not being cut off, stagnated and thereby created a recessional moraine.

The Lyell Glacier, as it appeared around 1880

The Holocene Epoch

The last 10,000 years have been classified as the Holocene epoch—a misleading name, for it implies that the glacier-dominated Pleistocene epoch is behind us. Notwithstanding global warming through man's zealous production of greenhouse gases, nothing could be farther from the truth.

Since 13,000 years ago, the unofficial start of the Holocene for the Sierra Nevada (when its glaciers had all but disappeared), the Yosemite landscape has changed very little. The massive face of El Capitan has weathered back only ¼ inch, if even that, though parts of it have spalled rockfalls. Rockfalls generally occur in winter and early spring, as water works its way behind large flakes, freezes and expands, and thereby pries the flakes loose. But even if Yosemite Valley were sealed inside a waterproof bubble, rockfalls would still occur. When the granitic rocks solidified 80 million years or more ago, they did so under great pressure, for they were several miles below the earth's surface. Today these rocks at the surface exist only under atmospheric pressure, and they expand under this release of pressure, a process known as sheeting. The sheets of exfoliating, curved flakes on Half Dome's northeast slope—the one with the intimidating cable route—are perhaps the best examples of this process in the Yosemite Valley area. However, examples of this unloading can be found almost anywhere granitic rocks exists, and some good exfoliation slabs are seen along Highway 120 between Olmsted Point and Tenaya Lake.

While all flakes are initially formed through unloading, they can be pried loose by processes other than freezing water. On March 26, 1872, John Muir, Galen Clark and others witnessed massive rockfalls due to the distant Owens Valley earthquake. A sufficient tonnage of rocks fell from Liberty Cap to momentarily dam the Merced River just above the brink of Nevada Fall.

Lightning can be another cause of rockfalls. A large-scale rockfall is unlikely to occur, but in June 1976 a lightning bolt broke off a 220-foot-high 1000-ton slab from Upper Yosemite Fall's massive wall.

Major rockfalls occur every few years in Yosemite Valley. The largest one identified is the prehistoric fall that dammed Tenaya Creek to create Mirror Lake. Gerald Wieczorek of the U.S. Geological Survey, who has been studying the Park's rockfalls, estimates this one to have been about 160 million tons. The 1987 Middle Brother rockfall, perhaps the largest historic one, pales in comparison at about 1.7 million tons. The Park's largest known rockfall is found, appropriately, in Slide Canyon (see page 34), and is estimated at 5.5 million tons.

While rockfalls built up talus slopes in Yosemite Valley and other parts of the Park, rivers and creeks worked ineffectually at removing them. Rivers and creeks were also ineffective at cutting through bedrock and they typically have carved only a foot or so into it in the last 13,000 years. Examine the brink of Vernal or Nevada falls and see just how little erosion the Merced River has done.

By the start of the Holocene epoch, all of the Sierra's Tioga-age glaciers had disappeared. However, small glaciers of relatively short duration—"little ice ages"—developed several times. The most recent one began about 1250 A.D. and became pronounced from about 1550 to 1850 A.D. This was the historic Little Ice Age, and John Muir was the first to discover a real glacier in the Sierra Nevada, not just a year-round snowfield. This was the Merced Peak glacier, which he discovered in 1871. By late 1977, a severe drought year, all traces of ice and snow there had disappeared. With man-induced climatic warming, this may be the fate of the few remaining Sierran glaciers.

Before closing this chapter on the evolution of the Yosemite landscape, we should look at the origin of its meadows. It had long been assumed that High Sierra meadows once were lakes that had developed after Tioga glaciers had retreated into oblivion about 13,000 years ago.

Actually, as Spencer Wood has shown, many of the High Sierra meadows, such as Tuolumne Meadows, were forested up to at least the start of the Little Ice Age, when colder conditions developed and the level of ground water rose, drowning the trees. We can therefore be thankful for the Little Ice Age, for without it we wouldn't have the many meadows from which we can view the snow-clad High Sierra landscape. The view-packed Yosemite Valley meadows are also in existence largely due to the presence of a high water level, the *water table,* but they have also been modified by the hand of man, as we'll see in the next chapter.

Chapter 5

The Living Yosemite

Who can forget his first visit to Yosemite—the enormous granite cliffs of El Capitan, Half Dome and Clouds Rest, the leaping, dashing waterfalls, the glaciated domes of Yosemite Valley and Tuolumne Meadows, the pristine, deep-blue waters of Tenaya Lake, the rusty, metamorphic peaks above Dana Meadows? Of these features only the waterfalls move, and none are living. For most visitors, memories of living forms—except for giant sequoias (Hike 93)—are likely to take a back seat to the inanimate landscape, although many out-of-state visitors will be duly impressed with the size of some conifers. But despite the barren peaks, cliffs and canyon walls, Yosemite is predominantly a landscape of forest green. Along all but a few of the Park's trails, conifers shade our way. In this chapter we'll delve into the "Living Yosemite"—the assemblage of plants and animals which we too often take for granted. We'll look at its *ecology,* or the relations between organisms and their environment. Because man too is an organism, we'll also look at him.

Driving up Highway 41, 120 or 140, you can't help noticing that the natural scene changes with elevation. The most obvious changes are in the trees, because they are the largest organisms and, unlike animals, they don't move around, hide or migrate in their lifetime. When you pay close attention, you notice that not only the trees but the shrubs, flowers, grasses and animals also change with elevation. You might wonder why you don't see the same plant and animal species in Tuolumne Meadows that you saw in Yosemite Valley. The answer is not as simple as it seems, for a combination of influences limits the distribution of each species. Standing in Tuolumne Meadows on even the warmest day, you'll certainly conclude that its climate is distinctly cooler than that of Yosemite Valley. Climate is probably the foremost limiting influence, but there are others. In the following pages we'll also look at the roles that topography, soil, fire and organisms play in regulating the distribution of plant and animal species.

Climatic Influences

Of all influences, temperature and precipitation are probably the most important. The pertinent climatic data for Yosemite National Park and the lands to the west and east of it are summed up in the following table. The climatic sites are arranged from west to east in ascending order to Mt. Dana, then in descending order on the Sierra's steep east slopes down to Mono Lake. Note in this table that temperature decreases with increasing elevation, but precipitation increases only up to mid-elevations, beyond which it decreases slowly to the crest, then rapidly beyond it.

Ellery Lake seems to be an exception. Its high precipitation figure is due to storm winds whipping through Tioga Pass, spreading out,

Left: **Some common Yosemite animals**
Top row (l. to r.): **mule deer, golden-mantled ground squirrel, California ground squirrel**
Middle row: **mountain chickadee, Clark's nutcracker, Steller's jay**
Bottom row: **blue grouse, western rattlesnake, rubber boa**

Table 1. Climatic data along a west-east transect of the Sierra Nevada

Site (plant community)	Elevation		Average annual temperature		Average minimum temperature in January		Average maximum temperature in July		Average annual precipitation		Growing season
	feet	meters	°F	°C	°F	°C	°F	°C	inches	cm	months
Merced (valley grassland)	160	50	63	17	36	2	98	37	12	30	9
Mariposa (foothill woodland)	2000	610	58	15	32	0	94	34	30	77	7
Yosemite Valley (ponderosa pine forest)	3970	1210	53	12	25	-4	90	32	37	94	6
Mariposa Grove (ponderosa pine forest)	6000	1800	48	9	20	-7	80	27	45	115	5
Crane Flat (sugar-pine/lodgepole-pine forest)	6200	1890	48	9	20	-7	80	27	45	115	5
Tenaya Lake (red-fir/lodgepole-pine forest)	8149	2484	43	6	17	-8	72	22	40	102	4
Tuolumne Meadows (mountain meadow)	8600	2620	39	4	15	-9	70	21	35	89	3
Tioga Pass (subalpine forest)	9941	3030	36	2	10	-12	60	16	30	76	2
Mt. Dana (alpine fell-fields)	13053	3978	32	0	0	-18	55	13	25	63	1½
Ellery Lake (subalpine forest)	9489	2822	37	3	10	-12	60	16	35	89	2
Mono Lake (sagebrush scrub)	6400	1950	48	9	20	-7	84	29	14	36	6

and depositing their snow down-canyon around this lake. In like manner, storm winds whip up the deep Middle Fork San Joaquin River canyon, cross the low Sierra crest and deposit a thick mantle of snow in the Mammoth Mountain ski area, giving it one of the longest lasting ski seasons in the state.

Because much of a winter's snow remains through late spring—and some remains throughout the summer—most of Yosemite's vegetation has an adequate water supply. In fact, the presence of the subalpine meadows is due to too much water, for conifers aren't able to survive in these seasonally water-saturated soils. However, on the rocky slopes of Mt. Dana, the Dana Plateau and other alpine slopes, the snow melts before the start of the growing season. On these dry slopes, then, the wildflowers are often dependent on summer thunderstorms for moisture. The winter snow on these slopes serves a different purpose for their perennial wildflowers: it buries and protects them. In extremely cold winter winds the equivalent wind-chill temperature can *easily* drop below −40°F(−40°C).

Physiographic Influences

The topography indirectly affects the distribution of plants and animals. As we have seen, a change in elevation means a change in temperature and precipitation, and irregular topography can create uneven distribution of snow. Well-named Snow Flat is at about the same elevation as Tuolumne Meadows, yet because it lies south of Mt. Hoffmann, it receives about twice as much snow as Tuolumne Meadows, which lies just north of the Cathedral Range. This range creates a "rain shadow" on its north side because storms lose most of their moisture on its southern flank. The Sierra crest creates an even greater rain shadow, which explains why Mono Lake, in the table, has such a low figure—about 30% of the maximum figure.

Topography also affects vegetation in other ways. A north-facing slope, because it receives less sunlight than a south-facing slope, is cooler, so evaporation and transpiration on it are less. Consequently, it can support a denser stand of vegetation. This denser stand produces more litter, which results in more humus, so ground water is retained better. In one soil survey conducted by the author, about 60% of the soil's weight on a north-facing slope was due to water,

whereas on a nearby south-facing slope, only about 5% was due to water. This was an extreme case, but, nevertheless, it helps one to visualize why north-facing slopes tend to be heavily forested while south-facing ones tend to be more open and sometimes brushy. At mid-elevations we see red and white firs on the shady slopes and Jeffrey pines and huckleberry oaks on the sunny ones.

Edaphic Influences

Yosemite's soils are derived primarily from granitic rocks. The decomposition of these rocks creates the soil that High Sierra hikers are so familiar with—gravel-size pieces of feldspar and quartz with a few flecks of mica. On mid-elevation slopes these weathered minerals can accumulate to produce a deep, well-drained soil, which will support a moderately dense forest of Jeffrey pines and white firs, such as on slopes below the back side of Half Dome (Hike 80). In soils that are extremely porous, a pure stand of Jeffrey pines can develop, as in volcanic soils of the Mono Basin, east of the Park. Where a gravelly Sierran soil is also shallow, huckleberry oak will largely replace Jeffrey pines.

It is the dark minerals of granitic rock that are important in supplying certain elements to plants. These dark minerals often are the first part of the bedrock to decompose, and they are often carried as ions in solution, only to be deposited lower down. Hence we find richer soils in flat areas, where these nutrients accumulate. Dense forests, particularly lodgepole forests, then develop, provided that the ground water is low enough. Where ground water saturates the soil—even for a short period each year—meadows develop.

A small fraction of Yosemite's soils are derived from metamorphic rocks, which are found mainly along the Park's highest elevations. At these heights an alpine plant definitely thrives better on the resulting metamorphic soils than on adjacent granitic soils. This is because metamorphic bedrock fractures into smaller pieces than granitic bedrock does, thus creating a greater water-storage capacity for plants. Furthermore, this rock is much richer in dark minerals, so it yields a more nutrient-rich soil. And, being darker in color than their granitic counterparts, metamorphic-derived soils absorb more heat—very important to plants at these alpine altitudes.

Biotic Influences

Soils can affect the type and amount of vegetation, but vegetation can also create and change soils. A soil is more than just a combination of loose, moist sand and gravel—it also has an organic component. Each year the Merced River deposits sterile silt, sand and gravel at the south end of Washburn Lake. Grasses and sedges take root in these new accumulations and stabilize them. Then, as these plants die they add an organic component to the sediments over the years, converting them to soil. As the soil develops here, it becomes ripe for invasion by willows, which further modify the new soil. Transpiration by both herbs and shrubs eventually reduces the water table sufficiently to allow another invasion—by aspens and lodgepole pines—to occur. In this way, a sterile beach eventually becomes—through activities by a *succession* of plant species—a rich forest soil.

Animals also influence the development of soils and thus affect the development of vegetation. Most of the Yosemite landscape stands above the range of the lowly earthworm, but at mid-elevations, nature has other soil processors. Foremost among these is the industrious pocket gopher, who works year round, even in the cold of winter when other rodents are either hibernating or living off stored foodstuffs. Winter is actually a safer time for the gopher to work, for it can burrow along at the base of a snowpack without danger from its summer predators—hawks, owls, gopher snakes, weasels, badgers, foxes and coyotes. After the snow melts, the gopher's winter tunneling appears as "gopher ropes." (After a gopher digs a tunnel through the snow, he later fills it with soil from his diggings in the ground beneath the snow. When the snow melts, this core of soil is then exposed, looking like a piece of rope).

In a mountain meadow a gopher population will churn up tons of soil each year. This process has numerous benefits all leading to the development of a richer soil. To a much lesser extent, burrowing and digging by ground squirrels, moles, badgers and coyotes also contribute to soil development.

And we must not forget the decomposers—bacteria, fungi, lichens, invertebrates and even a few plants—without whom dead plants and animals would continually accumulate until the entire forest lay smothered beneath their mass.

Decomposers—usually minute and unseen—busily convert dead plants and animals into litter and humus. However, because too much litter and humus can prevent seedling germination, fire is an integral part of the ecosystem in all but Yosemite's alpine areas.

It has been said that the giant sequoia, might not be around today were it not for the roles played by fire, the Douglas squirrel and a cone-boring beetle (Hike 93). Momentarily we'll overlook the role of fire and concentrate on the roles of organisms. More than 150 species of insects depend in part on the giant sequoia, and it is very dependent on one insect. This tree is not alone in this respect. In Yosemite, insect species outnumber plant species about ten to one. Without insects, most wildflowers would disappear for lack of pollination. Then too, wildflowers receive aid from birds and rodents in the form of seed planting and seed dispersal. Even preying on plants is beneficial; otherwise plants would undergo a population explosion, cover the earth, and die in their own debris.

An example of the complexity of plant-animal interaction is shown in the following chart, which shows some of the plants and animals that either directly or indirectly depend in part upon the gold-cup oak. The lines show who eats whom. For example, the mountain king snake, at the bottom right, preys on the western rattlesnake, the gopher snake and the western skink. The gopher snake also preys on the western skink, and also on the mole. The mole feeds on termites, and so on. The list of plants and animals could be extended indefinitely. If one were to remove the oak's parasitic mistletoe, perhaps the oak population would increase, but then, the animals that feed on the mistletoe and the animals that in turn prey upon them would be affected. Whenever you tamper with one of nature's components, you affect the whole system.

The Role of Fire

The presence or absence of ground fires can really alter the system, for it significantly alters the populations of ground-dwelling plants and animals and everything associated with them. Fires were once thought to be detrimental to the overall well-being of the ecosystem, and early foresters attempted to prevent or subdue all fires. Until 1971, fire suppression was a general, though sometimes contested, Yosemite policy. This policy, however, led to the accumulation of

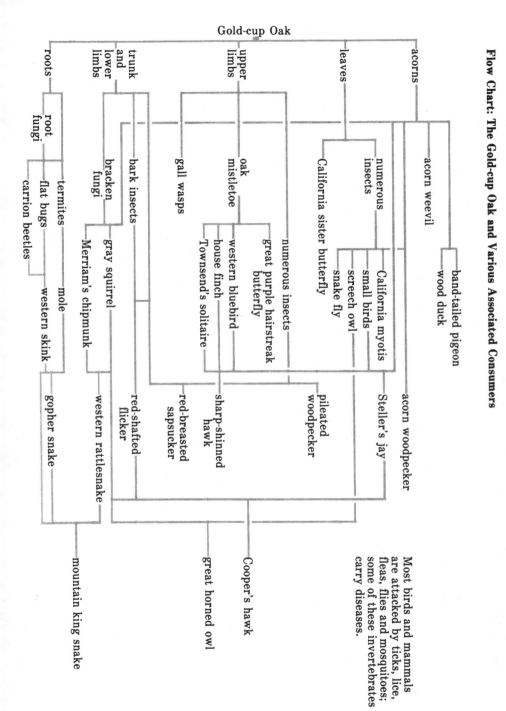

Flow Chart: The Gold-cup Oak and Various Associated Consumers

Most birds and mammals are attacked by ticks, lice, fleas, flies and mosquitoes; some of these invertebrates carry diseases.

thick litter, dense brush and overmature trees—
all prime fuel for a holocaust when a fire
inevitably sparked to life. It also led to a change
in the distribution of plant and animal species
and encouraged root rot (Hike 66).

Foresters now know that *natural* fires
should not be prevented, but only regulated.
These fires, if left unchecked, burn stands of
mixed conifers—such as those found in
Yosemite Valley—about once every 10 years.
At this frequency, brush and litter do not
accumulate sufficiently to result in a damaging
forest fire; only the ground cover is burned over,
while the trees remain generally intact. Thus,
through small burns, the forest is protected from
going up in smoke. Ultimately, however, stands
of trees mature, the trees die, logs accumulate on
the ground, and major fires occur, such as the
1988 Yellowstone fires.

Some trees are adapted to fire. The giant
sequoia, for example, releases its seeds after a
fire, as do numbers of conifers, shrubs and
wildflowers. Seeds of the genus *Ceanothus* are
quick to germinate in burned-over ground, and
some plants of this genus are among the primary
foods of deer (see Hike 8). Hence, periodic
burns will keep a deer population at its
maximum. With too few burns, shrubs become
too woody and unproductive for a deer herd. In
like manner, gooseberries and other berry plants
sprout after fires and help support several
different bird and mammal populations.

Without fires, a plant community evolves
toward a *climax,* or end stage, of plant
succession. Red and white firs are the main
species in the climax vegetation that is
characteristic of the Sierra's mid-elevations.
However, a *pure* stand of *any* species invites
epidemic attacks and therefore can be unstable.
In the past, pure stands of Yosemite's
lodgepoles have been severely attacked by
lodgepole needleminers—the larval stage of a
moth—which turned the living stands into
"ghost forests."

Fire is also beneficial in that it unlocks
nutrients that are stored up in living matter,
litter, topsoil and even rocks. Vital compounds
are released in the form of ash when a fire burns
plants and forest litter. Fire also can heat
granitic rocks enough to cause them to break up
and release their minerals. In one study of a
northern coniferous forest it was concluded that
the weathering of granitic rock in that area was
primarily due to periodic fires. A post-fire
inspection in Yosemite can reveal that fires do
get hot enough to cause thin sheets of granite to
exfoliate, or sheet off, from boulders.

Natural, periodic fires, then, can be very
beneficial for a forest ecosystem, and they
should be thought of as an integral process in the
plant community. They have, after all, been
around as long as terrestrial life has, and for
millions of years have been a common process in
most of the Sierra's plant communities.

Biogeography

We have just delved very briefly into the
influences regulating the distribution of plants
and animals. Of course, not every species is
equally affected by these influences. And
therefore every plant and animal has its own
range, habitat and *niche.* The range is the entire
area over which an organism may be found.
Some species have a very restricted range;
others, a very widespread one. The giant
sequoia, for example, occurs only in about 75
small groves at mid-elevations in the western
Sierra Nevada. An organism's habitat is the
kind of place where it lives. The habitat of the
giant sequoia is typically a gentle, forested,
periodically burned slope that is usually near the
ridge between two river canyons. An organism's
niche is the functional role it plays in its
community. For example, the giant sequoia
provides food and shelter for dozens of insects
that utilize the tree's needles, branches, bark and
cones, and additional organisms benefit from
soil changes created by the sequoia's roots. At
the same time, the sequoia receives essential aid
from the Douglas squirrel, from a long-
antennaed beetle and from fire (see Hike 93).
Thus the niche is a give-and-take relationship.

The sequoia's range, though not really large,
is great compared to that of a few alpine species
such as the snow willow. This "shrub"—usually
less than an inch high—is found only on a few
old, nearly flat surfaces on or close to the Park's
northeast boundary. Animals, having the ability
to move, generally have greater ranges than
plants, though the Mt. Lyell salamander has a
spotty, subalpine range about equal in north-
south extent to that of the giant sequoia. An
isolated population of this animal survives atop
Half Dome (Hike 80).

Some plants and animals have tremendous
ranges. For example, the bottlebrush
squirreltail—a grass of the Hordeae tribe found
in Yosemite—extends from Mexico north to
British Columbia and east to Texas and South
Dakota. It can be found in dry, open habitats
from sea level up into alpine fell-fields. Some

Plate 1. **Some common Yosemite trees—all conifers**
Top row (l. to r.): **gray pine (Digger pine), Jeffrey pine, whitebark pine**
Middle row: **western juniper, incense-cedar branches, mountain hemlock**
Bottom row: **red fir, red fir cone (top) and western white pine cone (bottom), western white pine**
        (silver pine)

Plate 2. **Some common Yosemite shrubs**
Top row (l. to r.): **chinquapin, tobacco brush, pinemat manzanita**
Middle row: **mountain ash, thimbleberry, mountain spiraea**
Bottom row: **red mountain heather, bog kalmia, Labrador tea**

256

Plate 3. **Some wildflowers of foothill woodlands and ponderosa pine forests**
Top row (l. to r.): **Indian pink, Indian hemp, miner's lettuce**
Middle row: **Lemmon's catchfly, mountain violet, common madia**
Bottom row: **fireweed, nude buckwheat, California stickseed**

257

Plate 4. **Some wildflowers of Jeffrey pine forests**
Top row (l. to r.): **mountain pride, pussy paws, sulfur flower**
Middle row: **Mariposa lily, spreading phlox, Applegate's paintbrush**
Bottom row: **scarlet gilia, single-stemmed senecio, mule ears**

Plate 5. Some wildflowers of red fir/lodgepole pine forests
Top row (l. to r.): **western spring beauty, bleeding heart, racemose false Solomon's seal**
Middle row: **spotted coralroot, pine drops, snow plant**
Bottom row: **white-veined wintergreen, dwarf lousewort, California Jacob's ladder**

Plate 6. **Some wildflowers of creeks, springs and bogs**
Top row (l. to r.): **ranger's buttons, cow parsnip, leopard lily**
Middle row: **elephant heads, common large monkey flower, red columbine**
Bottom row: **wandering daisy, arrowhead butterweed, broad-leaved lupine**

Plate 7. **Some wildflowers of meadows**
Top row (l. to r.): **sticky cinquefoil, corn lily, green gentian**
Middle row: **hiker's gentian, shooting star, marsh marigold**
Bottom row: **yarrow, meadow penstemon, Gray's lovage**

Plate 8. **Some wildflowers of subalpine forests and alpine fell-fields**
Top row (l. to r.): **alpine gold, timberline phacelia, shaggy hawkweed**
Middle row: **flat-seeded rock cress, alpine gentian, mountain sorrel**
Bottom row: **rock fringe, sphynx moth and Davidson's penstemon, alpine saxifrage**

other far-ranging plants seen throughout much of Yosemite are bracken fern, golden brodiaea, comb draba, Brewer's lupine, Applegate's paintbrush, woolly sunflower and common yarrow.

In the animal kingdom, the mule deer (see Hike 8), mountain lion, coyote, badger, long-tailed weasel, California ground squirrel and deer mouse are mammals that range through much of Yosemite. Many birds seen in Yosemite have migrated, if not from the south, then from the lowlands, and they follow the development of a food supply that occurs higher and higher as the winter snowpack retreats. In most of the Park you can expect to see the robin, junco, Brewer's blackbird, red-shafted flicker, white-crowned sparrow, chipping sparrow, dipper, red-tailed hawk and marsh hawk. Reptiles and amphibians, despite their limited mobility and their disadvantageous cold-blooded circulatory system, do include a few well-adapting species that have broad ranges. Seen from the foothills up into the subalpine zone are the western fence lizard, western toad and Pacific treefrog. The western rattlesnake is also widespread up to about 7000 feet, and a few individuals have made it up to the subalpine zone. Thus, some plant and animal species can adapt to environments and competitors better than others. Most of Yosemite's plants and animals have a more restricted distribution, each living in only several of Yosemite's seven plant communities, and some species live in only one community. We'll now look at some of these species found in the Park's communities.

Plant Communities and Their Animal Associations

When you hike in the mountains, you anticipate seeing certain plants and animals in a given habitat. You quickly learn, for example, that junipers don't grow in wet meadows, but corn lilies do. Corn lilies, in turn, don't grow on dry rock slabs, but junipers do. Likewise, you would expect to find garter snakes in wet meadows and western fence lizards on the dry rock slabs, but never the reverse. Thus you could group plants and animals by their habitat. In this book, as in other guides, this classification is based on the dominant *plant* or *plant types* of a habitat simply because these are the most readily observed life forms. Such a group of life forms is called a plant community, even though it includes animals as well as plants.

Because animals move, they can be harder to classify. Birds, for example, typically have a wide—usually seasonal—range, and therefore may be found in many plant communities. In the following list of communities, a species is mentioned in the community in which you, the visitor, are most likely to see it. In addition, only the more prominent and/or diagnostic species are mentioned. To mention all would fill an entire book—Yosemite Valley *alone* has about 400 species of grasses and wildflowers and thousands of insect species! Common names, particularly among wildflowers, vary from guide to guide, and the author has attempted to use either the most common name (e.g., sulfur flower) or the most descriptive name (e.g., gold-cup oak) for each species. To save space, grasses, ferns, lower plants, trout and invertebrates have not been included.

The following plant communities are listed in an approximate order of ascending elevation and decreasing temperature. These plant communities aren't the final word in plant-animal classification, since each community could be further subdivided. For example, Lionel Klikoff has identified *eight* vegetational patterns in the Gaylor Lakes area (Hike 46), near Tioga Pass. Each pattern is the result of a different set of microenvironmental influences.

Table 2. Yosemite's Plant Communities

1. Foothill Woodland

Trees: Digger pine, knobcone pine, blue oak, interior live oak, tanbark oak, California buckeye, red willow, arroyo willow, black cottonwood

Shrubs: scrub oak, poison oak, Parry manzanita, whiteleaf manzanita, chaparral whitethorn, yerba santa, toyon, western redbud, spice bush, bush poppy, bush monkey flower, mock orange, chaparral currant, bitter gooseberry

Wildflowers: Indian pink, soap plant, California poppy, miner's lettuce, Chinese houses, purple milkweed, star flower, western buttercup

Mammals: gray fox, bobcat, spotted skunk, ringtail, brush rabbit, Merriam's chipmunk, Botta's pocket gopher, dusky-footed wood rat, Heermann's kangaroo rat, brush mouse, pinyon mouse, ornate shrew, small-footed myotis (bat), western pipistrelle (bat)

Birds: California thrasher, wrentit, bushtit, plain titmouse, scrub jay, rufous-sided towhee, western bluebird, Nuttall's woodpecker,

Hutton's vireo, Bewick's wren, blue-gray gnatcatcher
Reptiles: common king snake, racer, striped racer, ringneck snake, western whiptail, southern alligator lizard, Gilbert's skink
Amphibians: foothill yellow-legged frog, California slender salamander, California newt, arboreal salamander
Where seen: Poopenaut Valley, Hetch Hetchy Reservoir (northwest side), Arch Rock-El Portal area, Alder Creek trail near its end

2. Ponderosa Pine Forest

Trees: ponderosa pine, incense-cedar, black oak, sugar pine, white fir, gold-cup oak, Douglas-fir, giant sequoia (restricted distribution), California laurel (bay tree), big-leaf maple, Scouler's willow, Pacific dogwood, white alder, black cottonwood
Shrubs: Mariposa manzanita, mountain misery, western azalea, creek (red) dogwood, buckbrush, deer brush, Sierra gooseberry
Wildflowers: broad-leaved lupine, harlequin lupine, narrow-leaved lotus, black-eyed Susan, common madia, scarlet monkey flower, blue penstemon, evening primrose, bleeding heart, wild ginger, false Solomon's seal, Indian hemp, umbrella plant (Indian rhubarb), mountain violet, waterfall buttercup
Mammals: black bear, raccoon, striped skunk, gray squirrel, long-eared chipmunk, big brown bat, hairy-winged myotis (bat)
Birds: Steller's jay, black-headed grosbeak, western tanager, Townsend's solitaire, acorn woodpecker, white-headed woodpecker, downy woodpecker, band-tailed pigeon, purple finch, solitary vireo, Nashville warbler, black-throated gray warbler, MacGillivray's warbler, winter wren, violet-green swallow, screech owl, spotted owl, golden eagle
Reptiles: California mountain kingsnake, rubber boa, gopher snake, northern alligator lizard
Amphibian: ensatina
Where seen: Yosemite Valley, Cherry Lake, Mather R.S., Pate Valley, Old and New Big Oak Flat roads, Alder Creek trail, Wawona, Mariposa Grove

3. Jeffrey Pine Forest

Trees: Jeffrey pine, red fir, white fir, incense-cedar, sugar pine, western juniper
Shrubs: huckleberry oak, greenleaf manzanita, snow bush, tobacco brush, sagebrush, white squaw currant, curl-leaved mountain mahogany
Wildflowers: mountain pride (Newberry's penstemon), Bridge's penstemon, showy

penstemon, Gray's lupine, single-stemmed senecio, mountain pennyroyal (coyote mint), mule ears, Douglas wallflower, shieldleaf (streptanthus), spreading phlox, scarlet gilia, pussy paws, sulfur flower, nude buckwheat, Leichtlin's Mariposa lily, Sierra sedum
Mammals: Sierra Nevada golden-mantled ground squirrel, mountain pocket gopher, bushy-tailed wood rat
Birds: mountain quail, fox sparrow, green-tailed towhee, Townsend's solitaire, olive-sided flycatcher
Reptiles: western fence lizard, sagebrush lizard, western rattlesnake
Where seen: El Capitan, North Dome-Indian Ridge, old Kibbie Lake trail, lower West Walker River, slabs above Lake Vernon and Agnew Lake. At most of Yosemite's rocky or dry-gravelly mid-elevation sites; widespread on the Mono Basin's higher slopes.

4. Red Fir/Lodgepole Pine Forest

Trees: red fir, lodgepole pine, western white pine, white fir, mountain hemlock, aspen, Scouler's willow, MacKenzie's willow
Shrubs: bush chinquapin, pinemat, manzanita, mountain spiraea, Labrador tea, red heather, Sierra laurel, Sierra gooseberry, sticky currant, service-berry, bitter cherry, mountain ash, Lemmon's willow, mountain alder
Wildflowers: common wintergreen, pine drops, snow plant, spotted coralroot, meadow rue, Richardson's geranium, arrowhead butterweed, larkspur, monkshood, red columbine, mountain blue bells (lungwort), alpine lily
Mammals: red fox, porcupine, marten, chickaree (Douglas squirrel), lodgepole chipmunk, western jumping mouse, dusky shrew, little brown myotis (bat)
Birds: blue grouse, dark-eyed junco, mountain chickadee, red-breasted nuthatch, golden-crowned kinglet, Williamson's sapsucker, Hammond's flycatcher, Cassin's finch, evening grosbeak, red crossbill, goshawk, great gray owl
Where seen: generally found between 6500 and 9000 feet—the elevation traversed by the bulk of Yosemite's trails; it is the most widespread plant community in Yosemite. Most accessible sites: Highway 120 from Crane Flat to Tuolumne Meadows, White Wolf, Pohono Trail, Badger Pass, Chiquito Pass

5. Mountain Meadow

Shrubs: alpine willow, caudate willow, Eastwood's willow, Sierra willow, western blueberry, dwarf bilberry

Wildflowers: corn lily, Jeffrey's shooting star, squaw root (Queen Anne's lace), swamp onion, carpet clover, Leichtlin's camas, marsh marigold, Lewis monkey flower, primrose monkey flower, alpine monkey flower, Lemmon's paintbrush, Brewer's paintbrush, alpine paintbrush, Sierra penstemon, whorled penstemon, slender cinquefoil, Brewer's cinquefoil, sticky cinquefoil, Drummond's cinquefoil, pussytoes, elephant heads
Mammals: Belding ground squirrel, white-tailed hare (jack rabbit), montane meadow mouse, water shrew
Birds: white-crowned sparrow, Brewer's blackbird, mountain bluebird, spotted sandpiper
Reptile: mountain garter snake
Amphibians: Yosemite toad, Pacific treefrog, mountain yellow-legged frog
Where seen: Tuolumne Meadows, Dana Meadows, Lyell Canyon, Grace Meadow, Kerrick Meadow, McGurk Meadow, Mono Meadow, Moraine Meadow, Lukens Lake, Cathedral Lakes, Dog Lake, Middle Gaylor Lake, Washburn Lake, Emeric Lake

6. Subalpine Forest

Trees: whitebark pine, lodgepole pine, western white pine, mountain hemlock
Shrubs: bush cinquefoil, alpine willow, Eastwood's willow, Mono willow, Sierra willow, red heather, white heather, Labrador tea, alpine gooseberry, sticky currant
Wildflowers: Sierra wallflower, Davidson's penstemon, Pierson's penstemon, Coville's lupine, alpine columbine, mountain sorrel, rock fringe, Lobb's eriogonum, cut-leaved daisy, alpine saxifrage, pink alumroot
Mammals: pika, yellow-bellied marmot, aplodontia, white-tailed hare (jack rabbit), alpine chipmunk, ermine (short-tailed weasel), little brown myotis (bat)
Birds: Clark's nutcracker, pine grosbeak, mountain chickadee, mountain blackbird, black-backed woodpecker
Amphibians: Mt. Lyell salamander, Yosemite toad
Where seen: most high lakes and passes, including Dorothy Lake, Peeler Lake, Benson Pass, Virginia Pass, Summit Lake, McCabe Lakes, Gaylor Lakes, Tioga Pass, Mono Pass, Ireland Lake, Vogelsang High Sierra Camp, May Lake, Ten Lakes, Clouds Rest, Half Dome, Post Peak Pass, Fernandez Pass, upper Chain Lake

7. Alpine Fell-Fields

Shrubs: snow willow, alpine willow, bush cinquefoil, alpine prickly currant
Wildflowers: sky pilot, alpine gold, Brewer's draba, Lemmon's draba, Sierra draba, dense-leaved draba, Coville's phlox, Davidson's penstemon, cut-leaved daisy, dwarf daisy, Muir's senecio, Whitney's locoweed, Sierra podistera, oval-leaved buckwheat, Muir's ivesia, pygmy lewisia, compact sandwort
Mammals: pika, yellow-bellied marmot, alpine chipmunk
Bird: gray-crowned rosy finch
Where seen: most of the Sierra crest from Matterhorn Peak south, including Mt. Dana, Parker Pass and Donohue Pass; also Mt. Hoffmann and Red Peak Pass

The Ahwahnechee

One animal that could be found in all of Yosemite's plant communities was *Homo sapiens*—the aboriginal natives of Yosemite Valley. Calling themselves the Ahwahnechee, these people roamed the Yosemite landscape for food gathering, trade, or tribal interactions. Generally, however, they found most of what they needed right in Yosemite Valley. Annually they burned the valley's floor, and this was a tradition that had definite benefits. Foremost, it maintained the oak population, and acorns from black oaks alone made up 60% of their diet. Fire also reduced brush and kept the forests open and parklike, thus reducing the chance of ambush. Today Yosemite Valley holds far more *Homo sapiens* (humans) than its resources could feed. We, however, carry in our own food or buy trucked-in foods. The Indians had to make do with the resources on hand, not only for food, but for all aspects of survival. They made extensive use of the Valley's resources and the resources of other nearby plant communities. The following table, based on unpublished work by Will Neely, a Park naturalist, gives one an idea of just how extensively they utilized the plants. Animals—both vertebrates and invertebrates—were also extensively utilized.

Table 3. Indian Uses of Yosemite Plants

Food

Acorns and large seeds: black oak, sugar pine, western juniper. When black-oak acorns were scarce, then the following were used: gold-cup oak, interior live oak, Digger pine, buckeye, pinyon pine (east of the Sierra crest)

Smaller seeds: bunch grass, western buttercup, evening primrose, farewell-to-spring, California coneflower

Bulbs, corms, roots: Leichtlin's Mariposa lily, golden brodiaea, blue camas, squaw root, Bolander's yampah

Greens: broad-leaved lupine, common monkey flower, nude buckwheat, California thistle, miner's lettuce, sorrel, clover, umbrella plant (Indian rhubarb), red columbine, alum root

Berries and fruits: strawberry, blackberry, raspberry, thimbleberry, wild grape, gooseberry, currant, blue elderberry, western chokecherry, Sierra plum, greenleaf manzanita

Drinks: Mariposa manzanita, western juniper

Medicine

Yerba santa, common yarrow, giant hyssop, Brewer's angelica, sagebrush, showy milkweed, Indian hemp, balsamroot, California barberry, fleabane, mint, knotweed, wild rose, meadow goldenrod, mule ears, pearly everlasting, California laurel (bay tree)

Soap

Soap plant, meadow rue

Rope and Twine

Indian hemp, showy milkweed, wild grape, soap plant

Baskets

Redbud, creek dogwood, big-leaf maple, buckbrush, deer brush, bracken fern, willows, California hazelnut

Bows

Incense-cedar, Pacific dogwood

Shelter

Incense-cedar

Western Man in Yosemite

In the late 1850s tourists, homesteaders and entrepreneurs began to flock to Yosemite Valley in increasing numbers. By 1864 the Valley was set aside ostensibly for "public use, resort and recreation," but also to protect it from these people so that future generations could enjoy its amenities. The surrounding high country, however, was not protected, and sheep (and cattle to a lesser extent) were driven up into virtually every High Sierra meadow. Tuolumne Meadows in particular was severely overgrazed

by sheep, resulting in deterioration of its soils. Overgrazing was certainly detrimental to the native fauna and flora, but by the mid-1890s, grazing had been virtually eliminated from all parts of the Park except Yosemite Valley, where a dairy herd grazed, not to mention everyone's horses. Fruit orchards competed with native trees.

All the introduced animals together with their masters inadvertently brought in unwanted alien plants, insects and associated diseases. Galen Clark, the Park's first guardian, noted that in the 30 years that passed after the Park was first set aside, the luxuriant native grasses and flowering plants of Yosemite Valley had decreased to only one-fourth of their original number. Part of this was due to grazing, part to other causes, and part to the new plant competition.

Overgrazing on the Valley floor resulted in trampled soil and bare spots, both inviting invasion by ponderosa pines and incense-cedars. Prohibition of fires insured the survival of young conifers which, as they matured, shaded out the once co-dominant black oaks. Finally, lowering the water table through blasting and ditching hastened this conifer invasion of the meadows. Today the Yosemite Valley plant community is largely a dense conifer forest with neatly defined, gardened meadows; it is no longer an open conifer-oak woodland.

The underfunded, understaffed Park Service is attempting to reverse some of the past damage. In particular, it is attempting to halt the slide toward extinction of peregrine falcons and great gray owls, and it has reintroduced bighorn sheep to east-border lands. But how do they deal with the top predator, man?

The rising flood of visitors often has been perceived as the foremost threat to Yosemite's fauna and flora. However, the most pernicious threats usually go unseen and are beyond the control of the Park Service: man-induced global warming, increasing atmospheric pollution, upper-atmosphere ozone depletion, and habitat loss in middle and lower elevations of the Sierra Nevada and elsewhere in the Americas. The latter is of particular concern for Yosemite's birds, which in the fall typically migrate to lower elevations or to lower latitudes, such as to Central America. But everywhere the mounting human population is destroying habitat and the life it once held. For example, each person added to California ultimately causes enough habitat destruction to destroy up to one ton of animals, plants and micro-organisms—something to ponder.

Recommended Reading and Source Materials

(The entries marked * are very technical and will not be understood by most readers.)

General

Brower, Kenneth. 1990. *Yosemite: an American Treasure.* Washington, D.C.: National Geographic Society, 199 p.

Browning, Peter. 1988. *Yosemite Place Names.* Lafayette, CA: Great West Books, 241 p.

Cameron, Robert. 1983. *Above Yosemite.* San Francisco: Cameron and Co., 144 p.

Ditton, Richard P., and Donald E. McHenry. 1989. *Yosemite Road Guide.* El Portal: Yosemite Association.

Medley, Steven P. 1991. *The Complete Guidebook to Yosemite National Park.* El Portal: Yosemite Association, 112 p.

Melham, Tom. 1976. *John Muir's Wild America.* Washington, D.C.: National Geographic Society, 199 p.

Muir, John. 1894 (1977). *The Mountains of California.* Berkeley: Ten Speed Press, 400 p.

Muir, John, and Galen Rowell. 1989. *The Yosemite.* San Francisco: Sierra Club, 223 p.

Osborne, Michael. *Waterfalls of Yosemite Valley.* El Portal: Yosemite Association, 48 p.

Robertson, David. 1984. *West of Eden: A History of the Art and Literature of Yosemite.* El Portal and Berkeley: Yosemite Association and Wilderness Press, 174 p.

Mountaineering

Darvill, Fred Jr. 1989. *Mountaineering Medicine.* Berkeley: Wilderness Press, 79 p.

Falkenstein, Chris, and Don Reid. 1992. *Rock Climbs of Tuolumne Meadows.* Denver: Chockstone Press, 192 p.

Graydon, Don, ed. 1992. *Mountaineering: The Freedom of the Hills.* Seattle: The Mountaineers, 447 p.

King, Clarence. 1872 (1970). *Mountaineering in the Sierra Nevada.* Lincoln: University of Nebraska Press, 292 p.

Reid, Don. 1991. *Yosemite Select: the Best of Yosemite Climbing.* Denver: Chockstone Press, 125 p.

———. 1993. *Yosemite Climbs.* Denver: Chockstone Press, 500 p.

Rowell, Galen A., ed. 1974. *The Vertical World of Yosemite.* Berkeley: Wilderness Press, 207 p.

Secor, R.J. 1992. *The High Sierra: Peaks, Passes, and Trails.* Seattle: The Mountaineers, 368 p.

Spencer, Mark, and Shirley Spencer. 1988. *Southern Yosemite Rock Climbs.* Oakhurst, CA: Condor Designs, 151 p.

History

Bunnell, Lafayette H. 1880 (1977). *Discovery of the Yosemite in 1851.* Olympic Valley, CA: Outbooks, 184 p.

Brewer, William H. 1930 (1966). *Up and Down California in 1860–1864.* Berkeley: University of California Press, 583 p.

Farquhar, Francis P. 1965. *History of the Sierra Nevada.* Berkeley: University of California Press, 262 p.

Muir, John. 1911. *My First Summer in. the Sierra.* Boston: Houghton Mifflin Co., 272 p.

Reid, Robert L., ed. 1983. *A Treasury of the Sierra Nevada.* Berkeley: Wilderness Press, 363 p.

Russell, Carl P. 1968 (1976). *100 Years in Yosemite.* El Portal: Yosemite Association, 210 p.

Sanborn, Margaret. 1989. *Yosemite: Its Discovery, its Wonders and its People.* El Portal: Yosemite Association, 289 p.

Geology

*Bailey, Roy A., N. King Huber and Robert R. Curry. 1990. "The diamicton at Deadman Pass, central Sierra Nevada, California: A residual lag and colluvial deposit, not a 3 Ma glacial till." *Geological Society of America Bulletin,* v. 102, p. 1165–1173.

*Bartow, J. Alan. 1991. *The Cenozoic Evolution of the San Joaquin Valley, California.* U.S. Geological Survey Professional Paper 1501, 40 p.

*Bateman, Paul C. 1983. "A summary of critical relations in the central part of the Sierra Nevada batholith, California, U.S.A." In

Circum-Pacific Plutonic Terranes (J. A. Roddick, ed.). Geological Society of America Memoir 159, p. 241–254.

Bateman, Paul C., and Clyde Wahrhaftig. 1966. "Geology of the Sierra Nevada" In *Geology of Northern California* (Edgar H. Bailey, ed.). California Division of Mines and Geology Bulletin 190, p. 107–172.

Christensen, Mark N. 1966. "Late Cenozoic crustal movements in the Sierra Nevada of California." *Geological Society of America Bulletin*, v. 77, p. 163–181.

Clark, William B. 1970. *Gold Districts of California*. California Division of Mines and Geology Bulletin 193, 186 p.

Cox, Allan, and Robert B. Hart. 1986. *Plate Tectonics: How It Works*. Oxford: Blackwell Scientific Publications, 392 p.

*du Bray, Edward A., and David A. Dellinger. 1988. *Potassium-Argon Ages for Plutons in the Eastern and Southern Sierra Nevada Batholith, California*. U.S. Geological Survey Bulletin 1799, 10 p.

*Ernst, Wallace G., ed. 1981. *The Geotectonic Development of California* (Rubey Volume I). Englewood Cliffs: Prentice-Hall, 706 p.

*_____. 1988. *Metamorphism and Crustal Evolution of the Western United States* (Rubey Volume VII). Englewood Cliffs: Prentice-Hall, 1153 p.

Fryxell, Fritiof, ed. 1962. *François Matthes and the Marks of Time*. San Francisco: Sierra Club, 189 p.

Fullerton, David S. 1986. "Chronology and Correlation of Glacial Deposits in the Sierra Nevada, California." *Quaternary Science Reviews* (special issue: *Glaciations in the Northern Hemisphere*), v. 5, p. 161–169.

Gutenberg, Beno, John P. Buwalda and Robert P. Sharp. 1956. "Seismic explorations on the floor of Yosemite Valley, California." *Bulletin of the Geological Society of America*, v. 67, p. 1051–1078.

Harland, W. Brian, and others. 1990. *A Geologic Time Scale 1989*. Cambridge: Cambridge University Press, 263 p.

*Howell, David G., ed. *Tectonostratigraphic Terranes of the Circum-Pacific Region*. Houston: Circum-Pacific Council for Energy and Mineral Resources, 585 p.

Huber, N. King. 1981. *Amount and Timing of Late Cenozoic Uplift and Tilt of the Central Sierra Nevada, California—Evidence from the Upper San Joaquin River Basin*. U.S. Geological Survey Professional Paper 1197, 28 p.

_____. 1987. *The Geologic Story of Yosemite National Park*. U.S. Geological Survey Bulletin 1595, 64 p.

_____. 1990. "Evolution of the Tuolumne River." *Yosemite*, v. 52, no. 1, p. 5–8.

_____. 1990. "The late Cenozoic evolution of the Tuolumne River, central Sierra Nevada, California." *Geological Society of America Bulletin*, v. 102, p. 102–115.

Jenkins, Olaf P. 1948. *The Mother Lode Country* (Geologic Guidebook Along Highway 49—Sierran Gold Belt). California Division of Mines and Geology Bulletin 141, 164 p.

Matthes, François E. 1930. *Geologic History of the Yosemite Valley*. U.S. Geological Survey Professional Paper 160, 137 p.

_____. 1950. *The Incomparable Valley*. Berkeley: University of California Press, 160 p.

_____. 1960. *Reconnaissance of the Geomorphology and Glacial History of the San Joaquin Basin, Sierra Nevada, California*. U.S. Geological Survey Professional Paper 329, 62 p.

*Nokelberg, Warren J. 1983. *Wallrocks of the Central Sierra Nevada Batholith, California: A Collage of Accreted Tectono-Stratigraphic Terranes*. U.S. Geological Survey Professional Paper 1255, 28 p.

*Nokleberg, Warren J., and Ronald W. Kistler. 1980. *Paleozoic and Mesozoic Deformations in the Central Sierra Nevada, California*. U.S. Geological Survey Professional Paper 1145, 24 p.

Oakeshott, Gordon B., ed. 1962. *Geologic Guide to the Merced Canyon and Yosemite Valley, California*. California Division of Mines and Geology Bulletin 182, 68 p.

*Oldow, John S., and others. 1989. "Phanerozoic evolution of the North American Cordillera; United States and Canada." In *The Geology of North America; An Overview* (The Geology of North America, Volume A, Albert W. Bally and Allison R. Palmer, eds.). Boulder: Geological Society of America, p. 139–232.

Ruddiman, W.F., and H.E. Wright, Jr. 1987. *North America and Adjacent Oceans During the Last Deglaciation* (The Geology of North America, Volume K–3). Boulder: Geological Society of America, 501 p.

Schaffer, Jeffrey P. 1977. "Pleistocene Lake Yosemite and the Wisconsin glaciation of Yosemite Valley." *California Geology*, v. 30, p. 243–248.

_____ . 1987. "A New Look at the Origin of Yosemite Valley." *Yosemite,* v. 49, no. 3, p. 6–9.

_____ . 1992. *The Geomorphic Evolution of Yosemite Valley, Sierra Nevada, California* [Ph.D. thesis]. Berkeley: University of California, Department of Geography, 250 p.

_____ . 1993. "California's Geological History and Changing Landscapes." In *The Jepson Manual: Vascular Plants of California* (James C. Hickman, ed.). Berkeley: University of California Press, p. 49–54.

Smith, George I., and others. 1983. *Core KM-3, a Surface-to-Bedrock Record of Late Cenozoic Sedimentation in Searles Valley, California.* U.S. Geological Survey Professional Paper 1256, 24 p.

Unruh, J.R. 1991. "The uplift of the Sierra Nevada and implications for late Cenozoic epeirogeny in the western Cordillera." *Geological Society of America Bulletin,* v. 103, p. 1395–1404.

*Wahrhaftig, Clyde. 1965. "Stepped topography of the southern Sierra Nevada." Geological Society of America Bulletin, v. 76, p. 1165–1189.

Geologic Maps

Alpha, Tau Rho, Clyde Wahrhaftig and N. King Huber. 1987. *Oblique map showing maximum extent of 20,000-year-old (Tioga) glaciers, Yosemite National Park,* central Sierra Nevada, California. U.S. Geological Survey Map I-1885.

Bailey, Roy A. 1989. *Geologic map of the Long Valley caldera, Mono-Inyo Craters volcanic chain, and vicinity, eastern California.* U.S. Geological Survey Map I-1933.

Bartow, J. Alan. 1985. *Map and cross sections showing Tertiary stratigraphy and structure of the northern San Joaquin Valley, California.* U.S. Geological Survey Map MF-1761.

Bateman, Paul C., and others. 1983. *Geologic map of the Tuolumne Meadows quadrangle, Yosemite National Park, California.* U.S. Geological Survey Map GQ-1570.

Bateman, Paul C., and Konrad B. Krauskopf. 1987. *Geologic map of the El Portal quadrangle, west-central Sierra Nevada, California.* U.S. Geological Survey Map MF-1998.

Calkins, Frank C., and others. 1930 (1985). *Bedrock geologic map of Yosemite Valley, Yosemite National Park, California.* U.S. Geological Survey Map I-1639.

Chesterman, Charles W. 1975. *Geology of the Matterhorn Peak Quadrangle, Mono and Tuolumne Counties, California.* California Division of Mines and Geology Map Sheet 22.

Dodge, F.C.W., and L.C. Calk. 1987. *Geologic map of the Lake Eleanor quadrangle, central Sierra Nevada, California.* U.S. Geological Survey Map GQ-1639.

Huber, N. King. 1983. *Preliminary geologic map of the Pinecrest quadrangle, central Sierra Nevada, California.* U.S. Geological Survey Map MF-1437.

Huber, N. King, and C. Dean Rinehart. 1965. *Geologic map of the Devils Postpile quadrangle, Sierra Nevada, California.* U.S. Geological Survey Map GQ-437.

Huber, N. King, Paul C. Bateman and Clyde Wahrhaftig. 1989. *Geologic map of Yosemite National Park and vicinity, California.* U.S. Geological Survey Map I-1874.

Kistler, Ronald W. 1966. *Geologic map of the Mono Craters quadrangle, Mono and Tuolumne Counties, California.* U.S. Geological Survey Map GQ-462.

_____ . 1973. *Geologic map of the Hetch Hetchy Reservoir quadrangle, Yosemite National Park, California.* U.S. Geological Survey Map GQ-1112.

Peck, Dallas L. 1980. *Geologic map of the Merced Peak quadrangle, central Sierra Nevada, California.* U.S. Geological Survey Map GQ-1531.

Saleeby, J.B., and others. 1986. *Centennial Continent-Ocean Transect #10: C-2 Central California Offshore to the Colorado Plateau.* Geological Society of America (incl. 1984 64 p. text).

Silberling, N.J., and others. 1987. *Lithotectonic terrane map of the western conterminous United States.* U.S. Geological Survey Map MF-1874-C.

Stewart, John H., John E. Carlson and Dann C. Johannesen. 1982. *Geologic map of the Walker Lake 1x by 2x quadrangle, California and Nevada.* U.S. Geological Survey Map MF-1382-A (first of a complete series of geological maps on this area).

Wagner, D.L., and others. 1981. *Geologic map of the Sacramento quadrangle, scale 1:250,000.* California Division of Mines and Geology Regional Geologic Map Series, Map No. 1A.

Biology

Basey, Harold E. 1976. *Discovering Sierra Reptiles and Amphibians*. El Portal: Yosemite Association, 50 p.

Beedy, Edward C., and Stephen L. Granholm. 1985. *Discovering Sierra Birds*. El Portal: Yosemite Association, 229 p.

Crampton, Beecher. 1974. *Grasses in California* (California Natural History Guide 33). Berkeley: University of California Press, 178 p.

Edelbrock, Jerry, and Scott Carpenter, eds. *Natural Areas and Yosemite: Prospects for the Future* (Yosemite Centennial Symposium Proceedings). El Portal: Yosemite Association, 667 p.

Gaines, David. 1988. *Birds of Yosemite and the East Slope*. Lee Vining: Artemisia Press, 352 p.

Gibbens, Robert P., and Harold F. Heady. 1964. *The Influence of Modern Man on the Vegetation of Yosemite Valley*. Berkeley: University of California Division of Agricultural Sciences Manual 36, 44 p.

Grater, Russell K., and Tom A. Blaue. 1978. *Discovering Sierra Mammals*. El Portal: Yosemite Association, 174 p.

Grillos, Steve J. 1966. *Ferns and Fern Allies of California* (California Natural History Guide 16). Berkeley: University of California Press, 104 p.

Hartesveldt, Richard J., and others. 1975. *The Giant Sequoia of the Sierra Nevada*. Washington, D.C.: National Park Service, 180 p.

Harvey, H. Thomas, Howard S. Shellhammer and Ronald E. Stecker. 1980. *Giant Sequoia Ecology: Fire and Reproduction*. Washington, D.C.: National Park Service Scientific Monograph Series No. 12, 182 p.

Hickman, James C., ed. 1993. *The Jepson Manual: Vascular Plants of California*. Berkeley: University of California Press, 1600 p.

Jameson, E.W., Jr., and Hans J. Peeters. 1988. *California Mammals* (California Natural History Guide 52). Berkeley: University of California Press, 403 p.

Keator, Glenn. 1978. *Pacific Coast Berry Finder*. Berkeley: Nature Study Guild, 62 p.
. 1980. *Sierra Flower Finder*. Berkeley: Nature Study Guild, 126 p.

Klikoff, Lionel G. 1965. "Microenvironmental influence on vegetational pattern near timberline in the central Sierra Nevada." *Ecological Monographs*, v. 35, p. 187–211.

Leopold, A. Starker, and others. 1951. *The Jawbone Deer Herd*. Sacramento: California Division of Fish and Game, Game Bulletin 4, 139 p.

McGinnis, Samuel M. 1984. *Freshwater Fishes of California* (California Natural History Guide 49). Berkeley: University of California Press, 316 p.

Niehaus, Theodore F., and Charles L. Ripper. 1976. *A Field Guide to Pacific States Wildflowers* (Peterson Field Guide 22). Boston: Houghton Mifflin, 432 p.

Ornduff, Robert. 1974. *An Introduction to California Plant Life* (California Natural History Guide 35). Berkeley: University of California Press, 152 p.

Patten, Duncan T., and others. 1987. *The Mono Basin Ecosystem: Effects of Changing Lake Level*. Washington, D.C.: National Academy Press, 272 p.

Peterson, P. Victor, and P. Victor Peterson, Jr. 1975. *Native Trees of the Sierra Nevada* (California Natural History Guide 36). Berkeley: University of California Press, 147 p.

Peterson, Roger T. 1990. *A Field Guide to Western Birds* (Peterson Field Guide 2). Boston: Houghton Mifflin, 432 p.

Petrides, George A., and Olivia Petrides. 1992. *A Field Guide to Western Trees* (Peterson Field Guide 44). Boston: Houghton Mifflin, 308 p.

Powell, Jerry A., and Charles L. Hogue. 1979. *California Insects* (California Natural History Guide 44). Berkeley: University of California Press, 388 p.

Stebbins, Robert C. 1972. *Amphibians and Reptiles of California* (California Natural History Guide 31). Berkeley: University of California Press, 152 p.

Storer, Tracy I., and Robert L. Usinger. 1964. *Sierra Nevada Natural History*. Berkeley: University of California Press, 374 p.

Thomas, John H., and Dennis R. Parnell. 1974. *Native Shrubs of the Sierra Nevada* (California Natural History Guide 34). Berkeley: University of California Press, 127 p.

Watts, Tom. 1973. *Pacific Coast Tree Finder*. Berkeley: Nature Study Guild, 62 p.

Weeden, Norman. 1986. *A Sierra Nevada Flora*. Berkeley: Wilderness Press, 412 p.

Whitney, Stephen. 1979. *A Sierra Club Naturalist's Guide to the Sierra Nevada*. San Francisco: Sierra Club, 526 p.

Zwinger, Ann H., and Beatrice E. Willard. 1989. *Land Above the Trees*. Tucson: University of Arizona Press, 487 p.

Index

Numbers in italics indicate photographs.

1995 Yosemite National Park update

(Each updating item that concerns geology is marked by a **G**.)

Since this guidebook is aimed at hikers, they ought to be aware of a service available to them. For many years shuttle buses have operated in eastern Yosemite Valley, and these have offered hikers the opportunity to get close to a trailhead without driving to it and adding to traffic congestion. Of course one could walk a mile or so to the trailhead, but this may not always be desirable. For example, let's say you are staying at Upper Pines Campground, and want to do Hike 70, the valley's north-rim traverse. This is difficult enough by itself, and you probably won't want to walk an additional 3 miles from the campground to the start of the Yosemite Falls trail, and so you take a shuttle. More recently, bus service has been offered so that hikers no longer have to retrace their steps to the trailhead or hitch a ride along a Park road back to it. You can now—for a fee, based on how far you go—take a bus from Yosemite Valley up along the Tioga Road and stop at any point, such as Yosemite Creek, Tenaya Lake, or the final destination, Tuolumne Meadows. Between Tenaya Lake and Tuolumne Meadows free shuttle buses offer many opportunities for hikers and tourists alike. Also, there are now free shuttle buses that operate between Wawona and the Mariposa Grove. Except for the free Yosemite Valley shuttle-bus service, all the other bus services operate only during the "summer" season.

p. 1: Day-hiking and backpacking. Wilderness-permit information is on the back side of the book's topographic map, but two changes regarding permits were made as of 1995. First, next to the valley's post office there now is a new Wilderness Center, where you can get permits as well as learn about the wilderness. Second, up to 50% of each trailhead quota may be reserved in advance, and this center now processes these wilderness-permit reservations *by mail only* (address: Wilderness Reservations, Wilderness Center, P.O. Box 545, Yosemite, CA 95389). There is a $3 charge for every person in your party, payable by check or credit card to the Yosemite Association. Send a letter including your name, address, phone number, number in your party, entry and exit dates, starting and ending trailheads, principal destination, number of stock or pack animals and, if applicable, alternative trailheads or dates you are willing to accept if your first choice is not available. For more information phone the center at (209) 372-0310.

Additionally, you ought to be aware of two issues. First, the Park Service is advocating backcountry use of bear-resistant food canisters, which you can buy or rent in the Sports Shop and Mountaineering Shop in Yosemite Valley, the Mountaineering Shop in Tuolumne Meadows, and the store in Wawona. If you have tried bear bagging, you will know what a hassle it can be, and so the food canisters are a very desirable

alternative. Second, mountain lions have been sighted with increasing frequency, and ultimately someone may be attacked. Consult the Park's free newspaper, the *Yosemite Guide*, for what to do should you encounter one.

p. 2: Accommodations. Yosemite Valley's two walk-in campgrounds are Sunnyside, which is across the road from the Yosemite Lodge complex, and Backpackers, which is along the north bank of Tenaya Creek immediately west of the Group Camp. The Backpackers Walk-in Campground is only for backpackers with wilderness permits who will be departing on a trail the next day (one-night stay maximum). Also of note, Yosemite Park and Curry Company's contract ended late in 1993, and starting in 1994, the facilities have been managed by Yosemite Concession Services, a division of Delaware North Companies, Inc., of Buffalo, New York. Some phone numbers have changed. For example, the reservations number (formerly 252-4848) now is 255-8345.

p. 3: Fishing. Special regulations for the Merced River in Yosemite Valley from Happy Isles footbridge west to Pohono bridge include catch-and-release only for native rainbow trout and no bait fishing. Only artificial lures or flies with *barbless* hooks may be used. Brown trout limits are set at five fish per day, ten in possession, and it is the responsibility of the angler to be able to identify fish species.

p. 4: Swimming and Rafting. New regulations were implemented in 1994. You can still bring your own non-motorized raft, but you can use it *only* between Clark Bridge and Cathedral Beach Picnic Area (a.k.a. Cathedral Picnic Area), and *only* between 10 a.m. and 6 p.m. You must have in your possession an appropriately sized U.S. Coast Guard approved Type I, II, or III personal flotation device for each occupant.

p. 5: Other activities. The *Yosemite Guide* is a seasonal newspaper, not a weekly one. Read it, since it has the most up-to-date information on campgrounds, reservations, permits, scheduled events, temporary closures or bans, etc. that could affect your visit.

p. 15, col. 1: 3½ million visitors per year. From 1992 onward there have been about 4 million visitors per year.

p. 23: Sonora Mountaineering. This went out of business in 1994, but was replaced by Sierra Nevada Adventure Company (SNAP), which occupies the same site and sells backpacking, mountaineering, and other outdoor-recreation gear.

G **p. 39, col. 2:** 80- to 90 million-year-old quartz monzonite. Most of the higher-elevation granitic terrain north of Tuolumne Meadows is composed of Cathedral Peak granodiorite, which has been dated at 86 million years old.

G **p. 51:** Tahoe glaciation at its maximum 75,000 years ago (also stated on 138, 198, and 241). Diverse, accumulating evidence from the mid-'80s onward indicates quite convincingly that this glaciation is considerably older, existing from about 170,000 to 130,000 years ago.

G   p. 67, col. 2: Long Gulch hike, Tioga-age glacier. This glacier began to diminish about 16,000 years ago, as stated on p. 241.

G   p. 70, col. 1: moraine of a Sherwin-age glacier. More likely this is a moraine of a Tahoe- or Tioga-age glacier. There are no Sherwin-age moraines west of the Sierra Nevada crest.

p. 73: Sunnyside Walk-in Campground. If this is full, then try the Backpackers Walk-in Campground (p. 2 entry). Reach it by walking or by taking the shuttle bus from Yosemite Lodge (Stop 8) over to North Pines Campground (Stop 18). Walk through that campground, then on a trail you bridge Tenaya Creek and find the campground just across the creek, immediately to the left of the trail. (The Group Camp is immediately to the right.)

p. 79, Trailhead: Tenaya Lake Walk-in Campground parking area. Parking area still exists, but campground was closed in 1992. This campground is also mentioned on pages 83, 90, 91, 92, 95, 96, 99, 100, 115. Also, currently you can drive 1.7 miles up the Old Tioga Road, but in the future this stretch may be closed to vehicles.

p. 83, Introduction: Tuolumne and Merced giant-sequoia groves. The road down to the Merced Grove has been closed to vehicles for quite some time, and in 1993 the road to the Tuolumne Grove was closed. It is now about a one-mile hike (or bike ride) down to that grove. There are about 20 mature trees in each grove.

p. 88, Trailhead: PORCUPINE CREEK sign. No sign in 1993. Park at an obvious turnout, which is the second one east of Porcupine Flat Campground.

p. 97, Pothole Dome: You can no longer cut across the boggy meadow to the dome, but must first walk northwest along the edge of the road to some trees and then head back over to it.

p. 116, col. 2: Sunrise High Sierra Camp. From here you could hike on the John Muir Trail (the first part of Hike 51 in reverse direction) north to Highway 120 (Tioga Road) and then take a shuttle back to your trailhead.

p. 120, col. 2: trail from Sunrise High Sierra Camp to Sunrise Lakes. Another option is to follow Hike 47 in the reverse direction down to its trailhead at Tenaya Lake and then take a shuttle back to your trailhead.

G   p. 120, col. 2: giant lateral moraine. In the first sentence of p. 121 I called this a Tahoe-age moraine, based on the Park's geologic map and on a very quick look at it where the trail crosses it. However, in 1993 I studied it in detail, and concluded it was unquestionably a bedrock ridge, not a moraine. Furthermore, the till, or glacial debris, strewn discontinuously atop it is Tioga age, not Tahoe age, and its ice surface here was at about

8700 feet. The Tioga-age moraines seen lower down are, like others just mentioned above, late-Tioga in age.

G   p. 121, col. 2: Moraine Dome. This has been the type locality to indicate the amount of weathering and erosion that has occurred since the El Portal-age glacier left the summit about 800,000 years ago. The critical assumption here is that the surface of the dome was completely smooth after glaciation, and that at least seven feet of denudation has occurred, based on the height of the dike of resistant aplite. Actually, about 20,000 years ago the Tioga-age glacier overflowed the summit. The ice was thin enough that pressure exerted on the bedrock was minimal—as was ice movement—and so very little erosion occurred. The dike was unaffected. The famous lateral moraine of Moraine Dome is late-Tioga in age, not full-Tioga.

p. 125, col. 2: underwater arch. Don't try swimming through it in high water; it is challenging enough in late-season slack water.

p. 126, col. 2: an even larger meadow. About 3.4 miles up the Rafferty Creek trail, a newer trail branches left to enter this meadow and climb about 1.6 miles to Tuolumne Pass. The older, forested route, about 0.3 mile longer, is abandoned.p. 130

p. 130, Trailhead: Mono County Road 158 actually is State Route 158.

p. 131, col. 2: recrossing the fork at the north edge of a subalpine meadow. The fork here has widened sufficiently so that it can be mistaken for the higher boulder-dotted pond.

G   p. 138, col. 2: Mono Basin. This basin and Owens Valley originated about 100 million years ago, and hence both are very old. However, downfaulting in them has occurred only in the last few million years. Before faulting, the Mono Basin's bedrock floor may have been at about 7000 feet elevation, not 10,000 feet.

G   p. 143, col. 1: Lake Yosemite. Actually, the lake was supposedly dammed behind the El Capitan moraine, which is opposite the base of the north face of Lower Cathedral Rock. As Stanford's Professor Blackwelder concluded back in 1930, there was no lake after the Tioga glaciation. My recent field evidence indicates that the last Lake Yosemite existed after the Tahoe glaciation, and it was filled in with sediments by the start of the Tioga glaciation about 26,000 years ago. The El Capitan moraine did not dam a lake, but it does act as a river dam—as do nearby rockfall block—so that in time of high runoff, water accumulates here and the valley floods. The current valley floor is a floodplain, not the top of lakebed sediments.

p. 144, col. 1: Devils Elbow Picnic Area. The beach is still open to the public, but the stretch of river bank along the road is closed to prevent further erosion. Gone is the rope tied high to a tree. This picnic area is also mentioned on p. 72 and 147.

p. 147, col. 1: El Capitan Picnic Area. This area is now closed due to environmental degradation along the

Merced River's bank. The trail, however, still passes through this area, although now it is devoid of picnic tables, etc. Its new site is on the north side of the valley's west-heading road, more or less opposite the old site's entrance road. Instead of watching the river flow by, visitors now can walk a few minutes north to watch climbers scale Ranger Rock.

p. 149: Sentinel Bridge. During 1993 and 1994 a new bridge was constructed, which replaced the old one. The photograph is from the old bridge.

p. 153, col. 1: gravel pit/garbage dump. This site now is a parking lot for backpackers only. (Be sure you get a wilderness permit before parking here.) Day hikers must use the day-use lot at Camp Curry. From it the "quieter route" (top of col. 2) starts southeast, joined by one or more use paths (the number subject to change over time).

p. 153, col. 2: Happy Isles area. The trail still angles southeast through this area, but it is a broad, paved one. In 1993 several broad, paved paths were laid down in this area, and a sizable restroom building was built near the shuttle-bus stop. Also, the area was intensively planted with native trees and shrubs.

p. 153, col 2: gaging station. See the p. 143 entry on Lake Yosemite.

G   **p. 154:** Medial Moraine, "I believe this west-trending ridge is a *moraine left by the retreating Merced Canyon glacier.*" I have to eat those emphatic words, which were written before had I completed my field work in the area. Analogies sometimes work; this one did not, since the Merced River's glacial system was more complex than that of the Stanislaus River's. The moraine is a recessional moraine left by the Tenaya Canyon glacier about 14,000-15,000 years ago.

G   **p. 156, col. 1:** Medial Moraine, cont'd. On revisiting this area with two U.S. Geological Survey geologists, none of us could find any certain glacier-transported boulders. Rather, it appears to be solely the remnants of an old rockfall.

p. 156, col. 2: cutting south through the Group Camp. You now cut south along the west edge of the Group Camp, since its western part was converted to the Backpackers Walk-in Campground.

p. 161, col. 2: Trail junction by Lehamite Creek. The June 1992 Dome Fire burned from the valley's rim north up to this environs, where trailside damage was minimal.

p. 162, col. 1: Inspiration Point/old Wawona Road. A rewarding side trip from the point is to continue 1.2 miles west (and 400 feet up) along the old road, this stretch being unmaintained. The last 0.4 mile is across a small part of a major August 1990 lightning-caused fire, and so you will encounter charred snags across the road. What makes this generally shady route so rewarding is that immediately after the road tops out where it crosses a ridge (that descends to the east end of Turtleback Dome—itself a ridge), you will find, on the right (north) side of the road a "bottomless pit." And, if you

scramble a minute or two south from the road, you will find a "rift gully." The local landscape here literally is falling apart! A major rockfall could be generated from here tomorrow—or in thousands of years. One is unlikely to occur while you visit it, but if you choose to explore this local landscape, then exercise caution due to drop-offs.

p. 169, col. 2: outhouses near site of La Casa Nevada. These have been removed and new ones have been placed lower down, just above the trail near the upper end of Emerald Pool.

p. 169, col. 2: once again meet the John Muir Trail (near the brink of Nevada Fall). At this junction are more outhouses. The one near the Nevada Fall bridge (p. 170, col. 2) has been removed.

p. 170, col. 2: a short half mile to another junction. Part of this stretch is now closed to both camping and day use. Day use is permitted east of the John Muir/Merced Lake trails junction, but camping is restricted to an area immediately east of the John Muir Trail and immediately north of the Merced Lake trail. North along the JMT from this junction you'll quickly encounter a trailside sizable outhouse complex. Bear-bagging no longer is necessary since there are metal bearproof boxes to store your food in.

p. 171, col. 1: summer ranger. In summer 1993 the "Little Yosemite Valley Ranger Station" was located northeast of the outhouse complex, across a minor creek. The station has treated, safe water. Hopefully you will find one or more signs to direct you along a path or two to this ranger camp. (Note: rangers often are out on patrol.)

p. 171: Half Dome. No camping on Half Dome's summit.

p. 171: notes on Liberty Cap, Mt. Broderick, Lost Lake and the Diving Board. Part of Liberty Cap's long east rib was burned in an early '90s fire. Be careful if you try to climb to its summit, since there is a lot of loose rock. Contrary to earlier accounts, the summit was topped by glacier ice during the Tioga glaciation. Apparently no glaciologist bothered to climb it to observe small remnants of fresh polish and striations on the summit area.

A surprisingly good use trail strikes west along the north slopes of Liberty Cap's long east rib, then skirts between Mt. Broderick's base and Lost Lake, and finally dies out on the saddle just west of and above the lake. A ducked cross-country route continues onward, and there are several possibilities for an ascent up to the Diving Board, easier ones being farther to the west. If you are the least bit intimidated on any ascent route, turn back. After about 600 feet of ascent, the gradient abates, and to avoid absolutely miserable brush above, traverse westward across gentle slopes to a viewful ridge and ascend it. Near the top, where the ridge dramatically steepens, nonclimbers will want to traverse east and ascend a use path directly up to the

Diving Board. Be forewarned that most people taking this route are expert climbers who then continue up the southwest face of Half Dome and descend the Half Dome trail. If you descend from the Diving Board, chances are good that you will not be able to find your ascent route, and instead will encounter drop-offs—luck, perseverance or a rappel rope is necessary. In short, virtually all nonclimbers will avoid this route. It is unfortunate that a trail does not climb to the Diving Board, since there is important glacial evidence in several places that has been wholly ignored—not surprisingly—by glacial geologists.

p. 171, col. 2: Half Dome. On a sunny summer Saturday, hundreds of people can be found trying to scale Half Dome. Congestion on exposed trail stretches and on the cables then can be a real problem. This situation could grow so bad that the cables could be removed, closing the route to all but rock climbers.

G **p. 175, col. 2:** Matthes on glacial erosion/*So* true. Not so true, since Little Yosemite Valley, Lost Valley, Echo Valley and the Merced Lake valley all were relatively wide before glaciation. Locally, glaciers were effective at excavating basins, Yosemite Valley (now filled in with sediments) being the prime example, but they were quite ineffective at widening canyons. Therefore, the statement on p. 174, that Moraine Dome was extensively steepened by glaciation, is not true. The slopes likely were nearly as steep before glaciation as they are today.

p. 186, col. 2: 1987 fire. An early '90s fire destroyed additional forest from Illilouette Creek over to the edge of Little Yosemite Valley.

G **p. 187, col. 1:** Illilouette Creek glacier. Evidence of early glaciation in the Illilouette Creek drainage is sparse. For these early times, totally imaginary glacial moraines and lake deposits have been described and mapped, none actually existing. Rather, what exists are Tioga-age outwash deposits derived from the glaciers of the upper drainage, and a Tioga-age moraine just up from the bridge across the creek. That moraine indicates that the Merced's Tioga-age glacier slightly overlapped onto the lower part of Illilouette Creek. Still, absence of silt and clay sediments implies that a lake did not form. Rather, Illilouette Creek flowed either beneath the main glacier or along its side.

p. 187, col. 2: Panorama Point. The trail now avoids this brushy point, which is liable to break away in a major rockfall in the near future.

G **p. 187, col. 2:** Junction with the Mono Meadow trail. Here a geologically significant Tioga-age lateral moraine diagonals across the trail.

G **p. 200-205:** Mariposa Grove of Big Trees. There is very interesting ongoing research on how the populations of giant-sequoia groves have fluctuated since the last glaciation, which may indicate how they will survive if climate change occurs. There also is completed research on sequoia groves and the number and sizes of their trees in them, and it shows that the Grizzly Giant is not the fifth largest; more than 25 trees are larger.

G **p. 232:** Early Volcanism. The volcanic deposits buried the extensive gold-laden deposits of the northern Sierra Nevada, which collected there because that area was not affected by the Cretaceous uplift.

G **p. 238, col. 2:** Matthes. On the basis of his quite extensive field work, Matthes by 1914 had derived a generalized, *essentially correct* picture of how the Yosemite Valley landscape had evolved. He emphasized that glaciers were *ineffective*. However, like others he could not quantify his views, and so in 1915 he abandoned his approach and used a quantitative method based on two hypothetical, untenable assumptions of his mentor, Harvard's Prof. William Morris Davis (p. 239, col. 1). Years before Professional Paper 130 was published, Davis essentially abandoned the most crucial assumption—pulses of rapid uplift—which was so crucial for Matthes. Given that the two wrote and visited each other, it is unlikely that Matthes would have been oblivious to this retraction. Despite his own field evidence to the contrary, Matthes plunged ahead, using Davis flawed views, producing an error-prone product that was, most unfortunately, declared a classic by Prof. Bryan, a successor to Prof. Davis.

G **p. 246, col. 1:** Preglacial width of Yosemite Valley. Based on further field work and calculations, I now believe it was more like 80% as wide, not half as wide.

G **p. 246, col. 2:** Medial Moraine. See the p. 154 entry.

p. 253: Gold-cup oak. This is more appropriately called the canyon oak. With the 1993 publication of The Jepson Manual, which replaces Munz very dated California Flora (both published by University of California Press), some common names of plants have changed, and these changes will be reflected in the new edition of my guidebook when it comes out. (My geology chapter in The Jepson Manual, written when I still believed in major, recent uplift is now somewhat dated because of that belief.)

p. 269: Schaffer, 1992. Based on my previous rate of productivity, I had expected to easily complete my dissertation by the end of 1992. Wrong. Field work supposedly was completed in 1993, but I've done additional work in '94 and '95.